Tracing the Connected Narrative

Arctic Exploration in British Print Culture, 1818–1860

JANICE CAVELL

UNIVERSITY OF TORONTO PRESS
Toronto Buffalo London

© University of Toronto Press Incorporated 2008
Toronto Buffalo London
www.utppublishing.com
Printed in Canada

ISBN 978-0-8020-9280-9

∞

Printed on acid-free paper

Library and Archives Canada Cataloguing in Publication

Cavell, Janice
　　Tracing the connected narrative: Arctic exploration in British print culture,
1818–1860 / Janice Cavell.

(Studies in book and print culture)
Includes bibliographical references and index.
ISBN 978-0-8020-9280-9

1. Franklin, John, Sir, 1786 – 1847 – Travel – Arctic regions – Bibliography.
2. Arctic regions – Discovery and exploration – British – History – Sources.
3. Arctic regions – Discovery and exploration – British – Bibliography. 4. Arctic
regions – Discovery and exploration – British – History – 19th century. 5. Arctic
regions – Discovery and exploration – British – Press coverage – Great Britain.
I. Title. II. Series.

PN5117.C38 2008　　　　910.9163'27　　　C2007-907632-7

University of Toronto Press acknowledges the financial assistance to its publishing
program of the Canada Council for the Arts and the Ontario Arts Council.

This book has been published with the help of a grant from the Canadian
Federation for the Humanities and Social Sciences, through the Aid to Scholarly
Publications Programme, using funds provided by the Social Sciences and
Humanities Research Council of Canada.

University of Toronto Press acknowledges the financial support for its
publishing activities of the Government of Canada through the Book
Publishing Industry Development Program (BPIDP).

Contents

Illustrations follow p. 116

Acknowledgments

This work was originally accepted as a doctoral thesis by the Department of History at Carleton University in 2003. I would like to thank my thesis advisers, Brian McKillop and David Dean, and the director of graduate studies, Bruce Elliott, for their invaluable support over the years and to gratefully acknowledge the financial support provided by Carleton and by the Social Sciences and Humanities Research Council of Canada.

As a researcher, I have been fortunate in many ways. In the summer of 2002 I was among the last to consult the John Murray Archive in its original home at 50 Albemarle Street in London. Both the setting and the warm welcome from Mrs Virginia Murray were unforgettable. At the Scott Polar Research Institute, Beau Riffenburgh offered essential aid and advice to a novice Arctic historian. Robert Headland, the late William Mills, Shirley Sawtrell, and Caroline Gunn all gave courteous and efficient assistance, and Anthony Voss kindly granted access to the Richardson-Voss Papers. The staffs at the Derbyshire Record Office, the National Maritime Museum, and the British Library were equally gracious and helpful. Thanks are also due to Jonathan Topham, who sent me a prepublication copy of his article 'John Limbird, Thomas Byerley, and the Production of Cheap Periodicals in Regency Britain,' and to Michael Bravo, who provided a copy of his doctoral dissertation. I would also like to thank Rob Tiessen of the University of Calgary Library and Lucinda Walls of the W.D. Jordan Special Collections and Music Library, Queen's University, for their kind help in obtaining illustrations for this book. Permission has been granted from the Trustees of the National Library of Scotland to quote from letters in the John Murray Archive. I am grateful as well to the Scott Polar Research

Institute, the British Library, the National Maritime Museum, and the owner of the Gell Collection. Finally, I am most grateful to Jill McConkey at the University of Toronto Press for her enthusiasm and expert advice.

Like my thesis, this book is for my children, Alex, Cecily, and Ben.

Illustration credits

John P. Robarts Library, University of Toronto
Departure of the *Erebus* and *Terror*; Fitzjames' cabin; James Fitzjames; officers of Austin's expedition; John Rae

National Portrait Gallery, London
John Barrow; Jane Griffin; William Penny

Queen's University, Kingston
'The Falls of Wilberforce' (Finden engraving), reproduced with permission from an original in the W.D. Jordan Special Collections and Music Library

University of Calgary Library
William Edward Parry; 'The Falls of Wilberforce, in the Arctic Regions'; John Franklin; map of 'the connected discoveries of Captains Parry, Ross, and Franklin'

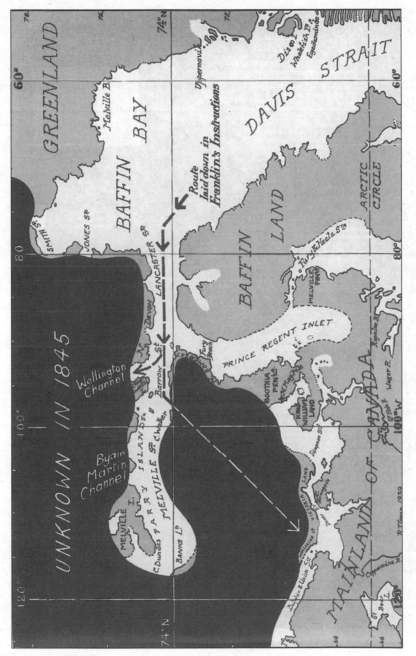

Map 1   The North-west Passage region as known in 1845, when the Franklin expedition sailed.

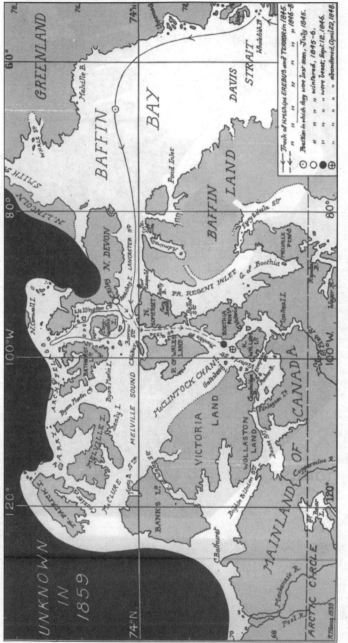

Map 2 The North-west Passage region as known in 1859, after the return of Sir Leopold McClintock.

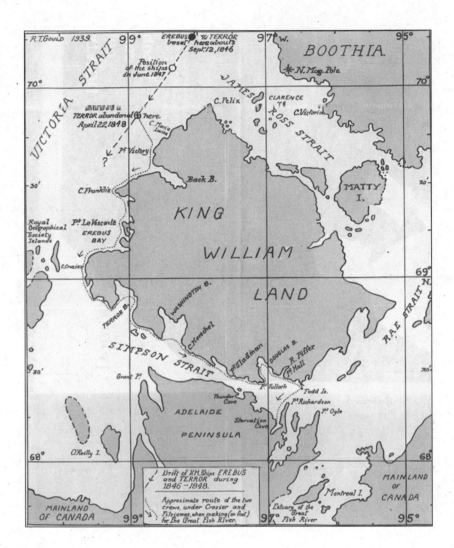

Map 3 King William Land, to illustrate the retreat from the *Erebus* and *Terror*.

TRACING THE CONNECTED NARRATIVE:
ARCTIC EXPLORATION IN BRITISH PRINT CULTURE, 1818–1860

Introduction

'Arctic exploration, in so far as it can be carried out from an armchair before a winter fire, has long been for me a pursuit that verges on a passion,' Stephen Leacock confessed in 1938. 'I have been with Franklin on that famous journey to the Coppermine that was the prelude to his last and fatal adventure. I remember no more thrilling episode in my life than when Franklin and I ... crossed the freezing Coppermine, running heavy with ice, in a craft made of willow sticks.'[1] There can be few book-lovers in the English-speaking world today who have never read anything at all about Sir John Franklin and the Northwest Passage. For some, as for Leacock, it is almost an obsession. A few have even taken extracts from the narratives on canoe trips, so as to read Franklin's words in the actual places they describe.[2] But the reading experience of the nineteenth-century audiences who followed the Arctic story with fascinated attention over the years from 1818 to 1860 is still a *terra incognita.* How did his contemporaries see Franklin, and why?

As I attempted to answer these questions, I realized that very few even among the affluent, educated middle class of nineteenth-century Britain would ever have read the book that gave Leacock such a vivid illusion of standing at Franklin's side, *Narrative of a Journey to the Shores of the Polar Sea in the Years 1819, 20, 21 and 22.* Instead, most of them would have learned about Franklin as they glanced over the newspaper at the breakfast table or listened to a family member reading aloud from a magazine by the fireside at night. Working men and women might have gathered around a literate neighbour to hear a poem about Franklin's lost expedition along with the latest political opinions from the Radical press. Nineteenth-century encounters with the Arctic in print were at once more varied and more embedded in the rhythms and routines of daily life than those of the twentieth and twenty-first centuries. So I would have to place Arctic exploration narratives in the broader context of the print culture of their time – newspapers from the *Times* to the penny press, periodicals, cheap popular literature. And, no matter how wide a range of publications I might study, whenever possible I would have to go beyond the texts and their authors to nineteenth-century readers and the varied ways they interpreted the Arctic story, for it was clear that class, gender, and political allegiance all had their effect, and that many readers understood Franklin's fate in ways that would not have been sanctioned by the political or cultural authorities.

The resulting book makes connections and raises questions that should be of interest to scholars in a variety of areas. The relationship between books and other forms of print culture, the naval hero as a national symbol, the development of the British identity during the nineteenth century, the links between masculinity and religion, and the place of populism in mid-Victorian cultural and political life all are examined. However, the major aim is to understand the British cultural construction of Franklin and other Arctic explorers on its own terms, as the readers of Franklin's own day would have understood it. I was often astonished, and not a little daunted, by the vast amount of nineteenth-century print devoted to Franklin and by the complexity of the processes I was studying. This evidence has led me to conclusions about the cultural dimension of British Arctic exploration that differ sharply from those of previous scholars, and especially Canadian scholars.[3] I would like to begin by examining the assumptions that underlie earlier Canadian work, though readers with little interest in academic debates may prefer to move on to the later sections of this introduction.

Exploration Narratives and Discourse Analysis

Many Canadian studies of Arctic exploration literature are strongly influenced by postmodern theories of discourse and by criticisms of British imperial culture. The false, misleading nature of exploration literature is a dominant theme. According to scholars such as Richard Davis and Ian MacLaren, the British construction of Canada's north was a preposterous distortion, which clearly demonstrated the ethnocentric limitations of British culture as a whole. In Davis's view, Franklin was primarily a 'solid representative of his imperial culture,' and the disasters of his first and last expeditions 'arose because Franklin, as did the culture that produced him, assumed the supremacy of his own values and wisdom, even as he placed himself in circumstances that demanded new ways of understanding … This was at the core of his failure.'[4] Not all contemporary Canadian writers on the subject share this highly critical stance, but such ideas have achieved wide acceptance not only among scholars, but among popular historians and novelists, including Pierre Berton, Peter Newman, Ken McGoogan, Margaret Atwood, and Rudy Wiebe.[5] A 2003 news story reports a movement among Arctic scientists to change the name of the research ship *Sir John Franklin* because of Franklin's ethnocentric attitude towards northern Aboriginal people.[6]

The perceived significance of the Arctic explorers, then, lies almost entirely in what their story means to Canadians today. For Davis and many others, Franklin's story is above all a cautionary tale, which can help Canadians to 'grasp one of the essential components of the national culture: the need to approach cultural differences with respect and humility, so that we [do not] repeat the mistakes that Franklin's ethnocentrism brought about.'[7] What the story meant to Franklin himself and to his contemporaries is a question rarely explored in any depth. The explanation usually given is brief and stereotyped: after the end of the Napoleonic Wars, naval officers required other employment, and the conquest of the Arctic was seen as an ideal way to demonstrate British prowess and superiority. However, the explorers' efforts were frustrated by the power of nature. Decades later, the failure of the last Franklin expedition and allegations that naval officers had committed cannibalism set off a terrifying wave of national self-doubt in an otherwise complacent mid-Victorian Britain. This drama was enacted by vague entities, sometimes personified by a single individual: 'the Navy' or 'the Admiralty' made decisions and took actions; 'the press' described the explorers' deeds in glowing terms; and 'the British public,' jingoistic yet docile, believed whatever it was told. 'The Admiralty' usually means John Barrow, the second secretary for most of the period from 1804 to 1845; 'the press' may be represented by Charles Dickens in his role as editor of *Household Words*; but 'the British public' remains a faceless, gullible mass.

There can be no unmediated access to the past, of course, and any attempt to understand it must necessarily reflect the time and place in which the work was written. But in the case of Canadian writings about British Arctic exploration the shaping factor has been unusually strong. This is due primarily to the idea that the far north has always held a central place in the Canadian psyche.[8] Shelagh Grant and Sherrill Grace, among others, claim that since the time of Confederation, the 'idea of north' has been the key to understanding Canada.[9] Even among writers who are strongly influenced by postmodernist ideas, the conviction that the far north is an essential part of the national being persists. Such ideas have given rise to the belief that because of their unique affinity with the north, Canadians are better suited than any others to understand Arctic exploration as a cultural phenomenon. Davis, for example, complains in a review of a British book on the Arctic in nineteenth-century culture that the author makes only 'superficial' use of Canadian scholarship. In Davis's view, this omission is 'especially unfortunate' because many Canadian writers 'have an excellent grasp on the reality of the Arctic.' Their perceptions of the subject could therefore serve as a 'standard against which to measure the constructed image that ... Britons have built through vicarious experience.'[10]

A dichotomy between Canadian reality and British illusion lies at the root of Davis's conceptualization of the subject. Though he has made extensive use of postmodern theory in his work on exploration literature,[11] it is evident that essentialist assumptions have shaped Davis's methodology. He implies that simple factual reality exists 'out there'; that those who are not blinkered by a false, constructed discourse can have unmediated access to it; and that it can be adequately represented in their written words. Reality is therefore prior to and independent of discourse. Grace makes this understanding of cultural construction explicit. She writes that representation 'is at best a necessary practice that mediates socially constructed images of the self and the world, ' but 'at its worst it can block the real by replacing it and directing our attention or desire away from complex lived experience of a heterogeneous reality towards a simulacrum.'[12] To put it in the simplest possible terms, there are good constructions that reflect lived reality and bad constructions that are false and misleading. Grace's aim is to clear away the bad (often racist and sexist) discourses, leaving only the best (by today's standards) representations of the Arctic as cornerstones of the national identity. Davis's and Grace's studies thus reject the main tenets of Michel Foucault's concept of discourse, even though both cite Foucault as a major influence on their work. Foucault's position is an extreme and intellectually rigorous one. He writes uncompromisingly, 'The purpose of history ... is not to discover the roots of our identity but to commit ourselves to its dissipation' and 'What is found at the historical beginning of things is not the inviolable identity of their origin; it is the dissension of other things. It is disparity.'[13]

An important question for anyone drawing on Foucault's ideas is how, if human reality is constituted through discourse, any individual can have unmediated experience of the real world. As Joan Scott has pointed out, experience itself is mediated and understood through the discourses that shape an individual's perception of events.[14] And, if there is no such thing as simple factual reality, it is difficult to see why nineteenth-century Europeans should be criticized for having failed to apprehend and represent it. By definition, there can be no unproblematic representation of the real world, since a representation is a cultural artefact rather than a mirror. Many contemporary writers seem to define authentic representations simply as those that are compatible with the discourses currently prevailing in the academic world. Their own access to the reality of the non-European world as it existed in past centuries is the unexamined assumption on which historical and literary studies of discourse are based. This contradiction is a major flaw at the heart of most postmodern academic discussions of exploration and travel literature. (And, with regard to Canadian perceptions of Arctic exploration, it must be remembered that the vast majority of Canadians have little or no personal knowledge of the far north. Very few have visited it even briefly, and fewer still have spent their lives there. None now alive experienced it as it was in the nineteenth century. Southern Canadians therefore inevitably understand the region's history only from the outsider's point of view. Leaving all discussions of postmodern theory aside, this fact in itself invalidates the dichotomy between a Canadian understanding based on experience and purely vicarious British representations.)

For those who accept the model of good and bad representations of the Canadian Arctic, the literature of British exploration appears as little more than a tissue of delusion and deception. The purposes for which nineteenth-century representations were created differ so dramatically from the purposes of present-day writers on the subject that it is easy to accept the notion that 'we,' aided by an intuitive insight born of our special relationship with the northern landscape, have grasped the truth, whereas 'they' were incapable of perceiving simple reality. British narratives of Arctic exploration were on the whole significantly less racist and ethnocentric than Davis and others have claimed.[15] However, it is certainly not my intention to argue that nineteenth-century British writers produced realistic, factual accounts of the Canadian Arctic.[16] Rather, my main contention is that for the purposes of historical study, an attempt must be made to understand the British discourse from within.

Arctic Exploration Literature and Nineteenth-Century Print Culture

In this book, I have tried to avoid preconceived ideas about what representations of the Arctic should be like. *Tracing the Connected Narrative* examines the process by which the British discourse was created and the interpretations to which it gave rise during the years from 1818 to 1860. The concepts and methodology are drawn from recent works in the history of print culture, especially the new interdisciplinary approaches to nineteenth-century periodical literature, and from studies in British cultural history by Gerald Newman, Linda Colley, Leonore Davidoff, Catherine Hall, and Patrick Joyce. In this sense, it is a study more in British history than in the history of the Canadian Arctic. (However, given the enormous impact that British culture had on Canada in the nineteenth and early twentieth centuries, a better understanding of what it was and how it functioned would surely enhance the field of Canadian cultural history as well.)

There is abundant, deeply fascinating, and readily available primary source material in the explorers' journals, letters, and narratives. The various motives and assumptions underlying the actions of naval officials and the explorers themselves can be elucidated through conventional archival sources such as journals and private correspondence. Publishers' archives contain additional valuable material about the explorers in their role as authors. Such a treatment of the subject would, however, still leave the press and the public unexamined. It is in the public sphere of journalism and reader response that the full meaning of Arctic exploration as a cultural phenomenon is to be found. This study is founded on the insight most memorably articulated by Marilyn Butler, who writes that periodical literature was not a mere reflection of nineteenth-century culture, but rather 'culture's medium.'[17]

Other writers on Arctic exploration have drawn occasionally on newspaper and periodical articles as a convenient source of background material. Used selectively in this way, these articles seem merely to confirm and supplement other evidence. However, when periodical literature is given a central place in the analysis, previous understandings of the place held by exploration narratives in British culture are transformed. Nineteenth-century British periodical literature was remarkable for its richness, complexity, and diversity. In newspapers, magazines, and reviews, journalists did indeed lavishly praise Arctic explorers and their books, but they also questioned, speculated, criticized, and interpreted from a broad range of ideological and literary viewpoints. As J.G.A. Pocock has remarked in a discussion of Pacific exploration, it should not be forgotten that all European ideas were 'profoundly contestable' within Europe.[18] Particularly during the years of the Franklin search (1848–59), the Arctic story was commonly used as a vehicle for protest:

only one publication, the *Times* of London, consistently supported Admiralty decisions, and many journalists bitterly denounced the conduct of the search as but one among many instances of governmental incompetence. Although a coherent metanarrative of Arctic exploration emerged from this welter of voices, the process by which it was constituted was anything but simple. It is evident that any dichotomy between all-powerful officials and explorer-authors on one side and a compliant, easily influenced press and public on the other should be avoided.

Recent studies in the history of reading emphasize that readers should not be considered as generic and passive; instead, it is essential to realize that they employed different reading strategies according to their circumstances and needs. These changed over time. The act of reading, as Wolfgang Iser called it in one of the earliest discussions of reader response,[19] is historically conditioned. And, while readers were often profoundly influenced by what they read, there was never a time when they could simply be manipulated. As Roger Chartier points out, 'We must recognize ... a major tension between the explicit or implicit intentions a text proposes to a wide audience and the variety of possible reading responses.' Chartier believes that it is 'necessary to place the notion of appropriation at the center of a cultural historical approach,' and that studies should focus on 'differentiated practices and contrasted uses of the same texts, codes, or models.'[20] Jonathan Rose also suggests that the study of 'hypothetical,' generic readers should be replaced, whenever possible, by an emphasis on 'the actual ordinary reader in history.'[21]

Although this study cannot pretend to fully elucidate the question of reader response, such evidence as does exist sheds new light on the place of exploration literature in nineteenth-century culture. Throughout the book, the specific physical form in which writings about the Arctic were available to the public is a central concern. A wealthy reader who had just paid several guineas for a new, lavishly illustrated exploration narrative clearly did not have the same experience as one who could afford to buy only a penny or twopenny magazine containing extracts from the book. Direct evidence of ordinary readers' strategies and responses is, unfortunately, scanty. However, periodical writers and reviewers can very usefully be considered in their role as readers of the latest Arctic news or the most recent Arctic narrative. Publishing strategies can be analysed in order to understand editors' and journalists' perceptions of the reading public and its demands. Such strategies changed significantly over the period from 1818 to 1860. Accounts of specific reading practices and experiences have been included whenever possible. Where there is no direct evidence, I have drawn on the indirect testimony of journalists seeking to gain the widest possible reading audience. In this way, both the broad, generalized sweep of the connected narrative as it unfolded over time and the concrete circumstances under which particular readers encountered it can be grasped. These matters are further discussed in chapter 1, which provides a more detailed introduction to the methodology employed.

A basic assumption in this book is that journalists and readers actively appropriated the Arctic story, interpreting it in accordance with their own needs and preoccupations, and that it was largely through these appropriations that the broader connected narrative was constituted. However, authorial intention is also considered. While authors' power falls far short of the ability to control the public's interpretation of their works, their personal motives and intentions cannot be disregarded altogether. As Nicolas Barker and Roger Chartier have argued, even though meaning is the outcome of collaborative social processes beyond the control of any individual, authorial intention makes a far from negligible contribution to the perceived significance of a work. Earlier models of the author's intended meaning as the key to full understanding[22] must be rejected, and the act of literary creation should be studied in the broader context of a work's editing, publication, sale, and reviews. Barker calls this process the transmission of a text, and he notes that 'both intention and reception … are abstractions, or, rather … neither can be discussed without reference to the fact of transmission, without which neither has any substance. Transmission … links intention and reception, and converts them into a historic process.'[23]

According to Chartier, an author is 'both dependent and constrained': dependent because 'his intentions … are not necessarily imposed either on those who turn his text into a book … or on those who appropriate it by reading it' and constrained 'in that he undergoes the multiple determinations that organize the social space of literary production and that, in a more general sense, determine the categories and the experiences that are the very matrices of writing.'[24] Many of these categories and experiences can best be grasped through the study of authors. The need for continued study of authorial intention has also been emphasized by Martyn Thompson. As Thompson observes, texts are inevitably read in multiple ways, and it is an essential part of the intellectual historian's task to explicate the varied understandings. However, an author's intentions are themselves the products of certain historical circumstances. While examining them in isolation from the processes of publication and reception would be of relatively little value, when set in a broader context they are an important subject of historical inquiry.[25]

Paul Magnuson's *Reading Public Romanticism* provides an excellent example of the type of study suggested in these theoretical articles. Magnuson argues, 'Only by reading the surrounding context of a work can one see the public mediation of its central tropes, the nuances of the individual words, and the resonances of its commonality.' To study an author's journals and correspondence, the drafts of a work, and its later editing and publication can elucidate a great deal, but only by placing the work in the context of the public discourse of its time can either authorial intention or reception adequately be understood. 'A work has public significance only if it is responsive and answerable,' Magnuson asserts. '[T]he frame enters the work as a determinant and expands by allusion outward to the exterior discourse.' Moreover, '[p]recise location within the discourse is essential for any reading of the connections' between the work and its context; that is, when and where a work was published, and why its author chose a certain form of publication, were key factors in the constitution of its original meaning. According to Magnuson, 'without precise location, there is no cultural significance.'[26] In the case of Magnuson's subject, Romantic poems, many were first printed in magazines or newspapers. The strategies of presentation used, along with previous and subsequent utterances in these and other periodical publications, shed new light on both the poets' intentions and the public's initial understanding. Later publications of the same poems in different locations gave rise to other meanings.

The public discourse of periodical literature illuminates the understanding of Arctic writers in a similar way. The intentions of four authors – John Barrow, John Franklin, Leopold McClintock, and Sherard Osborn – are given detailed consideration in this book. Barrow's books and periodical articles and the narratives of Franklin and McClintock were all published by the firm of John Murray. The Murray Archive supplies considerable background information on the writing, editing, and publication processes. Franklin's published journals and letters, the Franklin, McClintock, and Osborn correspondence in the Scott Polar Research Institute, the Gell collection of Franklin papers in the Derbyshire Record Office, and the draft of McClintock's narrative in the National Maritime Museum provide ample additional sources for a study of these explorers as authors. But only when these materials are studied in conjunction with the reviews and other articles does the interplay between intention and reception become clear.

For these Arctic writers, as for a now famous reader, Carlo Ginzburg's Menocchio, culture was 'a horizon of latent possibilities – a flexible and invisible cage' within which a 'conditional liberty'[27] could be exercised. The exploration narrative was a genre with well-defined rules: 'I hope I have not overstepped the proper bounds of a narrative, [and] I hasten to resume the details of the voyage,' commented Franklin's friend John Richardson after penning a somewhat unconventional passage.[28] Yet many authors, each in his own way, did overstep the bounds set by previous writings, pushing the genre to new developments, which in turn defined the boundaries for later explorers. Some of these innovations were warmly welcomed by reviewers; others were severely condemned. Only by what Franklin called the 'opinions of the public so positively expressed through their organs (the different Magazines and Reviews)'[29] could such innovations be validated as part of the discourse.

The book begins with McClintock, the leader of the last Franklin search expedition. His return to England in the autumn of 1859 precipitated one of the most strongly marked and widespread conflicts over the meaning of the Arctic story. The interpretation offered by the most highly regarded publication of the day, the *Times*, met intense opposition from a very broad range of other newspapers and periodicals. It is at this culminating point, where meaning was sharply contested, that the discourses surrounding Arctic exploration can most readily be examined. McClintock had discovered the long-sought answer to the mystery of Franklin's lost expedition, yet his news was dismissed by the *Times* as a matter of little consequence. In the ensuing outburst of print, journalists explained in great detail, and often with deep emotion, what the Arctic narrative meant to them and what they believed it meant to the nation. The book begins with the end of the story because at no other time was public attention so intensely focused on Arctic exploration. Throughout the years from 1818 to 1859 the attribution of meaning was a rich and complex process. In 1859 there was a strong retrospective element to the commentaries, as journalists and readers looked back and reflected on the story as a whole. These responses provide important evidence that periodical literature played an essential role in shaping perceptions of the Arctic enterprise over many decades. Chapter 1 contains a detailed examination of this aspect of the discourse and explains the assumptions that underlie the treatment of Arctic literature in all its forms as a connected narrative.

The writing of McClintock's narrative shows the Arctic discourse at its most powerful. McClintock was initially reluctant to publish at all, and his correspondence reveals how intensely he felt the constraints imposed by public expectations. A man of remarkable integrity and out-standing ability as an Arctic traveller, McClintock had no secrets or shortcomings to conceal, yet he clearly experienced great anxiety as to whether he could adequately fill the public role of an Arctic author. Almost paradoxically, his fears had their origin in his own profound internalization of the Arctic discourse. In a further fascinating twist, McClintock's genuine reluctance to enter the realm of public print was among the factors that added authority to his narrative and to the dis-course of which it formed a part.

McClintock's closest associate in the writing process was his fellow explorer Sherard Osborn, who had extensive experience as a journalist. Though they shared many of the same preconceptions and convictions, McClintock and Osborn were men of contrasting temperament, and they understood Arctic authorship in somewhat different ways. Despite their on the whole harmonious collaboration, there were disputes between them. Like the divergent press interpretations immediately following McClintock's return, these points of conflict reveal much about the discourse: at such moments, usually implicit assumptions are made explicit and defended. In addition, the relationship between McClintock's narrative and Osborn's journalism opens up a previously unexamined aspect of Arctic literature. Here, too, the events of 1859–60 offer important evidence, which has been of central importance in shaping the theoretical assumptions and methodology of this book.

Tracing the Arctic Narrative

In many ways, therefore, 1859 is the best starting point, but it is also true that without a detailed knowledge of the development of the discourse over time, the full power of the constraints operating on McClintock cannot properly be appreciated. Chapter 2 deals with the renewal of British Arctic exploration in 1818, and from this point on the approach is almost entirely chronological. The main focus in chapters 2 and 3 is on John Barrow. Barrow has frequently been described as a behind-the-scenes mastermind who successfully duped the British public into accepting ordinary naval officers as almost superhuman heroes of exploration. However, when Barrow's writings are placed in the context of their original publication in the *Quarterly Review*, they can be seen as part of a much broader process, one in which Barrow willingly partici-pated, but that neither he nor any other individual could control. This was the re-imagining of Britain described by Linda Colley in *Britons: Forging the Nation 1707–1837.*

Barrow adapted the concepts and language he employed in response to public opinion, and he was also clearly influenced by the writings of other journalists: those who attacked his Arctic enterprise forced him to develop and defend his ideas, while those who supported him were in some cases more closely attuned to readers' expectations. He was quick to echo and imitate writers such as these. As a result, the discourse that ultimately evolved was in some respects utterly unlike that which Barrow initially employed. His early writings on the Arctic were embedded in the rhetoric of eighteenth-century science, but by 1820 Barrow had espoused a romantic vision of northern discovery as a quest linking the nineteenth century to the nation's glorious Elizabethan past.

Chapter 2 deals mainly with the 1818 expeditions of John Ross and David Buchan and chapter 3 with William Edward Parry's 1819–20 voyage. In contrast to the failures of Ross and Buchan, Parry sailed for hundreds of miles into the previously unknown Arctic archipelago. His narrative recounted this exploit in a modest, restrained tone that was praised by every reviewer. The book did much to determine the paradigms of Arctic authorship. In particular, Parry's achievements as an explorer and an author provided the context for the public response to Franklin's first overland journey in 1819–22 – one of the most dramatic episodes in Arctic history. Chapter 4 offers a detailed analysis of the writing and reception of Franklin's narrative. Franklin's intentions as an author were in some ways in harmony with the wider discourse, but in others seriously at odds with it. He himself understood his experiences through the conceptual framework provided by his religious faith, and what had happened to him was in his own mind largely a private and individual matter. His letters to his fiancée, Eleanor Porden, indicate that it was extremely difficult for Franklin to accept the role of Arctic hero. Only through the concept of duty could he reconcile himself to the writing of a public account. Critical response, however, very effectively integrated Franklin's private perceptions with public understandings of religious belief as a key component in the national character.

By the early 1820s, then, Arctic exploration was linked in the public mind with emerging narratives of national history and identity. Chapter 5, the only purely thematic chapter, explores these dimensions of Arctic literature more fully. Chapter 6 covers the late 1820s, the 1830s, and the 1840s – a time when developments in print culture carried the Arctic narrative to an ever wider audience. Chapters 7, 8, and 9 examine the period of the Franklin search. By the 1850s, the reading public had expanded enormously. The search was prolonged, and there were many controversies surrounding the government's conduct of the various expeditions. At the same time, Franklin's second wife, Jane, became the object of public adulation through her sponsorship of private search efforts. The Arctic narrative was adopted by liberal and radical journalists as a means of expressing protest, and the search was widely perceived as a people's crusade, which demonstrated that the world of officialdom was dangerously out of harmony with the popular spirit. The narrative became more flexible in terms of gender, class, and even race, as Lady Franklin assumed a leading role in the public eye, bringing with her such unconventional Arctic heroes as whaler William Penny, métis fur-trader William Kennedy, and French naval officer J.-R. Bellot. Attitudes about race, however, hardened significantly in 1854, when John Rae repeated Inuit allegations that the men of the lost expedition had resorted to cannibalism.

Criticism of the government reached its culminating point in the months following McClintock's return. The success of his expedition – the last in the series of Lady Franklin's private ventures – seemed to demonstrate conclusively that the Admiralty had neglected its duty to the nation's naval heroes, leaving it to personal devotion and private initiative to bring the long Arctic story to a fitting end. However, McClintock himself, as a naval officer whose beliefs and standards of judgment had been shaped by the Arctic narrative in its more traditional form, had no wish to perpetuate such dissensions. One of his aims as an author was to promote a sense of reconciliation, and in this he was ultimately successful. As a result, the elements of opposition in the Arctic literature of the 1850s were to a large extent forgotten. Chapter 9 describes this final stage.

The Evolution of the Explorer-Author from the Elizabethans to Cook

Ideas about how and by whom exploration accounts should be written changed significantly between the Elizabethan era and the early nineteenth century. Only from the late 1700s on was it considered essential that the commander of an expedition should produce a book. This new belief arose from the critical response to the narratives of James Cook's first two voyages. The first narrative, written from Cook's journal by John Hawkesworth, was seen as inferior in many significant ways to the second, written by Cook himself. The contrast between Hawkesworth's writing and Cook's formed an important part of the intellectual context in which nineteenth-century exploration literature was understood.

In the sixteenth century, English readers were familiar with exploration accounts in two basic forms: the individually published story of a particular voyage, written by the captain, some other participant, or another writer, and compilations bringing together many shorter accounts by different authors. The word 'compiler' could mean either a literary man who produced a narrative based on the records of a voyage or someone who collected and published various exploration reports (sometimes related to one voyage or explorer, sometimes to many).[30] In Richard Hakluyt's famous collection, *The Principal Navigations, Voyages, Traffics and Discoveries of the English Nation* (1st ed., 1589; 2nd rev. ed., 1598–1600), first- and third-person accounts created for a variety of reasons were brought together. The contents ranged from narratives by or about adventurers such as Hawkins, Drake, and Raleigh to the business reports of hard-headed merchants.[31]

In the late seventeenth century, William Dampier took the individual narrative to new heights of popularity with his *New Voyage Round the World* (1697). This tale of privateering and adventure went through five editions in its first eight years.[32] Throughout the eighteenth century, exploration literature was a very popular genre. However, individual, separately published narratives written by the explorers themselves became the dominant form only towards the end of the century. Compilations including many reports were numerous and evidently sold extremely well.[33] In addition, George Anson's circumnavigation in 1740–4 offered a new prominence to compilers. The chaplain of Anson's flagship, Richard Walter, turned the documents of the voyage into a readable narrative. The book was described on its title page as 'compiled from papers and other materials of the Right Honourable George Lord Anson and published under his direction by Richard Walter.'[34] It was one of the great successes of the century. There were four editions in its year of publication (1748) and it remained a favourite of the reading public for over 100 years.

When John Byron, Samuel Wallis, Philip Carteret, and James Cook made their Pacific voyages, the Admiralty's original intention was to keep secret as much as possible of the information obtained. So overwhelming, however, were public interest and curiosity that after Cook's return it was decided accounts must be published. The eighteenth-century mania for perfect grammar and elegant style made sailors seem like very unsuitable authors. As a result, Dr John Hawkesworth was chosen to produce narratives of all four voyages. Hawkesworth assured Lord Sandwich, the first lord of the Admiralty, that he would do his best 'to make it another Anson's Voyage.'[35] In an awkward attempt to merge the personal account with the compilation, Hawkesworth wrote in the first person throughout, assuming the voice of each explorer in turn. He explained in his preface that, despite this practice, the opinions expressed were sometimes his own.[36] Hawkesworth claimed that the manuscript had been read to the four commanders, and that all had approved it – a claim later disputed by the explorers.[37]

The experiment met with disapproval from reviewers, even before the explorers' objections were known. 'It undoubtedly renders the narrative more animated and interesting; and yet there are frequent occasions where the reader would wish to discriminate, and to be certain whether a particular opinion or reflection flows from the Journalist or the Editor. In some places indeed the distinction is somewhat too apparent; particularly where the usual plain texture of the nautical narrative suddenly disappears, by the insertion of some splendid philosophical *patches* of a very different manufacture,' observed the *Monthly Review*. Incongruities necessarily abounded in a book 'where the same individual assumes the two very different characters of a sea-commander and of a speculative philosopher or metaphysician; and uses the very dissimilar language of the log-book, and of the portico.'[38] However, the reviewer was reconciled to these inconsistencies by Hawkesworth's claim that the explorers approved of all he had written.

The *Annual Register*'s reviewer was more critical. 'Neither are we quite convinced by the Doctor's reasons, that it was altogether necessary to narrate in the first person; and when in the preface we find the Doctor letting us into the secret, and discussing the point with us, it is not so easy afterwards immediately to fall into the deception, and believe that the Doctor was a party in the voyage, or that any of the captains, or voyagers, are the writers,'[39] he pointed out. Other critics were less restrained; so intense, in fact, were some attacks that when Hawkesworth died shortly afterwards, the cause was said to be a broken heart.[40] An irate letter writer in *Baldwin's London Weekly Journal* complained that Hawkesworth had earned the magnificent sum of £6,000 by his literary labours, while the voyagers themselves had received far less recompense. '[W]hy should not [the explorers] be supposed qualified to describe what they saw, felt, and suffered in Terms sufficiently vigorous and proper? Is any Man offended at the plain honest Language of our old Voyagers?' he demanded. There was no need for a 'learned Gentleman' to 'digest the Journals, and lick [them] ... into the Shape of modern Elegance.'[41]

Despite Cook's initial lack of confidence in his own literary abilities, he himself wrote the narrative of his second voyage. Like the earlier compilers who integrated journals, logs, and other records into a single coherent narrative, Cook drew on his subordinates' records as well as his own, and this remained a standard practice for explorers in the nineteenth century. The practice was not concealed or denied, but neither was it advertised, and the commander's name on the title page contributed to a widespread impression that the work was entirely his own. Either the praise or the condemnation of reviewers and readers would therefore be directed almost exclusively at the leader of the expedition.

In his preface, Cook made an apology for his narrative's shortcomings, asking his readers to 'recollect that it is the production of a man, who has not had the advantage of much school education, but who has been constantly at sea from his youth ... After this account of myself, the Public must not expect from me the elegance of a fine writer, or the plausibility of a professed book-maker; but will, I hope, consider me as a plain man, zealously exerting himself in the service of his country, and determined to give the best account he is able of his proceedings.'[42] The critics' response was extremely positive. '[T]he work ... is properly and *bona fide* his own,' the *Monthly's* reviewer noted approvingly. He thought Cook's apology was unnecessary: 'It does not perhaps require the keen eye of a professed *Reviewer* to discover ... inaccuracies [i.e., small grammatical errors]; but, on the other hand, we are never at a loss to discern his honest meaning; and think that these little negligencies furnish an additional testimony to the truth of his declaration.' Cook's style was described as 'natural and manly ... simple and affecting,' and as evidence that the writer possessed a 'a sensible, worthy, and feeling mind.'[43]

From the 1770s on, the questions of authenticity and authority were almost always addressed in prefaces. In the case of George Vancouver, who died before finishing his narrative, his brother John hastened to assure readers that 'the melancholy event which has retarded [the book's] completion' need not 'affect its authenticity in the public opinion.' The portion of the narrative that Vancouver had written before his fatal illness was 'now presented to the public, exactly as it would have been had Captain Vancouver been still living.' His papers relating to the remaining part of the voyage were printed 'as nearly as possible in his own words, without attempting any such arrangement of them, as might tend to diminish their authenticity, or bring into doubt that scrupulous veracity from which Captain Vancouver never departed.' Although there had been some condensation, nothing had been added: 'I have strictly adhered to the rough documents before me,' John Vancouver attested. [44]

A narrative written by the commander of an expedition in a plain, honest style thus became the paradigm for the best exploration literature. Any obvious attempt at literary effect was equated with artifice and insincerity, while some awkwardness or dullness in the writing was not only acceptable but seen as welcome proof of a book's authenticity. These ideas would be still further developed in reviews of nineteenth-century Arctic narratives. Such developments were not, of course, limited to Arctic reviews, but by the mid-1820s the Arctic heroes were held in particular reverence as men whose deeds and words exemplified the British national character.

1 The End of an Epic, 1859–1860

McClintock … went forth, like a knight of old, at a lady's call. Style the enterprise Quixotic, if that is any consolation to you, O sublime officials of the Admiralty: Quixotic! yes, and what would the world be worth without *such* Quixotisms? There were many men, despite sublime officiality, who *felt* that he would succeed … We know now on which side lay the truth. McClintock came back, bringing with him a story …

'The End of an Epic,' *Sharpe's London Magazine,* November 1859

From the autumn of 1859 to the spring of 1860 and beyond, British newspapers and magazines were filled with reports and commentaries on the return of Captain Leopold McClintock's expedition in search of Sir John Franklin. Only nine days after McClintock's arrival in England, the *Illustrated London News* described the story he brought with him as 'already more deeply imprinted upon the national remembrance than any occurrence of our time.'[1] A few months later, a journalist discussing the history of British Arctic exploration remarked that there was no need for him to list McClintock's achievements, since they were 'too familiar and too deeply impressed upon all who have heard them to need repeating.'[2] Summing it all up in April 1860, another writer commented that McClintock's report was 'received … with an amount of interest and enthusiasm which has rarely been equalled.' In this journalist's view, the news was of the greatest possible national significance: the explorers were 'entitled to congratulate themselves not only on the success which has attended their special effort, but on the incidental benefit which is conferred on a whole people by the story of their gallant and chivalrous exploit.'[3]

The public unfolding of the story began when McClintock's ship, the steam yacht *Fox*, anchored off the Isle of Wight on 21 September 1859. McClintock was a naval officer, but his expedition was not sponsored by the government; it had been paid for by Lady Franklin. Nevertheless, his first action was to write a long report to the Admiralty. When the report was finished, he added a covering letter, in which he expressed his confidence that his superiors would

> rejoice to hear that our endeavours to ascertain the fate of the 'Franklin expedition' have met with complete success. At Point Victory, upon the north-west coast of King William's Island, a record has been found, dated the 25th of April, 1848 ... By it we were informed that Her Majesty's ships Erebus and Terror were abandoned on the 22d of April, 1848, in the ice ... and that the survivors, – in all amounting to 105 souls, under the command of Captain Crozier, – were proceeding to the Great Fish River. Sir John Franklin had died on the 11th of June, 1847.
>
> Many deeply interesting relics of our lost countrymen have been picked up upon the western shore of King William's Island, and others obtained from the Esquimaux.[4]

McClintock went ashore at Portsmouth and took the train to London, carrying with him his report, the record found at Point Victory, and two cases filled with objects belonging to the members of the lost expedition. His intention was to call on Lady Franklin and inform her in person of the expedition's results, but he found that she was in the south of France. She had spent every autumn since 1849 in England, waiting for news of the search expeditions, but in 1859 her doctor insisted that she go abroad. Nor was Sir Roderick Murchison, the president of the Royal Geographical Society and one of Lady Franklin's most devoted supporters, in London. Both he and McClintock's friend and fellow Arctic explorer, Sherard Osborn, were in Aberdeen, where the British Association for the Advancement of Science was meeting.

Late that evening, at the United Service Club, a tired McClintock wrote a letter to Lady Franklin, apologizing for his 'hasty scrawl.' It was a difficult task at best to break the news of her husband's death to a devoted wife, and, faced with the unexpected necessity of doing so in writing, McClintock made an awkward job of it. The rather abrupt style of his letter contrasts sharply with the well-rounded phrases of the official report. 'My dear Lady Franklin,' he wrote, 'Hoping to find you in Town, I did not write any letters for you, and now have only time to say we have returned all well. I am sure you entertained no high hopes of survivors being found, and this understood, you will, I think, receive our news as good news. Brief records have been found ... Sir John Franklin died on 11th June, 1847.'[5]

On the morning of 22 September McClintock presented himself at the Admiralty. At 10:30 a.m. a short, unemotional note was written: 'The Secretary of the Admiralty presents his compliments to the Editor of the *Times*, and forwards the accompanying letter for insertion.'[6] The note, McClintock's report with his covering letter, a list of the relics, and a copy of the Point Victory record duly appeared in the next day's *Times*. They were prefaced by a leading article which declared that there was one fact above all the others now revealed deserving of the public's attention: Franklin had died in 1847, only two years after his ill-fated expedition left England, and so there had never been the slightest chance of saving his life. The men Franklin had commanded were also dead before the end of 1848; they had 'all shared the fate of their chief, dropping down one after another until the last man perished.' All the expeditions sent out in search of them between 1848 and 1857 (many of which the *Times* had strenuously opposed) had therefore been misguided and unnecessary. The tragedy was cause, indeed, for grief, because Franklin and the others were brave men; yet the *Times* went so far as to call it 'wicked' to have sent out still more brave men in attempt after fruitless and risky attempt 'to gratify a curiosity which deserves almost to be called morbid, in order to furnish us with the exact particulars of the circumstances under which so many strong hearts and devoted souls were taken from us for ever.'

The message conveyed by the *Times* was that McClintock's return had a very simple meaning: the quixotic search for Franklin was over. '[T]here can be no longer those sad wailings from an imaginary Tintagel to persuade the credulous that an ARTHUR still lives,' the leading article proclaimed. By implication, though it was never directly stated, this last expedition was unnecessary, like all the others. Franklin and his men had died years before, and only those possessed by an 'almost ... morbid' curiosity could have wished to know the exact details of their passing. The *Times* acknowledged, although very briefly, that others would likely dispute this claim. The leader-writer observed: 'the duty of government is often graceless; it must often be in antagonism to the aspirations and desires of the governed, and here it is its duty, as it appears to us, to say, "Let the dead bury the dead." The report of Captain McClintock will close this sad eventful history.'[7]

Lady Franklin's absence from London was not mentioned in the *Times*'s initial report, and it therefore appeared that as soon as McClintock arrived in England, as a matter of course he had delivered his news to the Admiralty rather than to her. The Admiralty, with equal promptitude, had passed the story to the *Times*. As a result, the newspaper's interpretation of events seemed to have official sanction. This was a common enough situation. Many government departments released information through the *Times*; readers were well aware of the paper's close ties with officialdom, and its early access to news. Much of the *Times*'s prestige and its ability to influence public opinion stemmed from this situation.[8]

McClintock was thus placed in an awkward position, for both the Admiralty and the *Times* had long opposed the continuation of the Franklin search. For the past five years, advocates of the search had tried in vain to influence the *Times* in their favour by behind-the-scenes manoeuvring, in the hope that, if the newspaper changed its stance, the Admiralty might be forced to follow suit. One of them wrote despairingly in 1856, 'the world is governed by the Times – at least England is,' adding that he did not think the public 'ought to be so grossly misled.'[9] McClintock was a cautious man, without the wealth and family connections that often proved crucial to a naval officer's career, and his decision to command Lady Franklin's expedition had not been an easy one. As he wrote to her niece and devoted companion, Sophia Cracroft, early in 1857: 'unless the Admty favoured it I certainly wd not like to embark in it, because failure, would give them a [illegible] for gratifying their hostile feelings, by "shelving" one for life.'[10]

McClintock must have been aware that the Admiralty would likely release his news with the least possible fanfare and applause. This in itself would not have troubled him, for like most naval officers he was conditioned to regard publicity seekers with contempt. Nevertheless, having risked much to take part in the search for Franklin, he can hardly have been pleased at the thought of seeing his success belittled. However, any course other than the one McClintock chose might offend those on whom his future prospects depended. Particularly in Lady Franklin's absence, he had no alternative but to accept the Admiralty's method of releasing his report. His response to the leading article is not recorded, but a few days later, an officer signing himself 'An Arctic Navigator' wrote an indignant letter to the editor, describing it as an 'unkind slap'[11] to McClintock and his fellow searchers.

The anonymous officer need not have made this reply, for events quickly demonstrated that it was not within the *Times*'s power to determine the public understanding of McClintock's news. The 23rd of September was a Friday. On Saturday the 24th the other daily papers and a few weeklies began to offer their very different perspectives. The weekly papers included some of the most widely read and influential middle-class periodical publications, such as the *Illustrated London News*, the *Athenaeum*, the *Spectator*, and the *Saturday Review*. As well, there were the working-class *Weekly Dispatch*, *News of the World*, *Lloyd's Weekly Newspaper*, and *Reynolds's Newspaper*, all with a strong radical bent. By October, the weeklies were in full cry. The floodgates of publicity had been opened, and the expedition (which had set out two years earlier amid considerable scepticism about its chances of success) was hailed as 'the end of an epic'[12] – one of the greatest epics of the English nation. The interpretation put forward so confidently by the *Times* was soon under serious attack. 'While there was hope that but one lived to tell the tale of heroism and suffering, ten thousand Englishmen were ready to go forth to the rescue. Now ... a nation mourns their loss, and recounts for the admiration of future ages such details of their adventures and sufferings as, by the equal courage of after explorers, have been rescued from obscurity,'[13] wrote the *Weekly Dispatch*. The onslaught was continued in many monthly magazines. Dozens of voices insisted that the story of Franklin's last expedition should never be put aside; instead, it should be told and retold for the benefit of the present and future generations. '[T]o our children's children will the stirring tale be told,'[14] predicted one. 'Sir John Franklin and his companions have left behind them, memories that shall endure as long as their land's language lives,'[15] declared another.

In late December McClintock's narrative, *The Voyage of the 'Fox' in the Arctic Seas*, was published by John Murray, resulting in numerous reviews and other articles. The first edition of 10,000 copies sold out almost immediately.[16] Throughout 1860 periodicals continued to discuss the book, with some quarterlies making their contributions to the debate long after McClintock's return (in the case of the *Westminster Review*, more than a year afterwards). Finally, in a sort of summing-up as the Arctic story lost its immediacy, Thomas Hood's elegaic poem 'The Lost Expedition' appeared in the December 1860 issue of *Macmillan's Magazine*.

By November 1859 it was quite evident that the *Times*'s initial advantage in publishing the story first, with official sanction, had not been sufficient to create a general trend in press commentary. The majority of journalists were determined to present McClintock's news not as the relatively inconsequential confirmation of what all sensible people had realized long before – that there could be no survivors of the lost expedition – but rather as the final magnificent episode in an epic tale of British greatness. As one observer put it, 'The ephemeral at a penny and the portly quarterly up to six shillings all alike joined in the general exultation.'[17] According to the *Illustrated London News*, the exultation was shared by 'millions of sympathizing souls'[18] among the reading public. On 30 December the *Times* capitulated, and published a review of *The Voyage of the 'Fox'* in which the search for Franklin was described as a noble and chivalrous enterprise.

The coverage of McClintock's return could be used for a case study in mid-Victorian publicity, featuring a comparison of the various publications' opinions and strategies. In the history of the British periodical press, 1859 was an important milestone. As Richard Altick points out, in that year 'the most talked-of aspect of the publishing scene ... was the tremendous increase in the number and variety of periodicals.'[19] During 1859, 115 new journals began publication in London alone.[20] One of the older weeklies, *Chambers's Edinburgh Journal*, observed humorously that 'the Millennium of the Periodical Writer is at last arrived,' and it predicted that England's population might soon consist entirely of editors and contributors, with no audiences left to read their productions.[21] Periodicals from the well established to the newly fledged and from the highbrow to the popular joined enthusiastically in the coverage of McClintock's exploit. *Blackwood's Magazine*, which had reported on Arctic matters since 1818, published one of the longest reviews of McClintock's narrative. A steady stream of articles and reviews in the *Athenaeum* had provided one of the most important sources of information on northern exploration from the time the journal was founded in the late 1820s, and this tradition was continued. The *Illustrated London News*, which began publication in 1842, covered the story from Franklin's departure in 1845 onward, and in 1859 it devoted many pages to McClintock's discoveries, including numerous pictures and a facsimile of the Point Victory record. The *London Journal* was a penny weekly established in 1845. It specialized in melodramatic serial fiction and achieved the highest circulation of its day. Here McClintock was celebrated in verse as the hero who

> in sorrow's last extremity
> When man's strong heart had fail'd him, and each eye
> Turn'd from the task away – when Franklin's name
> Had passed from living lips to hist'ry's fame –
> ... Force[d] from the grave the all that she could say,
> The when, the how, his spirit pass'd away.[22]

The new weeklies *Once a Week* and *Everybody's Journal* published articles by explorer Sherard Osborn, a close friend of McClintock. The phenomenally successful first issue (January 1860) of the monthly *Cornhill Magazine*, which sold between 110,000 and 120,000 copies, contained excerpts from the journal of one of the *Fox's* officers. (The issue was released just before Christmas; Tennyson read the *Fox* article aloud to his wife, Emily, on Christmas Eve.)[23] The fourth issue (February 1860) of another new monthly, *Macmillan's*, included a long article on 'Arctic Enterprise and Its Results since 1815.'

In order to understand how this debate was so resoundingly won by those who rejected the *Times*'s claim to omniscience, it is necessary not only to look at which periodicals, addressed to which audiences, advanced which views, but to consider the ways periodicals fitted into the lives of their readers. British audiences had been reading about the Franklin search since 1848 and about Arctic exploration since 1818. Not only was the explorers' goal, the Northwest Passage, useless from any practical point of view,[24] but it was exceptionally difficult to find. Expedition after expedition set out, only to be baffled by the geographical complexities of the Canadian north. It appears to be a story of frustration and failure, but when the *Times* expressed this opinion, an overwhelming number of other journals disagreed, insisting that Arctic exploration was of great, perhaps even central, importance to the life of the nation, and that its heroes deserved the full support of their fellow citizens. It seems unlikely that so many periodical writers would have made these claims if the majority of their readers agreed with the *Times*. Yet in many respects the Victorian fascination with the Arctic is at first difficult to understand, for there were few triumphant successes or tangible rewards to rouse public enthusiasm.

Here it is useful to turn to the work of literary critics on reader response and on serial publication. The work of Linda K. Hughes and Michael Lund focuses on serialized fiction, but it also forms an excellent starting point for research into this non-fictional topic. Hughes and Lund argue that two major issues regarding serial publication have received insufficient recognition: first, that 'the serial embodied a vision, a perspective on stories about life, intrinsic to Victorian culture,' and second, that 'the dynamics of serial reading' played a major role in the interpretation of fictional works.[25] Victorian readers liked to envision expansive stretches of time, and Hughes and Lund suggest that they found serial publication of fiction especially appealing because of this. The telling of long stories, rich in detail, was particularly well suited to serial publication, since the pauses between instalments gave readers time to reflect on every nuance in the tale. A reader holding an entire novel could skim through it in a short time or cheat by looking ahead to see 'how it came out'; a reader with only a few instalments to go on had to carefully ponder whatever evidence he or she had been given. (The serialization of a novel usually lasted one or two years, which was the same length of time most expeditions remained in the field.)

Some readers likely reflected in solitude, but there is ample evidence, with regard to both fiction and exploration reports, that reading aloud and discussion in social groups played a large part in the process of interpretation. Reading aloud was a well-established practice in middle-class families. Some working-class families followed suit, and workers with an interest in literature sometimes pooled their resources to buy periodicals and cheap books. Henry Mayhew recorded in *London Labour and the London Poor* (1862) that literate slum dwellers willing to read to their neighbours would always find an eager audience.[26]

In an 1848 review of *Jane Eyre* and *Vanity Fair*, Elizabeth Rigby commented, 'A remarkable novel is a great event for English society. It is a kind of common friend, about whom people can speak the truth without fear of being compromised, and confess their emotions without being ashamed ... We fly with eagerness to some common ground in which each can take the liveliest interest.'[27] Two years later, another reviewer referred to 'the friends of Sir John Franklin,' and explained that by this term he meant 'the whole English public.'[28] Like Jane Eyre and Becky Sharp, Franklin had become so constant a theme of conversation that he seemed like 'a common friend' to all those who had read about him.

Hughes and Lund's insights into the ways periodical publication of novels influenced reader response are valid for reports of exploration as well, since much of what they observe about the intersection of periodical rhythms with the rhythms of readers' lives holds true for all topics covered on an ongoing basis. The long time span covered by the search for the Northwest Passage was more of an advantage than a disadvantage to nineteenth-century reading audiences. As William Scoresby, a former Arctic whaling captain, wrote in 1850, 'Notwithstanding ... the perpetual failures, as to the main object, of the numerous modern expeditions, – the explorations themselves have ever been regarded with general, and, not infrequent[ly], *absorbing* interest.'[29] The failure of so many expeditions mattered less when they were perceived as parts of a larger whole, and as episodes whose true significance might not be apparent until the story was finished.

Moreover, the Victorians understood Arctic exploration not merely as a series of intensely interesting events, but as a story which had naturally and of its own accord taken on a literary form. The term *epic*, used by so many periodical writers, was not hastily or ignorantly chosen. '[T]he whole story of the Arctic Expeditions,' wrote one journalist in the fall of 1859, 'is to me a Poem. If I call it an Epic, I think I do not use too lofty a word.'[30] Other writers claimed that the story was a romance, in which 'England's naval chivalry'[31] sought the Northwest Passage as King Arthur's knights had sought the Holy Grail. The *Leisure Hour*, for example, described Franklin as 'the Bayard of the seas and shores,' adding, 'to poets it may now be left to celebrate the wild romance of the modern Odyssey, and to sing the praises of the Penelope of England [Lady Franklin].'[32]

If Arctic exploration was a story in the literary sense, it was a story that had so far appeared in instalments. In 1856 a reviewer wrote of the 'deep interest' felt in the 'long story of Arctic adventure ... occurring as it has done in our own times, in a succession of striking episodes prolonged through now many years.'[33] In the autumn of 1859 many editors took pains to direct their readers' attention back to other instalments so that, now the full story was available, they could consider it as a whole and more readily grasp its true significance. Some periodicals merely made general references to previous coverage,[34] while others, for example, the *Leisure Hour*, provided lists of earlier articles. The editor of the *Illustrated London News* was the most explicit in his remarks on the purpose of such lists, noting that they were published 'with a view to aid such readers as are anxious to trace the connected narrative of this most melancholy chapter in the History of Discovery.'[35]

Exploration narratives were, of course, central to the 'connected narrative,' but they did not supersede other forms of publication. After the appearance of an explorer's own account in book form, it naturally took its place as the most authoritative source of information. However, many members of the reading public, no matter how fascinated by the story, likely read the narratives only long after their publication, or even not at all. The price of newly published books in nineteenth-century England was very high in relation to the prices charged by American publishers. British publishers preferred smaller but more costly editions, while American publishers favoured large print runs and low prices. The standard cost of a three-volume novel was established at 31 shillings and sixpence in the 1820s and did not drop until the 1890s.[36] Exploration narratives often cost even more, being published in lavish quarto editions with many illustrations. This was especially true in the 1820s. For example, the first edition of Franklin's *Narrative of a Journey to the Shores of the Polar Sea* cost 4 guineas, and the second, in two octavo volumes without illustrations, 24 shillings.[37] A number of reviewers commented that such prices were, as the *Gentleman's Magazine* put it, 'an insuperable bar to ... wide circulation.'[38]

Matters had improved somewhat by the late 1850s, and the first edition of *The Voyage of the 'Fox'* was an octavo volume priced at 16 shillings. Nevertheless, this was a substantial sum, and buyers got one book for just over half the price of three volumes of fiction. McClintock's narrative was unquestionably a luxury item. Despite the growth of subscription libraries, even in the middle decades of the century there must have been many readers who gained their knowledge of Arctic exploration mainly from newspapers, magazines, and secondary works. Inexpensive reprints of novels and standard works of non-fiction were common by the 1850s, but Arctic narratives were not often among the reprinted books. John Murray, the publisher (and copyright holder) of most Arctic narratives, was not particularly active in the field of cheap reprints. In the late 1820s abridged, reasonably priced editions of Parry and Franklin were brought out, but there were no further republications. As one of Murray's friends wrote to him, 'You are not, and cannot be a cheap book-seller ... It would require a large return of profit to reconcile me to your making your venerable establishment into a kind of old-clothes shop.'[39] It was not until 1869, a decade after its first publication, that *The Voyage of the 'Fox'* appeared in a cheap (5 shilling) edition. (Although almost all the volumes printed were sold, the result was a net loss for Murray, showing that inexpensive books were indeed not the firm's forte.) [40]

However, as periodicals costing only a few pence became more numerous from the 1820s on, the potential for exploration reports to reach a very wide audience was achieved. As Richard Altick has pointed out, the vast majority of the literate population of England 'formed a market for cheap periodicals alone.'[41] Some of the least expensive and most widely circulated periodicals, including the *Mirror of Literature, Amusement, and Instruction*, *Knight's Penny Magazine*, and *Chambers's Edinburgh Journal*, printed extracts from the narratives, which would have provided the only exposure some readers had to these primary accounts. The *Mirror* (1822–49) sold from 15,000 to 80,000 copies per issue; the *Penny Magazine* had a circulation of about 100,000 in its first year (1832), 160,000 in the second, and 200,000 in the third, but declined thereafter and ceased publication in 1845. *Chambers's* also began publication in 1832, with circulation at about 30,000–50,000 copies per issue; the second series (starting in 1844), sold about 80,000, and this level was apparently maintained through the 1850s.[42]

Yet there was far more to the question than price. Even those upper- and middle-class readers who could afford to buy, or otherwise managed to obtain copies of, the published narratives, would very seldom have come to them without extensive prior information and many preconceptions gained from the reading of periodicals. On the contrary, the more interested a reader was in the expeditions, the more likely he or she would be to follow periodical coverage closely. The expeditions did not set off in a blaze of newspaper publicity, vanish from the public eye for a year or two, and then return to a second quick burst of ephemeral print, followed by the speedy publication of one or more narratives. Instead, the rhythms of periodical publication combined with the rhythms of Arctic travel. An immense amount of information was published not only before the appearance of the narratives, but in many cases before the return of the expeditions. From 1818 on, editors were well aware of the appeal these reports held. In the 1820s William Jerdan, the editor of the *Literary Gazette*, went to great lengths to obtain the earliest possible news and recorded that as a result of his efforts the *Gazette's* circulation rose substantially.[43] In the *Blackwood's* review of Parry's first narrative, the author commented with mock ruefulness: 'throughout the whole time that these northern voyages have occupied public attention, we have been so assiduous in picking up recent information respecting their progress ... and so fortunate in obtaining it accurate and minute, we find ourselves now ... forestalled of our matter out of our own mouth.'[44]

Such information appeared according to a reasonably predictable pattern, which contributed to readers' sense of Arctic exploration as an ongoing story. Before the flowering of the illustrated press in the late nineteenth century, the departure of an expedition did not usually receive extensive coverage. However, letters, and sometimes journals, written by officers and brought back by whaling ships and Hudson's Bay Company ships, or in some cases sent overland from the Arctic to Montreal and then on to England, were widely published in magazines ranging from the scientific to the popular. Reports received through these channels (and later, during the Franklin search period, through returning relief expeditions) could be looked for during the late summer, fall, and early winter. The silent periods between were often very effective in heightening readers' anticipation of what would come next. When an expedition returned, letters from its members to friends and family again found their way into the press. And, since literary piracy was then almost a way of life, the letters were often reprinted in other publications.[45] *Blackwood's*, for example, published an 'Account of the Expedition to the North Pole' (led by John Ross), which was 'drawn up from original letters from Captain Ross and Lieut. Robertson of the Isabella' in October 1818.[46] In the November issue came news from David Buchan's expedition in the form of a 'Letter from an Officer Concerning the Polar Expedition' written 'to a friend in Scotland.'[47] In December 1818, after Ross's return, the news of his expedition was conveyed through a letter from an unnamed officer, apparently written directly to the editor.[48] A year later, in December 1819, *Blackwood's* printed a 'Letter from the Arctic Land Expedition' (the first Franklin expedition) by 'J.R.,' presumably Dr John Richardson. The editor explained that he had 'been favoured with a copy of the following interesting letter, addressed to a Lady in this neighbourhood.'[49]

Richardson's letter was reprinted in the February 1820 issue of the *Gentleman's Magazine*,[50] and the *Gentleman's* printed another letter, likely from Franklin himself, in January 1821.[51] This letter also appeared in the *Literary Chronicle* on 17 March 1821.[52] In November 1821 the *Dumfries Courier* published a letter from Richardson 'to a gentleman in that part of the country,' which was reprinted in the *Literary Gazette* on 24 November.[53] A letter recounting the 'Progress of the Arctic Land Expedition under the command of Lieutenant Franklin,' which had been read to the Wernerian Society in December 1820, was printed in the *Edinburgh Philosophical Journal* in January 1821.[54]

The *New Monthly Magazine* published letters from two unnamed officers of Ross's expedition in October 1818,[55] a letter 'from an officer of the Isabella to Captain Napier' in November,[56] and an 'Extract of a Letter from on board the Dorothea' in December.[57] In September 1821 an 'interesting letter from one of the gentlemen employed' on Parry's second expedition appeared.[58]

On occasions when the last report had provided something of a cliff-hanger, followed a year later by news of a surprising or dramatic nature, public interest was correspondingly strong. In the case of McClintock, the *Fox* sailed in early July 1857. Letters sent back by the whaling fleet duly made their appearance in the press during November.[59] (Despite the *Times*'s reluctance to give the expedition favourable publicity, McClintock's letters gained publication in its columns by a very simple expedient: the recipients quoted them in their own letters to the editor.) No more was heard until August 1858, when the news was of a distinctly discouraging nature.[60] McClintock reported that the *Fox* had spent the winter trapped in the middle ice of Baffin Bay. This obstacle was the first to be encountered by vessels sailing west from Greenland towards Lancaster Sound (the gateway to the Arctic archipelago). It seemed that Lady Franklin's last effort was destined to meet with even worse fortune than most of the expeditions that had gone before. No progress of any kind could be placed to McClintock's credit: in the spring of 1858 the *Fox* had not yet even entered the archipelago. However, a quiet determination to make every possible effort despite the loss of a year's work was the predominant theme of McClintock's letters home. Further letters printed in November 1858 were written from Lancaster Sound, indicating that there was at least some possibility of success.[61] McClintock's triumphant return in the next year was rendered all the more dramatic because of his early trials. After the publication of his narrative, many reviewers harked back to the discouragements of the expedition's first year and lauded McClintock's perseverance.[62]

Letters printed in the press gave readers access to the explorers' personal correspondence, and such glimpses of distant events were unparallelled for their vividness and sense of immediacy. In cases such as McClintock's, his feelings in a difficult and frustrating situation could be expressed far more strongly in letters to family and friends than in an official report, and likely evoked a correspondingly greater sense of sympathy. For many readers, the effect of these letters must have been to make them feel that the explorers were actual acquaintances, writing directly to them from the icy North. The young Brontës, for example, incorporated Parry and Ross into their private world of fantasy. Emily Brontë adopted 'Pare' as her special hero, while Anne, so young that she could not pronounce his name properly, chose 'Trott' (Ross). Their knowledge of the explorers was much more likely derived from the letters and other articles in *Blackwood's* than from the narratives. The Brontës' biographer Winifred Gerin believes that *Blackwood's* was the source 'of their phenomenally precocious knowledge on matters of history, literature, politics, travel and art; and, more striking still, of the very shape and direction their imaginative writings took.' As an adult, Branwell Brontë wrote that the magazine had 'laid a hold on my mind which succeeding years have consecrated into a most sacred feeling. I cannot express ... the heavenliness of associations connected with ... articles ... read and re-read as a little child ... "Blackwood" formed my chief delight.'[63] Though few other children were so talented or precocious, many must have experienced similar emotions.

In addition to the letters, detailed reports of sledging journeys and scientific work were published in the press with increasing frequency, and after 1830 lectures given to the Royal Geographical Society were not only printed in the Society's journal, but reported on in publications ranging from the *Times* and the *Athenaeum* to the *Penny Magazine* and the *News of the World*. During the Franklin search, reports of government committees' deliberations, with extensive evidence in their appendices, were published. Extracts from and comments on these Arctic blue books were to be found in a wide range of periodicals. Then, after the narrative of an expedition was published, periodicals offered further commentary in their reviews. These frequently contained very long extracts, making at least the more striking and dramatic passages familiar even to people who did not read the books.

What Derek Roper has called the 'guided tour' method of reviewing, in which summarizing a book's contents through judiciously selected extracts was seen as an important part of the reviewer's task,[64] survived from the eighteenth century well into the nineteenth. This ensured that interested readers could examine long passages from a recently published book, even if to purchase it would have been far beyond their means. Reviews were thus an extremely important means of disseminating both information about the expeditions and ideas about the larger significance of exploration, and, like all periodical literature, they were available to a wider audience than the books themselves. They would have provided readers who had been following the story as it unfolded a strong sense of belonging to an interpretive community.[65] Given the enormous amount of information available in periodical form, even those who did not read the narratives in full could regard themselves as knowledgeable about the subject and qualified to participate in the process of interpretation.

In terms of richness and detail, then, the periodical reports of polar exploration were not inferior to published narratives, and the sense of intimacy and privileged insight to be gained from reading explorers' letters to family and friends may have been even greater than that derived from reading the narratives. The exact nature of readers' responses does, however, remain somewhat elusive. As has often been pointed out, evidence about the reading experience is usually difficult to come by. There are many general contemporary statements about the intense fascination of Arctic exploits; according to William Scoresby, for example, the return of any Arctic expedition 'usually excited the most lively interest,' and the expeditions in search of Franklin 'called forth the public solicitude and sympathy through the length and breadth of the land.'[66] An anonymous writer in *Chambers's Edinburgh Journal* agreed in 1867 that Arctic adventure 'seems to be the only kind of travel of which neither adventurers nor readers weary.'[67] However, more detailed accounts of how exploration reports and narratives were read are rare.

Fortunately, the ingenious solution hit upon by Hughes and Lund – that of considering writers in their capacity as readers – can also be applied to exploration literature. Reviews of individual instalments of serialized novels were published by many weekly newspapers; Hughes and Lund have found that the reviews contain a great deal of evidence about how episodes were considered both in themselves and as part of a larger, unfolding whole.[68] As they point out, the reviewers cannot be taken as entirely typical readers, yet their responses must have had much in common with those of the general public. In the case of Arctic exploration, periodical writers often mentioned their personal reactions to the reading of the latest report or narrative. Such references could be extremely specific about the form in which information was received and the circumstances under which reading was done. An anonymous author, using the pen name 'Joven,' began his article in the November 1859 issue of *Sharpe's London Magazine* by recounting his experiences as a reader and by speculating about how typical they were. Joven quoted a passage by Sir Humphrey Gilbert, which he had read in Hakluyt's *Voyages*, and also a sentence from McClintock's report to the Admiralty. 'We have here,' he then wrote,

the first and the last notable words that have been written on the subject of Arctic discovery; and no careful reader can fail to see that the spirit of both is identical. With McClintock's words we are all familiar: it is but a few weeks since we read them in the newspapers. Humphrey Gilbert's are less known to us. Probably not very many of my readers have ever disinterred Sir Humphrey's treatise from the dust of old libraries, or pored over it in the pages of Hakluyt's "Collection of Voyages and Travels." I have done so, and with very strange feelings. I have looked at the old black-letter volume, and tried to realize for myself the sensations with which it would be read when it first appeared, more than two centuries and a-half ago. That first edition of Hakluyt is a handsome and a portly book still, and I have tried to think of it as a *new* book – *new* as when it came to the dwellers in Elizabethan England.[69]

Joven was acutely aware that one aspect of his reading experience (seeing McClintock's report in a newspaper) was common to most of the literate population of England, but another (having access to a first edition of Hakluyt) was restricted to an educated and bookish minority. In his role as a periodical writer, he hoped to draw a connection between the two types of reading that others would find useful and relevant. Furthermore, he attempted to recount his experience in such a way that his audience would mentally project themselves back into the Elizabethan age and picture themselves opening Hakluyt with the same sensations they had felt when reading a newspaper report. They could then, in imagination, comprehend both the vast sweep and the essential unity of the epic that had just ended.

If the evidence to be found in periodicals is treated with proper caution and sometimes read against the grain, it seems entirely appropriate to use it as a means of approaching the question of reader response. Periodical writers undoubtedly had ideological aims, and their representations of themselves as readers are not simple mirrors of nineteenth-century reality. Nevertheless, there is a great deal these articles can tell us, and, particularly in the absence of other extensive sources, reviews and other published responses to Arctic exploration must form the basis of any study of this topic. Another advantage in considering writers as readers is that it works against a rigid 'top-down' model of discourse.

The power of reviews is undeniable: explorers themselves could be strongly influenced by reviewers' opinions and deeply stirred by their rhetoric. Parry, for instance, returned from his second voyage in search of the Northwest Passage in October 1823. Franklin's narrative of his first overland expedition had been published in the previous spring, and it was reviewed by John Barrow in the *Quarterly Review*.[70] Shortly after his arrival, Parry wrote a highly emotional letter to Franklin. 'I have not yet seen your book, and have only read the Quarterly Review. This latter was put into my hand at Shetland [where Parry's expedition landed], and I need not be ashamed to say that I cried over it like a child,'[71] he told his fellow-explorer. This particular review had an exceptionally strong influence on the meaning many people attributed to the achievements of British Arctic explorers, and it was frequently quoted or paraphrased in other nineteenth-century accounts (a topic that will be dealt with in later chapters). Its effect on Parry is of great interest, since he had three roles to play in relation to the discourse: those of explorer, writer, and reader. In none of these was he either entirely a free agent or entirely constrained by prevailing discourses about exploration. The narrative Parry had published two years earlier, in 1821, added important new elements to the discourse within which Barrow's review of Franklin was written. It is thus difficult to say where the chain of cause and effect that led to the explorer weeping over the *Quarterly* began – or where it ended.

By 1859 the significance attributed to the Arctic metanarrative was vast. For most British periodical writers, Arctic discovery was not only a source of exciting news stories but a national epic with deep roots in the past. Arctic exploration was seen as a characteristically British achievement, which illustrated the nation's greatness in an especially striking way. 'The history of Arctic adventure and discovery,' wrote the *Illustrated London News* in October 1859,

> forms a noble chapter in the annals of Great Britain. Among all the brilliant deeds of our countrymen by sea and land, from the days of Elizabeth to those of Victoria, the achievements of such men as Ross, Parry, Franklin, and, last of all, McClintock, and their brave comrades, stand out pre-eminent for unselfish heroism, and for almost epical grandeur ...
>
> Foreigners who read of the pertinacious efforts made by our people, rather than by our Government, in this direction, ask why it is left to the hardy mariners of these isles to discover the North-West Passage? ... The reason seems to be that the love of maritime adventure lies deep in the heart of our population; at the very root, as it were, of our British nature. It is an instinct or a passion that courses in our blood, palpitates in our pulses, and forms one of the main elements of the strength and glory of the nation.[72]

Just how far back the true beginning of the epic lay was a matter on which there was less clear-cut agreement. The *Illustrated London News* traced it to the Elizabethan period and even beyond, back to 'the "Sea Kings," our old Danish and Scandinavian ancestors.'[73] This was a common practice, but readers were not always directed so far into the past. Three time frames can be discerned. The first dated the process of Arctic exploration from the sixteenth century, thus linking it to the period when England first achieved true greatness as a nation, and to the beginnings of the empire. As well as this long-term framework, there was a middle term, which considered mainly events since the ending of the Napoleonic wars and the subsequent renewal of Arctic exploration in 1818. This time frame, like the first, correlated well with the story of Britain's growth as a nation and an empire, since the period of definitive supremacy dated from the defeat of Napoleon. Finally, the shortest term began either with Franklin's departure in 1845 or with the beginning of the search for him in 1848. While lacking the broad sweep of the other two, for many periodicals (including the *Illustrated London News*) it was the more practical choice, since it was more or less within this time span that they themselves had commenced publication. However, the middle term also served periodicals' self-image as opinion makers, since the *Quarterly Review* in its heyday had provided much of the original impetus for the renewal of Arctic voyages.

In many ways, the closure provided by McClintock's return – the 'sense of an ending' – was more important than the exact date of the beginning, and the epic could be seen as having commenced three centuries, four decades, or fourteen years before with little difference to the presumed meaning of the story. Whatever beginning date was chosen, the vision of northern exploration as an epic was an effective refutation of the *Times*'s claim that what had ended was a mistaken enterprise, of little consequence in the larger scheme of things. For most periodical writers, the story was a grand one, and the dramatic value of the closing episode served to heighten their sense of its overall importance. The correlation between the periodicals' own extended coverage of the story and its ongoing, epic nature over many years further reinforced the implicit arguments against the *Times*'s interpretation.

This study attempts to do as the editor of the *Illustrated London News* suggested: trace the connected narrative of Arctic exploration in the major (and as many as possible of the minor) nineteenth-century British periodicals. The explorers' narratives are placed within this context, so that despite the wide range of forms in which written representations were available, the literature of polar exploration can be seen as a unified whole. The time frame is the middle term, from 1818 to 1859–60. I have begun with the ending in order to emphasize the form the story ultimately took in the mid-Victorian mind. This form, quite obviously, was not necessarily implicit in the articles published in the 1810s, yet an awareness of it can sharpen the analysis of periodical literature over the decades by directing attention towards the literary qualities that actual events could take on in this medium. In particular, the constitution of a national epic in periodical writings, which have often been considered ephemeral and therefore of less importance than books, shows the power this form of publication had in nineteenth-century culture. The 'epic' comparison so often made by periodical writers would almost certainly have been considered less valid if narratives in book form had not

existed. However, the books might not have been perceived as epics without the surrounding framework of interpretation in periodicals: the
interplay between the two forms of publication was complex and fruitful.

In terms of the history of print culture, the analysis of Arctic exploration as it was understood through periodical literature reveals an ongoing, continuous process (the gradual development of a metanarrative)
during a period that saw a great deal of change (the rise of the weekly
paper, the decline of the quarterlies, the advent of cheap illustrations,
the enormous expansion of the reading public). By examining the 'serialization' of a non-fictional topic, the coverage of which was spread over
four decades, the work done on serialized fiction can be extended and
enriched. In terms of the history of exploration, such an approach also
has much to offer. The topic of Arctic exploration in the nineteenth-
century press has been dealt with by only two recent writers, Beau
Riffenburgh in *The Myth of the Explorer: The Press, Sensationalism and
Geographical Discovery* and Robert David in a chapter of *The Arctic in the
British Imagination, 1818–1914.* Both restrict their analyses to newspapers
in the second half of the century, when more sensationalized coverage
and illustrated papers had become the norm.[74] In Riffenburgh's case
this is quite appropriate, since newspaper sensationalism is his topic.
David, however, claims to offer a broader picture of the Arctic in British
culture from 1818 to 1914. He argues that there is a great need for more
sophisticated and wider-ranging approaches to the topic of polar exploration, and he believes that this can be achieved by expanding the subject matter beyond printed texts to include visual images. His focus is
therefore on the illustrated press.[75]

David's account moves from 1855, when the stamp tax on newspapers was abolished, to the 1890s, with the earlier half of the century receiving very little attention. Since the metanarrative of Arctic
exploration had its roots in this earlier period, David misses many of
the key links made between Arctic journeys and the British national
character. The construction of Arctic heroism began in elite periodicals like the Tory *Quarterly Review,* but by the 1850s the story had developed a strong populist tinge, as it was enthusiastically taken up by
mass-circulation journals, including the *Illustrated London News* and
Cassell's Family Paper. It also made its way to Liberal and moderately
Radical middle-class papers, most notably the *Daily News, Leader,* and
Sun, and to working-class journals such as the *Weekly Dispatch* and *News
of the World.* This fascinating process of development is missed in studies that begin at mid-century.[76]

Another flaw in David's methodology is that he considers only a few of the vast number of daily and weekly papers published in nineteenth-century Britain. The *Times* is the only daily he examines in any detail, and his analysis of its coverage is open to criticism on a number of points. He suggests that popular interest in polar exploration was fostered mainly by the illustrated papers, and in order to substantiate his contention that earlier coverage was of fairly minor consequence, he notes that the *Times*'s reporting of Arctic expeditions was 'very low-key.' This observation, however, proves nothing about press coverage as a whole, since the *Times* was notorious for its strong opposition to most of the Franklin search expeditions. David points to the low number of articles about McClintock's expedition in the *Times* as proof that before the 1870s, the daily press had relatively little to say about the Arctic.[77] Again, the *Times*'s coverage was not typical, and David has missed a few of the articles that did appear in its pages. For example, the *Times* did not publish a large number of book reviews, but a select few publications, deemed to be of particular importance, were given notices. The enthusiastic review of *The Voyage of the 'Fox'*, mentioned earlier in this chapter, is not included in David's list; presumably, he counted only news items and leading articles. But this review was an important piece, as its very appearance indicated that the *Times* had abandoned its earlier editorial position in response to public opinion. Such a capitulation was an unusual event in the history of the *Times*,[78] and it shows that far from being of little interest to the reading public in the 1850s, Arctic exploration was a site where meaning was fiercely contested. While David's determination to consider visual images as well as printed texts is undoubtedly a positive development, his own fairly narrow focus on the illustrated weeklies does limit the validity of his conclusions. This study examines mainly printed texts, taking in a far wider range of publications over a longer period of time, and, when read in conjunction with David's analysis of pictorial representations, it should help to provide a fuller overall view of the subject.

It also seems necessary to question the assumption made by both David and Riffenburgh that only sensational coverage could command a significant degree of public attention. Riffenburgh notes that early newspaper and magazine articles were far longer than would now be considered acceptable, and that they were written in what he describes as a 'dull' and 'understated' style.[79] Because the style of these articles is so different from that which had evolved by the second half of the century, Riffenburgh and David believe that readers took relatively little interest in them. On the contrary, it appears that the quieter, but very extensive, early coverage was widely and enthusiastically read, and that it wielded a correspondingly large degree of cultural power.

The theoretical framework proposed by David, based on Bernard Smith's work, has both advantages and difficulties. In his *Imagining the Pacific in the Wake of Cook's Voyages*, Smith places great emphasis on the differences between explorers' journals and drawings made on the spot and the later transformations of these words and images by others who had never travelled to the Pacific. Smith acknowledges the power of European cultural models to produce distortions in written descriptions and artistic portrayals of the non-European world. However, he also insists that the sailors, scientists, and artists who accompanied Cook did have the ability and the motivation to produce realistic, adequate representations. From this point of view, their journals and field sketches are far more satisfactory than the later versions produced for circulation in Europe. According to Smith, the artists were forced to abandon their realistic vision as they reworked their first impressions into images that would meet the public's expectations. Other artists without any first-hand experience at all produced further distortions, resulting in the type of misrepresentation deplored by Edward Said. Smith devotes a chapter to such distortions in European portrayals of Pacific peoples and landscapes and another to literary and artistic representations of Cook himself in his role as hero. He concludes that a similar process, whereby realistic eyewitness accounts were replaced with stereotyped images, worked to 'heroize' the explorer. Though Cook, as a historical individual, unquestionably had many admirable qualities, the resulting heroic figure must be seen as a cultural construct that does not in any serious way reflect reality.[80]

David reaches a similar conclusion in his study of the Arctic. He argues that a few standard images of the Arctic were repeated over and over in the illustrated papers with only slight variations, and that they eventually became a kind of shorthand that represented the far north in the popular imagination mainly through clichés and stereotypes.[81] While positive portrayals of northern Aboriginal people and the land itself could occasionally be found in the press and popular literature, the representations as a whole were seriously lacking. David's view is thus similar to Said's contention that Orientalist discourse was characterized by its uniform, unvarying quality, and that Europeans were, in effect, prisoners of their own cultural creation: in Said's words, they were 'constrained in what they could either experience or say' about the non-European world.[82] Both Smith and David depart slightly from

Said's views, believing that adequate representations of non-European reality were possible though extremely rare. If they existed at all, it was at a very early stage in the process of cultural transmission, and they usually went unnoticed amid so many derivative and false representations.

For all its merits, Smith's work unfortunately does not directly consider the nature of representation and discourse. It is unquestionably true that in terms of cultural interaction, primary source accounts are far more complex than secondary works, arising as they did from actual experience of unfamiliar environments. A gradual process of transformation is apparent when the representations of both Aboriginal peoples and the European explorers themselves are traced over the years following an expedition's return. Yet precisely why this process occurred and how it worked are questions not answered in any detail by either Smith or David.

It is tempting to follow Smith, and to see certain representations of Arctic exploration as authentic and others as derivative and false – mere discourse, as opposed to realistic accounts. The Pacific and Arctic explorers, although products of European culture, were often able to engage with the unknown in a surprisingly complex, sophisticated manner. A close examination of British Arctic journals and narratives shows that many of the explorers were, in fact, remarkably sensitive to other cultures. This suggests that these explorers have themselves been the victims of discourse, and that they have been culturally (re)constructed to serve the purposes of a post-colonial era. However, it should not be assumed that the experiences the explorers recorded in their journals, letters, and narratives were not conditioned by discourse – or, in other words, that there was a straightforward reality of exploration which has been ignored by nineteenth- and twentieth-century secondary writers alike, and which may now be recovered and contrasted with the distortions perpetuated in the secondary literature. It does, however, seem to be the case that the explorers' experiences, and their manner of recording them, stemmed from other discourses that postmodern and post-colonial writers have not taken into consideration.

The extreme complexity of the subject is shown by the fact that men with direct experience of the Arctic, who in their role as explorer-authors could produce subtle and often very positive portrayals of its landscape and people, could also assume the journalist's role and contribute to the heroizing process deplored by Smith and David. Exploration narratives sold well, yet the nineteenth-century public also formed an insatiable market for the (from our point of view) far less impressive secondary works. To understand the more stereotyped accounts as some sort of official ideology imposed by a central power clearly is not possible, since, as the controversy surrounding McClintock's return demonstrates, the metanarrative of Arctic exploration emerged from the interplay between many different forms of print culture, and the closest approach to an official version was quickly and effectively contested. Nor is the tendency to see popular representations as inferior and debased necessarily the most useful approach. Though they are in many ways unsatisfactory as representations of the non-European world, when viewed from another angle they constitute a fascinating (and far from simple or static) cultural phenomenon.

Sherard Osborn is the most striking example of an explorer who engaged in different forms of authorship.[83] He took part in two Franklin search expeditions, wrote a narrative of his own, and edited two others: one with credit given to him on the title page, and one without (apparently at his own request). In addition, he published widely in periodicals, sometimes signing his articles and sometimes publishing them anonymously. Osborn was unquestionably a maverick. Though a naval officer who eventually rose to the rank of rear admiral, he had an abiding dislike for formality, for 'old fogies,' and for bureaucracy of all kinds. His friend Clements Markham summed him up as 'a man of fascinating personality, who was beloved by all who served under him. When he had his own way ... he was a perfect subordinate. Still, he was a better man for those who served under him than for those under whom he served.'[84] 'Combative he undoubtedly was,' wrote another of Osborn's associates, 'but the sailor-like frankness and largeness of the man disarmed all rancorous antagonism.'[85]

Osborn's first Arctic experience came during Horatio Austin's 1850–1 expedition, when he commanded H.M.S. *Pioneer.* He and Austin were frequently in conflict, and after the expedition's return to England, Osborn was one of the few officers who did not receive promotion. He published an excellent narrative, *Stray Leaves from an Arctic Journal; or, eighteen Months in the polar Regions, in search of Sir John Franklin's Expedition, in the Years 1850–51.* The style is direct, almost jaunty, often humorous, and very readable. In 1852–4, Osborn served again in the Arctic under Sir Edward Belcher, who was even more of a naval martinet than Austin. As a result, Osborn went back to England as a prisoner, under threat of court martial for insubordination. (He was promptly set free, with an official commendation of his conduct.)[86] Osborn was on the friendliest terms with Lady Franklin and Sophia Cracroft, her niece and confidante. He continued to be a strong advocate of further expeditions long after the search fell out of favour in official circles. However, he also felt free to publicly state his views even when they were opposed to Lady Franklin's. For example, Osborn accepted Robert McClure's claim to be the first discoverer of the Northwest Passage, even though Lady Franklin stubbornly (and, as it turned out, correctly) refused to do so, on the grounds that her husband's missing expedition might have discovered it first. Osborn's support of McClure was a source of considerable distress to her.

Osborn found authorship much to his liking, and during a period when his health made him unfit for active naval service, it became a financial necessity as well. After his return from Belcher's expedition, he wrote a narrative of McClure's voyage, based on the latter's journal. It was published under the title *The Discovery of the North-West Passage: From the Logs and Journals of Capt. Robert Le M. McClure* (1856). In 1857 he published *Quedah; or Stray Leaves from a Journal in Malayan Waters*, an account of his experiences as a midshipman in the late 1830s. Osborn then served with distinction in the Crimean War. He also served in China and in the squadron that escorted Lord Elgin on his 1857 mission to Japan. It was after this service that Osborn returned to England as an invalid. He was able to make ends meet by publishing articles on his Japanese experiences and other non-Arctic topics in *Blackwood's Magazine*. (According to the *Dictionary of National Biography*, he 'laboured unremittingly with his pen.') 'A Cruise in Japanese Waters' was serialized in *Blackwood's* beginning in December 1858, then published in book form in 1860.

Osborn and McClintock were friends, although, as Markham noted, 'No two men could be more different.'[87] Osborn considered McClintock too subservient in his attitude to officialdom. He complained to Sophia Cracroft that he could not 'understand [McClintock's] want of independence of a parcel of besotted old gentlemen in the Admiralty – and it simply riles me to hear him talk of trusting to them.'[88] Osborn helped to prepare McClintock's journal for publication and 'saw it through the press,'[89] a remarkably speedy process, as the narrative was published only a few months after the expedition's return. He was deeply involved in the production of the book from the beginning. 'I send you the Journal and will call for it & your opinion on Wednesday next,' Osborn wrote to Murray in early October. 'It wants much editorship. I'll gladly do, and get done all in my power in that respect.'[90] A draft of the narrative preserved in the National Maritime Museum[91] has corrections and annotations by Osborn, and he apparently made further corrections at a later stage: in late November, he sent Murray revises 'complete ... up to page 336.'[92]

At the same time, Osborn wrote a number of articles for periodical publication. Some were signed: 'Arctic Discovery and Sir John Franklin' (*Everybody's Journal*, 15 and 22 October); 'The Last Voyage of Sir John Franklin' (*Once a Week*, 22 and 29 October); and 'The Search for Sir John Franklin' (*Once a Week*, 5 November). Others were published anonymously, and unfortunately it is not possible to be sure how many of these he wrote. A letter from Sophia Cracroft to John Richardson dated 14 October originally contained clippings from the *Illustrated London News*, and Cracroft told Richardson that these were by Osborn.[93] As the enclosures have been separated from the letter, there is now no way of telling which articles this comment referred to. It seems likely that they were part of the supplement published on 1 October. Osborn wrote at least two anonymous reviews of *The Voyage of the 'Fox'*, published in *Blackwood's Magazine* and the *Times*.[94] (His triumphant appearance in the columns of 'our old enemy,'[95] as Lady Franklin called the *Times*, must have been a source of particular satisfaction to him.)

Neither review contains the slightest indication that the reviewer played so important a part in the writing of the narrative. The style is floridly romantic: 'the hair-breadth escapes from wreck and famine; [the] firm manly reliance in God, and their own energy; [the] proofs of a courage which no danger could daunt, and an endurance which no suffering could subdue, thrill the landsman as he reads them, and must ever stimulate future generations of seamen to emulate such deeds of "high emprize,"'[96] Osborn wrote in the *Times*. In *Blackwood's* he commented that no failure had daunted McClintock. The *Fox* expedition was a 'chivalrous enterprise,' and the explorers' purpose was 'to dare all things.'[97]

Osborn's reviews were restrained in comparison with his articles in *Everybody's Journal* and *Once a Week*. The latter provide an example of the heroizing process at its most extreme. Osborn described the search for the Northwest Passage as a quest in which 'many an aspiring spirit essayed to do that deed whereby bright honour and immortality were to be won.' According to Osborn, 'The veil which hid from human ken the mysteries of the Arctic zone was not to be rent by one bold stroke.' Instead, 'it was to be the test of British perseverance, patience, and hardihood. ... The dread realms of frost and silence were only to be penetrated by the labours of two generations of seamen and travellers. The consummation of the discovery of the north-west passage was to be obtained but by the self-sacrifice of a hundred heroes.'[98]

Osborn described the death of Franklin and the hopeless last march of the surviving members of the expedition as if he had been an eyewitness to these events, and he represented the explorers as meeting their ends with the utmost courage, resignation, and nobility:

Poor lost ones, we mark them day by day, growing weaker ... we hear the cheering appeal of the gallant officers to the despairing ones, the kind applause heartily bestowed to the self-sacrificing and the brave ... they pass from sight into the snow-storm, which the warm south wind kindly sends to shroud the worn-out ones, who gently lie down to die; and they died so peacefully, so calmly, with the mind sweetly wandering back to the homes and friends of their childhood; the long-remembered prayer upon their lips, and their last fleeting thoughts of some long-treasured love for one they would someday meet in Heaven.[99]

Through McClintock's courage and devotion, the story of the lost expedition had been rescued from oblivion: 'As those men fell ... their prayer must have been that their countrymen might learn how nobly they accomplished the task they had voluntarily undertaken. That prayer has been granted. As long as Britain exists, or our language is spoken, so long will be remembered and related the glorious fate of the crews of the Erebus and Terror.'[100]

In late December the *Once a Week* articles, with the addition of some new material, were published in book form by Bradbury and Evans as *The Career, Last Voyage, and Fate of Captain Sir John Franklin*. 'I have arranged the republication of my Once a Week Papers shall come out at Christmas so as to keep the ball rolling and keep interest directed to the subject,'[101] Osborn told Murray. The book was reviewed by C.R. Weld in the *Athenaeum* on 28 January. Weld had written about Arctic literature for many years, and having a family connection with Franklin (he was the explorer's nephew by marriage), he was sympathetic to the search even in its more quixotic manifestations. Yet Weld felt obliged to point out that Osborn's account was based far more on imagination than on ascertained fact. He took particular exception to Osborn's account of Franklin's funeral, about which McClintock had brought back not the slightest evidence, and commented that the incident was 'apparently, so palpable to [Osborn] that he has embodied the burial scene in an engraving. This would have been better suppressed.'[102] (Not all reviewers, however, were quite this severe: one described Osborn's book equivocally as a 'heart-stirring, albeit partly imaginary, sketch ... drawn up ...

upon such data as were available,'[103] while another cheerfully and uncritically incorporated quotations from Osborn into his own reconstruction of the explorers' last days.)[104]

It is clear that Osborn had gone beyond what his more fastidious contemporaries considered permissible in speculating about events where solid evidence was lacking. But despite his financial situation in 1859, Osborn was no second-rate literary hack, churning out melodramatic accounts of an Arctic he had never seen. He was, rather, an extremely intelligent individual, with many unconventional views and the force of character to express them even when it was not to his advantage. He had previously produced an Arctic narrative with a refreshingly down-to-earth tone, full of humour and realistic details.

Moreover, in his reviews of McClintock, Osborn praised his fellow explorer above all for his restrained, modest, and natural writing style. He claimed that McClintock's unadorned, straightforward prose stood as the best guarantee of the narrative's truthfulness and innate value. Osborn began his *Blackwood's* review by commending McClintock's 'simple and sailor-like narrative,' and further remarked that the 'modesty and unassuming nature of real worth' had 'seldom been more charmingly exemplified.'[105] In the *Times*, he described the book as a 'truthful, unpretending tale,' so inherently affecting that it needed 'no fine language to touch our hearts.'[106]

In his role as reviewer, Osborn presented the book to the public as a straightforward reflection of McClintock's own sterling character rather than as the result of literary artifice of any kind.[107] Osborn's letters show that he wished to keep his involvement in the production of the book from public knowledge. On this issue, however, he encountered firm opposition from McClintock himself. McClintock, too, felt an overriding concern with the public perception of his work and its authenticity, and though he shared many of Osborn's assumptions, he came to a different conclusion about the proper course under the circumstances. In McClintock's mind, the important fact was that he had not written his journal with an eye to later publication. Therefore, when preparing it for the press he required the help of a friend more experienced in the ways of the publishing world. To McClintock, it seemed absolutely essential that Osborn's role be known, as otherwise his own integrity and good faith might be doubted. His great dread was that he might be perceived as a publicity seeker who had participated in the Franklin search in the hope of profit and fame. McClintock had already written to Sir Roderick Murchison that at first he had been determined not to publish anything, '& it is Lady Franklin who is getting it done. I wish you to know this.' Murchison had agreed to write the preface to *The Voyage of the 'Fox,'* and in a strong hint as to the desired content, McClintock told him, 'I leave it to your good taste & your knowledge of my own wishes, to say as little as possible about me.'[108] Murchison accordingly wrote that McClintock had kept his journal with 'no idea whatever of publishing it,'[109] and that he had consented to write the narrative only in response to the entreaties of Lady Franklin and other friends.

When Osborn objected to the proposed acknowledgement of his help in the dedication, McClintock's response was uncompromising. '[T]he passage is an important one, & bears out Sir Roderick's introduction,' he told Murray. 'It is due to Sir R.M[.] & to myself that this passage is inserted, also to Lady F; to the public to assure them that the book is not a cooked up affair, so all things considered Osborn must allow himself to be all wrong he must "shut up" & say amen to it.'[110] Osborn was little accustomed to giving in, but on this issue it seems he did shut up and say amen. The published dedication informed readers that 'To ... SHERARD OSBORN, I am greatly obliged for his kindness in seeing [the book] through the press.'

Despite their differences, the aim of both McClintock and Osborn was to avoid any suspicion that the book was 'a cooked up affair,' and both firmly believed in the authenticity of the account they had produced. The question of authenticity was, in fact, central to the discourse of polar exploration literature. McClintock's official biographer, Clements Markham (himself a veteran of Austin's expedition), wrote that *The Voyage of the 'Fox'* was the 'best and most interesting of all Arctic books ... It is ... a story modestly and simply told ... and yet with such unconscious force and pathos that the reader becomes enthralled by the living interest of the narrative ... Unconscious of his own power, McClintock unintentionally impresses the reader with his supreme ability and consummate leadership.'[111]

For Osborn, Markham, and many reviewers, the overtly romantic style in which they themselves at times wrote[112] would have been painfully out of place in a narrative published by the leader of an expedition, as would any indication of egotism on the part of the explorer-author. Reviewers could be brutal to explorers who ignored this unwritten rule: for example, Sir Edward Belcher's *The Last of the Arctic Voyages*, published in 1855, was widely condemned. Belcher, unlike McClintock, appeared in his narrative as anything but modest, presenting himself instead as all too conscious of his power both as a naval commander and as an author. The

British Quarterly Review observed with scathing sarcasm, 'Till we read his book we were scarcely aware of the divinity which hedges in a captain in the Royal Navy. He appears to write in full uniform ... In fact, after turning over a few pages of the work, we felt as if we ought to peruse the remainder cap in hand, and to wind up every section with numerous expressions of gratitude to the writer for his condescension in communicating his sentiments to mankind.'[113] The books that received reviewers' approbation were those in which the writer called the least attention to himself as a hero. This attitude seems to stand in puzzling contrast to the elaborate rhetoric with which non-explorers, or explorers writing as commentators rather than recounting their own exploits, clothed the epic of Arctic exploration and its leading figures. The effects that Arctic narratives had on their readers were described with much appreciation, and in some cases an almost reverent awe, but reviewers seemed determined to believe that such effects had been achieved without any forethought or literary strategy. (It is extremely important to note that the narratives themselves laid no claim to the status of epic or romance; these claims were made on their behalf by reviewers.)

To gain approval, the explorers had to appear (in Markham's phrase) 'unconscious of [their] own power.' Their books had to seem as if they had been created through a natural rather than a cultural process. The narratives' resemblance to the literary genres of epic and romance was firmly believed to have arisen from an unusual congruence between literary form and reality. The claim that literary artifice played no part in the writing of exploration narratives was repeated again and again in periodical literature. The review of Elisha Kent Kane's *Arctic Explorations* in *Chambers's Edinburgh Journal* expressed this belief with particular force and clarity: the reviewer declared that Kane's book was 'above all common praise, on account of the simple, manly, unaffected style in which the narrative of arduous enterprise and firm endurance' was told. It was 'obviously a faithful record of occurrences, made by a man who was quite aware that what he had to tell needed no extraneous embellishment.' There was, however, 'so much of artistic order in the mind of the narrator, that the unvarnished record ... naturally shaped itself into a work of distinguished excellence upon literary grounds.'[114]

For Osborn to claim, from behind the cover of anonymity, that a book he himself had helped to write was a mirror-like reflection both of events and of its author's character might seem like hypocrisy and deception. Yet in a historical account it is surely more useful to reflect upon the seeming dichotomy between the plain style of the most successful narratives and the floridly rhetorical writing of many secondary accounts than to condemn it. The opposition and contradiction that twenty-first-century observers see may not have existed in the minds of nineteenth-century writers. (To view them as hypocrites would, of course, be to assume that they were aware of the contradiction and consciously chose to perpetuate it.) The literary collaboration of McClintock and Osborn shows that there can be no simple separation of authentic, first-hand accounts on one hand and derivative, distorted works on the other. The primary and secondary works influenced one another at countless points. It is better to see the literature of polar exploration as a whole, and to make an attempt to understand it in all its complexity, than to divide it into categories and elevate one type of writing over another.

Tracing the connected narrative through a broad range of publications can heighten awareness of the many forms in which representations of Arctic exploration could reach the public, and it can contribute to a better understanding of the complex process through which the discourse of polar heroism took shape. The temporal dimension of the narrative, from 1818 to 1859, has another advantage besides those already mentioned. To begin in 1818 is to link the Victorian literature of Arctic exploration with its Romantic roots. In turning to the periodical literature of the late 1810s and early 1820s, which in both practical and literary terms laid so much of the groundwork for later developments, it is essential to keep in mind the specific cultural context within which these articles were written, published, and read. Reviews of Arctic narratives can be found next to reviews of Byron, Shelley, Keats, and Scott (and indeed occasionally seem to have been deliberately placed beside commentaries on these writers' work). When Arctic literature is separated from this context it loses much of its original meaning.

During the 1980s and 1990s, the links between Romanticism and British imperialism were largely ignored.[115] The postcolonial re-evaluation of nineteenth-century European literature that began with Said's *Orientalism* (1979) did not posit any key links between the imperial enterprise and the Romantic movement. Much greater emphasis was placed on imperialist ideology as part of the Enlightenment narrative of progress through reason and science. In Said's work, Romanticism is viewed as little more than an interest in the more exotic aspects of otherness. It has been claimed by Said and others that Europeans constructed themselves as rational, scientific, progressive, and therefore unalterably superior to the primitive non-European 'others,' and that European political dominance was justified primarily through Enlightenment ideals.[116] Said believes that for all imperialists, the conquest of the non-European world, like the conquest of nature, appeared to be an inevitable and necessary part of human progress.

However, the Romantic revolt against eighteenth-century philosophy provided many of the most important paradigms of nineteenth-century thought.[117] It was of particular importance in Britain, where the Enlightenment was often viewed with hostility in the 1790s and after: according to Burke and his followers, revolutionary France was the Enlightenment in action.[118] The relationship between British imperialism and eighteenth-century philosophy was an extremely problematic one, since the worship of reason was seen as an attribute not of the British national character but of the French 'other.' The dominant strand in nineteenth-century British imperialist thought was romantic and conservative rather than utilitarian and liberal, and in many ways the British constructed themselves in opposition to the Enlightenment narrative. It was often claimed that Englishmen were warm-hearted, generous, practical, and brave, while the French, though highly intelligent, had cold natures and were ruled by logic and theory. As Edmund Burke wrote, 'it seems as if it were the prevalent opinion in Paris, that an unfeeling heart, and an undoubting confidence, are the sole qualifications for a perfect legislator.' These 'men of theory,' who 'value[d] themselves on being systematic,' aimed at 'a geometrical and arithmetical constitution.'[119] Their attempt to construct a utopian society along lines dictated by reason led only to the Reign of Terror.

Such beliefs are of immense importance for the study of British polar exploration literature. Romanticism lay at the core of the ideology this literature expressed. Nineteenth-century British Arctic explorers were not predisposed to see their work as part of the triumphant conquest of nature; rather, they believed that only by submitting to the power of nature could they benefit and learn from their experiences. Clements Markham, one of the most ardent advocates of polar exploration, defined it as 'a great but unequal conflict with the powers of nature in order better to understand the laws of nature.'[120] In the polar regions, the idea that nature could be conquered appeared highly unrealistic, and it seems to have been because it provided the opportunity for contact with nature at its strongest and most impressive that such exploration was believed to be of value.

While the explorers certainly hoped to gain scientific knowledge from their endeavours, and while science was of key importance to their self-understanding, their beliefs about the value of their enterprise were strongly coloured by Romanticism and by the Christian beliefs that many of them (including Franklin and McClintock) held. This combination was also to be found among reviewers: for example, David Brewster, a Scottish scientist who was also a Presbyterian minister, took a keen interest in northern exploration from 1818 until the end of the Franklin search, and wrote many reviews of Arctic literature. Brewster declared in 1852, 'It is man's duty to complete the survey of the planet which he owns. Reason demands it of him as a tribute to the All-wise; and Revelation calls upon him to discover the secrets of His wisdom, and make known the marvels of His power.'[121]

In recounting their adventures, the Arctic explorers frequently referred to their reliance on the power of God. 'It has pleased God to accord us a deliverance in which His merciful protection contrasts – how strongly! – with our own utter helplessness ... Thus forcibly does His great goodness come home to the mind!'[122] wrote McClintock in *The Voyage of the 'Fox,'* describing his ship's escape from the dangers of the northern pack ice. Such passages were to be found in almost every Arctic narrative. Joshua Fitch, reviewing McClintock's book in the Methodist *London Quarterly Review,* insisted that the Arctic expeditions had 'illustrated a form of heroism quite peculiar in its character ... There is required here rare calmness, and that steadfast patience and endurance which is often the sternest form of trial.' The patient courage of Arctic explorers bore no resemblance to 'the brutal and purposeless hardihood which seeks danger for its own sake, and goes forth to encounter difficulties in the mere wantonness and triumph of physical strength.' In Fitch's opinion, the Bibles and other religious books found by McClintock among the relics of the Franklin expedition proved that even in apparent defeat, 'as they dropped down to die,' Franklin's men were 'cheered by a sense of the Divine presence.'[123] Another reviewer remarked, 'Locked among ice under the Arctic night, our voyagers from first to last have been impressed not only with a new sense of the Almighty power, but with living trust in the beneficence by which they are sustained.' This writer praised McClintock for his geographical and scientific researches, but thought that his narrative would 'be read more widely for the heart that is in it, for the manly simplicity with which it tells [the] story.'[124]

For many advocates of Arctic exploration, the immediate success or failure of the expeditions did not really matter; so long as the explorers' faith and devotion stood as examples to the nation, the enterprise had fulfilled its most important aim. The utilitarian calculations of the risk and the monetary cost of the search that were so important to the Admiralty and the *Times*, on the other hand, could easily be characterized as a betrayal of true national ideals. 'It seems to me so un-English to coldly reason upon the advisability of seeking Franklin ... that had I not heard it advanced I could not have believed such indifference could exist,'[125] Osborn wrote in a letter to the *Times* in 1850. In 1859 the *Illustrated London News* described the utilitarian attitude as 'cold, stolid, selfish,' and a 'stigma' on the national record.[126] The Admiralty bureaucrats, in this view, were a blinkered minority, seriously and perhaps dangerously out of touch with the popular spirit.

The beginnings of the Arctic metanarrative lay in the years around 1820; that is, in the period when some of the greatest Romantic literature was being published and when the evangelical revival of religion was at its height. Romance was the first literary genre through which the story of polar exploration took shape in the British imagination, and its power was sustained throughout the nineteenth century. Even more specifically, the discourses that shaped the literature of British Arctic exploration arose from the literary and ideological battles between Tories, Whigs, and Radicals as they were fought out in the pages of such journals as the *Quarterly Review*, the *Edinburgh Review*, and the *Examiner*.

2 The Dreams of Romance, 1818–1820

Glowing anticipations are confidently formed ... which would scarcely be hazarded even in the dreams of romance.

John Leslie, 'Polar Ice, and a North-West Passage,'
Edinburgh Review, June 1818

Forty years before Leopold McClintock's return to England, in the summer of 1819, readers of the *Quarterly Review* were taking up a newly published issue[1] containing a review of Captain John Ross's *A Voyage of Discovery, made under the orders of the Admiralty, in His Majesty's Ships Isabella and Alexander, for the purpose of exploring Baffin's Bay, and inquiring into the probability of a North-west Passage.* The long (forty-nine-page) unsigned article was written by John Barrow, the second secretary of the Admiralty, a fact of which many readers would have been aware.[2] Barrow began by describing his disappointment with both Ross's deeds and his written words, and he made it clear that he felt entitled to criticize the explorer from an exceptionally lofty and privileged point of view:

The lively interest we have taken in discussing the question of a northern communication between the waters of the Pacific and the Atlantic, and the sanguine expectations which we had formed, on no slight grounds, as we thought, of the speedy solution of this problem ... will sufficiently account for the disappointment we experience ... at the total failure of the two Expeditions which had so much excited the attention of Europe ...

The failure of the Polar Expedition [under Captain David Buchan] was owing to one of those accidents, to which all sea voyages are liable ... Of that of the other [Ross's] we hardly know in what terms to speak, or how to

account for it. We have the story before us, such as it is, told by the officer
most interested in making it good ... [but] we cannot conscientiously pronounce it any otherwise than unsatisfactory ... We ... are actuated solely by
a sense of duty ... unmixed with a single particle of personal hostility; for
we are most willing to think [Ross] ... an active and zealous officer in the
ordinary duties of his profession: at the same time however he must excuse
us for believing that, in accepting the command of a Voyage of Discovery,
he had not given due consideration to the nature of his qualifications. It is
a service for which all officers, however brave and intelligent they may be,
are not equally qualified; it requires a peculiar tact, an inquisitive and persevering pursuit after details of fact not always interesting, a contempt of
danger, and an enthusiasm not to be damped by ordinary difficulties.[3]

Despite his claim to impartiality and his half-hearted tribute to Ross's
abilities, Barrow went on to pen an exceptionally vituperative review, in
which his personal feelings of disappointment and spite clearly played a
role. Ross's performance as both an explorer and a writer was called
into question, and it was strongly implied that he must be either incompetent or dishonest, and perhaps both. The reasons for Barrow's enmity
would have been apparent to readers who knew or guessed the
reviewer's identity. In his official capacity at the Admiralty, and in three
articles published in the *Quarterly Review*, Barrow had strenuously
advocated that an expedition be sent to Baffin Bay in order to explore
its unknown northern reaches and to discover whether any of its
western branches, especially Lancaster Sound, might be the gateway to
the Northwest Passage. Ross had returned with the unwelcome (and,
Barrow rightly suspected, erroneous) report that Lancaster Sound was
closed at its western end by mountainous land.

Barrow's article was in many ways typical of its time. Both the Tory
Quarterly and its great Whig rival, the *Edinburgh Review*, were known for
their merciless treatment of authors who incurred their displeasure
('having come before the public,' Barrow grimly observed of Ross, 'he
must be content to undergo the usual ordeal').[4] Writers in both journals
frequently made judgments based far more on politics than on purely
literary considerations. In many cases, they used the books being
reviewed merely as pretexts for essays in which their own views on literary and political matters were expounded at great length.[5]

This new, highly critical and combative approach was markedly different from that of the eighteenth-century reviewers, who usually provided
summaries of, and long extracts from, the books in question, sometimes

adding prescriptive comments on matters of literary treatment and style. As most reviews were owned by booksellers with an interest in increasing sales, favourable notices predominated. Derek Roper describes Sir Walter Scott's claim that these periodicals gave 'applause to everything that reached even mediocrity' as somewhat exaggerated, but essentially correct. According to both Scott and Roper, it was because the *Edinburgh* and *Quarterly* reviewers (in Scott's words) 'squeezed into their sauce plenty of acid' that their work had such a great impact, becoming 'popular from novelty as well as from merit.'[6]

The change was one Ross understandably deplored. He strongly resented the intense scrutiny to which he was subjected in the public sphere of the new periodical writing,[7] and he believed that as a naval officer under Admiralty orders he was obliged to answer for his actions to his official superiors alone, not to the public. Indeed, he was convinced that he ought to have been shielded from published commentary. That Barrow could publicly attack him from behind the cover of anonymous publication was especially galling to Ross. He vainly protested that 'if the officers of His Majesty's Navy shall be subject to have their conduct canvassed before the Public in this very improper manner,' future explorers' power of decision-making would be hampered by the fear that they might be unjustly condemned by those 'unacquainted with nautical affairs' and hence 'unable to judge of such questions.'[8]

Looking forward to the developments that were to come rather than back on those that had already occurred, Barrow's comments on the desired qualities of an Arctic discoverer show how great were the changes that took place between 1819 and 1859. The image of the polar explorer as a romantic, knightly hero, noble yet modest and unpretending, had not yet been constructed, and though Barrow clearly wished to heighten his readers' condemnation of Ross's failings by measuring him against what Clements Markham would later call the 'beau ideal' of an explorer,[9] no such ideal figure was then available in fully realized form.

The Arctic metanarrative did not spring from a preconceived plan. If any individual can be held responsible for the course British Arctic exploration took in the first half of the nineteenth century, that individual was surely John Barrow. He was the epitome of the behind-the-scenes manipulator; as his biographer, Christopher Lloyd, has written, 'From whatever angle one looks at the history of his times ... Barrow's figure appears in the background, planning, advising, promoting.'[10] (Besides his role in determining naval policy, Barrow advocated the acquisition of the Cape Colony by Britain; chose St Helena as Napoleon's place of exile; founded the Royal Geographical Society; and wrote nearly 200 articles for the *Quarterly Review*.) Not only was he a powerful official, but his articles in the *Quarterly* had an immense influence on both events and perceptions. As a periodical writer, he wielded a very high degree of cultural power. Yet what happened, in terms both of events and of interpretations, was nothing like what Barrow had planned in the 1810s. Barrow did not foresee a forty-year epic quest for the passage, culminating in a decade-long search for a missing expedition; rather, he anticipated a fairly quick and efficient process of discovery in which the advancement of scientific knowledge would be the primary aim. The discourse employed by Barrow in 1819 was significantly different from the discourse that had evolved by 1859. He did not begin as a Romantic, but as the years passed he made significant contributions to the emergence of a romantic metanarrative. Clearly, there were strong elements of continuity in the process of evolution, but the elements of discontinuity must also be given full weight.

Barrow's review was typical of its time, and that time was exceptionally complex, both culturally and politically. Barrow was born in 1764 and died in 1848, just as the long Franklin search was beginning. In 1816, when he wrote his first article on northern exploration, he was fifty-two years old, and many of his assumptions were those of an earlier period. He was a farmer's son, who had risen to a position of wealth, power, and influence in the eighteenth-century way, by finding patrons to advance his career. Barrow had a firm belief in the intrinsic value of scientific knowledge. He justified the risk and expenditure involved in Arctic exploration on the grounds that 'to the liberal and honourable mind that thinks the pursuit of science for the sake of science, worthy of a great, a prosperous, and an enlightened nation like England ... the benefits of science are not to be calculated ... [The] expeditions may fail in the main object of the arduous enterprize [*sic*]; but they can scarcely fail in being the means of extending the sphere of human knowledge; and if they bring back an accession of this, they cannot be said to have been sent out in vain – for "knowledge is power."' In these early articles, the characteristics that Barrow described good explorers as possessing were the eighteenth-century virtues of zeal, industry, perseverance, and, when in circumstances of danger, a 'cool and steady resolution.'[11] There is little in his writing at this point that shows Romantic affinities, except perhaps his brief evocation of the colourful Elizabethan voyagers. Barrow described the search for the Northwest Passage as 'peculiarly a

British object,' and he predicted that the reign of George III would 'stand conspicuous and proudly pre-eminent in future history, for the spirit with which discoveries were prosecuted, and the objects of science promoted.'[12] He felt it would, therefore, be particularly fitting that the centuries-old search for a northern passage should be concluded during that reign. This line of argument has clear affinities with many periodical writings from 1859, but it is still far removed from the *Illustrated London News*'s claim that 'an instinct or a passion' for maritime exploration lay 'at the very root, as it were, of our British nature.'[13]

For all his belief in science and progress, Barrow had lived through tumultuous times, and, like many powerful men in that reactionary period, he felt that the established order of things was under siege. The most immediate threat ended with the defeat of Napoleon, but the postwar period brought divisions and dissent within British society to the forefront, as what the *Quarterly* called the 'hundred tongues of Radicalism' propounded 'doctrines equally anti-social, anti-moral, and anti-christian.'[14] Science itself, in this context, could provide serious cause for alarm. Like many nineteenth-century Englishmen, Barrow held to a firm religious faith and believed that the claims of reason and of revelation were not incompatible. Following Paley, to whose work he frequently referred,[15] Barrow saw the workings of divine providence behind the phenomena of nature, and he believed that while reason could lead to a better understanding of nature, it should not directly be applied to the study of religion. 'Scepticism in matters of religion is generally productive of bad consequences – in those of science it is just the contrary,' he declared at the beginning of one of his *Quarterly* articles.[16] Yet Barrow could not ignore the fact that the rise of science was creating an intellectual climate unfavourable to religion.

Barrow was completely in sympathy with the principles on which the *Quarterly Review* was founded by the publisher John Murray in 1808. The journal's aim was to counter the corrosive effects of scepticism and liberal doctrines, particularly as they were expressed through the *Edinburgh Review*. The *Edinburgh* was founded in 1802 by a group of intelligent young lawyers, who found themselves with spare time on their hands because their liberal opinions hampered the development of their careers. So ardent on occasion were their criticisms of the established order that even other Whigs were shocked: one furiously kicked a particularly radical issue out into the street.[17] The wit and elegant malice of its articles made the *Edinburgh Review* an unprecedented success. In 1797 circulation figures for the older reviews stood at 5,000 for the

Monthly Review, 3,500 for the *Critical Review* and the *British Critic*; and 1,500 for the *Analytical Review.*[18] The *Edinburgh* soared to 7,000 in 1807; 11,000 in 1809; and 13,000 in 1814.[19]

In 1807 Murray suggested the project of a Tory review in a letter to George Canning. 'There is a work entitled the *Edinburgh Review,* written with such unquestionable talent that it has already attained an extent of circulation not equalled by any similar publication,' he wrote. 'The principles of this work are, however, so radically bad that I have been led to consider the effect that such sentiments, so generally diffused, are likely to produce, and to think that some means equally popular ought to be adopted to counteract their dangerous tendency.'[20] The *Quarterly's* contributors (who included, besides Barrow, Sir Walter Scott, Robert Southey, and Barrow's colleague John Wilson Croker, the first secretary of the Admiralty) shared a strongly conservative outlook. Their high ability as writers made the enterprise as successful as the *Edinburgh,* and the *Quarterly* soon joined its rival as one of the most influential British periodicals. It commonly sold 10,000 to 13,000 copies per issue and, according to Southey, it reached 'fifty times ten thousand' readers.[21] It should be considered an important part of the cultural process described by Linda Colley in *Britons: Forging the Nation, 1707–1837.* Colley argues that the British upper classes responded to the challenges of the late eighteenth and early nineteenth centuries not by clinging to their traditional system of beliefs and values in a purely negative, reactionary way, but rather by reinventing themselves culturally. She believes that they displayed great cultural strength, establishing a new imagined community of patriotic Britons and thereby uniting the different classes and regions of the country in a sense of common cause against their French opponents. Colley's account emphasizes the creativity of this response, perhaps in answer to earlier historians, particularly E.P. Thompson, who described the upper and middle classes in the revolutionary period as frightened and repressive.[22]

Colley does not refer specifically to periodicals such as the *Quarterly* in her analysis, but they are clearly part of the movement she describes. Both the creativity detailed by Colley and the underlying fear emphasized by Thompson can be detected in the pages of the *Quarterly* generally and Barrow's articles in particular. According to Jon Klancher in *The Making of English Reading Audiences, 1790–1832,* the English reading public fragmented during the 1790s and the bitter debates over the French Revolution. By the 1810s and 1820s periodicals were a literary battleground where meaning was fiercely contested. Through reviews and magazines, groups of writers with shared ideological and aesthetic aims sought to mould the tastes, perceptions, and interpretive strategies of the reading public – a process that was seen as particularly important in the prevailing climate of political uncertainty. As a result, many readers came to define themselves culturally and politically through the periodicals they chose to read.

Moderate liberal opinion was represented by the older *Monthly Review*, founded in 1749, and the *Eclectic Review*, which began publication in 1805 and had strong ties to the Dissenting churches. More extreme liberalism, verging at times on radicalism, could be found in the *Edinburgh Review*, the *Monthly Magazine* (founded in 1796), and (far more radical than the *Edinburgh*) Leigh Hunt's weekly, the *Examiner* (1808). Radicalism in its most unalloyed form could be found in cheap weekly papers such as William Cobbett's *Political Register* (founded in 1802), William Hone's *Reformists' Register and Weekly Commentary* (1817), Thomas Wooler's *Black Dwarf* (1816), and Richard Carlile's *Republican* (1819).[23] These papers were far more overtly political and less literary than the magazines and reviews and so to some extent stood outside the cultural battles described by Colley and Klancher. However, their very existence, and their success (in 1816 the *Political Register* had a circulation estimated at 40,000 to 50,000, and perhaps as high as 70,000, while the *Black Dwarf* sold 12,000 copies per issue in 1819) were enough to stoke conservative fears that a major political crisis was imminent. Broadsides and pamphlets by these radical journalists sold at a phenomenal rate: Cobbett's 'Address to the Journeymen and Labourers,' first published in the 2 November 1816 issue of the *Political Register* and then reprinted separately, sold 200,000 copies in two months. Hone's satire 'The Political House that Jack Built' went through forty-seven printings in 1819 alone and sold 100,000 copies.[24]

On the Tory side, in addition to the *Quarterly*, were the *Gentleman's Magazine* (published since 1731), the *British Critic* (1793–1826) and the *Anti-Jacobin Review* (1798–1821). Two Tory monthly magazines were founded in response to liberal publications: the *New Monthly Magazine* (1814), which opposed the *Monthly Magazine*, and *Blackwood's Edinburgh Magazine* (1817), intended, like the *Quarterly*, as a rival to the *Edinburgh Review*. *Blackwood's* too achieved striking success in this role, soon reaching a circulation of 10,000 or more. Two weekly literary papers, both with Tory sympathies, appeared on the scene in the late 1810s: the *Literary Gazette* in 1817 and the *Literary Chronicle* in 1819. The *Gazette* was particularly successful, owing to the talent and energy of its editor, William Jerdan.

Finally, there were two religious magazines supported by evangelical members of the Church of England: the *Christian Observer* (1802) and the *British Review* (1811).[25]

Klancher identifies the twelve months from the autumn of 1816 to the autumn of 1817 as a crucial time,[26] when competition among those seeking to provide the reading public with an interpretive framework became more fierce and self-conscious than ever before. The year 1819 was even more critical in terms of political events: the Peterloo Massacre took place in August and the repressive Six Acts were passed in December. By the beginning of 1820 the *Quarterly* was inveighing bitterly against 'the noxious fecundity and the unspeakably malignant power of the Radical press,' which it claimed was 'conducted by men alike bankrupt in fortune and in principle.' Their success, should such a catastrophe occur, would lead to 'orgies too dire for description' and 'the paroxysms of a sanguinary anarchy.'[27]

To avert these calamities, Barrow and his colleagues strove to formulate a vision of the nation that could stand as a bulwark against revolutionary change. Barrow himself never wrote on obviously political topics, specializing instead in exploration and travel literature.[28] Many years later he declared, 'My opinion has always been that the Quarterly should always appropriate a portion of its pages to Naval Exploits and discoveries, and to adventures by sea and land – these next to Biography, are more suited to the [hoi polloi] than long prosy dissertations on Puseyism [and] Socialism.'[29] This view was in accordance with Scott's and Murray's shrewd realization that the journal could achieve wide popularity only if it offered readers informative and entertaining articles on a variety of topics along with its political commentaries.[30]

In Barrow's earlier articles, the background of political turmoil can be detected, if at all, only between the lines, in hints and indirect allusions. His sponsorship of Arctic exploration at first made him vulnerable to attack by the *Quarterly*'s adversaries, but ultimately it became a powerful source of status and authority for his writing. As Barrow's position became stronger during the early 1820s, his references to the *Quarterly*'s political and cultural opponents grew more specific, as did theirs to him. But while Barrow could use reviews of Arctic narratives as a platform for his political opinions, his enemies found it increasingly difficult to respond in kind. By the mid 1820s the Arctic heroes and their champion Barrow occupied a nearly unassailable position as upholders of the nation's honour.

The first indication of Barrow's Arctic interests came in his review of Lord Selkirk's *A Sketch of the British Fur Trade in North America*, which appeared in the October 1816 issue of the *Quarterly*. In his book, Selkirk recounted the clashes between the two rival fur-trading companies, the Hudson's Bay Company (HBC) and the North West Company, and charged that the North West Company deliberately encouraged violent and immoral practices by its traders. Barrow summarized Selkirk's accusations at considerable length. He observed that, if they were true, the matter was a very serious one, but reserved his judgment until further evidence was available. However, he flatly refused to accept Selkirk's panegyrics on the Hudson's Bay Company.

Turning the review from Selkirk's concerns to his own, Barrow pointed out that the HBC had done very little in the way of exploration: 'The great leading feature on which their petition for an exclusive charter was grounded, the discovery of a North-West Passage ... has not only been totally neglected, but ... thwarted by every means in their power,' he charged. Barrow remarked that the Nor'Westers were at least energetic men of business; the HBC traders, on the other hand, were characterized by their torpor. Whereas the early Elizabethan voyagers had shown 'unabated zeal' and 'extraordinary perseverance' in northern waters, the 'Company of Adventurers of England trading into Hudson's Bay' did as little as they could: 'From the moment this body of "Adventurers" was instituted, the *spirit* of adventure died away; and every succeeding effort was palsied by the baneful influence of monopoly, of which the discovery of a north-west passage was deemed the forerunner of destruction.' In the late eighteenth century, while the government was 'vigorously prosecuting new discoveries,' the HBC remained in 'that state of apathy which seems most congenial to their habits and interests.'[31]

If the Northwest Passage had not yet been discovered, it might well be because no one had bothered to look in the right place. Barrow thought that the western side of Baffin Bay held the most promise. To the possible objection that the enterprise would have little practical benefit, Barrow retorted that purely practical considerations should 'have little weight with those who have the interests of science at heart, or the national honour and fame.'[32] And in any case, commercial benefit was not entirely out of the question: should the passage prove to be in a relatively low latitude, it might provide a far shorter route to the North West Company's Pacific trading posts than the long voyage round Cape Horn.

In a footnote near the end of the article, Barrow referred to the meteorological logs published in the *Transactions of the Wernerian Society* by William Scoresby, a whaling captain from Hull. When compared with the records from Constantine Phipps's northern voyage in 1773, they seemed 'to sanction the idea of a decreasing temperature'[33] in the Arctic regions. During the summer of 1817 the possibility of climactic change was again raised: Scoresby and other northern whalers reported that they had found the sea near Greenland freer of ice than it had been within living memory.[34] Barrow carefully examined the whalers' logs in search of data to support his project for northern voyages.[35] In the autumn of 1817 Scoresby wrote to Sir Joseph Banks, the president of the Royal Society, suggesting that scientific expeditions be sent to the Arctic. Banks in turn wrote to the first lord of the Admiralty, Lord Melville, endorsing the suggestion. Banks's letter, dated 20 November,[36] echoes many of the phrases in Barrow's *Quarterly* articles. (On the basis of this resemblance, Christopher Lloyd believes that Barrow drafted the letter for the elderly Banks, who played only a minor role in the Arctic project; Michael Bravo, on the other hand, argues that Banks, not Barrow, was the true moving spirit behind the plan, and that Barrow acted only as his assistant or junior partner.)[37] Melville made a favourable reply on 10 December.[38]

Barrow conveyed this news to the public in a *Quarterly* article titled 'On the Polar Ice and Northern Passage into the Pacific.' (Lieutenant Edward Chappell's *Narrative of a Voyage to Hudson's Bay* provided a convenient pretext. The book was summarized, condemned, and dismissed in the first paragraph of the twenty-four-page article.) There were to be two expeditions, each taking a different route towards the 'polar basin' or 'open polar sea' that Barrow thought must lie beyond the dissolving barrier of ice.[39] He believed that if there was no land around the pole, the sea would almost certainly be open and navigable. In any latitude, he argued, 'It is the narrow seas only, and those without tides or currents, that freeze over. The ice-bergs, or mountains of ice, are generated on the land.'[40] One expedition would sail northward between Greenland and Spitzbergen, in an attempt to pass over the pole itself, and so on toward Bering Strait, while the other would make its way to the northwest, through Davis Strait and Baffin Bay, hoping to find an opening to the west not far from the northern coast of America.

The issue containing 'On the Polar Ice and Northern Passage into the Pacific' was published on 21 February 1818 and sold just over 12,000 copies on that day alone.[41] Barrow's article provided the first public indication that the search for the Northwest Passage was to be renewed.[42] It was both a skilful summary of what had already been made known to the public about the unusually ice-free condition of the northern seas and a sort of news release on behind-the-scenes developments at the

Admiralty. This was typical of *Quarterly* articles and part of a deliberate strategy on the part of the publisher and editor. As Murray wrote in 1808, 'we must avail ourselves of any valuable political information we can command.' Walter Scott agreed. '[N]othing,' he wrote, 'will render the work more interesting than the public learning, not from any vaunt of ours, but from their own observation, that we have access to early and accurate information on points of fact.'[43] To today's reader, the article, with its extensive data on such matters as ocean currents and its lengthy speculations on the past and future climate of Europe, does not seem designed to create a sensation. However, create a sensation it did. The notion that the Arctic regions, after having for so long been closed to inquisitive Europeans by a barrier of ice, might at last be ready to yield up their secrets, evidently had immense public appeal.

Two days after 'On the Polar Ice' appeared, the *Literary Gazette* commented, 'The Number of the *Quarterly Review* just published contains one of the ablest tracts upon this subject, that it was ever the good fortune of any periodical work to produce ... As a matter for the imagination to dwell upon, we can conceive nothing more attractive ... our whole faculties are absorbed in extraordinary speculations.'[44] Many other periodicals testify to the great public interest that was immediately aroused. According to the *Edinburgh Magazine*, few other voyages of discovery had ever attracted 'so great a share of general attention'[45] as those announced by Barrow, and the *Monthly Review* referred to the 'present eager appetite of the public for every sort of information connected with the arctic regions.'[46] The poet Eleanor Porden was so fired with enthusiasm after reading the 'very able and delightful article in the last Quarterly Review' that she insisted on visiting Deptford, where the ships were fitting out. That same day, Porden composed 'The Arctic Expeditions.' She urged,

'Sail, sail adventurous Barks! go fearless forth,
Storm on his glacier-seat the misty North ... And you, aspiring Youths! heroic band!
Who leave, by Science led, your native land;
Undaunted steer where none have mark'd the way ...'[47]

One of the 'aspiring Youths' was Buchan's second-in-command, John Franklin. He wrote in a letter to his sister, 'If the sanguine hopes and best wishes of the country could command success we certainly should obtain it – never *surely* was there any thing that excited such general

Interest and attention – in all places and every Society the expedition is the grand topic of conversation and the very circumstance of belonging to it seems to be a sufficient introduction any where.'[48] To another sister he reported, 'Deptford has been crowded with carriages and the ships with visitors every day.' Franklin noted with pride that 'men of scientific eminence' were taking a keen interest in the expeditions, and he added that the 'Ladies' had been especially 'forward and kind in their attentions and good wishes.'[49] Franklin may have been thinking of Miss Porden: after reading her poem he asked to be introduced to her and, by her own later account, 'An eye-witness of their first interview ... saw at once how their acquaintance was likely to end.'[50] Five years later they were married.

The expeditions sailed in April 1818. According to *Blackwood's*, they departed amid 'universal cheers.'[51] To the *Edinburgh Review*, such interest in any enterprise promoted by its rival was cause for alarm. Its June number contained a long article by John Leslie of Edinburgh University. Leslie employed elaborate scientific arguments in an attempt to refute Barrow's claims about the possibility of voyages into the unknown regions of the Arctic, insisting that no change in the northern climate had taken place. He wrote haughtily that 'a very flimsy and spurious kind of philosophy, however trifling or despicable it may appear in the eyes of the few who are accustomed to think profoundly, has gained currency among certain classes of men, and engendered no small share of conceit.' Barrow was said to have employed 'much loose reasoning' and to have indulged in 'visionary declamation. Glowing anticipations are confidently formed ... which would scarcely be hazarded even in the dreams of romance.'[52]

This seems to have been the first use of the term *romance* to describe Arctic voyages, and that it was meant to stem public interest does not make it any less significant. It reveals much about the context of the time that this term, intended to trivialize Barrow's project, had precisely the opposite effect. The connotations of the word were exceptionally complex, and were enmeshed in political as well as cultural debates. The situation is explicated by David Duff in *Romance and Revolution: Shelley and the Politics of a Genre*. Duff points out that during the eighteenth century views of romance were ambivalent, with negative perceptions and responses outweighing positive. It was, in general, 'a term of derision and abuse – usually to be found alongside terms like "chimerical," "fanatastic," "extravagant," "unnatural." Romance, from this perspective, was a language of the absurd.'[53] The figure of Cervantes' Don Quixote was always at hand to illustrate the folly and the dangers of romantic enthusiasm.

It was certainly in this negative sense that Leslie understood romance. However, since the 1790s the cultural importance of the genre had expanded immensely, and this development was closely linked to political debates. Duff believes that the publication of Burke's *Reflections on the Revolution in France*, with its famous lament that 'the age of chivalry is gone,' marked an important turning point. Burke eloquently argued that the crude indignities inflicted on the French royal family, and especially on Marie Antoinette, demonstrated that the revolutionaries were incapable of the nobler emotions. He described them as heartless monsters, exulting in their power over the king and queen. In his view, had reasonable reform of political abuses been their true aim, they would have felt no need to insult and terrify the king, their lawful sovereign, or his wife, who, like all women, was entitled to honourable treatment simply by virtue of her sex. Both his nostalgia for the age of chivalry and his championship of Marie Antoinette, who was widely believed to be an unfaithful wife, seemed to offer Burke's enemies the perfect weapons with which to demolish his arguments. He was promptly lampooned as a deluded, quixotic 'Don Dismallo,' bent on rescuing 'the peerless and immaculate Antonietta of Austria from ... durance vile.' Yet this ridicule proved, in the long term, remarkably ineffective. As Duff points out, a taste for romance had been on the rise throughout the late eighteenth century, and by the 1790s the genre had a very strong appeal. Moreover, the chivalric code contained many virtues that the radicals themselves cherished. In the very process of exploring the language of romance as a means of discrediting Burke, they apparently came to realize its cultural power. Many tried to appropriate it for their own purposes, representing themselves as stainless heroes battling the dark forces of reaction. From the 1790s on, images and metaphors derived from romance were widely employed in political discourse. Conservatives probably benefited most from this development (of the liberal Romantics, only Byron achieved great popularity during his lifetime) but such language was, in Duff's words, 'peculiarly unstable and ambivalent' and 'always susceptible to inversion.'[54] With respect to the Arctic debate, the most important point is that the language of romance was most effective when employed in a positive sense; as a means of ridicule it was more likely to harm than to help the cause of those who used it.

Leslie had therefore chosen a tactic fraught with danger. In addition, he unwittingly aided his opponent's cause through a clumsy and unconvincing article. Its criticism was purely negative, and it made very dull reading, with long stretches of scientific disquisition unrelieved by anything likely to interest the general reader. The 'science' on which Leslie rested his condemnation of Barrow's supposed 'romance' seemed to be little more than petty carping over details, not tied to any large principles. He admitted, somewhat grudgingly, that it was 'befitting the character of a great maritime nation, to embrace every chance even of improving geographical knowledge, and of extending the basis of natural science,'[55] yet his claim to be one of the 'few who are accustomed to think profoundly' smacked too much of arrogant pedantry for the public taste. As Leslie's scientific colleague, geologist Robert Jameson,[56] later observed in the *Edinburgh Philosophical Journal*, 'The public took a deep interest in speculations like [Barrow's], where the dry details of hydrography were enlivened by discussions and schemes almost bordering upon romance ... the general expectation of advancing the interests of natural science, and of practical investigation, would not permit itself to be damped.'[57] Romantic the enterprise was, and Barrow cannot have failed to notice that public enthusiasm did not wane when Leslie pointed this out. Because Leslie, unlike the radical political writers, made no attempt to weave romantic imagery into his own discourse, the language of romance was left to Barrow. Though he apparently had little prior inclination to do so, he learned to wield it effectively.

This development, however, did not become apparent for some time. In 1818 the debate proceeded along more traditional lines. Other Tory periodicals predictably took Barrow's side against the *Edinburgh*. '[S]trange to say,' observed the *New Monthly Magazine*,

> men of science, instead of waiting, in common with their more simple countrymen, for the history of this voyage, have set themselves in battle array ... there are men of such warped judgments and jaundiced eyes, as to view every thing in a bad light that is presented in a quarter to which they have a radical enmity. Hence some learned professors, who by being nearer the pole possess less ardent imaginations than we southern inquirers, have ... positively determined that ... our navigators have gone upon a fool's errand, for want of consulting the northern Delphos.[58]

The phrase 'radical enmity' was surely chosen with intent, and the link between liberal politics and poorly timed criticism of an enterprise which had caught the public imagination was a shrewd move. That Leslie's criticism appeared only after the expeditions had departed seems to have worsened the impression it made. *Blackwood's* insisted that Barrow's opinions had 'met with the approbation of the great body of intelligent and thinking readers,' and it characterized the *Edinburgh's* carping as a slur not only on him but indirectly on the explorers themselves. This was carefully linked to the weakening of national pride and resolve which both *Blackwood's* and the *Quarterly* identified as an effect of political dissent. According to *Blackwood's*,

> the vessels of discovery had scarcely disappeared from our horizon, accompanied with the anxieties and good wishes of every man who loved either science or his country, when a prophetic lamentation was sounded ... We certainly did not expect that the spirit of damping, so common ... in the calculation of political probabilities, would have shown itself so openly in the peaceful empire of science; but we fear, that within her sacred limits, there is an opposition as active as that which animates the body politic ... we cannot but question the feelings and motives of the men, who interrupted the universal cheers which followed the departure of our intrepid countrymen.[59]

Here, even more openly than in the *New Monthly*, patriotism was associated with support of the explorers, while radical opinions, unrest, and selfishness were described as the characteristics of those who opposed their enterprise.

In September, letters and dispatches written by Ross and his officers in Baffin Bay at the end of July were brought back by the whaler *Dexterity* of Leith. They reflected considerable optimism about Ross's chances of success, and consequently a large number made their way into print. '[T]hough the following letters are not official, they have an equal claim to confidence as coming from intelligent officers employed in this arduous service, and who in writing with familiarity to their friends are more likely to be minute in their remarks, than persons engaged in drawing up formal dispatches,'[60] wrote the editor of the *New Monthly*. The letters were indeed informative and entertaining reading, and Arctic correspondence quickly became a staple of press coverage.

To the general surprise (since they were equipped for wintering), both expeditions returned in November. Buchan had encountered extremely heavy ice, and it was plainly impossible for him to proceed northward. He was the first to return; the November issue of the *British Review* printed the news along with a report from the whaling fleet that Ross's ships had last been seen on 4 August, 'standing in a north-westerly direction, *the sea being clear and open as far as the eye could reach from the main-top gallant-mast head.*'[61] However, Ross too was soon back in England. He reported that his progress had been stopped by land at the western end of Lancaster Sound. This in itself was unwelcome news to Barrow, who was keenly aware that the *Edinburgh* was only too ready to ridicule him for the failure of his plans. However, when he heard that only a few officers other than Ross himself claimed to have seen the land, that Ross had not investigated to ensure it was not an optical illusion, and that the second-in-command, William Edward Parry, doubted Ross's conclusions, Barrow reacted with suspicion and hostility.

Ross's biographers have been at a loss to adequately explain the vindictiveness with which Barrow treated him.[62] Since the land Ross claimed he saw was indeed an optical illusion, they admit that his performance in this regard was deficient, but they point out that he undoubtedly had many virtues both as a person and as an explorer, and they can see no adequate reason for Barrow's extreme hostility. These writers, however, view their subject's life and the history of Arctic exploration in isolation from British history as a whole. In the prevailing political circumstances, success or failure in finding the Northwest Passage had far more than geographical significance. Not only Barrow's status as an Admiralty official,[63] but the prestige of the *Quarterly*, and through it the political principles Barrow espoused, all were at stake. Had Ross been able to report beyond all doubt that the land existed, and had his officers confirmed his account, Barrow would simply have had to make the best of it. As it was, not only did Ross make an unwelcome report, but the more it was questioned, the more obdurate he became in refusing to admit the possibility of a mistake. Barrow therefore viewed Ross as an enemy, who either deliberately or out of incompetence had publicly embarrassed the Admiralty. Barrow seems to have felt that only by sacrificing Ross could he safeguard his own position and limit the possible political damage. He therefore made the controversy over Lancaster Sound public with no apparent compunction. Ross naturally experienced great emotional distress, and he believed that Barrow had maliciously set out to damage his career.

Soon after the expedition's return, in November 1818, rumours spread that Ross's officers had contradicted his reports. In December, a letter by an unidentified officer appeared in *Blackwood's*. It provided an emotionally charged account of ardent enthusiasm for discovery blocked by a strangely reluctant commander. The writer recounted that, as the ships entered Lancaster Sound, 'every heart panted to explore' it, and so strong were the indications of a passage that

> I firmly believe every creature on board anticipated the pleasure of writing ...
> from ... the Pacific. ... Every breast beat high, and every one was desirous to

mount the crows-nest, to look out for the opening that should conduct us to
the Polar Sea … We had not run, however, above ten leagues within the
inlet, when the *Isabella* bore up, and of course, the *Alexander* did the same,
and we stood out of the inlet; why, we could not conjecture … It is impossible to describe to you the gloom that was immediately spread over every
countenance … At the very spot where the *Isabella* bore up, the depth of
water was 650 fathoms … the *Alexander* was about four or five miles a-stern of
her consort at that time; but not the least appearance of land was visible in
the direction of the inlet from her crows-nest.[64]

The writer did not claim that Ross was wrong, but he very emphatically
stated that there were no adequate grounds for taking it as proven that
Ross was right.

One of Ross's friends described this letter as 'a most insidious and
jesuitical' document, and speculated that it had been written by
Barrow.[65] The accusation seems unlikely, as many of the officers were
indeed sceptical of Ross's claim, but it is equally unlikely that any of
them would have ventured to publish such a letter without Barrow's
encouragement. The letter was reprinted in the *Literary Gazette,* with the
comment that it 'confirms our opinion … that nothing has been ascertained' as to the existence or non-existence of the Northwest Passage.[66]
At about the same time, another anonymous account was published in
the first issue of Richard Phillips's *New Voyages and Travels.* This officer,
too, emphasized the many indications of a passage, and he confirmed
that those in the *Alexander* had seen no land, though observers in the
Isabella were 'fully convinced' of its existence.[67]

Throughout this period (the fall of 1818 and the early months of
1819), reviews of a new book by Barrow were appearing alongside the
news of the expeditions. As many reviewers pointed out, its publication
had evidently been timed to 'prepare the public mind for the anticipated fortunate results of the two expeditions';[68] instead, the first
reviews coincided with the news of their unexpected return, and later
commentaries were as concerned with the controversy over Lancaster
Sound as with the book in itself.[69] Barrow's volume, titled *A Chronological
History of Voyages in the Arctic Regions; undertaken chiefly for the purposes of
discovering a North-East, North-West, or Polar Passage between the Atlantic and
the Pacific: from the earliest periods of Scandinavian Navigation, to the departure of the recent Expeditions, under the Orders of Captains Ross and Buchan,*
added a new twist to the debate, which until then had centred around
the question of science. Barrow had originally justified the expeditions by claiming that Britain's high rank among nations could not

be maintained without great voyages of scientific discovery; the *Edinburgh* retorted with Leslie's denial that the proposed enterprise was scientifically respectable. In *A Chronological History*, Barrow turned to the past as a way of legitimizing his plans. His main focus was on the Elizabethan period, when the quest for the passage had begun, and he reproduced much colourful material from the pages of Hakluyt and Purchas. Many reviews quoted the book's epigraph, taken from the latter (complete with seventeenth-century spelling), which praised the 'heroicke courage' of England's 'marine worthies.'

Blackwood's gave the book an extremely favourable review and awarded Barrow the victory over Leslie. Both science and history, in the reviewer's opinion, supported Barrow's position. The *New Monthly*'s reviewer reserved his judgment on the scientific and geographical aspects of the controversy until a fuller account of Ross's voyage was available. But he declared that as a Briton he felt 'honest pride' when reading about the daring deeds of the Elizabethan explorers. 'Long may the historians of Britain, arbitress and queen of nations, have to enrol in the splendid annals of her glories, similar and equally bloodless achievements,' he wrote with fervour.[70] The historical approach persisted as a means of linking the great traditions of the past with the achievements of living sailor-explorers. From 1819 until the end of the Franklin search a surprising number of reviews and other articles opened with long historical discussions derived from *A Chronological History*. These passages appear dull and repetitive to today's reader, but clearly, they held great appeal for nineteenth-century audiences.[71]

Barrow's position was thus extremely strong, but Ross refused to capitulate. In his narrative (published by Murray in March 1819),[72] instead of admitting that he could have been wrong, Ross stated in the most emphatic terms that he felt no doubt his report was correct. The land was marked on his chart as a definite discovery, and he even published a sketch of it. Reviewers' responses were varied. Barrow's scathingly negative assessment in the *Quarterly* has already been described. He supported his criticisms by quoting sections of Parry's journal, which showed that Parry, like his two anonymous colleagues, had not been convinced that the decision to turn back was justified. In April, Edward Sabine published a description of the Greenland 'Esquimaux' in the *Quarterly Journal of Science, Literature and Art*. At the end of his account, Sabine added his testimony to that of the others who doubted Ross's report of land.[73] When Sabine read Ross's narrative, he was outraged to find that his scientific observations were presented there in such a way as to give the impression that the work had been done by Ross himself. Sabine publicly accused Ross of plagiarism in a pamphlet titled *Remarks on the Account of the late Voyage of Discovery to Baffin's Bay*, which also appeared in April. This dispute between Sabine and his former commander had no direct bearing on the Lancaster Sound controversy, but it contributed to the atmosphere of doubt now surrounding Ross. The *Monthly Review* accordingly echoed both the content and the tone of Barrow's criticism.[74]

On the other hand, the definite statement by Ross – an officer with an unblemished record of service – gave many critics pause. The prestige acquired by the navy during the Napoleonic wars was a factor on which he as well as Barrow could draw. The *New Monthly* decided in his favour,[75] and even those who did not unreservedly accept Ross's claim worded their criticisms carefully. *Blackwood's* wrote that the narrative had 'impressed us with a high opinion of the skill and judgment of Captain Ross. Unfortunately, in Sir James Lancaster's Sound there appears to have been a haste on the part of Captain Ross which ... leaves a disagreeable impression with the public, which we regret we cannot remove.' Ross's claim that Lancaster Sound did not lead to a northwest passage was derived from 'false premises, or, at least, from premises that were not proved.'[76] Robert Jameson, writing in the newly founded *Edinburgh Philosophical Journal*, agreed that Ross's report could not be taken as conclusive, but he too was careful not to overstate his criticism.[77] The *British Review* criticized the Admiralty's orders to Ross, calling them 'vague and unsatisfactory.' Barrow was not mentioned by name, but it was well known that he had drafted the instructions. It was therefore implied that Barrow was more to blame than Ross for the expedition's poor results. However, the reviewer clearly felt little enthusiasm for either Ross himself or his 'ostentatious and expensive volume.' He believed that Scoresby, rather than a naval officer, should have been put in command.[77]

The *Edinburgh*, of course, supported Ross and ridiculed Barrow, but its attack was not especially effective. The review began with a rather laboured joke at Barrow's expense, which, perhaps inevitably, included a reference to Don Quixote: 'The antient [*sic*] connexion of the Basin and the Pole, is well known to that part of the learned world which has devoted itself to the study of our sign-posts, and the head armour of Don Quixote: – and we suppose it is to this venerable association that we are indebted for the happy phrase of the *Polar Basin*, of which it has been our lot to hear so much for the last twelve months.'[78] The unidentified reviewer[79] went on to imply that Barrow refused to accept Ross's report only because it did not conform to his preconceived theories on Arctic geography. He described this attitude as 'very ungrateful dissatisfaction' and went on to state that Ross appeared 'to have done his duty ... and to have told his story ... honestly.' However, 'we cannot say that [Ross] has made a very interesting or entertaining book of it ... on the contrary ... we have found this work very heavy reading.' As for the disputed sighting of land, the *Edinburgh*'s stance was somewhat equivocal, and may reflect a disagreement between the author of the article and the editor. At two points the reviewer agreed that Ross had proved there was no Northwest Passage, but elsewhere he wrote that he was 'rather surprised at the positive manner in which the non-existence of the passage is here stated.' The author confessed that he felt tempted 'to drop the subject altogether.'[80] To drop the subject, at least for the time being, was indeed the wisest course. The Admiralty had already sent out another expedition, under Parry's command, to settle the question. As over-emphatic predictions on either side of the argument ran the risk of embarrassing their authors when Parry returned, the controversy was allowed to fade into the background.

3   The Threshold of a World Unknown, 1820–1821

On thus reaching the limit of former discovery, the mind is irresistibly impelled to look back upon the records of previous navigators, who also attained to this point, but failed in penetrating beyond; leaving to Lieutenant Parry and his associates the honour of having first passed the threshold, as it were, of a world unknown.

'Parry's Voyage of Discovery,' *Gentleman's Magazine*, June 1821

As had happened with John Ross's expedition, reports from Edward Parry were brought back to England by whalers in the autumn after his departure. Then in February 1820 there was a rumour that his ships had been seen at the mouth of the Coppermine River.[1] After this, no more was heard until 4 November, when the *London Gazette* printed a letter from Parry to John Wilson Croker, the first secretary of the Admiralty, sent to England in advance of his arrival by the whaler *Lee* of Hull (Parry had remained in the Arctic for a few more weeks in order to complete a survey of Davis Strait). Parry reported that his two ships had safely wintered in longitude 112 1/2° west, between the 74th and 75th parallels of north latitude, and that he had discovered twelve new islands. On the same day, William Jerdan of the *Literary Gazette* made his own independent, and reasonably correct, announcement that Parry had wintered in latitude 75° north, longitude 115° west. Jerdan pointed out what Parry's letter did not – that this meant Parry had sailed westward 'several hundred miles'[2] beyond the point where Ross claimed he had seen solid land. '[E]ven in the midst of our politics,' Jerdan wrote, the news 'excited a marked sensation throughout the country.'[3] Another periodical writer thought that the intensity of the public's response to Parry's news 'was without any former example.'[4] On 5 November Barrow wrote to John Murray that Parry would 'publish individually – the sooner the better,'[5] and on the 6th Murray offered 1,000 guineas for the narrative. Parry accepted the next day.[6]

Parry's return was a triumphant moment for John Barrow. The early reports were quickly supplemented by an Admiralty chart showing the impressive extent of Parry's westward advance.[7] As a result, Ross became the object of considerable scorn in some quarters and seemed destined to be remembered, if he was remembered at all, only as a man who had been proved wrong.[8] Parry's account (published in the spring of 1821) was full of adventurous moments and striking incidents, all narrated in the straightforward prose considered appropriate for naval explorers. In his first letter to Murray, he expressed his wish that the work should be 'as complete, and as far from *book-making* as possible.'[9] By 'book-making' Parry apparently meant a self-consciously literary, artificial style. Unlike the unfortunate Ross, who had been goaded into boasting of discoveries that were later proved illusory, Parry recounted his substantial achievements with charming modesty. A few journalists expressed sympathy for the defeated Ross, refusing to share Barrow's almost paranoid conviction that he had deliberately attempted to dupe the Admiralty and the public. Nevertheless, the combination of Parry's triumph in Lancaster Sound and his success as a writer made him unquestionably the hero of the hour. Since he took care to avoid any remarks in his narrative that might seem like gloating over his former commander, even those who felt distaste for Barrow's more extreme attacks on Ross did not hesitate to describe Parry as the ideal polar hero. And, unlike Ross (who was plain and middle-aged), the handsome young Parry made a dashing public figure.

Earlier controversies faded in the response to Parry's return and the publication of his narrative. Almost with one voice, periodicals from every part of the political spectrum described him as a credit to the nation he served. The *Edinburgh* alone took refuge in silence, tacitly leaving the field to the victorious Barrow. While some Tory publications, such as *Blackwood's*, were among those refusing to speak ill of Ross, no Whig journals attacked Parry. The *Monthly Magazine* gave the narrative only a short and not very enthusiastic notice, but this was mainly due to the intense competition to profit from public interest in the expedition. The *Monthly's* publisher, Richard Phillips, preferred to direct readers towards the letters by an anonymous officer of the expedition that were about to appear in his *New Voyages and Travels*.[10] There the price was

3 shillings and sixpence, or only one-twentieth of the cost of Parry's narrative.[11] The narrative, consisting of '300 pages of dull text, and 200 of preface and appendix,' was hardly worth 3 guineas: indeed it 'ought in truth, in a voyage undertaken at the public expence [sic], to have been detailed in a five shilling pamphlet.' The author himself, however, was awarded praise: '[his] style is good, and he has made the utmost of his inconsiderable materials,'[12] the reviewer conceded.

Surprisingly, Jerdan of the Literary Gazette, a stalwart Tory, published similar remarks. Jerdan had worked exceptionally hard to obtain the first full account of the expedition's activities. He managed to get on board the expedition's ship, the Griper, as it came up the Thames, and elicited enough details from the officers to write an informative article. By going for sixty hours without sleep, Jerdan had his article ready for publication by the next Saturday, 25 November. That issue of the Gazette sold an extra 500 copies, and the increased circulation was maintained. (As Jerdan himself noted years later, 'in th[o]se piping times of shilling sheets,' the increase 'was equal to about a thousand pounds a year.')[13] The next week, he wrote with mock indignation that his article had 'since occupied the pages of almost every print in the metropolis,' and perhaps even in the country.[14]

Jerdan was understandably eager to print more Arctic material. Several of the officers, on whom he had evidently made a very favourable impression, gave him their contributions to the expedition's newspaper, the North Georgia Gazette and Literary Chronicle. Jerdan decided to publish these poems and short humorous articles in several numbers of his paper. He had the first one in type when a letter came from Parry, stating that he intended to publish a book containing all the contributions, and that the officers had agreed to give their copyrights to him.[15] When the book appeared, Jerdan criticized its high price. 'Readers,' he pointed out, 'must now exhibit their half-guinea for what in our pages would not have cost them half-a-crown.'[16]

Despite eager hopes that it would appear within a month or two of his return, Parry's narrative was not published until mid-May 1821. In accordance with Admiralty practice, the officers' journals had been collected for the commander's use as he wrote up the official account. They were returned on 21 April. Jerdan had persuaded the expedition's surgeon, Alexander Fisher, to publish a narrative with Longmans, the owners of the Literary Gazette.[17] By more feverish work, Jerdan had the narrative ready for publication on 30 April, two weeks before Parry's long-delayed book. This unprecedented speed led to suspicions that

Fisher had kept a secret copy of his journal. He was exonerated at an official inquiry. The ever-resourceful Jerdan reported the entire episode in the *Gazette*, thus printing Arctic news of his own making. He also published long extracts from Fisher's book. (The rival *Literary Chronicle*, which until this point had shown far less interest than the *Gazette* in Arctic matters, now resorted to a four-part retrospective, reviewing Phipps's *A Voyage towards the North Pole* [1774], the new edition of Daines Barrington's *The Possibility of approaching the North Pole asserted* [1818], Barrow's *Chronological History*, and Ross's narrative.)[18]

When Parry's narrative finally appeared, the *Gazette* accorded it an odd mixture of praise and blame. The content was described as sometimes 'minutely tedious,'[19] but Parry's 'candid,' 'perspicuous,' and 'gentleman-like' writing style was singled out for praise. 'Though he apologizes for writing like a sailor, we can only observe that we should be very glad to see no small number of our literati acquire the same style,' Jerdan observed. However, he added severe censure of the narrative's high price (£3 13s 6d, versus 12 shillings for Fisher's less ambitious volume). Jerdan pointed out that a 'man in the middle rank of life, of decent fortune, say from 600*l.* to 1000*l.* per annum, even though devoted to literature,' could not 'afford to purchase in the course of the year more than eight or ten of these extravagant quartos.' In his view, by encouraging publication in so lavish a form the Admiralty was 'defrauding the country of the intelligence to which it has a just right and title.'[20]

This criticism, in comparison with that formerly published in the *Edinburgh*, was a mere tempest in a literary teapot, and Jerdan went on to maintain excellent relations with the Arctic officers, to their and the *Gazette*'s mutual benefit. He was always ready to give the explorers favourable publicity, and in the last years of his life he wrote nostalgically of 'that illustrious band.'[21] Even at the time, Jerdan's piqued remarks had little effect on public opinion as a whole, since other periodicals awarded Parry unalloyed praise. The *Literary Chronicle* declared: 'The narrative of Captain Parry is all that we could wish: it is ... circumstantial without being tedious, explicit without being commonplace, and interesting without the least art or attempt at effect ... we know not which to admire most, his enterprizing and undaunted character, his amiable disposition as a commander, or the modesty with which he narrates his success ... his work is entitled to the highest praise, and might serve as a model for journals of this description.'[22] *Blackwood's* wrote, '[Parry has] incidents to tell of a romantic and unusual character, and talents for telling them, which, in despite of his modest excuses about his education, it is difficult to imagine that he should not suspect were respectable, for, in truth, they seem to us first-rate. Without a care or a fear, therefore, he seems to have written, with singular facility and precision, whatever came in order, and to have thus given the world a volume ... replete with interest almost throughout.'[23] The *London Magazine*, which was founded in 1820 as a rival to *Blackwood's*, supported the so-called Cockney School of poets, which *Blackwood's* habitually maligned. The *London* might therefore have been expected to take an opposing line on Parry, but instead it too expressed complete approval. Noting the 'universal interest' aroused by the expedition, the reviewer went on to say that there could certainly 'be but one opinion as to the zeal and capabilities of Captain Parry.'[24] The Nonconformist *Eclectic Review* not only praised Parry, but joined Barrow in condemnation of Ross. Its reviewer declared that the voyage reflected 'the highest credit, not only on ... Captain Parry, but on the talent and decision manifested by Mr. Barrow ... amid all the discouragements which Captain Ross's representations were evidently designed to perpetrate.'[25] Since Barrow supported the established church as firmly as he did the monarchy and the administration, this attitude at first appears rather startling. However, it is most likely an indication of that coming together of various segments of society described by Linda Colley. Parry's success was frequently linked, either implicitly or explicitly, with conservative moral values. To the Dissenting authors of the *Eclectic Review* and to their readers, these values probably appeared preferable to the much discussed irreligion of many radicals. The Tory *Literary Chronicle* followed its review of Parry with one of Shelley's *Queen Mab*, leaving a fairly obvious conclusion to be drawn by the reader. While Parry was a man of the utmost courage and integrity, Shelley furnished 'one of the most striking and melancholy instances of the perversion ... of genius, that we have ever met with.' The reviewer declared that he felt 'some portion of pity for a man of enlarged intellectual powers thus debasing himself,' but he was also filled with 'disgust at [Shelley's] licentious and incestuous principles, and horror at his daring impiety ... [He] would shake off all laws, human and divine, and have a society rioting in lust and incest.'[26]

It was not only Parry's impressive performance as an explorer that made this strategy possible. His expedition, unlike Ross's, had wintered in the Arctic, in what was then considered an exceptionally high latitude. Cut off from all human contact, either European or Aboriginal (there were no Inuit in the area), they formed a tiny society of their own. Parry resolved to keep his crew in excellent health both physically and mentally, and he resorted to some unusual means in pursuit of his goal. Besides giving careful attention to diet and exercise, he provided a number of entertaining or useful pastimes. Several plays were written and staged, and, as previously mentioned, a newspaper appeared throughout the winter. There was also a school in which officers taught illiterate sailors to read and write. Almost every reviewer commented favourably on what the *Literary Gazette* described as Parry's 'paternal care' of his men.[27]

Parry appeared not only as the beau ideal of a daring explorer, but as the benevolent ruler of a Britain in microcosm, complete with class structure. The *Edinburgh Philosophical Journal* expressed its approval of 'the prudence and moderation ... with which he managed his little colony.'[28] Parry's success seemed to demonstrate that it was not revolution, but more innovative rulers, that society required. The sailors had responded to their commander's care with exemplary conduct; as *Blackwood's* expressed it, the events of the voyage proved how well British sailors could behave 'when well treated ... repaying, as they always do, such treatment ... with confidence, attachment and good humour.'[29] The Tory *British Critic* likewise praised the sailors for their 'cheerfulness, sobriety, discipline, [and] patient endurance of fatigue and hardship.'[30] The liberal *Examiner* joined in the chorus of enthusiasm, commending Parry's writing as 'lucid, and peculiarly unaffected and modest' and his treatment of his men as 'above all praise.' The reviewer ended with the statement that it was 'scarcely possible to conclude ... without an expression of complacency at the proofs this voyage supplies of the intrepidity, perseverance, and honourable spirit of enterprise which it is possible to infuse into every class of our countrymen. It forms another example of our British practical superiority when discipline is rectified by prudence and humanity.'[31]

Parry's literary style was plain, modest, and on the surface entirely apolitical; he offered readers a convincing account of events, but did not enter into interpretations. As he himself explained, echoing Cook, 'The extent of my aim has been, to give a plain and faithful account of the facts which I collected, and the observations which were made by myself and others, in the course of the voyage; and these ... may be relied on as scrupulously exact. It is for others, better qualified than ourselves, to make their deductions from those facts.'[32] The narrative was, to all appearances, exactly what Parry and the reviewers declared it to be: a straightforward tale written by a man intent on telling the truth.

And that Parry cunningly constructed it to give that impression, while deftly hiding unpleasant realities,[33] is not necessarily the case. The role of the plain sailor writing out the facts to the best of his ability stood ready for him to step into, and there is no reason to believe that he did not conscientiously strive to fulfil it. It shaped his behaviour just as it shaped his readers' responses: the construction of the ideal polar hero lay at a far deeper and more complex level than any individual's conscious intentions. Parry does appear to have been a man with a strong sense of duty and great practical ability. The combination of the cultural context with an individual so well fitted to carry out the role of Arctic hero had far-reaching effects. Ross's narrative gave rise to conflicting interpretations and to politically based, intensely hostile controversy; Parry's book brought reviewers (and presumably readers) together. A range of broadly similar, but not identical, understandings were possible: Anglicans and Dissenters, Tories and liberals alike, could find qualities to praise, and all could agree that as Britons they felt immense pride in his achievements.

The narrative made no claims to any special place in the realm of literature. Like Cook, Parry wrote as if the whole question of literary genre was meaningless to him; he seemed, as *Blackwood's* reviewer so approvingly claimed, simply to have 'written ... whatever came in order.' But just as the book gave rise to much politically oriented commentary despite its lack of overt political content, reviewers provided the literary reflections in which the author appeared to have no interest. Many judged it in relation to the prevailing taste for romance, especially when mixed with gothic horror. The disapproval felt by conservatively minded reviewers when confronted with literature of this type is evident from J.W. Croker's evaluation of *Frankenstein* in the January 1818 issue of the *Quarterly*. Croker (who, besides his work as first secretary of the Admiralty, was the *Quarterly's* most prolific contributor)[34] described Mary Shelley's novel as 'a tissue of horrible and disgusting absurdity.' It was powerfully written in 'strong and striking language,' but 'the greater the ability with which it may be executed the worse it is – it inculcates no lesson of conduct, manners, or morality; it cannot mend, and will not even amuse its readers, unless their taste have been deplorably vitiated ... it gratuitously harasses the heart, and wantonly adds to the store, already too great, of painful sensations.' (Croker dismissed the book's description of the Arctic with the amused comment that it had unfortunately been written before 'our Review ... enlightened mankind' on the subject.)[35]

The *Monthly Review* specifically commended Parry's narrative because it did not pander to the 'morbid but too fashionable taste' for sensational incidents and extreme emotions. The reviewer praised its 'gentleman-like style and sterling merit' and went on to describe it as 'a plain, unvarnished, and modest relation; a very faithful transcript, we can easily believe, of the occurrences of the voyage; and devoid of the tricks and pretensions of authorship.' He remarked that although the 'sober, and somewhat unvarying tenor of the narrative' was 'little calculated to gratify that morbid but too fashionable taste, which can be stimulated only by scenes of fiction or the poignancy of satire,' nevertheless, the book could not 'fail to be duly appreciated by the lovers of truth, and the advocates of national honour.'[36] In a similar vein, the *Examiner's* reviewer pictured the irritation many readers (especially female readers), who had eagerly anticipated a thrilling tale of adventure, must have felt when the book was actually in their hands. The reviewer believed that a large part of the reading public was not sufficiently 'reflective' to appreciate its merits properly.[37] The *British Review* agreed that only 'those, in whom the natural appetite for truth is not vitiated by fiction' were likely to enjoy the book. These discerning readers would 'rise from the volume amused and instructed, with a just impression of the simple elegance of its style, and the authentic character of its narrations.'[38]

It was not, however, that the narrative completely lacked romantic elements. On the contrary, it was romantic in a new and better way. The *Eclectic Review's* writer noted that Parry had encountered 'horrors that would have overwhelmed spirits of inferior mould' in his navigation of dangerous ice fields. Determined to press forward despite these hazards, he had shown 'that absorbing and intense enthusiasm which courts the extremest hazards as steps to the attainment of its object.' However, far from giving way to his emotions (as the unfortunate Dr Frankenstein had done at crucial points in his career), Parry won through by the exercise of 'steady and intrepid self possession.'[39] He was a hero equal to the most perilous quest.

The *British Review* focused on the romantic aspects of the setting in which Parry's adventures took place. Many popular writers of the time set their stories amid lush southern landscapes, and in contrast to these, the Arctic presented only 'scenes of utter desolation, apparently the sepulchre of nature.' Yet readers of Parry's book could not 'but be delighted to dwell on the glorious visions so peculiarly the privilege of the polar skies, the coruscations and colours of the Aurora Borealis, the halos, the prismatic parhelia, and other novelties.' They would 'experience the *immixto horrore voluptas*, when conducted under the brows of ice-bergs a hundred and forty feet high, – those stupendous monuments of the power of frost, which seem erected by winter, on the confines of his dominions, as samples of the dread magnificence of his reign.' Finally, they would 'imagine with breathless interest, the struggle to escape from a closing barrier of ice which approaches in hideous shapeless masses, to destroy the vessels in its rugged embraces.' It was, all in all, 'impossible not to follow with sympathy and admiration the track of these daring adventurers; to participate in their struggles and disappointments, and in those scanty pleasures which seem, as it were, wrung from the churlishness of the region, and prove the energy and buoyancy of man's spirit.'[40]

The review in the *Gentleman's Magazine* arrived at the language of romance through a summary of the expedition's geographical results. Whereas it had previously been speculated that the North American mainland might extend up the western side of Baffin Bay, to join the mass of Greenland further north, it was now clear that beyond Lancaster Sound there lay an archipelago of large islands, 'intersected by numerous channels; and it is but fair to presume that the number of these inlets will be increased by future observation.' The Northwest Passage would most likely be (as, in fact, it is) a winding path through an ice-clogged and geographically complex region. The *Gentleman's* reviewer pointed out, more clearly than most, that although Parry had proved the passage almost certainly did exist, he had also proved that it would not easily be discovered. Nevertheless, the reviewer was confident that 'perseverance in following the clue with which we are now presented, may enable us at length to unravel the mazes of this ... labyrinth.'[41]

This comparison would echo through all future Arctic literature. It was an apt way of describing the geographical realities of the Canadian north, and it also had powerful literary resonances, linking Parry's tale to the conventions of medieval romance. The revival of romance was of central importance in the culture of the time on both sides of the political debate. Tory reviewers like Croker evidently feared as well as disdained its more extreme, sensational forms, with their potential destabilizing and radicalizing effect, but on the whole the genre was more compatible with conservative than radical visions of history and society. It was not merely that many romances were set in the Middle Ages, thus fostering admiration and nostalgia for a golden age of tradition, hierarchy, and unquestioning religious belief. In the hands of conservative writers like Scott, romance was a powerful tool for popularizing Burke's vision of British society as one that had changed and evolved slowly, through historical processes so gradual that they resembled the processes of nature. Either implicitly or explicitly, the British acceptance of slow change over time was contrasted to the French revolutionaries' arrogant rejection of the past and their misguided attempts to build a wholly new society. Conservatives sought to maintain a sense of continuity with the past and its chivalrous, aristocratic ethos, and they portrayed radicals as the implacable enemies of these traditions. The radical romances of poets like Shelley found only a limited audience at the time of their publication, while Scott's novels were best-sellers.

A romance, in the strict sense, is a tale dealing with chivalry and adventure, usually involving a quest. The hero makes a journey, which takes him through dark and desolate landscapes fraught with peril; some episodes, however, take place in regions of enchanting beauty. The romance is almost always a love story, with the hero's deeds being performed for the sake of a lady. Marvellous events and supernatural powers frequently figure in the tale; enchanters, enchantresses, and their spells are stock elements. The pattern of the hero's quest involves descent into a world of darkness and danger; this may be a literal descent into a labyrinth or cave, or it may be a more symbolic descent, such as wandering in a dark forest or wilderness of some sort. The early nineteenth-century revival of chivalric romance reached a wide audience, especially after the publication of Sir Walter Scott's immensely popular poems *The Lay of the Last Minstrel* (1805), *Marmion* (1808), and *The Lady of the Lake* (1810). These helped to create a fashion for all things medieval. Scott then turned to prose, and transferred many elements of both epic and romantic poetry to his historical novels. In its nineteenth-century form, which owed much to Scott, the romance (either in prose or in verse) could more loosely be defined as an adventure story in which the hero undertakes a quest of some sort. Beginning with *Waverley* (1814), Scott's novels fed the public's appetite for tales of adventure. They were often set in the Middle Ages (for example, *Ivanhoe, Quentin Durward, The Talisman,* and *The Fair Maid of Perth*) and so contained many of the expected trappings of romance as integral elements of the plot. Even in those with more recent settings (*Waverley, Old Mortality, Redgauntlet, Rob Roy, Kenilworth, Woodstock*), characters and events took on added glamour because they were embedded in past times, when the ideals of chivalry still played an active role in society.

The heroes of Scott's prose romances – always gentlemen both by birth and in character – were caught up in tumultuous events such as the conflicts between Normans and Saxons or the Jacobite rebellions.

Men like Waverley might admire and sympathize with the oppressed, whether Saxons or Scots, but they did not in the end join the revolt against lawful authority. Instead, having won and married his lady, Scott's typical hero returned to everyday life as a wiser man, dedicated to a middle way between warring factions. Scott implied that true historical progress was made through unpretending, practical men such as these, rather than by zealots and extremists.[42] No matter how striking the incidents they contained, Scott's novels were ultimately an affirmation of conservative political principles. Such principles, indeed, could be regarded as the treasure the hero brought back from his quest.

Scott thus shaped fictional narratives containing much accurate historical detail around an archetypal literary pattern. In doing so, he made the idea of chivalry all the more appealing: his heroes lived and acted in the 'real' world of history rather than in the realm of poetic fantasy. The historical events and characters depicted might have a certain glamour, owing to their distance in time, but they had actually occurred, and the stories did not require plot devices involving spells, charms, or visions to move them forward.[43] The poetry of romance was brought significantly closer to the prose of ordinary life.

The development was new and startling enough to cause some initial distrust even in Scott's own Tory literary circle: the *Quarterly*'s reviewer praised *Waverley* as a novel of exceptionally high quality, but he expressed doubts about the value of 'what may be called historical romance, in which real and fictitious personages, and actual and fabulous events are mixed together to the utter confusion of the reader, and the unsettling of all accurate recollections of past transactions.' He thought that the author should have employed his talent and his knowledge of the past in writing an authentic historical account of the 1745 uprising, since the novel would likely always be regarded 'as a *mere* romance, and the gratuitous invention of a facetious fancy.'[44] However, by the early 1820s Scott's new genre was fully approved by readers and critics alike. According to John Ruskin, Scott's novels were 'the chief source of delight in all households caring for literature.' Even before he could read, Ruskin heard the books read aloud by his father each evening. 'I can no more recollect the time when I did not know them than when I did not know the Bible,' he wrote in his autobiography.[45] A *Quarterly* reviewer noted that 'Kings, crusaders, knights, and outlaws' were characters 'we never hoped ... to meet with in serious narrative,' but through the magic of books like *Ivanhoe* they had 'become as familiar in our mouths as household terms.'[46] Throughout the nineteenth century, books, paintings, and other cultural media celebrated the ideal of chivalry and insisted that it was no anachronism. Instead, chivalry was seen as a moral code relevant to every aspect of daily life for men and women of all classes.[47]

The literature of Arctic exploration played a central role in this development. The Arctic was in many ways an ideal setting for romance. Not only did it have an aura of strangeness and adventure because of its geographical remoteness, but it was a place where atmospheric phenomena and the patterns of day and night were utterly different from those Europeans were accustomed to, making it appear as a magical realm of terrifying danger, but also of surpassing beauty. The bleak, barren landscape was plunged into darkness for months at a time. But even during the Arctic winter all was not mere desolation. The sun, though it never rose above the horizon, produced delicate colours in the sky, while the moon and stars shone with a 'splendour unknown in the more southern and temperate regions.'[48] The moon was frequently surrounded by haloes and paraselenae, or mock moons.[49] Then there were the brilliant displays of the aurora borealis, the cause of which was at that time still a mystery.

The prolonged days of the Arctic summer offered even stranger and more dazzling visions to the European eye; the *New Monthly* described these as 'fantastic illusions of light and colour, with which Nature seems to amuse herself in these dreary solitudes, as if, secure from the prying impertinence of man, she might descend to downright gambol with her powers.'[50] 'Magic' and 'enchantment' were words readily employed by explorers and reviewers alike when attempting word pictures of Arctic scenery. William Scoresby, for example, described the dramatic effect when a fog suddenly lifted and revealed icebergs sparkling under the 'ethereal brilliancy of the polar sky': such a scene, he wrote, 'bursts on the senses in a brilliant exhibition, resembling the production of magic.'[51] (Passages such as this were among the most likely to be reprinted in reviews.) Parhelia (mock suns) and optical illusions like the one seen by Ross contributed to the belief that the Arctic was a special realm, where the evidence of the senses could not always be relied on. When the true nature of the region was revealed by Parry, it was evident that only through a prolonged quest could the passage be found. The use of the term *labyrinth* to describe the archipelago soon became commonplace.

No reviewer of Parry's narrative made these literary connections in so explicit a fashion. However, the familiarity of literary men and women with romance in all its forms, and of the wider reading public with Scott's poems and novels, was unquestionably of crucial importance in the reception of Arctic literature. The cumulative effect of all the literary comparisons in the various reviews is a factor that cannot be ignored. Most readers with an interest in the subject presumably read many reviews. Even if the readers did not, Parry and his fellow explorers certainly did,[52] and the reviews cannot have failed to influence their future work as writers. Literary form and reality could almost be said to have entered into a new relationship, each reinforcing and enriching the other. The story had all the elements of imaginative literature, yet it could not be dismissed as mere fiction. Parry was not only a successful explorer but a hero of romance; the romance was not just a romance but the unvarnished truth. It was romantic, but not gothic; plainly written, yet exciting. Like Scott's novels, Arctic narratives brought the fantasy of romance closer to believable reality. The scientific aspect of the quest played a key role here, for it was part of the explorers' task to investigate and explain the strange phenomena of the Arctic. As one reviewer pointed out, 'the brilliant auroras, parhelia, and lunar halos' could 'gratif[y] both the vulgar and the scientific eye.'[53] Over the decades to come, these ideas would be elaborated into a powerful interpretive framework. The language of romance and the trope of the plain-speaking nautical explorer on the surface appear incompatible, but in Arctic reviews they gradually came together in what proved to be an exceptionally persuasive combination. And, with the *Edinburgh's* silence, there was no voice to contest the authority of this new language.

Barrow's review must be considered both separately and in relation to the others. It was not among the first to appear (the *Quarterly*, as usual, was published behind schedule) and so did not set the tone for the other periodicals. Parry's success was already ensured, and in terms of literary interpretation Barrow was more a follower than a leader. He was not a literary man, and even with the impetus provided by Leslie's introduction of the term *romance* into the Arctic debate, it seems unlikely that he would have developed the romantic imagery of exploration discourse entirely on his own. 'We may now say "the ice is broken," the door opened, the threshold passed, and the first stage of the journey accomplished,' he began, in what may have been an echo of the *Gentleman's* review. As did all the other reviewers, Barrow paid tribute to Parry's plain and modest style. 'In this work,' he wrote, 'we find no display of self-importance ... no marvellous stories ... but, on the contrary, a plain statement of facts and occurrences, and a detail of scientific observations, made with unimpeachable accuracy, and recorded in the clearest and most simple and unaffected language.'[54]

Barrow then went on to produce an image daringly unlike any that had previously occurred in his writing. Parry was compared to a hero of romance, armed with a magic weapon, who conjured away the barrier placed in his path by Ross (by implication cast as an evil enchanter). Barrow wrote that Parry had 'transformed, as with a touch of Harlequin's sword, the magnificent and insuperable range of mountains … into a broad and uninterrupted passage.'[55] However, there were no more such comparisons. In the rest of the review, Barrow's increasing romanticism is evident, but the focus of his attention was on the Arctic explorer as a hero more like the Elizabethans than like Cook and the other great scientific navigators of the eighteenth century. The defining characteristic of the Elizabethans, as Barrow represented them, was their daring: in their small ships, and without adequate knowledge of science to guide them, they had ventured almost recklessly into the unknown. Barrow had always admired their courage, but he originally regarded Cook as by far the greatest of all explorers because of his scientific attainments and his steady, prudent, methodical character. In his review of Matthew Flinders's *A Voyage to Terra Australis* (1814), Barrow suggested that readers should not blame Flinders because his narrative was less interesting than Cook's. Cook had painted a 'comprehensive picture' of formerly unknown parts of the globe; so vast was the area his voyages encompassed, and so outstanding his ability as a scientific observer, that he 'left nothing to future navigators but to fill up the minuter parts, and add here and there a few touches of light and shade.'[56] But in a sharp change of opinion, Barrow now declared that Cook fell short of Parry in many respects.

Parry too was a scientific explorer, but having passed the threshold of the Arctic, he found himself in a strange new world full of dangers, the like of which Cook had never encountered. Indeed, Cook, like Ross, had turned back at the threshold Parry so boldly crossed. Both in the Antarctic (latitude 71° 10' south) and the Arctic (latitude 70° 41' north), Cook had prudently retreated when faced with a barrier of ice. 'But how stands the case with Captain Parry?' Barrow asked.

After working his way, and struggling almost without intermission for three months, through such fields and floes of ice as were never before encountered by ships with impunity, he was frozen up for ten months in the high latitude of 75°, during three of which the sun never shed one cheerful ray, and the thermometer was generally from 40° to 50° below zero … under such circumstances it required no small share of mental energy to preserve the health and spirits of the people entrusted to his care … and his efforts

were crowned with such success, that he was enabled to bring home every
man (with the exception of one who carried out with him an incurable dis-
ease) in as high health as when they left England, and the two ships as perfect nearly as on the day in which they left the docks.

For all Cook's undoubted greatness, Barrow was prepared 'to assert,
without fear of contradiction ... that in no part of his career of discovery had he occasion to call into action all those personal exertions and
mental energies, which were perpetually demanded in, and essential to
the safety of, the late expedition.' Barrow wrote that no book he had
ever reviewed inspired in him 'more respect for the character of the
author' than Parry's. He claimed that no one could 'rise from its
perusal without being impressed with the fullest conviction ... that the
resources of [Parry's] mind are equal to the most arduous situations,
and fertile in expedients under every circumstance however difficult,
dangerous or unexpected.'[57]

Here the discourse of scientific exploration was not rejected; it was
recast in more romantic terms. The Arctic environment, in so many
ways like the landscape of romance, had called into action higher qualities of character than even the greatest of eighteenth-century explorers
had been required to demonstrate. As Britons sailed northwest in the
wake of their Elizabethan forebears, the old days of chivalrous daring
were revived. In pursuit of their scientific aims, Arctic explorers had to
encounter not only danger, but danger of the most extreme kind, in an
environment utterly different from any they had known before. Parry
went farther than Cook in a merely geographical sense, but there was
much more to his achievement than that. Beyond the threshold of the
Arctic world, only leaders who excelled even the great Cook in daring
and resourcefulness could hope to succeed.

By the time Barrow's review appeared, Parry had set out once again
for the Arctic, hoping to follow the coastline of the continent westward
from Hudson Bay to the Pacific. 'The chances of a failure must insepara-
bly be annexed to all enterprizes [sic] of the nature of that on which
Captain Parry is employed,' Barrow admitted. 'One thing, however, we
will fearlessly assert, that, if a passage is to be effected by human means,
Captain Parry is the officer most likely to accomplish it.'[58] But before
further news was heard from Parry, a second Arctic explorer returned
with an even more dramatic tale to tell.

At several points in his *Quarterly* review of Parry, Barrow made reference to reports from the Arctic land expedition, commanded by

Lieutenant John Franklin. The public had as yet heard relatively little of this venture or of its leader. Franklin was, however, the Arctic officer with the most practical knowledge of exploration and the greatest determination to make a career in geographical discovery. His overland expedition, though it had less initial public appeal than Parry's daring voyage, achieved instant fame on its return to England in October 1822.

Franklin, born in 1786, had resolved on a naval career at the age of twelve, on the day when he first saw the sea.[59] His father strongly disapproved of his choice, but after much argument arranged for him to go on a merchant voyage to Portugal as a cabin boy. Mr Franklin hoped that this would cure his son of any romantic illusions about the sailor's life. However, it had precisely the opposite effect and made John more determined than ever. He entered the navy as a midshipman in 1800, and soon after fought at the battle of Copenhagen.

In 1801–4 Franklin served under Matthew Flinders during his survey of Australia in H.M.S. *Investigator*. From Flinders, one of the navy's outstanding surveyors, he learned much that qualified him for employment on later expeditions. The governor of New South Wales was so impressed by young Franklin's earnest study of surveying and astronomy that he jokingly referred to the boy as 'our Mr Tycho Brahe.'[60] But there was a darker side: the expedition involved personal tragedy for Flinders, and Franklin's response to his commander's misfortunes reveals a great deal about his personality during the early and less studied part of his life. Franklin had gained a place on the expedition through his aunt, Ann Chappell, who married Flinders shortly before the expedition sailed. Flinders hoped to take Ann with him to Australia, leaving her at Port Jackson while the survey was carried out. Unfortunately, he kept this plan (and his marriage itself) a secret from the Admiralty. When it was discovered, the attempt at secrecy brought him into serious disfavour, and he was promptly ordered to leave Ann behind.[61] The newlyweds' separation was to be far longer than anyone could have expected at the time. On the return voyage, Flinders's ship was wrecked near Torres Strait. The survivors were rescued, but it was not possible for them all to return in the same vessel. Franklin made his way back to England without difficulty. Flinders, on the other hand, was detained at Mauritius by the French governor. He was accused of spying and kept prisoner until 1810.

It was therefore almost a decade before husband and wife were reunited. Franklin, then on leave in London, was paying a call on Ann when Flinders arrived, several days before he was expected. So great was the emotion of the moment that Franklin, unable to reply coherently to Flinders's enquiries after their old shipmates, rushed out of the house. The next morning he wrote to Ann that he had 'scarcely yet recovered' from his 'agitation of mind.'[62] To Matthew he explained, 'I felt so sensibly the affecting scene of your meeting Mrs. Flinders that I could not have remained any longer in the room, under any consideration.'[63] Flinders lived only four years after his return: his health had already been undermined by his long imprisonment (although he was only thirty-six in 1810, his hair had turned almost completely white), and it suffered more as he struggled to complete the narrative of his voyage. He died just before it was published. Despite praise by reviewers, the book sold poorly, and in the end his widow had to make good the publisher's net loss of £51.[64]

It might be expected that the personal suffering the *Investigator* voyage inflicted on both Matthew and Ann (who, after all, were not mere acquaintances, but family members with strong feelings of affection for Franklin) might have given him reason to pause before deciding to devote all his own energies to further exploration. However, this was emphatically not the case. In some of his letters, especially two written to Ann Flinders in 1815 and 1818, Franklin appears deliberately obtuse and insensitive, ignoring the distress he caused her by his determination to make his name through geographical discovery (see chapter 4, below). Franklin usually demonstrated an easygoing, very affectionate nature in his interactions with family and friends, but in matters relating to his career he evidently had an exceptionally strong drive towards success.[65]

Those who knew him in later life unanimously agreed that Franklin was remarkable for his lack of egotism and self-seeking. His early letters demonstrate that this had not always been so. Nevertheless, Franklin's biographers have presented his life as forming a coherent whole, with an easily comprehensible linear development from the boy fascinated by the sea and its promise of adventure to the man resolved to do his duty by finding his way through the Northwest Passage. The raw edge of ambition shown in his letters, particularly during the years immediately after the close of the Napoleonic wars, is either passed over quickly or not mentioned at all.

A possible underlying motive was his family's economic situation. The Franklins had once been a landowning family on the borderline between well-to-do yeomen and minor gentry, but both John's great-grandfather and his grandfather were so improvident that his father, Willingham Franklin, had to make his own fortune by trade. Willingham

Franklin ran a successful drapery shop and a banking business in Spilsby, Lincolnshire, married the daughter of a prosperous farmer, and purchased a small country property for his retirement. However, the family fortune once again took a turn for the worse through John's eldest brother, Thomas. He too went into business, but with disastrous results. Thomas Franklin died in 1807, leaving substantial debts and other financial entanglements. As a result, the Franklin parents had to live in a much reduced style. To counteract these financial and social setbacks would certainly have been a reason for John's drive to distinguish himself. He also knew that he could not count on his parents for financial assistance if his naval career faltered, as so many did after 1815.[66]

As this is not a biographical study of Franklin, a more detailed inquiry into the roots of his ambition lies outside its scope. Nevertheless, the issue is relevant to the study of his narratives, since it seems to have been through the experience of his first overland northern expedition and the writing of his first book that Franklin's personality underwent a transformation. He had never been indifferent to religion, but while he was in the Arctic it gained a central place in his life. From a somewhat pushing youth, consumed by thoughts of promotion and worldly success, he became a man whose outstanding characteristics were widely considered to be humility, kindness, and unselfish concern for others. At the same time as he experienced this profound inward change, Franklin was constructed in print as a Christian hero. He found many aspects of this public process distasteful, but it was an important step in the evolution of Arctic discourse. In the end, Franklin's narrative proved even more valuable than Parry's to the conservative re-imagining of Britain.

The relationship between Franklin's individual intentions as an author and the public understanding of his narratives is a highly complex matter. He was certainly a man with a strong and fairly simple sense of patriotism, who would not have dissented from the proposition that British rule over much of the world had been ordained by divine providence. Yet to see him as entirely in agreement with, or constrained by, the wider discourse in which his words were embedded would be an error. There was an underlying tension, and sometimes contradiction, between his individual understanding of his experience and the evolving Arctic metanarrative. In Franklin's mind, his new-found religious faith belonged entirely to the private sphere and had no place in public representations. Though his narrative was based very closely on his journal,[67] the process of transforming a private document into a public account caused him deep emotional distress. For Franklin, reluctance to appear as an author was far more than an assumed rhetorical stance. As he himself stated, only 'an imperious sense of duty' impelled him to undertake and complete the task.[68] Yet the very sincerity with which Franklin yearned to avoid public attention made him all the more convincing as a modest, manly hero. It was apparently because of such initial disjunctions between authorial intention and collective interpretation that the discourse became so powerful. And it may also have been for this reason that it could evolve yet further, be appropriated by new interpreters, and give rise to other perceptions about the wider meaning of Arctic exploration. A detailed consideration of Franklin's experiences as an explorer and then as a writer should therefore suggest new ways of approaching Arctic exploration literature.

4   A Romance in Real Life, 1821–1824

There are instances of real courage and fortitude above the loftiest flights to which fiction ever soared; and which cast into shade the most graphic descriptions of poetry and fancy. There are 'romances in real life;' events and sufferings which could not be à priori supposed possible; which we read with an astonishment that partakes of incredulity; and which tempt us occasionally to ask – 'Can these things be?' Of such a character is the volume before us.

'Franklin's Journey to the Polar Sea,' *British Review*, May 1824

Between his return from Australia and the end of the Napoleonic wars, John Franklin was fully employed on active service, and distinguished himself on several occasions, but to his frustration, he was not promoted beyond the rank of lieutenant. After the end of hostilities, his mind turned again to geographical discovery. For obvious reasons, his aunt Ann Flinders did not think highly of exploration as a means to fortune or happiness. She expressed her views very plainly (and often with considerable bitterness) in her letters.[1] Nevertheless, in 1815, when Franklin heard rumours of a projected expedition to the Congo, he asked her to approach John Barrow on his behalf. Although doubting the wisdom of such a course, she complied.[2] She did not know Barrow well and felt some hesitation in writing to him, but Franklin evidently pressed her to do so. Under the circumstances, his later expression of concern as to whether the matter had caused her 'any sacrifice of feeling or the slightest uneasiness' rings somewhat hollow. Franklin also cheerfully disregarded Ann's forebodings about the fate his ambition might lead him to. He readily admitted that promotion was 'uppermost in my thoughts hopes and wish[es]' and told her that he hoped his requests for help would 'rather be approved than condemned by all who are my sincere Friends.' He went on to say that he would 'ever congratulate myself on the conviction that no effort of either mine or of my Friends has been wanting to draw forth [Barrow's] notice and consideration to my services and on the consciousness of having offered for any employment or occupation however hazardous and unpleasant that could possibly lead to my Professional advancement.'[3]

Franklin was eventually appointed as second-in-command of Buchan's Arctic expedition through the influence of Sir Joseph Banks.[4] In February 1818 he wrote to Ann that he was 'not surprized [sic] that the word Discovery should not possess many charms with you,' but hastened to add, 'My present expectations however open much brighter than I could possibly look for. The voyage I am about to engage in is one of the greatest Interest in every point of view, and appears to occupy the closest attention of all the men of Science in this great Metropolis ... The Service I apprehend will not be one of danger though of considerable fatigue.' Promotion would be likely, and success as an explorer 'would always insure my future employment.' And besides, 'the Emoluments are very handsome.'[5]

Buchan's ship, the *Dorothea*, was badly damaged during a gale in the pack. Franklin's vessel, the *Trent*, was comparatively unharmed. When Buchan decided to return, Franklin requested that he be permitted to go on alone. However, to ensure the safety of those on board the *Dorothea*, the two ships had to remain together. Buchan therefore refused.[6] After their return, Franklin promptly drew up a proposal for another expedition. C.R. Weld later described the plan as 'remarkable' for its 'originality and boldness.' Franklin wrote, 'Should it be questioned whether seamen would be equal to the fatigue and labour involved in this enterprise, I can only say, I would willingly participate with any who would embark in so interesting a cause.'[7] The proposal was not accepted, but Franklin had evidently made the desired impression on Barrow. He was quickly appointed to lead a small party to the northern shore of the North American continent, with the aim of obtaining information that might be useful to the commander of a ship seeking the Northwest Passage.

At the time, slightly more was known of the western than the eastern Arctic. The continental coastline had been visited by Europeans at three widely separated spots: the mouth of the Coppermine River (Hearne, 1771), the mouth of the Mackenzie River (Mackenzie, 1789), and Icy Cape in Alaska, the farthest point reached by Cook on his third voyage

(1778). It seemed highly likely that if Parry were successful in sailing west-ward through Lancaster Sound, he would eventually arrive in this area. Franklin was therefore sent out to chart the coastline eastward from the mouth of the Coppermine; it was hoped that he might meet with Parry's ships, but, if not, he was to leave reports in cairns for Parry's use.

Franklin and his companions (midshipmen George Back and Robert Hood, naval doctor John Richardson, and seaman John Hepburn) left England on board the Hudson's Bay Company ship *Prince of Wales* in May 1819, shortly after Parry sailed for Lancaster Sound. They then accompanied the fur-traders' brigade from York Factory to Cumberland House on the Saskatchewan River. Franklin had been told in London that he would receive extensive help, particularly in the form of food supplies, from the Hudson's Bay Company and the North West Com-pany. However, he found that the rivalry between the two companies (which was then at its height) had led to a serious shortage of provisions throughout Rupert's Land, and that the traders were unable to help him to the extent he had been promised.

During the winter of 1819–20 Franklin, Back, and Hepburn trav-elled on snowshoes to Fort Chipewyan on Lake Athabasca, in order to obtain information on possible routes to the Arctic Ocean. Hood and Richardson followed them in the spring. At Fort Chipewyan, in June 1820, Franklin heard the very welcome news that Willard Ferdinand Wentzel, an experienced employee of the North West Company, wished to join the expedition, and that he had persuaded a Native named Akaitcho and his band, the Yellowknife,[8] to serve as hunters and guides. It was evident that without such assistance the explorers would have not the slightest hope of success, and Wentzel's offer was gratefully received by Franklin.

In July, the explorers and a hired crew of voyageurs joined the Natives at Fort Providence on the north shore of Great Slave Lake. The party then proceeded to the winter quarters suggested by Akaitcho, within easy reach of the Coppermine River. Back and Hood made a brief reconnaissance of the Coppermine, while the others built a house they named Fort Enter-prise. Here they spent the winter of 1820–1. During the winter months, Franklin's mind turned to the subject of religion with a new intensity. He read the Bible, Law's *Serious Call to a Holy Life*, and Doddridge's *Rise and Progress of Religion*.[9] Of the latter two books he wrote in a letter to his sister Henrietta Wright (the wife of a clergyman) that he had previously found them of little interest, but now they provided him with 'grounds of hope, comfort, and support.' 'Serious reflection,' he explained, will soon convince the sinner of his guilt and of his inability to do anything of himself, for every day's experience proclaims to him with a powerful voice that he is weak, irresolute and unprofitable ... If, haply, under this conviction he should inquire, How, then, can I be saved? would it not be joy unspeakable for him to find that the Gospel points out the way? Christ, who died for the salvation of sinners, is the way, the truth, and the life. Can anything be more cheering than these assurances, or better calculated to fill the mind with heavenly impressions, and lift up the heart in grateful adoration to God?[10]

In June 1821 the expedition at last set out for the Arctic Ocean, travelling down the Coppermine in birchbark canoes. At the river's mouth, Akaitcho's band and Wentzel turned back, while the explorers, with the voyageurs and two Inuit interpreters, Augustus and Junius, sailed eastward along the coast as far as Point Turnagain on the Kent Peninsula. Wentzel and Akaitcho had agreed to leave supplies at Fort Enterprise for the explorers' use on their return. Franklin, perhaps reluctant to turn back without substantial geographical results, continued his explorations farther than was wise. Winter set in early that year. To go back the way they had come would take far too long, and Franklin decided to travel overland to Fort Enterprise. He expected that they would be able to live off the resources of the land, but the caribou had begun their southward migration earlier than usual. Game proved extremely scarce, and the men were often reduced to eating a lichen known as *tripe de roche*. The party divided, Back and the strongest voyageurs being sent ahead to bring back the supplies they expected to find at the fort. When Back did not reappear, the main party divided again: the weakest men made what progress they could while Franklin and some others went on at a quicker pace. The weakest of all was Hood, who could not digest the *tripe de roche* and suffered from severe diarrhea. Hood suggested the division, and Franklin believed that he did so in order not to hinder the others' progress. Richardson and Hepburn, both still relatively strong, volunteered to stay with him.

The most sensational events of the expedition occurred in the party left behind. Richardson came to believe that one of the voyageurs, an Iroquois named Michel Teroahauté, had murdered two of his companions and eaten their bodies, sharing the meat (which he claimed was that of a wolf) with the others. When Hood was found dead of a gunshot wound, there was very strong circumstantial evidence that Teroahauté had murdered him. Fearing that the voyageur would kill again, Richardson shot Teroahauté.[11] Richardson and Hepburn, the only survivors of the party, then joined Franklin at Fort Enterprise, where, contrary to their expectations, no supplies had been left. Back had gone on again in search of Akaitcho. While those at the fort waited for relief, more men died of hunger. 'Last year at the same season, and still later, there had been very little snow on the ground, and we were surrounded by vast herds of rein-deer. Now there were but few recent tracks of these animals, and the snow was upwards of two feet deep,' Franklin wrote.[12] Death seemed almost certain. Franklin later told his brother that he had 'never experienced Such ... happiness from the comforts of religion as in the moments of greatest distress, when there scarcely appeared any reason to hope that my existence could be prolonged beyond a few days.'[13] The survivors were eventually rescued by Akaitcho's hunters, who fed and cared for them. In all, eleven of the twenty men on the expedition had perished.[14] The Natives accompanied the survivors to Fort Providence, where they arrived on 26 November 1821. After another winter in the northwest, the explorers sailed for home with the Hudson's Bay Company fleet. They landed at Stromness early in October 1822.

Franklin's letters to his family from Stromness show that he expected the Admiralty to have published many (if not the most sensational) details about the expedition, which his official report had already made known to them. The report had been sent 'by Canada' the previous spring, and he thought that it must have reached London about a month earlier. (It was not received, in fact, until 13 October.)[15] Franklin therefore assumed that 'through the Newspapers you have gained all the intelligence the Great Men choose to publish previous to our arrival.' He had sent a letter to his brother Willingham at the same time as his report, detailing the sufferings of the overland march. Though he noted the high death toll, he said nothing about murder or cannibalism. He had no way of knowing whether this letter had been received, or whether the more sensational 'particulars' had yet been 'more fully imp[a]rted'[16] to the public. As he was unsure of how much his relatives knew, Franklin said very little, but he assured them that they would receive a full account when he arrived home.

In fact, nothing about the dramatic events that occurred in the autumn of 1821 was publicly known until a few days before the expedition's return. On 4 October a brief, and reasonably accurate, report from the Montreal *Herald* of 17 August was reprinted in the *Times*. It stated that Franklin had proved the mouth of the Coppermine River to be in a more southerly latitude than Hearne had claimed,[17] that he had surveyed a few hundred miles of coastline, and that '[s]everal deaths had occurred, among whom was Mr. Wood [sic], nine Canadians, and one Esquimaux.'[18] On 18 October the *Times* reprinted a longer, and far more sensational article,[19] copied from the 11 September issue of the Montreal *Gazette*, which hinted at cannibalism. The Admiralty at last took action: an official account was printed in the evening papers on the 18th and reprinted in the *Times* the next morning.[20] The deaths of Hood and Teroahauté were described in some detail, but nothing was said about cannibalism. On the 19th Eleanor Porden received a letter sent from Stromness, and in her reply, written the same day, she told Franklin that 'the accounts in the last two days['] papers were enough to frighten all your friends.'[21]

The members of the expedition, meanwhile, were making their way south from Stromness. On 18 October Franklin and Richardson arrived in Edinburgh, where they had an interview with the first lord of the Admiralty, Lord Melville.[22] By the 23rd Franklin was in London, while Richardson spent a few days with his family in Scotland. Franklin wrote to the doctor on the 24th, informing him that 'both those of the Colonial Office and the Admiralty have expressed in a very strong manner their entire Satisfaction at all our proceedings and especially on the point regarding Michel which naturally interested you to no small degree. They justly say no other step could have been taken.'[23] Within a week, Richardson too was in London. On 9 November, a luridly phrased, exaggerated account of his reasons for believing Teroahauté was a cannibal as well as a murderer appeared in the *Literary Gazette*.[24] Once again, the indefatigable Jerdan was first in the field with exciting Arctic news.

Before these articles appeared, it seemed unlikely that Franklin's achievements could rival Parry's in either geographical novelty or thrilling incident. Franklin's older brother Willingham, who felt a keen interest in his career, had feared that this would be the case. Willingham was an extremely ambitious man, both for himself (he was a barrister) and for his remaining brothers, James (who entered the East India Company's service) and John. Franklin had been raised in rank from lieutenant to commander during the early part of the expedition. He himself anticipated that this would be considered sufficient reward, and that further promotion would be withheld.[25] Willingham had expected to be in England when his brother returned and he had planned a vigorous campaign to secure John's advance to captain. Willingham's own career then took a major step forward with his appointment as puisne judge of the supreme court of Madras. This meant that he would not be available to forward John's cause. In July 1822 he wrote, '[if I had remained in England], I might have used my best exertions to obtain for you that ultimate Honour in the possession of which I have ever been so anxious to see you. Distance I am afraid will render all my efforts vain – but I think if the Admiralty will trust you with the publication of yr. voyage you may be able by that work to do more for yourself with them, than I cd. do for you were I present.'[26]

In Willingham's eyes, a narrative was the key to distinction and worldly success. For reasons that are not entirely clear, he believed that Barrow might well refuse permission for Franklin to publish. Willingham apparently feared that another Hawkesworth would be hired to write on Franklin's behalf, or even that there would be no publication at all. 'Rely not on Mr. Barrow,' he advised Franklin emphatically. Willingham thought that because of decreased expenditure on the navy in peacetime, 'few but young men of great interest or personal intimacy with Lord Melville, Mr. Croker and Mr. Barrow are certain of success'; they would 'naturally provide for their friends.' Such friends, 'together with a few relations of the other Lords and the relations of men of great Interest' were 'the only persons who can look forward with any confidence to promotion.' Because of Barrow's 'vanity' and his 'desire for Distinction,' it was unlikely that he would patronize men of 'humble merit.' According to Willingham, 'his first cares' would 'alway[s] be *himself* & *the Great.*' Willingham suspected that Barrow might be worse than indifferent: he might actively seek to thwart Franklin's efforts. '[A]gain I say, beware of him,' he cautioned John a second time towards the end of his letter. 'He has already sacrificed you to Mr. Parry & that is not the worst kick he will give you if it be in his power to do it – one effort of that kind will be made in preventing you from writing the history of your voyage, (as I suspect) so you must therefore watch his motions in that quarter & counteract them if you can.' Willingham did not explain what he meant by Barrow's having 'sacrificed' Franklin to Parry, but he may have been angered when Barrow utilized Franklin's early reports to the Admiralty in his review of Parry's narrative. Possibly Willingham believed that Barrow had lowered Franklin in the public esteem through the implication that his reports were of interest not in and of themselves, but only as they cast light on Parry's prospects of success during his next voyage. He urged John to make independent publication his first priority, and reassured him that his letters home had already shown that he had ample material for 'a very interesting and valuable account.'

Willingham mentioned three of his legal friends, Tinney, Amos, and Clinton, who were 'literary men' and would give John any assistance he required. 'I would however mainly rely upon myself as your powers are by no means unequal to composition, but on the contrary very fit for it,' Willingham concluded.[27]

Franklin himself expressed regret that Willingham would not be at hand to help him, 'having always Calculated on receiving his constant assistance.'[28] While still in Rupert's Land, he had discussed the subject of publication with Richardson, who 'often recommended and insisted that the work should appear cheap to the public, yet be well executed and be ready as Soon as possible.'[29] To his sister Isabella he wrote from Stromness that the book 'must be speedily commenced and executed with all the expedition possible or the public mind will lose the interest in its contents it may at first feel.' He went on to say that he did not 'look upon the task ... with any degree of complacency, not on account of the close application I must make ... but because I do not consider myself qualified to compete with the numerous excellent writers of voyages & travels in the present day. I have no doubt however of the incidents ... of our voyage being Sufficient to afford ample material for a useful & interesting narrative if judiciously arranged.'[30] To another sister, Elizabeth, he confided, 'The prospect of having to become an author is by no means gratifying to me, indeed nothing but a sense of duty would prompt me to undertake the task. My objection partly arises from a consciousness of my inability to equal the stile [sic] and language of most of the Modern travellers, and partly from the strong dislike I have always had to appear in a conspicuous station before the public, or rather being what is termed one of the *Lions* of the day.' Here Franklin was not completely honest: the letters he wrote in 1818 make it clear that he had greatly enjoyed his first taste of public recognition. But as the commander of an expedition, he could now expect far more in the way of fame than had been his lot as a second-in-command, and, in his new-found intensity of religious faith, the prospect had become distasteful. He told Elizabeth that he felt 'pain' at the thought of the 'injudicious' attentions that might be bestowed on him 'with respect to my publication.'[31]

On Franklin's arrival in London it immediately became evident that Willingham's fears were groundless. Barrow did everything in his power to encourage the publication of a successful narrative, and he later wrote a *Quarterly* review even more glowing than that he had given Parry. If he had not been so before, Franklin now became a young man 'of great interest' as well as 'personal intimacy' with Barrow. His promotion was secured within a month,[32] and shortly after reaching London he reported to Richardson that 'Croker and Barrow are quite hot for an early publication of our journals.' Franklin concluded that Barrow had spoken to Murray on his behalf even before he arrived, 'for the identical gentleman popped into the Admiralty a few minutes after me and the consequence of his appearance was as you may judge that I had a speedy communication with him on the Subject of publication. He confessed his great desire to get the work because Barrow had told him the narrative was the most painfully interesting of any he had ever read.' Franklin was about to leave London for a short visit to his family in Lincolnshire, and he told Richardson, 'I shall hope to hear of your having found a convenient lodging before my return that we may go to work as Soon as is convenient … I hope you will bear in mind your kind promise and endeavour to assist me as much as possible, for you are aware I do not feel quite competent to the task … Barrow has handsomely offered to revise every sheet, as he did Parrys [sic].'[33] Richardson provided extensive help and advice during the writing of the narrative, and Franklin drew on Richardson's journal as well as his own at many points.

However, even with such support, authorship was a problematic role for Franklin. He found it immensely difficult and emotionally draining to the point that it almost damaged his closest personal relationships beyond repair. He became engaged to Eleanor Porden soon after his return, and their correspondence shows that the stress of writing the narrative precipitated misunderstandings which led her to consider breaking off the engagement. Franklin's letters, formerly lively and entertaining enough (if a little sententious at times), became exceptionally stiff and pompous, a fact on which Eleanor did not fail to remark.[34] Then he denounced authorship in such bitter terms that Eleanor, who had every intention of continuing to write and publish after they married, was both hurt and seriously alarmed.[35] This turmoil is particularly surprising because Franklin's earlier correspondence showed him to be precisely the type of ambitious, capable young officer who could have been expected to step unhesitatingly into the role sketched out for him by Willingham. He had always demonstrated an eager desire to advance himself in his profession by every available means. Authorship brought him public approval, a substantial sum of money, and the praise of the woman he loved, yet he described the experience of writing as so painful and distressing that he longed to escape from it.

For all the sensibility (to use the term current at the time) that Franklin demonstrated on the day of Flinders's return in 1810, he evidently could not then imagine that a fate in any way resembling his former captain's could ever fall to his own lot. This youthful optimism, verging on arrogance, had vanished forever by the time he returned from the Arctic in 1822. A letter of congratulations and good wishes from Ann Flinders, written in early February 1823, went unanswered. When he received it, as he later explained to her, 'I was deeply engaged in preparing for the press the most painful pt. of my narrative – & the recollection of scenes which had been soothed by time and reflection, so distressed me that I felt quite unequal to correspondence with any of my friends. My letters from Lincolnshire even remained for weeks unanswered … Such then, was the state of ferment in wh. my mind was at that period.'[36] This was no mere excuse for his negligence as a correspondent. It was at the same time, although Franklin did not mention it to Ann, that Eleanor Porden began to comment uneasily on his antipathy to 'every thing which bears the least affinity to Literature.' She conjectured that his mind was 'harassed and over-wrought by application to your work,'[37] and hoped that his strange mood would quickly pass. Only after the book's publication in April were they able to discuss and resolve her fears.

Franklin went on to lead another expedition and write another narrative without any of the agonies that marked his first effort. He continued to advance his career whenever possible. Nevertheless, he had become a different man from the brash young lieutenant who almost aggressively solicited the help of his 'Friends' and who was so anxious to make a favourable impression on powerful men like Barrow. Instead, he shunned social occasions during which he might be showered with adulation for his exploits. He explained to Eleanor, who found this diffidence hard to understand, that he felt 'the more averse to entering into such parties because from the circumstances which have recently occurred every one feels himself at liberty to pay some unnecessary compliment to me.' He was apprehensive that 'such attention may prompt me to assume individual merit for results which are entirely to be ascribed to the superintending blessing of a Divine Providence.'[38] Franklin returned again and again to the incompatibility between the role of hero and true religious faith: 'I have sought earnestly in the Scripture for the grounds of my faith and hope, and the result of my enquiries, whilst it has given me the greatest conviction of my own unworthiness, has also afforded me the fullest confidence in the divine goodness and mercy,'[39] he wrote in July 1823.

Throughout the rest of his life, Franklin continued to assert that any success he had attained was not his own work but God's. His unostentatious piety and his lack of egotism were described as Franklin's defining qualities by all who knew him. In an account of the second overland expedition, Richardson wrote of 'the hold [Franklin] acquires upon the affections of those under his command, by a continued series of the most conciliatory attentions to their feelings, and an uniform and unremitting regard for their best interests.'[40] In 1892 Sir Henry Elliott, who had once served as Franklin's private secretary, agreed that 'Franklin's great characteristic was his thoughtfulness for others and his complete absence of all thought for himself; deeply religious, his duty to God and man was at all times his sole and only guide; and, when he had once decided what that duty was, no earthly consideration could turn him a hair's breadth from it ... identifying himself with the interests and welfare of those over whom he was placed, he won their love in an extraordinary degree.'[41]

It was apparently the difficulty of reconciling his new outlook on life with the public role he was required to play that lay at the root of Franklin's uncharacteristic behaviour in early 1823. Even as he came to see self-abnegation as a virtue, he was thrust into public view as a hero. Moreover, there had been a vividness and intensity to his Arctic experiences that Franklin had never before known, and yearned to recapture. 'How often,' he wrote to Eleanor, 'have I wished since those afflicting scenes have passed over which we encountered at Fort Enterprise that I could again enjoy the course of meditation and reflection I entertained during their progress, but I can scarcely hope for a return of those pleasurable sensations. The parties and cares of mixed society and an active life tend to dissipate such emotions. I experienced this with regret during my residence in London.'[42]

'Why should you shun the praise which is justly your due?' Eleanor argued. 'As a Christian you have indeed done no more than your duty, for more than that you cannot do; but as a man you have well performed it, and it is but just that your fellow men should give you credit for having done so, and that you should bring down your proud spirit to endure the expression of their good opinion.' Franklin was not convinced. It seemed to Eleanor that he was on the verge of converting to Methodism, and she found evangelical fervour repellent. 'You *must* have had such strong emotions that all now appears tame; but remember that there is no nourishment in pepper,' she admonished him near the end of a long letter criticizing excessive religious enthusiasm.[43] 'The emotions I have had were indeed strong, they afforded me the greatest consolation at the time, and thanks be to God continue to do so,' he replied.[44] But as he was clearly inclined to be moderate and conciliatory on other points, assuring her that he had no wish to curtail her literary activities, they were married in August 1823. The marriage was a happy one, though Eleanor continued to be made uneasy at times by his intensity on matters of religion. 'Mild as you usually are, your looks and voice have actually terrified me,' she wrote to him in September 1824.[45]

Emotions strong enough to terrify an intelligent woman are not part of the conventional picture of Franklin. In his narrative, he appears as an honest, conscientious, and somewhat plodding author, stoically recording facts even in the most hair-raising circumstances. A tale of starvation, murder, and cannibalism was surely never recounted in a plainer, more down-to-earth style. For all the emotional anguish and exaltation he had experienced, Franklin told his story in the modest, empirical fashion that the discourse of British exploration required. This suited him well on several counts, since he had no wish either to open his inmost experiences to the public or to be celebrated for his accomplishments. And, however little the resulting narrative suits current conceptions about the appropriate manner of representing experiences such as Franklin had undergone, it was perhaps even more enthusiastically received than Parry's book.

Although Franklin did not offer the reader much access to his thoughts and feelings, he did at many points refer to the profound solace he and his companions derived from their religious convictions. As the *Christian Observer's* reviewer remarked, the book was 'interspersed with little facts and observations which strongly betoken the habitual influence of religious and Christian principles; and all these facts and remarks occur so naturally and so incidentally that they bear the strongest marks of genuine sincerity.'[46] Even when describing a meal of burnt deerskin and *tripe de roche*, Franklin assured his readers, 'We looked ... with humble confidence to the great Author and Giver of all good, for a continuance of the support which had hitherto been always supplied to us at our greatest need.'[47]

This religious sentiment in itself added a new dimension to his narrative. Explorers had often concluded their accounts of dangerous episodes with a remark on the mercy shown to them by divine providence. However, few had undergone so prolonged and terrifying an ordeal as Franklin, and in no other narrative was religious feeling so closely woven into the very texture of the book.[48] The story was indeed one that rivalled fiction, but the sensational events of the expedition were not recounted in the language of gothic horror. Instead, Franklin made them the occasion for quiet but obviously heartfelt religious reflections.

'A more affecting tale of physical suffering was never recorded. Reality may here be said to outstrip romance,' the *Christian Observer* noted, adding that the narrative was 'calculated to excite feelings of the most painful interest.' The book had been received with 'lively interest,' yet its 'mixture of pious reflection and resolute conduct' raised it far above the level of common romances. Franklin and his men had 'given the world [an] edifying example of the efficacy of religious principles, hopes, and prospects, in supporting the human mind under the severest bodily distresses, and enabling it to sustain them, not only without murmuring, but with cheerful resignation.'[49] It could not be said of this book, as Croker had said of *Frankenstein*, that it 'gratuitously harasse[d] the heart' without offering any moral lesson to compensate for the 'painful sensations' inflicted on the reader.

The narrative's restrained, sober, truthful tone almost paradoxically heightened readers' sense that as they read they were witnessing exceptionally dramatic and meaningful events, and it is plain that many reviewers were deeply moved by it. One wrote that it 'appeal[s] with an energy, that may not be resisted, to the best sympathies of our nature, unlocking the deepest springs of our compassion, or hurrying us out of ourselves to hunger and freeze in the howling desert, until we start, as from a painful dream.'[50] Richardson's account of Hood's last days, which was included in the narrative, was frequently quoted by reviewers. Richardson described how he and Hood had comforted each other by reading religious books aloud: 'We ... found that they inspired us on each perusal with so strong a sense of the omnipresence of a beneficent God, that our situation, even in these wilds, appeared no longer destitute; and we conversed, not only with calmness, but with cheerfulness, detailing with unrestrained confidence the past events of our lives, and dwelling with hope on our future prospects.' Richardson declared that if it had not been for Hood's murder, 'I should look back to this period with unalloyed delight.' He recorded that Hood had evidently been reading Bickersteth's *Scripture Help* at the very moment of his death, for Richardson found the book beside his friend's body, as if it had fallen from his hands as he died.[51] This detail was mentioned by many reviewers. Richardson described Teroahauté as a basically good man and attributed his moral breakdown to a lack of religious conviction. Richardson knew that Teroahauté – an Iroquois born near Montreal – had likely been raised as a Catholic; however, it appeared to the explorers that he had abandoned his faith. 'His principles ... unsupported by a belief in the divine truths of Christianity, were unable to withstand the pressure of severe distress,' the doctor wrote.[52]

The other survivor of Richardson's party, John Hepburn, did not speak for himself in the narrative, but his religious convictions were accorded a prominent place by both Franklin and Richardson. Throughout his description of the return across the barren lands, Franklin drew a sharp contrast between Hepburn's conduct and that of the French-Canadian voyageurs. Franklin emphasized that he and his naval companions had never believed reliance on God meant they were not obliged to do their utmost to save themselves; on the contrary, they were convinced that the greater a man's faith, the more strenuously he must endeavour to deserve the gifts of providence. To Franklin's great and evident frustration, the voyageurs did not share this belief. He described them as averse to planning ahead and fatally prone to despair. Although physically stronger than the officers and admirably courageous in most situations, according to Franklin they were more of a burden than a help on the return march. 'The men now seemed to have lost all hope of being preserved; and all the arguments we could use failed in stimulating them to the least exertion,' he wrote at one point. Hepburn, on the other hand, was 'animated by a firm reliance on the beneficence of the Supreme Being, tempered with resignation to his will,' and he was 'indefatigable in his exertions.'[53] Franklin later told Eleanor Porden that, by Hepburn's own account, the latter's conduct was 'influenced by a sense of duty which the Scriptures had taught him.'[54] In the narrative, both Franklin and Richardson made it clear that their survival was in no small measure due to Hepburn's loyalty and zeal.

The religious dimension of the narrative was perfectly suited to Barrow's purposes as a *Quarterly* writer. The defence of religion as one of the cornerstones of traditional society had always been central to the *Quarterly*'s discourse. Parry, like Franklin, was a deeply religious man, but this side of his character was not evident in his narrative. And, though the good relations between Parry and his men were widely held up as an example, none of the sailors on his expedition had played so important a role as Hepburn. They did not appear as fully rounded individuals or as actors in their own right, but in Hepburn the lower deck gained its own Arctic hero. Richardson described him as 'a man, who, by his humane attentions and devotedness [to Hood], had so endeared himself to me, that I felt more anxiety for his safety than for my own.' Later, when Richardson collapsed from exhaustion after a march over rocky ground, he too was cared for by Hepburn. 'If Hepburn had not exerted himself far beyond his strength, and speedily made the encampment and kindled a fire, I must have perished on the spot,' Richardson recorded.[55]

Franklin's narrative therefore outshone Parry's as an illustration of both the spiritual and the social value of religion, and it offered an unforgettable story of comradeship between men of widely different class backgrounds. It was through his book that Arctic exploration literature became an truly integral element in the conservative re-imagining of Britain. 'Read this, ye Hunts and ye Hones; and if you be not as insensible to the feelings of shame and remorse, as to those consolations which the Christian religion is capable of affording, think of Richardson, Hood, and Hepburn,' Barrow wrote triumphantly in his review.[56] Overt references to his political opponents were rare in Barrow's periodical writings, and presumably he altered his usual practice on this occasion because he felt that victory was certain.

Of all the radical journalists, Leigh Hunt and William Hone were, along with William Hazlitt, the objects of the *Quarterly*'s greatest scorn in the early 1820s. Hone's *The Apocryphal New Testament* had been very harshly reviewed in the July 1821 issue: 'Nothing but the execution of a public duty would have tempted us to defile one line of our Journal with the notice of a wretch as contemptible as he is wicked,' the reviewer declared.[57] Hone responded with a letter to the *Quarterly*'s editor; receiving no reply, he had the letter printed in the *Examiner.*[58] In a review of Hazlitt's *Table Talk* in the next (October 1821) issue of the *Quarterly*, Hunt, Hone, and Hazlitt were referred to as three 'asses' who, were they not 'more vicious than stupid,' would deserve pity. Hazlitt's essays, although concerned with culture rather than politics, were pronounced dangerously subversive; according to the reviewer, 'the disciples of the Radical School lose no opportunity of insinuating their poison into all sorts of subjects: a drama, a novel, a poem, an essay, or a school-book, is in their hands an equally convenient vehicle. A direct attack upon the constitution of the country puts the reader effectually on his guard; it is the oblique stroke, like that of the tusk of the boar, which most dangerously assails the unwary.'[59] The same issue contained reviews of William Godwin's *Of Population* (a reply to Thomas Malthus) and Shelley's *Prometheus Unbound.* Godwin was described as the possessor of 'a mind of such overweening confidence in its own powers, as rashly to pull down, in its imagination, whatever had been held most venerable and valuable in society, in order to erect upon the ruins a visionary fabric of its own.'[60] The verdict on Shelley was that 'his works exhale contagious mischief ... in exposing to the public what we believe to be the character and tendency of his writings, we discharge a sacred duty.'[61] Hunt replied in the *Examiner,* attacking the *Quarterly*'s 'flagrant craft and

Jesuitism.' He presented an analysis of the October 1821 issue intended 'to catch misrepresentation "living as it rises," or in other words to press more speedily upon the public attention the literary principle and practice of the most cultivated, confirmed and pliable Toryism.'[62]

It is hardly surprising that Barrow was so 'hot for an early publication' of Franklin's account. It provided him with a strong weapon in the *Quarterly*'s ongoing cultural battles, and he used it deftly. However, as in the case of Parry's book, Barrow's review did not appear until three months after the publication of the narrative, and he therefore cannot be seen as the leader of public opinion. The early reviews were uniformly favourable. The narrative was published on 12 April 1823;[63] on 1 May Eleanor wrote to Franklin, 'Your book was exactly what I expected from my knowledge of you; but had anything been wanting to confirm my esteem and admiration of the writer, it would have done so. It is therefore with no ordinary feelings of pride and pleasure that I find the same sentiments expressed by what I may term the public voices of my country.'[64]

The *Literary Gazette's* review was the first to appear. It was published in two parts, on 12 and 19 April. Jerdan described the book as 'indeed a powerfully interesting production: the personal narrative most affecting, the scientific details equally valuable and amusing, and the manner in which the volume is printed and embellished ... such as to excite our admiration, and demand our warmest praise. The spirit and character of the whole ... render it, to use the bookselling phrase, one of the best got up volumes that has appeared even in these improving times.'[65] The engravings by Edward Finden, based on drawings by Back and Hood, had added considerably to the price of the volume (4 guineas), which Barrow originally thought should be no more than 3 guineas.[66] Franklin was eager to have as many illustrations as possible, and Barrow agreed that Finden's work was 'superlatively beautiful.'[67] These illustrations gained far more praise than had William Westall's contributions to Parry's narrative. Jerdan called the engravings in Franklin's book 'exquisite: they perfectly come up to our often-expressed idea of the style in which such illustrations ought to be executed.'[68] Affluent readers evidently agreed, for despite its high price the edition sold out quickly. In late July, Franklin noted that Murray had 'long ago Sold every copy.'[69] Richardson described the rapidity of the sale as 'almost unprecedented.'[70] Several months later, Franklin reported that second-hand copies were much in demand, selling for up to 10 guineas each.[71]

The first part of the *Gazette's* review must have generated an unusual amount of comment, for the next week Jerdan wrote, 'Were an Echo susceptible of pleasure, we might feel some gratification in the thanks and commendations we have received for the manner in which we introduced Captain Franklin's delightful work to the public in our last Number. But we feel too entirely that we were only the echo of attractive sounds, to appropriate any part of the praise to ourselves. The narrative is altogether so interesting, and the volume published in a style so creditable to the English press and arts, that it is impossible to describe the latter, or quote from the former, without producing an effect whose force is intrinsic and independent of our praise.' The first instalment contained long extracts, and Jerdan went on to print more, explaining, 'We do not know that we can, for the present, do better for our distant readers, who cannot yet have seen much of the work itself, than take it up where we left off, and select the leading features for their perusal.'[72]

The *Literary Chronicle* also confined itself mainly to printing extracts, at even greater length than the *Gazette*: the review extended over four issues (19 and 26 April, 3 and 10 May). The *Chronicle* introduced the first extracts by observing, 'The difficulties and hardships encountered by our brave countrymen in this expedition, heart-rending as they are in the recital, seem to have had no other effect on them, than that of arming them with patience and perseverance; and the account of their adventures, as detailed in Capt. Franklin's Narrative, independent of its value as a scientific work, renders it one of the most important and interesting volumes that has issued from the press, since Capt. Parry's Journal, to which it forms so suitable a companion.'[73] In conclusion, the *Chronicle's* writer reflected that it was 'a remarkable circumstance in the Narrative of this honourable but disastrous expedition' that his countrymen 'bore their disasters, dangers, and sufferings, better than the Canadians, who were accustomed to the climate, and brought up from infancy to constant fatigue.'[74]

The *Gentleman's Magazine*, the *London Magazine*, and the *New Monthly* published their reviews in May. The *Gentleman's* declared that the 'perseverance and dauntless courage of our countrymen, in their arduous and perilous researches, must ... excite the admiration of the civilized world.' As for the book in itself as a physical object, 'the costly and superb manner in which this interesting work is embellished ... reflects considerable credit on the talents of the Artist, and the munificent spirit of the Publisher.'[75] The *London Magazine's* reviewer noted, 'We have seldom opened a volume with higher expectations than the present; and those expectations have not been disappointed.' The geographical and scientific information was deemed 'of decided importance,' while '[i]n other lights' the book was 'extremely interesting, as a record of spirit and perseverance, of exertion and suffering, which have seldom been surpassed, and will not speedily be paralleled.'[76] According to the *New Monthly*, 'The enterprizing [*sic*] spirit, undaunted resolution, and indefatigable perseverance of Captain Franklin and his companions are now consigned to immortality ... their memories must for ever be entwined with the glories of their native country.'[77]

In June, notices appeared in the *Eclectic Review* and the *Edinburgh Magazine*. The *Eclectic*'s reviewer related that the voyageurs were 'a great annoyance ... they thought only of the present moment ... The high sense of duty, and the hope of reward and fame, which actuated the Commander and his officers, did not exist for their subordinate agents; and it must have required a continual exercise of firmness and temper, to over-rule their tendency to resist, and to keep their spirits from absolute despondency.' Franklin was praised for 'the perfect combination of prudence, courage, and ability, which he displayed throughout,' and Hepburn was described as 'a man of admirable qualities.'[78] The *Edinburgh Magazine* printed one of the most restrained commentaries. Nevertheless, the reviewer commended Franklin both as an explorer and as a writer. 'Although this expedition, through the serious and terrible obstacles which it encountered, was able to accomplish only a small part of the objects contemplated, and though it effected its return only through a fearful train of disaster, it was yet executed in a manner creditable to the individuals concerned, and has brought by no means a trifling accession to our geographical knowledge,' he observed.[79]

Barrow's *Quarterly* article appeared in July 1823, and a two-part review was printed in the September and October issues of the *Monthly Review*. Both these long commentaries developed and expanded on the themes of the shorter early reviews. They did so in such similar ways that it almost seems they were written by the same person. However, a letter from Franklin to Richardson names Robert Jameson as the author of the *Monthly* article.[80]

Barrow began by stating that the perusal of the narrative had 'not only afforded us many new lights on that portion of the globe of which it treats, but excited in our minds an intense and painful interest. The unstudied and seaman-like simplicity of the style is not the least of its merits; and the illustrations and embellishments ... are of a very superior kind.' After this brief recapitulation of earlier comments, he went on to pen one of the most influential passages in the entire literature of Arctic exploration, which would be quoted and paraphrased again and again throughout the nineteenth century. 'The narrative of Captain Franklin,' he wrote,

> adds another to the many splendid records of the enterprize [*sic*], zeal, and energy of British seamen – of that cool and intrepid conduct, which never forsakes them on occasions the most trying – that unshaken constancy and perseverance in situations the most arduous, the most distressing, and sometimes the most hopeless that can befal [*sic*] human beings; and it furnishes a beautiful example of the triumph of mental and moral energy over mere brute strength, in the simple fact that, out of fifteen individuals enured from their birth to cold, fatigue, and hunger, no less than ten were so subdued by the aggravation of those evils to which they had been habituated, as to give themselves up to indifference, insubordination, and despair; and, finally, to sink down, and die; whilst, of five English seamen, unaccustomed to the severity of the climate, and the hardships attending it, one only fell, and *he* – by the murderous hand of an assassin. A light buoyant heart, a confidence in their own powers, supported by a firm reliance on a merciful Providence, never once forsook them, nor suffered the approach of despondency, but brought them safely through such misery and distress, as rarely, if ever, have been surmounted.

Barrow returned to the contrast between the voyageurs and the British sailors later in the article, remarking that on the march across the barrens, the former, 'becoming alike indifferent to promises or threats, seemed to consider themselves as liberated from all control.' Franklin, on the other hand, did not falter even when he arrived at Fort Enterprise only to find it 'desolate – no provisions … no Mr. Wentzel, nor any letter from him to point out where the Indians were!' Placing his trust in God, 'this gallant officer never once uttered a murmur, nor gave himself up to despair.' Hood and Richardson demonstrated similar courage: 'Never certainly were the blessings of religion more strongly felt than in the case of these excellent men, when to all human appearance their case was utterly hopeless; yet nothing like despondency, not a murmur ever escaped their lips.'[81]

At the end of the review, Barrow once again linked the qualities of courage and religious faith to the British national character, this time contrasting the conduct of Franklin, Richardson, Hood, and Hepburn with that of French sailors and soldiers placed in a similar position. 'Excepting in the case of the French ship, Méduse, we hardly know a more lamentable instance of the fatal effects of insubordination and disobedience … nor, we may add, a stronger contrast than is afforded

by the conduct of the two parties on the two unfortunate occasions,'
he wrote.[82] J.B. Savigny and Alexandre Corréard's *Naufrage de la Frégate
La Méduse* had been reviewed, most likely by Barrow,[83] in the October
1817 issue of the *Quarterly* (the same issue in which the renewal of the
search for the Northwest Passage was announced). The *Méduse* was
wrecked while carrying French administrators, scientists and soldiers
to Senegal in 1816. Since there were not enough boats for everyone on
board, a raft was hastily constructed. Most of the soldiers were placed
on it, with very little food. At first the raft was towed by the boats, but
within hours the tow ropes were cast off and the 150 men on the raft
left to their fate. According to Savigny and Corréard, the only thought
which could console their companions was that of taking revenge on
the boats' crews for abandoning them. Many died from starvation and
exposure; some of the bodies were eaten by those who still survived. A
group of soldiers attempted to murder their officers but were themselves killed. When only thirty men remained alive, the weakest were
thrown overboard by the strong in order to conserve food. Fifteen
were eventually rescued, but six of them died shortly after. In recalling
this incident to his readers' minds, Barrow heightened the contrast
between Britons and 'others.' Franklin's voyageurs and the soldiers on
the raft – all French – had quickly given way to despair.[84] Especially in
the case of the *Méduse*, the result was moral breakdown and anarchy.
The British, by contrast, had maintained order both within their own
minds and in their interactions with others. Their sense of duty and
their perseverance had transformed otherwise disastrous events into a
moral victory.

Jameson employed many of the same arguments and strategies in the
Monthly, although with slightly less force and eloquence. He, too, turned
quickly from the events chronicled by Franklin to their broader significance for the nation. 'Had the expedition ... been undertaken merely
to gratify an individual's thirst for knowledge or for fame, its present
unvarnished history would still have roused the attention and excited
the sympathies of every generous mind,' he wrote. '[B]ut, when viewed
in combination with the series of national efforts to explore the arctic
latitudes ... it cannot fail to awaken the most lively and patriotic sensations. We hasten, therefore, to lay before our readers some notices of a
narrative which has such urgent claims on their regard, and which the
enlightened portion of the community will peruse with the mingled
feelings of commiseration and applause.'[85]

After outlining the events of the expedition, Jameson observed: 'A
more truly afflicting record ... has seldom fallen under our cognizance:

but, fortunately for the public, it is not a theme of barren regret or blighted expectation, the main specific object of the enterprize [*sic*] having been at least partially attained, much valuable scientific information collected and registered, and another illustrious example exhibited of what British valor, under the guidance of education and religious dependence, can endure and achieve.' Jameson ended with the usual commendation of Franklin's straightforward writing style, observing that, when viewed 'merely in the light of a literary composition,' the narrative possessed 'one of the fundamental properties of good writing, namely, unity of design.' Franklin and his fellow explorer-authors 'never deviat[ed] into useless discussion or sentimental digressions, but adher[ed] pertinaciously to their subject, and relat[ed] with plainness and perspicuity the events and circumstances, precisely in the order of their occurrence.'[86]

The *Christian Observer* also published a long and enthusiastic review, but not until the issue of Feburary–March 1824. The edition reviewed was the two-volume set without illustrations, priced at 24 shillings, and the *Observer* expressed pleasure that Franklin's work was now available to a wider audience in 'a more portable and less expensive form.' The reviewer felt that the expedition's scientific and geographical aims 'would have imparted a considerable interest' to the book, even if it had not contained 'a narrative of some of the most extraordinary sufferings, hardships, and privations that ever were encountered: as it is, it has excited a strong and general sympathy in the public mind.' He claimed that this sympathy had been 'wrought up in feelings of the highest respect and admiration towards Captain Franklin and his four British companions.' The reviewer very strongly shared these feelings, since to 'the fortitude of the enterprising traveller, they appear to have added, what renders the volume to us ten-fold interesting, the piety of the serious Christian. They have given the world one more edifying example of the efficacy of religious principles, hopes, and prospects, in supporting the human mind under the severest bodily distresses, and enabling it to sustain them, not only without murmuring, but with cheerful resignation.'[87]

At even greater length than Barrow, the reviewer contrasted the courage of the British with the despair of the voyageurs, and he too attributed the difference to religious faith. The voyageurs had demonstrated the 'most unaccountable and infatuated improvidence.' In contrast, it was

truly delightful and edifying to observe the steady piety of the English party, and the efficacy of right religious feelings and principles, in enabling them to hold up under a pressure of suffering which overwhelmed those who had nothing better to lean upon than their animal spirits. The Canadians had an advantage over the English, with respect to bodily strength, and the habit of being exposed to the hardships and severities of a North American winter. Yet they all sank ... while their less robust companions weathered and outlived the storm. Some may be disposed to ascribe this to the greater fortitude inspired by superior reflection and intelligence. We attribute it far more to the operation of religious hopes, feelings, and principles, kept alive by frequent acts of devotion[.]

The *Observer* accorded more space than either the *Quarterly* or the *Monthly* to Hepburn. '[W]e cannot withhold our feeble tribute of applause and admiration from the honest seaman,' the reviewer declared. 'He was foremost in encountering perils and hardships, and always at hand to administer to the relief of his companions. His courage and fortitude seem to have inspired the whole party.' Yet for all his strength and resourcefulness Hepburn had never forgotten his place in the naval hierarchy: 'he appears to have been free from all improper forwardness and pretension, perfectly submissive to his superiors, and disposed to distinguish himself in no other way than by a patient persevering industry, in the discharge of his arduous and painful duties.'[88]

The reviewer concluded by comparing Franklin's narrative favourably with those by earlier travel writers. No specific authors were named, but he seems to have been thinking of eighteenth-century explorers like Samuel Hearne. 'We confess,' he wrote, 'that, when we compare these traits of Christian piety and resignation with that lurking scepticism or cold insensibility to religious considerations which characterizes the narratives of too many travellers, they appear to our view like so many spots of verdure and fertility, amidst a wide encircling desert. They shed a moral warmth and beauty over the scenery of the *barren grounds*.' The records of Franklin and Richardson left 'no room for that painfulness of reflection which arises in a Christian mind, from the view of sufferings unsanctified and unimproved.' In the reviewer's opinion, 'It cannot be denied that, in travellers not previously fortified by sentiments of piety, and by the principles of true religion, a rambling curiosity ... [has] some tendency to confirm sceptical opinions and to increase irreligious practice.'[89] Like Barrow, then, though for slightly different reasons, the *Observer's* reviewer ranked the Arctic explorers above their eighteenth-century predecessors.

Another late review in a religious periodical appeared in the quarterly *British Review* of May 1824. The author began by outlining the events of the preceding thirty years. In his view, Britain had been the victim of a conspiracy of nations, led by France. Her 'conduct and character' while under attack 'cannot be regarded by the patriot, the philosopher, or the Christian, without sentiments of respect and wonder.' For it was at this time of great peril that many 'institutions for the advancement of religion, which have identified the name of Britain with a hallowed and therefore with an imperishable glory, had their birth.' Thus, the British victory was due chiefly to the religious faith of the people. Then, with the coming of peace, '[e]very measure, which could extend the boundaries of domestic prosperity, enlarge the stores of scientific discovery, or increase the benign influence and empire of Christianity, and with it the sum of happiness and hope to man, was eagerly adopted, and vigorously pursued.' Among these enterprises was the renewed search for the North-west Passage. Despite the great obstacles that would have to be overcome, the reviewer declared that he could not 'be of the number of those who think lightly of these attempts. They are suited ... to the generous character, they are worthy of the chivalrous feeling of Great Britain.'[90]

In this author's eyes, the Franklin expedition was clear proof of the special favour in which divine providence held the British people. The explorers passed through 'a series of fatigues and hardships, which cannot be read without feelings of the most painful emotion,' until they came at last to 'a climax of wretchedness, from which there could have been no return, had not the providence of God interposed to make them monuments of his sustaining and delivering mercy.' Their 'simple and sincere devotion' was 'a palpable and triumphant proof of the superiority of that courage, which emanates from a religious dependence upon the power and promise of God, over that which is supplied by mere instinct and constitution.' The reviewer drew the usual contrasts between this quiet faith and the despair of the 'others': the voyageurs 'possess[ed] indeed the courage which thoughtlessness supplies, but fail[ed] under the pressure of severe and protracted suffering.' As in Barrow's review, the case of the *Méduse* was cited as further proof that such fortitude and faith were characteristically British. 'Let any man read that harrowing account of the loss of ... La Meduse ... Let him compare it with the pages of this book! Let him judge of the difference between them! And then let him ask, to what principle is that difference to be attributed,' the author urged. [91]

By 1824 a consensus on the evaluation of Arctic writing had emerged among reviewers. The desired qualities were empiricism and modesty; the narratives might be overly detailed and at times repetitive and dull, but this was no real cause for censure. Instead, an abundance of factual material, listed in a sober scientific fashion, was a guarantee of authenticity. Readers seem to have eagerly concurred in this understanding. Decades later, during the Franklin search, an enthusiastic young volunteer, Joseph-René Bellot, recorded his thoughts on rereading Franklin's narratives. 'What admirable simplicity, and what real superiority is apparent in these unpretending phrases, which say only what these eminent men have seen in a clear manner, yet poetical withal, for they are faithful painters of nature,' he wrote in his journal. 'In reading these voyages … we are possessed with implicit confidence; and, without analysing our feelings, we are instinctively prompted to believe the writers; and yet they never deal in high-sounding empty phrases, but give us facts in every line … we feel how substantial and dignified, how full of instructive matter are their narratives, as we can tell by the sound of a cask struck with a finger whether it is full or empty.'[92]

At the same time as this literary standard of judgment was firmly established, the perceived significance of Britain's Arctic heroes was clearly defined in relation to national history and the national character. The interest of a narrative lay mainly in the indirect and unintentional revelation of its author's character; the role of the critic was to provide an exegesis in which such half-hidden traits were revealed for all to see and admire. The two outstanding characteristics of the Arctic explorers were considered to be perseverance and faith. Each of these qualities sustained and reinforced the other, while the combination of the two ensured that the achievements of any explorer who possessed them would be of far more than geographical or scientific importance alone. These men were admirable as individuals, and they also had special standing as embodiments of all that made Britain great. Exploration had become a matter of self-definition on both the personal and the national levels.

The Arctic narrative and its place within broader understandings of British history and nationhood are examined in chapter 5. The matter raises a number of thematic issues not easily discussed in all their implications within a chronological framework. The relationship between the Arctic and the British identity can be fully understood only when it is realized that there existed a larger narrative structure within which the emerging narrative of Arctic exploration was contained. This narrative claimed that a love of and natural affinity with the sea and maritime adventure were among the most important qualities of the British national character. The navy was thus exalted as the national institution that embodied these traits and allowed them their fullest scope for development. In the early nineteenth century, the very existence of a strong, successful navy was held to be a sign that Britons were fulfilling the role intended for them by divine providence. That in times of peace some naval officers should turn to discovery in far northern waters – just as their Elizabethan ancestors had done – demonstrated even more clearly that a special destiny was being fulfilled.

This metanarrative of British history drew on tropes that had originated in the Elizabethan era and then gathered strength in the late eighteenth and early nineteenth centuries. It continued to evolve throughout the rest of the nineteenth century, reaching new heights of importance in the 1890s and the early years of the twentieth century. The Arctic narrative both depended on and added new elements to it. Both had reached a coherent form by the mid-1820s and underwent important further developments between then and the 1850s. Chapter 5 outlines these developments in general terms; chapter 6 provides a more detailed analysis of Arctic expeditions and publications during the period from 1823 to 1848. In these years, northern exploration proceeded slowly but steadily. Particularly during the 1830s and early 1840s, British activity in and attention to the Arctic were less intense than they had been between 1818 and 1827. Nevertheless, the Arctic narrative continued to grow ever more rich and appealing until, in the late 1840s, as journalists and the public awaited the return of Franklin's third expedition, they were ready to greet his expected discovery of the Northwest Passage as an event of major importance in their nation's history.

Developments in print culture during this period were undoubtedly an important contributing factor. The 1820s and 1830s saw the first cheap mass circulation periodicals aimed at entertaining and informing the working class. These brought the story of northern discovery to an ever wider and more varied reading audience. The purposes the story served and the understandings it gave rise to shifted accordingly. By the 1850s the time when elite journals like the *Quarterly* led public opinion had long since passed. However, it was a writer in the *Quarterly* who in 1847 hit on a phrase that summed up the perceived importance of Arctic explorers to the nation: standing at the point where the discourses of naval supremacy and geographical inquiry overlapped, they were 'the Nelsons of discovery.' The full meaning of this phrase to readers of the time is a complex matter, and one that illuminates many aspects of nineteenth-century British beliefs about the nation's identity and destiny.

1 John Barrow. Portrait by John Jackson, ca. 1810.

2 William Edward Parry, after Samuel Drummond. Frontispiece to the *Mirror of Literature, Amusement and Instruction*, Vol. 6.

3 'The Falls of Wilberforce.' Engraving by Edward Finden, based on a drawing by George Back, in Franklin's *Narrative of a Journey to the Shores of the Polar Sea in the Years 1819-20-21-22.*

4 'The Falls of Wilberforce, in the Arctic Regions.' *Mirror of Literature, Amusement, and Instruction*, 24 May 1823.

5 John Franklin, after Thomas Wageman. Frontispiece to the *Mirror of Literature, Amusement, and Instruction*, Vol. 5.

6 Jane Griffin, later Lady Franklin, in 1816. Drawing by Amélie Romilly.

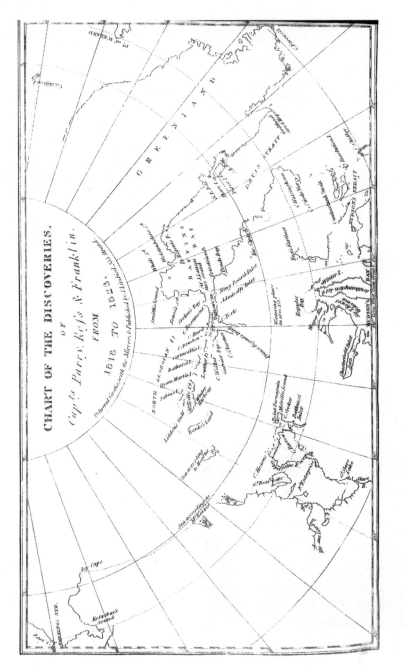

7 Map 'exhibiting the connected discoveries of Captains Parry, Ross, and Franklin.' *Mirror of Literature, Amusement, and Instruction*, special supplement, 17 November 1823.

8 Departure of the *Erebus* and *Terror*. *Illustrated London News*, 24 May 1845.

9 Fitzjames's cabin in the *Erebus*. *Illustrated London News*, 24 May 1845.

10 James Fitzjames. *Illustrated London News*, 13 September 1851.

11 William Penny. Portrait by Stephen Pearce.

12 Officers of Belcher's expedition. Left to right: Sherard Osborn, Mr Allard, Leopold McClintock, W.J.S. Pullen, G.H. Richards. *Illustrated London News*, 1 May 1852.

13 John Rae. *Illustrated London News*, supplement, 28 October 1854.

5 The Nelsons of Discovery

Thirty years have elapsed since one of our colleagues first addressed himself to the task of directing the public mind to the subject of Arctic exploration. He has lived to see many of his expectations justified – and we hope he may yet see others of them realised. ... with interest which accumulates by the hour do we watch for the return of those two vessels which are, perhaps, even now working their southward course through Behring's Straits into the Pacific. ... we are of opinion that the Erebus and Terror should be moored henceforth on either side of the Victory, floating monuments of what the Nelsons of discovery can dare and do at the call of their country[.]

Lord Ellesmere, in the *Quarterly Review,* June 1847

The evolution of the nineteenth-century naval metanarrative of British history began with the celebration of Horatio Nelson and other naval heroes of the Napoleonic wars by their contemporaries. It was continued by such authors as John Barrow,[1] J.A. Froude, and Thomas Macaulay, who reflected on the role played by sailors during the sixteenth, seventeenth, and eighteenth centuries, as well as in their own day. They adapted representations of England as a sea power found in the literature of earlier periods, Barrow and Froude drawing on Hakluyt and Purchas[2] and Macaulay on Pepys and Lord Halifax.[3] Froude's article 'England's Forgotten Worthies' (first published in the *Westminster Review* in 1852) and his *History of England from the Fall of Wolsey to the Defeat of the Spanish Armada* (1856–70) were key texts, which focused attention on the sixteenth century as the era when greater daring in maritime enterprises first brought out the characteristic genius of the English people. While these writers sought to help the public understand the historical roots and development of Britain's naval greatness, the construction of Nelson as a national hero was continued in the work of his biographers. As the period that gave rise to the naval narrative receded in time, the Napoleonic wars too became part of the mythical past. At the same time, a new generation of nineteenth-century naval officers had their lives enshrined in biography, a process traced by C.I. Hamilton.[4] These biographies both placed their subjects within the naval metanarrative and provided new elements and meanings for it to incorporate.

The metanarrative can be studied in two ways: first, by listing and analysing the component parts of the story, so that the broad understanding of British history and identity it promoted can be grasped, and second, by recording its evolution during the course of the nineteenth century. It was never entirely stable and fixed; rather, it shifted slightly over and over again to incorporate new elements, and was not precisely the same in any two decades of the century. To define its relationship to the narrative of Arctic exploration is sometimes a difficult matter. Both narratives were continually in the process of change and had a reciprocal influence on one another. In addition, very little scholarly work has been done on the place of the navy in nineteenth-century British culture,[5] and it is therefore often impossible to determine with certainty which aspects of the Arctic story added something new to the wider narrative and which were similar to what already existed. In a few cases, it is clear that arguments about the navy require modification when representations of Arctic heroes are taken into account. For example, according to Hamilton, one of the key elements in the Victorian biographies he studied was the characterization of naval officers as Christian heroes, sustained in their endeavours by religious faith. He believes that this was a new development of the 1850s. However, as chapter 4 demonstrates, Franklin and his men were presented to the public as Christian heroes in the early 1820s. In the case of religion, the Arctic explorers clearly broke new cultural ground.

The two narratives were closely tied to the prevailing concept of Britain's national character. Both naval and Arctic heroes were revered above all because they were seen as exemplars of the traits that distinguished Britons from 'others.' As a result, their stories had an immensely important role to play in shaping both the individual characters of their countrymen and the destiny of the nation as a whole. Gerald Newman defines the national identity or character as a 'mythic ideal,' a 'stylized phenomenon elaborated over and over in countless ways' until at last it becomes 'the central object of individual identifications within the group' and thus 'a pattern of enculturation.' A national identity is at first a cultural construction rather than a description of reality, but over time it takes on a degree of reality, as individuals shape their behaviour in accordance with the prevailing ideal.[6]

Newman suggests that the great strength of national character as a means of enculturation was that through it individuals could feel an enhanced sense of worth both personally and as component parts of the nation. He notes the affinities of such developments with Romantic literature: the individual self was of central importance to Romantic writers, who were also intensely interested in national folkways and historical traditions. These interests reinforced the belief that each nation had a unique essence, which sprang from deep roots in the past and must be carefully fostered in the present to ensure strength and prosperity in the future.[7] By developing their true natures, individuals could contribute to the larger growth of their nation. So close was the perceived bond between character and the nation that by the mid-Victorian years good character, rather than social standing or the ownership of property, was considered to be the main qualification for taking part in political life. Stefan Collini notes that 'the language of "interests" and "balance," which still occupied the centre of the stage in 1832, had ceded considerable ground to the language of character by 1867. Discussion of the Second Reform Bill, both in and out of Parliament, turned to a considerable extent on the question of whether the moral qualities of the respectable urban artisan were such that he should be entrusted with the vote.'[8]

The proper development of the self was a frequent theme in nineteenth-century writings, and it was commonly asserted that there were two types of personal growth, one conducive to the larger national good and the other mere self-indulgence. In an essay on Rousseau printed in the February 1822 issue of *Blackwood's*, the second way was (perhaps inevitably) identified with a Frenchman. The article implied that the first and better way was characteristic of the British and should in the future become ever more so. The author defined two types of self-consciousness, that of mind and that of temperament. Rousseau's genius was the genius of temperament, which, 'enchanted with the task of self-contemplation, lingers there, and considers as the goal of its course, what the other regards but as the entrance. Like a child, it becomes enamoured of its playthings, and refuses to advance into maturity.' Rousseau had remained a self-centred child all his life, viewing his

emotions and sensual urges with endless fascination. '[T]he unfortunate children of temperament,' the author remarked, 'mistake the fret-
ful irritability of their nerves for a yearning of soul.' The self-
consciousness of mind, on the other hand, 'after having explored its
own feelings and principles, and become acquainted with its internal
organization, passes on, out of itself, into the expansive regions of
knowledge.' Individuals possessing this higher type of self-awareness 'do
not live to contemplate alone, but to progress ... The eye of mind is
turned upon itself, not to seek a theme of pleasure or of pain, but to
perfect an instrument of power – to acquire the self-knowledge, the
intuition, the judgment, to be employed on worthier and more remote
objects.'[9] Such men (and occasionally women) would live for the
greater good of society. This type of self-development was essential for
the development of the nation, while the other could only hinder it.

The relationship between the hero, the ordinary individual, and the
collective national being was discussed in the writings of Thomas
Carlyle, Froude, Samuel Smiles, and many other nineteenth-century
authors. In *On Heroes, Hero-Worship, and the Heroic in History* (1841),
Carlyle argued that the significance of great heroes lay in their ability to
serve as a pattern for ordinary people to follow.[10] He claimed that 'Universal History ... is at bottom the History of Great Men' not because he
thought that heroes alone were worthy of study, but because they were
'the modellers, patterns, and in a wide sense creators, of whatsoever the
general mass of men contrived to do or to attain.' The hero's role was
not to command the masses so much as to inspire them to the best type
of self-development. If every individual took great men as a model, then
what Carlyle called the 'blessedest result' might ensue: 'a whole World
of Heroes.'[11] Froude agreed that the nation's youth, in particular,
needed the stories of great men to guide and inspire them. Such positive examples would be far more effective in producing moral behaviour
than any negative regime of threats and punishments. 'It is a very old
story,' Froude observed, 'that to forbid this and that ... is to stimulate a
desire to do it. But place before a boy a figure of a noble man ... and
depend on it, you will kindle his heart as no threat of punishment here
or anywhere will kindle it.'[12]

A popular statement of these theories was provided in Smiles's *Self-
Help: With Illustrations of Conduct and Perseverance* (published, appropri-
ately enough, by John Murray only a month before Leopold McClintock's
The Voyage of the 'Fox'). Smiles proclaimed that the 'spirit of self-help' was
'the root of all genuine growth in the individual; and, exhibited in the

lives of many, it constitutes the true source of national vigour and strength.' He defined character as 'human nature in its best form. It is moral order embodied in the individual.' Like Carlyle, Smiles believed that the true importance of great men lay in the example they held up to the masses. According to Smiles, 'whoever has left behind him the record of a noble life, has bequeathed to posterity an enduring source of good, for it serves as a model for others to form themselves by.'[13]

The British citizen's task, therefore, was to gain power over himself so that he might begin the shaping of his character. According to novelist Edward Bulwer-Lytton, the first step in this process was self-knowledge: 'Every man has his strong points – every man has his weak ones. To know both ... is the first object of the man who means to extract from himself the highest degree of usefulness.' The next was to further strengthen the strong points and to remedy the defects. Bulwer-Lytton claimed that the self could be 'changed or modified ... by circumstance, by culture, by reflection, by will, by conscience.' Further, 'Not a man has ever achieved a something good or great, but will own that, before he achieved it, his mind succeeded in conquering or changing some predisposition.' Only through such an effort of will in fashioning the self could an individual reach his fullest potential: 'In one completed Man there are the forces of many men. Self-control is self-completion.'[14]

Because inspiring exemplars were so important in the process of self-development, Arctic explorers took on added significance as models their fellow-citizens would be eager to emulate. Such exemplars as the Arctic heroes could ease the difficult task of character building. The regular naval service and the merchant marine yielded valuable benefits, such as the extension of commerce and the building up of a force of trained seamen, but in the long years of the Pax Britannica they lacked the glamour, excitement, and appeal of Arctic exploits. The heroic stories of men who had faced the dangers of the frozen north could rouse others not merely to do similar deeds but, far more important, to foster in themselves the same traits of character. Only a select few would actively engage in polar exploration – an enterprise from which very little could be expected in the way of practical results – but the qualities they displayed were of the utmost importance in every area of national life. 'They err, and err grievously, who ... measure only by the value to the merchant of the at last discovered passage,' the religious periodical *Good Words* declared in 1860. 'Is it nothing to have lighted amid those dreary wastes a beacon-fire for all the ages to come, around which are echoed from a hundred voices, tales of heroism and adventure as stirring as those of Greece or Rome? ... If the time shall ever come, as who can tell how soon it may, when perils from foes more deadly still than the iceberg or the snow-drift, shall menace our own shores, the lessons ... taught by their example to thousands of kindred hearts at home, shall not be found to have been barren or unfruitful.'[15]

The link between self-development and the national character, though so frequently made, was a complex one. In many ways the discourse of national character encouraged Britons to believe that heroic traits were a birthright, an essential part of their being, derived from the very soil and air of their native land. At other times, however, it was asserted that strenuous endeavour was necessary to form the self in a heroic mould.[16] Narratives of Arctic exploration were compatible with both these approaches and, in fact, allowed them to blend in a unique way. This was possible because the explorers were naval officers placed in a hazardous northern environment. Their heroic qualities were in part attributed to the demanding environment they faced, but such qualities were also believed to be typical of British naval officers as a class. The true significance of the Arctic lay in its ability to raise these characteristically British traits to the highest pitch of development: the Arctic heroes showed what heights of greatness all their countrymen were capable of reaching. Their courage and perseverance could be described both as at least latently present in all Britons and as the result of encounters with an exceptionally challenging environment.

That the Arctic explorers could be perceived in this manner was the outgrowth of a new narrative of national history centring on the navy. In the seventeenth and eighteenth centuries, national pride in naval victories was naturally strong, but the most influential construction of British history emphasized the growth of constitutional liberty. It was believed that Britain was unique because of its ancient constitution, a heritage from the early Saxons, which had been defended against the forces of tyranny and oppression through the centuries. This view remained extremely popular during the nineteenth century, but it had republican overtones, which sometimes caused uneasiness in the aftermath of the French Revolution. According to this doctrine, all Britons inherited certain rights and were not obliged to submit to arbitrary measures on the part of their rulers. Should a monarch exceed the limits set to his power by the constitution, his subjects were entitled to oppose him, by force if necessary. A knowledge of their birthright had inspired the Saxons to resist the encroachments of their Norman conquerors; eventually the

Norman barons, inspired in their turn by Saxon ideals, had moved to limit royal power by forcing King John to sign Magna Carta. Centuries later, first in the Civil War and then in the Glorious Revolution of 1688, the people had deposed a monarch who intended to establish royal absolutism. On the first occasion, Charles I was replaced by Oliver Cromwell, who became little more than a military dictator; in 1688, however, constitutional monarchy was the choice of the people.

The political discourse of constitutionalism could be used to justify both resistance and the status quo. Especially as it was formulated in the late eighteenth and early nineteenth centuries by Burke and his followers,[17] it promoted the belief that the British political system, with its protections against arbitrary government, was superior to all others and thus highly unlikely to require sweeping change. Except in rare moments of dramatic upheaval such as the Glorious Revolution, constitutional change was slow and gradual. This in itself was an important guarantee of British liberties, since slow change would not bring with it violence and injustices like those committed during the French Revolution.

Barrow and his fellow writers made extensive use of constitutionalist discourse in the *Quarterly*. Nevertheless, they were well aware that it was a site where meaning could and would be contested by their opponents. Radical writers frequently claimed that the monarchy and the aristocracy were corrupt and intent on undermining the constitution through the exercise of arbitrary power. Events like the Peterloo Massacre made such claims all the more credible. The radicals presented themselves as the true defenders of the Briton's birthright, and, as E.P. Thompson has written in *The Making of the English Working Class*, 'In 1819 the reformers appeared *more* powerful than they had ever been before, *because* they came forward in the rôle of constitutionalists. They laid claim to rights, some of which it was difficult to deny at law, which had never been intended for extension to the "lower orders." But if these rights were gained, it meant, sooner or later, the end of the old régime.'[18] Writers like William Cobbett were particularly adept at employing the language of constitutionalism for radical purposes.[19]

Under these circumstances, another and less easily disputed vision of national identity was welcome. During the late eighteenth and early nineteenth centuries a new narrative developed. It claimed that the British owed their national character above all to their unique relationship with the sea. The great popularity of Nelson and other naval heroes of the Napoleonic wars facilitated acceptance of the new interpretation. As

Gerald Jordan and Nicholas Rogers point out, 'It was entirely predictable that [periodicals like] the *Anti-Jacobin* should invoke the long-
standing heritage of British naval supremacy for conservative purposes
and appropriate naval victories for the cause of King and Country.'
From the late 1790s on, 'British seamen were increasingly projected as
the crucial line of defense against the Napoleonic threat, the para-
gon[s] of patriotism and liberty.'[20] The *Gentleman's Magazine* wrote in
1803 that 'the anchor of Great Britain' was the 'courage of her seamen,'[21] among whom Nelson stood pre-eminent. Nelson's daring tactics
endeared him to the public, and his death in the hour of victory at
Trafalgar ensured that he would be remembered as among the greatest
of all national heroes. As Robert Southey declared in an 1810 *Quarterly*
review, 'if the chariot and the horses of fire had been vouchsafed for
Nelson's translation, he could scarcely have departed in a brighter blaze
of glory.' Southey added, 'He has left us … a name which is our pride,
and an example which will continue to be our shield and our strength.'[22]
Southey's short biography of Nelson, published by Murray in 1813, was
intentionally 'concise enough to become a manual for the young sailor,'
which he might carry about with him until he had 'treasured up the
example in his memory and in his heart.'[23]

Nelson was constructed as the most recent and the greatest in a long
line of England's naval sons. Southey described the ocean as 'that element upon which, when the hour of trial comes, a Frenchman has no
hope.'[24] For all Napoleon's military might and skill, when matched
against Britain's sailor heroes his defeat was certain, for the sea was their
heritage. The narrative of Britain's growth as a naval power claimed that
only when Britons turned to the sea did their nation began to develop
its true character. According to this view, England had fallen short of
national greatness so long as it lacked a navy. Then, during the sixteenth
century, the Tudor monarchs at last realized the importance of sea
power. They wisely ordered the building of warships and encouraged
voyages of discovery. As Barrow put it in *A Chronological History*, 'the
spirit of discovery and foreign enterprize [*sic*] burst forth in the reign of
Henry VIII., and flourished in full vigour under the fostering hand of
Elizabeth.'[25] Many years later, near the end of the century, Froude gave
this part of the story one of its most concise and coherent re-tellings in a
series of lectures titled 'English Seamen in the Sixteenth Century.'
Under Henry VIII, according to Froude, 'after a sleep of … many hundred years, the genius of our Scandinavian forefathers suddenly sprang
again into life.' In the reign of Elizabeth, the English sea dogs were able

to defeat the mighty Spanish Armada, thus securing the liberty of Protestant northern Europe. In Froude's words, the Spanish 'were looking for new worlds to conquer, at a time when the bark of the English waterdogs had scarcely been heard beyond their own fishing-grounds ... And yet within the space of a single ordinary life these insignificant islanders had struck the sceptre from the Spaniards' grasp and placed the ocean crown on the brow of their own sovereign.'[26] The greatness of Henry and Elizabeth lay in their instinctive understanding of England's natural development: through their support of seafaring enterprises, they were the foster-parents of the national character.

However, the seventeenth century was a difficult period for the navy. The naval history of this time, with its many controversies, was retold during the nineteenth century by Macaulay in his immensely popular *History of England*.[27] The navy won important victories under Cromwell, but after the Restoration issues of class threatened to seriously impair its efficiency. The officers of Cromwell's day, despite their important practical experience of the sea, were replaced by aristocrats with influence at court but little knowledge of seamanship. The new officers were ridiculed as 'sea fops,' and their incompetence brought the monarchy into disrepute.[28] The solution proposed by Samuel Pepys when he was secretary of the Admiralty was to persuade upper-class families that their sons should be entered in the navy at an early age. In this way, officers would possess both an appropriate class background and a thorough knowledge of their profession. As Lord Halifax wrote in 1693, if a gentleman officer 'smelleth as much of pitch and tarre as those that were swadled in a sayle cloath, his having a Scutcheon will bee so farre from doing him harme that it will set him upon the advantage ground. It will draw a reall respect to his quality when so supported, and give him an influence and an Authority, infinitely Superior to that which the meer Seaman can ever pretend to.'[29] The policy was a great success: in the eighteenth century naval pre-eminence was firmly established, and Britain acquired a vast overseas empire. In war and voyages of discovery alike, the Royal Navy ruled the waves.

Both at the time and during the nineteenth century, this development was the focus of much comment. One captain predicted in 1756 'that the gentlemen of the navy will bring more laurels to their country than were ever brought in any former time.'[30] Another, looking back in 1830 on eighteenth-century developments, praised Admiral Sir Edward Hawke as 'the founder of that more gentlemanly spirit, which has since been gradually gaining ground in the navy.' He contrasted Hawke's 'gentlemanly deportment and propriety of conversation' with 'the coarseness of language and demeanour which disfigured too many of the old school.'[31] During the eighteenth century naval life become more formal and regulated by protocol; officers' uniforms, for example, were introduced in 1748.[32]

Greg Dening's *Mr. Bligh's Bad Language: Passion, Power and Theatre on the Bounty* contains many fascinating reflections on issues of class and authority in one of the most famous eighteenth-century voyages. It is Dening's thesis that the mutiny occurred because Bligh did not know how to exercise power in the manner expected of a gentleman: in Dening's words, he did not 'grasp the metaphors of being a captain.'[33] Bligh's very high degree of competence as a seaman was unquestionable, and the historical record shows that he was not the sadistic tyrant portrayed in twentieth-century films about the mutiny. But he repeatedly offended his subordinates through conduct and language that they considered unsuited to his social and professional rank. Dening links the elaborate, almost theatrical ritual of the eighteenth-century navy to Foucault's theories of discipline. The outward, ceremonial signs of authority and obedience were 'a language that both described and created relations of power'; Bligh's failing was that for some reason he could not 'sustain the drama.'[34]

It was not, of course, on episodes such as the *Bounty* mutiny (or the later mutinies at Spithead and the Nore) that the naval metanarrative focused. Instead, the exploits of Vernon, Jervis, Hawke, Anson, and Cook were described as the characteristic achievements of the eighteenth century. Then, at the beginning of the next century, sea power once again preserved Europe from a tyrant, and naval officers proved themselves to be not only brave heroes but the greatest champions of British liberty. According to Barrow, the cultural role of explorers in the nineteenth century was to make the public aware that the navy was far more than a powerful fighting machine: it embodied the moral values Britons held dear. 'The *physical* power of the navy of England,' he wrote in 1846, 'has long been duly appreciated ... its *moral* influence, though less the object of publicity, requires only to be more extensively known to be equally felt and esteemed; and nothing can be more conducive to this end, than the results to be derived from voyages of discovery.' Exploration narratives and other accounts led readers to 'appreciate [the explorers'] several characters and conduct, so uniformly displayed in their unflinching perseverance in difficulties of no ordinary description – their patient endurance of extreme suffering, borne without murmuring, and with an equanimity and fortitude of mind under the most appalling distress, rarely if ever equalled, and such as could only be supported by a superior degree of moral courage and resignation to the Divine will.' Barrow believed that such stories could 'not fail to excite the sympathy and challenge the admiration of every right-feeling reader.'[35]

The suffering which Arctic exploration so often entailed demonstrated that the fortitude of naval officers was more than outward show: it was part of their inmost being. In the Romantic era, the theatre of power described by Dening continued to be an essential component of naval discipline. But as the eighteenth century gave way to the nineteenth, in terms of public representation more than an effective exercise of authority was required from naval heroes. The great significance of Franklin's first expedition for his contemporaries lay in the fact that, when far from their ships and all the trappings of power, in an alien land, and surrounded by 'others' who could not comprehend their demands for obedience, the explorers had retained command over themselves. Even in the midst of hardship far beyond that ordinarily endured by men of their class, they would not abandon their moral code. Instead, such circumstances served only to show the full extent of their faith, discipline, and courage. Barrow and other writers (for example, Clements Markham later in the century) suggested that such testing had, in fact, been an important function of Arctic voyages since the sixteenth century. Because Frobisher, Davis, and other Elizabethan captains had played so prominent a part in the early days of the search for the Northwest Passage, it was frequently described as a uniquely English endeavour. But the place of the passage in nineteenth-century naval mythology was more complex than this.

The English mariners had sought a trade route far to the north because the more southerly routes were dominated by other nations, particularly Spain and Portugal. England's great rival, Spain, also possessed an apparently inexhaustible source of wealth in its Mexican and South American colonies. The English found no passage and no gold in the north, but it was often suggested that this was ultimately for the best. The Victorians believed that the very success of the Spanish made them greedy and lazy; the English, on the other hand, were naturally hardy and energetic because of their northern environment, and the harsh conditions they met on their Arctic voyages served to make them even tougher and more persevering. What the English achieved in the Arctic was the development of their national character. Nineteenth-century writers therefore constructed the Arctic as the environment that for centuries had most effectively called forth and developed the highest traits of the English character.

Barrow wrote about the Elizabethan explorers in phrases that echoed the key passage from his *Quarterly* review of Franklin: 'Persevering in difficulty, unappalled by danger, and patient under distress, they scarcely ever use the language of complaint, much less that of despair; and sometimes, when all human hope seems at its lowest ebb, they furnish the most beautiful examples of that firm reliance on a merciful and superintending Providence which is the only rational source of true fortitude in man.'[36] Such literary tactics were extremely effective in creating the impression of continuity between sixteenth- and nineteenth-century exploits. It was because they were thought to carry forward a great national tradition that the Arctic expeditions and narratives of their own day were of far more than ordinary interest to nineteenth-century writers. 'When ... it is considered that in the field of Northern Discovery England laid the foundation of her maritime pre-eminence, and that the men who have earned in it the greatest glory were chiefly British, it will be admitted that the history of their adventures must have a peculiar charm for the English reader,' as the authors of one popular secondary account put it.[37]

The narrative of England's self-realization as a naval power was central to the rhetoric of imperialism. It was believed that the empire, which had been won and was held mainly by naval power, was the almost inevitable result of England's affinity with the sea. This naval empire was thought to be essentially different from other empires based on military power. Great military power was seen as likely to debase a nation, since it could readily become the tool of internal despotism; naval power, on the other hand, could not so easily be used by a tyrant to oppress either his own people or those of other nations.[38] The English believed that they were not a military people, and along with the nineteenth-century idealization of heroic soldiers there went a persistent distaste for and distrust of the swaggering, bullying side of the military character. The courage of army officers, like the courage of Franklin's voyageurs, was frequently referred to in belittling terms, as purely physical rather than moral courage. As the *Illustrated London News* observed in 1859, 'The soldier is not the prime favourite of the people. That high place is reserved for the sailor ... The feeling has its roots in the very heart's blood of our people.'[39]

From the middle of the century on, soldiers who could be portrayed as Christian heroes (for example, Sir Henry Havelock and Charles George Gordon) were increasingly popular, and these men have been the subject of much recent scholarly attention.[40] However, it should not be forgotten that earlier attitudes persisted. At the turn of the century, many of Rudyard Kipling's poems and stories referred to the popular prejudice against soldiers. What the speaker in Kipling's 'Tommy' indignantly called 'makin' mock o' uniforms that guard you while you sleep' was evidently as common as the idealization of soldiers, at least in times of peace.

Soldiers were thus the focus of profoundly contradictory attitudes, but despite the memory of eighteenth-century captains like Bligh, naval heroes suffered from far less ambivalence. It was believed that the rise of English sea power had set the nation free to develop its unique characteristics, which included a love of liberty; then, during the struggle against Napoleon, the navy helped to free the peoples he had conquered, and one of the aims of British sea power was to secure the freedom of the seas for all nations.[41] In terms of both Britain itself and its relation to the world, naval officers played a highly positive role. Their heroism, almost by definition, had a strong moral dimension, since the navy was the guardian of all that was finest in Britishness.

The contrast between physical and moral courage was strongly drawn in representations of Arctic explorers. As early as 1821 an Arctic reviewer remarked that the 'animal courage' shown on the battlefield was merely an 'instinctive passion,' which 'in the estimate of unbiassed judgment ... sinks to the lowest point of the scale of intellectual heroism.' Parry and his men, on the other hand, had demonstrated courage of a higher type.[42] The idealism of the Arctic quest, carried out as it was in the hope of scientific knowledge rather than commercial gain, made naval explorer-heroes perhaps even more impressive than those sailors whose renown had been won in battle. Or, it might be more accurate to say that their exploits were seen as a necessary complement to the wartime victories of heroes like Nelson. Nelson himself had served as a midshipman on Constantine Phipps's northern voyage, and almost every nineteenth-century book on polar exploration referred to this episode in the hero's life. Another link between Nelson and the Arctic story was provided by an anecdote about Franklin's early naval career: as signal-midshipman of H.M.S. *Bellerophon* at Trafalgar, young Franklin was likely the officer who deciphered the famous message, 'England expects every man to do his duty.'

In Victorian eyes, Arctic exploration served the dual purpose of maintaining the navy's characteristic qualities at a high level, thus ensuring that in the event of future wars other Nelsons would be ready, and of asserting that the navy's deepest purpose transcended victory in battle. When Lord Ellesmere referred to Arctic explorers as 'the Nelsons of discovery,' the comparison was no superficial one.[43] The suggestion that the *Erebus* and the *Terror* should be moored beside Nelson's flagship was a pointed reminder that, as well as being the most powerful fighting force in the world, the navy had a higher meaning both for England and for other nations, and that it was such a powerful force precisely because it had that higher meaning. For the navy, strength and idealism, rather than being opposed to one another, were interdependent.

The history of the navy and the history of the national character could not be separated: the naval officer was more representative of the nation than any other figure. As Robert Louis Stevenson wrote, naval heroes were 'typical in the full force of the word … and what we admire in their lives is a sort of apotheosis of ourselves.'[44] For all the consistency with which this was proclaimed, the naval hero was a complex cultural phenomenon. Issues of class and gender were central to the representation of naval officers generally and the Arctic heroes in particular, and, in terms of both these categories, the naval and Arctic narratives possessed a surprising degree of flexibility. Naval officers were of course gentlemen, and this was of great importance, but they were gentlemen of a special kind. Sent to sea at the age of twelve or thirteen, they were educated in the school of experience rather than in those bastions of privilege, the public schools and universities. '[A] Man of War was my University,'[45] one eighteenth-century admiral wrote, and though his ostensible reason for pointing this out was to excuse his poor spelling, a certain amount of pride can be detected in his words. No matter how distinguished their ancestry or how wealthy their families, midshipmen were trained in obedience and practical skills, and they were required to live in spartan surroundings. They were seen as uniquely suited to exercise authority because, unlike the seventeenth-century 'sea fops,' what they demanded of others they could themselves endure if necessary. Though some eighteenth-century captains were denounced as tyrants addicted to 'rum, sodomy and the lash,' naval officers as a group were far less open to the accusations of effeminacy and corruption that radical writers so frequently made against members of the aristocracy who remained on land.[46] And, when they entered the literary sphere as authors, they were accorded special respect precisely because their formal education was of a very limited nature: as practical men with training in empirical observation rather than literary composition, their accounts of faraway places and peoples were presumably based on fact, not fancy. (See the discussion of Cook as an author in the introduction.)

However, if freedom from the taint of effeminacy was seen as characteristic of naval officers, the nineteenth-century naval hero was not purely masculine in the twentieth-century sense of the term. 'Nelson had a feeble body and an affectionate heart,' Robert Southey wrote at the beginning of his *Life of Nelson*. Throughout the book, Southey emphasized Nelson's frail physique and frequent illnesses. His original physical shortcomings were further exacerbated by the loss of an eye and an arm. That he overcame so many handicaps made Nelson's dauntless courage even more admirable. Southey quoted Nelson's own account of the great turning point of his life, which occurred after he had been in India for eighteen months. Tropical diseases had 'reduced [him] almost to a skeleton.' Nelson suffered from severe depression, believing 'that I should never rise in my profession. My mind was staggered with a view of the difficulties I had to surmount, and the little interest I possessed. ... After a long and gloomy reverie ... a sudden glow of patriotism was kindled within me, and presented my king and country as my patron. "Well then," I exclaimed, "I will be a hero! and, confiding in Providence, I will brave every danger!"' Southey explained that from that time on 'a radiant orb was suspended in his mind's eye, which urged him onward to renown.' Because of Nelson's adulterous affair with Lady Hamilton it was difficult to place him in the role of Christian hero, but the image of the small, sickly, yet utterly fearless man with an 'intuitive genius' for naval tactics was a sufficiently powerful contribution to the national mythology.[47]

Nelson's courage was deemed more admirable than the courage of physically stronger men; true manliness was thus constructed as a matter of character rather than of the body. This theme was developed even further in representations of the Parry and Franklin expeditions. Some writers expressed the opinion that the chapters dealing with the Arctic winter were among the most interesting in Parry's book. The *Blackwood's* reviewer, for example, thought that 'really this gallant young officer loses half his fame, when his exertions, guided by good sense and good feeling, on this trying occasion, are not distinctly appreciated.'[48] Here the explorers' manly qualities of boldness and determination were less prominent; instead, they were required to wait patiently through the months of winter darkness and to focus, while they waited, on maintaining a healthy social environment in their small, isolated community. In other words, they behaved more like women making and managing a home than like men 'penetrating' into the unknown. (The *Eclectic* commented with approval on the 'snug and comfortable' appearance of the ships during the winter, as shown in one of the engravings.)[49] Parry proved himself to be a sensitive and resourceful manager of personal relations between officers and men: the *Monthly* declared that his conduct during the months of inaction showed Parry's 'intelligent mind and feeling heart' to their best advantage.[50] While emphatically not effeminate, Arctic explorers were thus required to develop a feminine side to their characters. Patience and perseverance, which were among the qualities most often praised in Arctic heroes, could certainly be considered more feminine than masculine.[51] A balance between masculine and feminine qualities seems to have been the ideal standard against which explorers were judged. As one periodical writer observed, 'A man is a real hero, who can be either active or passive as circumstances demand; and if ever we envied men's properties and tempers, we would rather envy captain Parry and his followers, than most men we have ever known.'[52] Three decades later, the title page of Parry's biography, written by his son, bore the epigraph 'Both sex's [*sic*] virtues were in him combined.'[53]

Gentleness, another 'feminine' characteristic, was also believed to be typical of Arctic heroes. '[T]he best and greatest of these travellers have usually been among the gentlest and mildest of men,' declared Charles Dickens in 1859.[54] Smiles agreed that 'True courage and gentleness go hand in hand,' and he cited Franklin as an example.[55] The incident usually referred to when such claims were made was recorded by George Back. On a later expedition, Back again received help from Akaitcho's band. One of the hunters, Maufelly, remarked on Back's somewhat aggressive attitude towards mosquitoes, and expressed surprise that he was 'so unlike the old chief.' This prompted Back to explain: 'It was the custom of Sir John Franklin never to kill a fly; and, though teased by them beyond expression, especially when engaged in taking observations, he would quietly desist from his work, and patiently blow the half-gorged intruders from his hands – "the world was wide enough for both."'[56] Parry later remarked that Franklin 'was a man who never turned his back upon a danger, yet of that tenderness that he would not brush away a mosquito.' Parry's comment was quoted by Smiles.

During the first Franklin expedition, British officers were reduced to a state of extreme physical weakness. Franklin described their helplessness in vivid detail. '[E]very exertion began to be irksome; when we were once seated the greatest effort was necessary in order to rise, and we had frequently to lift each other from our seats,' he wrote, adding later that, 'owing to our loss of flesh, the hardness of the floor, from which we were only protected by a blanket, produced soreness over the body, and especially those parts on which the weight rested in lying, yet to turn ourselves for relief was a matter of toil and difficulty.' Richardson wrote that he and Hepburn were 'accustomed to the contemplation of each other's emaciated figures,' but on their return to Fort Enterprise, 'the ghastly countenances, dilated eye-balls, and sepulchral voices of Mr. Franklin and those with him were more than we could at first bear.' When Akaitcho's hunters arrived, they 'set about every thing with an activity that amazed us,' and 'contrasted with our emaciated figures and extreme debility, their frames appeared to us gigantic, and their strength supernatural.' Franklin detailed the dirt and disorder of the fort, and his own and his companions' unwashed state. The Natives (so often portrayed in European literature as repulsively dirty) were appalled by the filth. They at once 'began to clear our room of the accumulation of dirt and pounded bones.' Next, 'These kind creatures ... turned their attention to our personal appearance, and prevailed upon us to shave and wash ourselves. The beards of the Doctor and Hepburn ... were become of a hideous length, and peculiarly offensive to the Indians.' Later, on the way to Fort Providence, 'the Indians prepared our encampment, cooked for us, and fed us as if we had been children.'[57]

It might be expected that the scenes presented to the public in Franklin's narrative, with Britons in the position of helpless children, dependent on 'Indians' to feed and clean them, aroused anxiety and disgust. However, reviewers contemplated this part of the story not only with equanimity but with enthusiasm. This was because the explorers' moral strength had remained intact. Their suffering was a test of true manliness, and they were deemed to have acquitted themselves well. Given that no dishonour to the British officers was involved, reviewers were happy to commend the behaviour of the Natives: the London Magazine referred to the 'kindness and sympathy' they showed to the white men;[58] Barrow commented in the Quarterly that '[n]othing could be kinder and more humane' than their conduct;[59] the Monthly described their actions as 'tender' and 'compassionate';[60] and the Christian Observer dedicated several paragraphs to praising Akaitcho's character and intelligence.[61] Several reviewers echoed Franklin's comment that the Natives had shown 'humanity that would have done honour to the most civilized people.'[62]

Naval heroes and Arctic explorers thus added an important dimension to the idea of the Christian hero (and they did so well before the 1850s, which scholars working in this area have invariably identified as the period when the concept enjoyed its greatest popularity). In The Sinews of the Spirit: The Ideal of Christian Manliness in Victorian Literature *and Religious Thought,* Norman Vance writes, 'It was inevitable that manliness and Christianity should be sometimes uneasy together. The entertaining and healthy activism of the manly hero, whether in fact or fiction, was bound to jar with the less vivid religious imperatives: patience and heroic martyrdom, self-abnegation and the discipline of the will ... To be successful in worldly terms, and to be interesting in fiction, the Victorian hero needed qualities of self-assertion and determination rather than the humbler, more passive qualities of patience and heroic martyrdom.'[63] Vance bases his arguments mainly on an analysis of muscular Christianity as it was portrayed by such mid-Victorian writers as Charles Kingsley and Thomas Hughes. However, the literature of Arctic exploration demonstrates that passivity and suffering were indeed compatible with the ideal of Christian manliness. In the Romantic era such near-martyrdom greatly enhanced the appeal of Franklin and Richardson. (The botanist Joseph Dalton Hooker vividly recalled a visit by Richardson to his family in the late 1820s; Hooker, then a boy of eleven, was fascinated by the explorer, 'regarding him as more than human' because of the sufferings he had endured.)[64]

The literature surrounding the Franklin search, which is discussed in chapters 7 and 8, shows that this appeal persisted into the 1850s. In 1854 the *Leisure Hour,* a religious periodical, praised Franklin's 'ardour and energy,' but placed the greatest emphasis on the fact that he had been 'taught by as many perils as ever fell to the lot of an individual his entire dependence upon the God of providence. The lesson was not thrown away. Not in the spirit of self-confidence, but humbly relying upon the merciful care of the Almighty, did he go forth to wrestle with the storms, snows, ices, and rigours of the North.'[65] The great cultural achievement of the Arctic explorers was that they combined an ability to endure passive waiting and suffering with firmness and resolve great enough to meet even the most demanding ideal of manly strength. As another periodical writer put it in 1850, they demonstrated 'the most active bravery in surmounting difficulties, and the most patient endurance of inevitable suffering.'[66] Through this blending of qualities, they appeared as heroes with considerable depth and complexity of character, who could evoke the sympathy of a broad range of readers.

In terms of gender, then, the naval and Arctic narratives offered a fluid and adaptable vision of the heroic British character. The same was true of class. An 1857 article in *Chambers's Journal* denounced the aristocratic military model of heroism, in which 'tragic glory' and 'undying fame' were achieved 'by a single effort,' usually made amid 'the pomp and circumstance of war and the glare of publicity.' The author felt that stories of such heroism did only harm to the general public, especially to boys and young men, because they made readers unfit for the realities of everyday life. Although class issues are not made explicit in this article, the author clearly saw military heroism as reserved almost entirely for the aristocracy, and he described the 'stage-effect and brilliant éclat' that surrounded it with hostility. In his opinion, the contemplation of dashing army officers and their deeds would only foster resentment and discontent among those in humbler walks of life. 'The truest heroism,' the author claimed, 'requires for its exhibition calm reflection and deliberate will, rather than excitement. Instead of the heat of the affray ... its groundwork is a sense of duty ... Such heroism as this ... lies as much within the reach of the man of peace as of the warrior.' Those who achieved true heroism would be raised 'far beyond the ranks of those who plant the standard on a well-won breach.'[67]

The writer of this article did not refer to Arctic explorers, but they were obviously better models than army officers for a hero-like attitude towards the challenges of everyday life. The reviews of Arctic literature printed in cheaper periodicals such as the *Penny Magazine* and *Chambers's* repeatedly pointed out that calmness and patience were the key traits required for success. Elisha Kent Kane's narrative, for example, showed that 'Every step in his arduous path [was] taken only after the exercise of deliberately matured forethought.'[68] The perils encountered by the members of George Back's 1836–7 expedition 'were of a nature which demanded all the force of mind and all the consolatory resources of which they could avail themselves, in order to meet them without being cast down.'[69] Books that emphasized Arctic science were singled out for special praise in *Chambers's*, because the 'mere idea of a man sitting down calmly and patiently to interrogate nature in the cold and gloom of an arctic winter, has in itself an element of grandeur that is well calculated to arrest favourable attention.'[70] Such examples as these could guide men and women no matter what their situation in life.

This interpretation was made more plausible by the fact that naval officers represented a wider social range than army officers. While naval officers were generally expected to be of good birth, this was quite broadly defined, and so long as the ideal of gentlemanliness remained paramount, some blurring and bending of class distinctions was not only possible, but very favourably regarded. The navy was widely seen as a means for the sons of the poorer gentry to rise to a position of command, if they had enough talent. Nelson was the son of a clergyman in

'straitened' circumstances,[71] and though he had some useful family connections, it was primarily through merit that he advanced so rapidly in
his career (he was a captain at the age of twenty). Though he came from
the lower ranks of the gentry, he ultimately stood as high as, or higher
than, the sons of the aristocracy. Nelson himself evidently took a very
lofty view of the position held by naval officers, seeing them as a kind of
aristocracy in their own right. '[T]he word of every captain of a British
man-of-war is equal, not only to mine, but to that of any person in
Europe, however exalted his rank,' he once said.[72] Neither Parry nor
Franklin had aristocratic family connections: Parry's father was a doctor
and Franklin's a merchant. Franklin himself was a sturdy advocate of
upward social mobility. 'Instead of feeling regret at having derived my
birth from a person engaged in trade, I see in that circumstance an
additional reason for giving assistance to the fair prospects of others
similarly circumstanced, and I thank God the door of hope is not closed
to such persons in this country,' he declared.[73] Jane Austen mocked those
who resented the success of naval officers from families like Franklin's in
Persuasion (1818). The snobbish baronet Sir Walter Elliot complains that
the navy is 'the means of bringing persons of obscure birth into undue
distinction,' and that he has been forced to yield precedence on social
occasions to 'Lord St. Ives, whose father we all know to have been a
country curate, without bread to eat.'[74]

Men of great ability from even lower on the social scale than Nelson,
Franklin, or Lord St. Ives could become successful naval officers if they
were perceived as gentlemen by nature. According to G.J. Marcus,
'From the great country houses came many an admiral; from the
smaller manor-houses, the parsonages, and the like, a large proportion of the captains; from the farmsteads and the modest residences of
merchants and ship-owners, the masters, pursers, gunners, and other
warrant officers ... a few of whom attained to commissioned rank.'[75]
Promotion of common seamen to lieutenant or even captain 'was by
no means unusual.'[76] The example of Cook, who was the son of a farm
labourer and began his career as an ordinary seaman on a merchant
ship, was often cited. Other instances were scattered through naval
literature: Southey, for example, praised Nelson's coxswain John
Sykes, who twice saved the admiral's life. Nelson intended to obtain a
lieutenant's commission for him, a plan that was thwarted by Sykes's
death. Southey commented that Sykes's 'manner and conduct ... were
so entirely above his situation, that Nature certainly intended him for
a gentleman.'[77]

Arctic heroism had the potential to cut even more dramatically across class lines: ordinary men like Hepburn, though not destined to rise from the ranks like Cook, could become objects of widespread public admiration along with the Parrys and the Franklins. 'His character indeed is one, upon which the mind delights to dwell,' the *British Review* declared of Hepburn. 'It throws a relief and beauty of the highest moral description over these scenes of wretchedness.'[78] Character, not rank, was allegedly what counted most, and even the sailors who did not show Hepburn's exceptional qualities were brought into an unprecedentedly close relationship with their social superiors. Barrow wrote that, if they were to be successful, Arctic officers must always be 'kind and attentive to those under their command' (though he hastened to add that 'a ready and willing obedience' would still be 'strictly' required).[79] Punishments of any kind were rarely inflicted during Arctic expeditions, and flogging was almost unknown.[80] Journalists writing in Tory and Radical publications alike were ready (though naturally for very different reasons) to praise this development. Although the literature of Arctic exploration exalted the ideas of gentlemanliness and chivalry, and was most extensively used in its early years by conservative writers, it had considerable appeal for readers outside the aristocracy and gentry.

This was most obviously true of the middle class. Despite the aristocratic aura surrounding the revival of romance, the movement was in many ways most closely linked to the cultural formation described by Leonore Davidoff and Catherine Hall in *Family Fortunes: Men and Women of the English Middle Class, 1780–1850*. As Davidoff and Hall point out, a claim to 'moral superiority was at the heart' of the middle-class challenge to aristocratic hegemony in the late eighteenth and early nineteenth centuries. This claim was 'refracted through a gendered lens.'[81] Middle-class males who could make no claim to an exalted ancestry were constructed as gentlemen by virtue of their moral and manly qualities. A high moral character was presented as an integral component of their masculinity, with important implications for their status in both the public and the private spheres. They were deemed fit to exercise authority in all areas of their lives not because they were well born, but because they demonstrated true manliness.

The Arctic officers, though of middle-class origin, were lauded as chivalrous heroes by what Eleanor Porden proudly called 'the public voices of my country.' Joven wrote in 1859 that a knight 'armed with his sword and lance, and clad in complete steel, would rather stare if he were introduced to Dr. Richardson, with a microscope in his hand, and attired in a plain black tail-coat; but the difference between them is merely in externals.'[82] The well-regulated, almost domestic shipboard routines portrayed in narratives like Parry's could only add to the general confidence in men of the middle class as paternal rulers. Middle-class readers could thus take special pride in their accomplishments. The reviews are in and of themselves sufficient proof of this, since the great majority of periodical writers belonged to the middle class.

The nature of the working-class response is far more difficult to determine, and indeed it is impossible to state with complete certainty that there was any such response. It is nevertheless important to make some attempt at tracing it through the 1820s and 1830s, in order to understand the broad appeal the Franklin search undoubtedly had in the 1850s. Developments in print culture during these decades made the story more available to working-class readers. If they wished, they could learn about the Arctic in magazines costing only a penny or twopence. In *The Intellectual Life of the British Working Classes*, Jonathan Rose argues that working-class readers were strongly attracted by the material their social superiors endorsed as suitable reading for them. As one Aberdeen factory hand wrote of the 1820s, 'The Wizard of Waverley had roused the world to wonders, and we wondered too.'[83] This was not from intellectual subservience, but because such literature genuinely met their needs. By engaging with the canon, they gained a true sense of worth as intellectual beings, and these books could be read in ways that inspired social activism. Rose points out that in a 1906 survey of Labour MPs' early reading, most listed standard authors as major influences on their lives and ambitions. The top three places went to Ruskin (who in the opening sentence of his autobiography proclaimed himself to be 'a violent Tory of the old school; – Walter Scott's school, that is to say, and Homer's'),[84] Dickens, and the Bible. Carlyle and Henry George stood fourth and fifth. Scott was in sixth place, with one more vote than John Stuart Mill. Eighth was Shakespeare, followed by Burns and Bunyan.[85]

Rose's study offers ample proof that working-class readers not only could, but frequently did, interpret texts very differently than might have been expected either by the elites of the time or by scholars in the present day.[86] One author in the 1820s, naval officer John Frederick Dennett, somewhat naively suggested that the story of Arctic exploration would benefit the lower classes by making them aware of the Aboriginal 'others' whose lives, in material terms, were in his opinion so much bleaker than their own. Dennett expected that when one of his readers was 'introduced to a knowledge that there are many of his fellow men who have a very limited supply even of the necessaries of life, with the almost entire privation of those social and other comforts which are placed within the grasp of almost every individual of the British empire,' he would 'be led to be satisfied in the station of life assigned him.' Dennett was convinced that 'to draw such conclusions' was 'the proper duty of the reader; and then only education becomes useful to society.'[87] However, it seems highly unlikely that many workers followed Dennett's concept of their 'proper duty.'

Compilations of Arctic material like Dennett's began to appear on the market in the mid 1820s, and Murray published relatively inexpensive, abridged editions of the Arctic narratives in the late 1820s and early 1830s.[88] However, if workers read about Parry and Franklin, it would most likely have been in periodicals, especially the *Mirror of Literature, Amusement, and Instruction* and the *Penny Magazine*. Rose's study, while it provides extensive information on the reading of books, reveals less about periodical reading. However, it is clear from his and other accounts that the narratives of Anson's and Cook's voyages were eagerly read by members of all classes;[89] Cook's narratives, in particular, would often be found in working-class homes, even those where only a few books were owned.[90] In 1849 a clergyman reported that in his village's library, many books remained 'upon the shelves unread,' but 'we require duplicates over and over again of such works as Bunyan's *Pilgrim's Progress*, *Robinson Crusoe*, Cook's *Voyages*, and works of that description.'[91]

Readers familiar with these books likely turned with interest to Arctic material. Certainly, publishers and editors seem to have expected that this would be the case: Dennett's book was advertised as 'an appropriate companion to Jacques and Wright's edition of the Voyages and Discoveries of Captain Cook, which are printed in a uniform manner with this work.'[92] The large number of articles on northern exploration in cheap periodicals is strong indirect proof that poorer readers were interested in the topic: these magazines depended on a high volume of sales for their profits, and editors evidently had reason to see Arctic stories as a sure means to popularity and success. Although northern geographical discovery was a slower process between 1827 and 1848 than in earlier years, with fewer sensational incidents, there is every indication that the Arctic romance was slowly diffusing into the popular consciousness. Events during the 1850s – when some young readers of the 1820s and 1830s became writers in the radical press – would prove that it had there undergone a transformation.

However well the naval and Arctic narratives originally served conservative purposes, by the 1850s there was abundant evidence that over the decades, readers had reinterpreted and appropriated them in unexpected ways. Nor did the navy's great popularity mean that anything its members did would be approved. Instead, when naval officers and officials demonstrated behaviour that was inconsistent with the representations contained in popular literature, they were exceptionally vulnerable to the force of public opinion. They were measured against the ideal constructed in the metanarrative and bitterly condemned if they fell short of it. Arctic explorers who met the standard established by representations of Parry and Franklin could attain exceptional heights of popularity, but those who did not were viciously attacked in the liberal and radical press. From 1849 until the end of the search, Admiralty officials and some explorers, particularly Sir Edward Belcher, were repeatedly pilloried for their perceived arrogance and incompetence. In 1850 William Scoresby claimed that the search for Franklin was an enterprise which 'we, as the people, *have recognised ... as our own.*'[93] He and other writers suggested that the public therefore had the right to pass judgment on the government's rescue plans and the performance of the naval officers who carried them out. Indeed, it was seen not only as the people's right but as their responsibility to ensure that their hero Franklin and his men were found. This new relationship between the public and the explorers had its origin in the 1820s and 1830s.

6 Their Tribute from the General Voice, 1823–1848

The peevish objections of those to whom a ready commercial return, or a direct tangible payment are the sole objects of intellect have been disregarded, as they deserved to be, by the great majority of our countrymen; and the heroic exertions of our Seamen have met their full tribute of gratitude from the general voice[.]

'North-West Passage,' *British Critic*, May 1824

It was through the *Mirror of Literature, Amusement, and Instruction* that the Arctic story first came within the reach of a mass reading audience. The *Mirror*, which began publication in late 1822, is of particular interest because its publisher, John Limbird, and its editor, Thomas Byerley, were not members of the upper class seeking to reconcile workers to their lot. As Jonathan Topham has demonstrated, they were part of the radical publishing underworld so vehemently denounced by the *Quarterly Review*. Limbird was an associate of Thomas Dolby, who printed many of William Cobbett's publications, including the *Political Register*. Dolby and Limbird jointly issued pamphlets on the Peterloo Massacre and the Queen Caroline affair. The exact nature of Limbird's political opinions is not known, but it would certainly appear that his sympathies lay with the radicals.[1] However, in the early 1820s economic necessity forced many radical publishers to try new and less overtly political means of making their profits.

The taxation imposed through the Six Acts in late 1819 had forced radical publishers to raise their prices; weeklies like the *Political Register*, formerly sold for twopence, now cost sixpence, which was beyond the means of many readers. (The 'taxes on knowledge,' as they were called, remained in place until 1855.) The radicals were thus effectively deprived of the mass audience that had ensured their profits. Despite this, many attempted to continue in much the same way as before; journals like the *Black Dwarf* struggled on into the early 1820s, only to falter and cease publication. Limbird, however, was clearly a pragmatic and very adaptable man of business. Perhaps anticipating what was to come, he had already associated himself with a more 'respectable' journal, the *Literary Chronicle*, although its Tory sentiments were strongly at odds with those expressed through Limbird's other ventures in printing.[2]

Limbird then went on to found the *Mirror*, a weekly miscellany priced at only twopence. He thus sought to recreate the success of cheap periodical publications in the late 1810s, drawing on the techniques he had learned in earlier years and adding the new feature of one or two illustrations in each issue. He was able to reduce his costs through stereotyping, a recent development in the technology of printing. Limbird kept up his association with the world of radical publishing – the *Mirror's* early issues were printed by Dolby – but his new venture was resolutely apolitical, containing nothing that could provoke further repressive measures. Limbird was rewarded with remarkable success: the *Mirror's* first issue is said to have sold 150,000 copies, and though this high circulation was not maintained, it regularly sold about 15,000 copies per issue – slightly above the *Quarterly*, the *Edinburgh Review*, and *Blackwood's Magazine*. Particularly appealing issues could sell up to 80,000 copies.[3]

The *Mirror's* editor, Thomas Byerley, also edited the *Literary Chronicle*. The self-taught son of a carpenter, Byerley is described by Topham as 'the archetypal Grub Street hack.'[4] Like Limbird, he was energetic and highly practical, with a keen sense of what would interest the public. It is apparent that in his view Arctic exploration fell into this category. Their experience with the *Chronicle* had made both men aware of its potential to increase sales. They very clearly wished to imitate the success of Jerdan's Arctic articles in the rival *Gazette*: since 1820 the *Chronicle* had published many articles on the topic, and Byerley made use of the *Mirror* to promote the *Chronicle* as 'a periodical which has devoted much attention to the subject of Arctic discoveries.'[5]

Arctic coverage in the *Mirror* began with its twenty-sixth issue (26 April 1823), two weeks after the publication of John Franklin's narrative. A short biographical sketch of the explorer was provided.[6] The next issue (3 May) offered a copy of one of the illustrations in his narrative. Although the rather crude wood engraving could not approach the detail and delicacy of Edward Finden's work, it must have been well received, since another appeared three weeks later. The 3 May issue also gave a brief commentary on the expedition, which was described as '[o]ne of the most arduous enterprises ever undertaken even by British sailors, whose very nature it is to set difficulties and dangers at defiance.' The explorers, despite 'the most dreadful privations,' regretted only that they had accomplished relatively little. '[T]hus it ever is with Britons, who ... sink all personal considerations in zeal for their duty to their country,'[7] the writer noted. This was followed by information about the Dog-Rib people, taken from the narrative. A second illustration in this issue showed two 'Esquimaux Indians' who had been brought to London by an American, Captain Hadlock. Hundreds of Franklin's readers had flocked to see them, 'as they are in some degree illustrative of the work,'[8] and Byerley evidently hoped the *Mirror* could profit from their appeal. In the 24 May issue, the engraving of Wilberforce Falls, 'one of the most romantic natural scenes [in] the Arctic Regions,'[9] was accompanied by a descriptive extract (see figures 3 and 4).

Parry's return in October 1823 prompted a fresh spate of articles. The *Literary Gazette* and the *Chronicle* each provided a letter from an officer in their 25 October issues. These letters were very widely reprinted. Even the editor of the *Wesleyan Methodist Magazine,* which had the largest circulation of any periodical of the time, evidently felt that he must print the latest Arctic news in order to maintain his journal's standing. Although the magazine had until then demonstrated little interest in Arctic matters, the editor removed other articles 'of a less temporary' character from the November issue in order to include the letters. He explained that this was done 'to gratify the curiosity of that large portion of our Readers, who may not otherwise have speedy access to them'[10] (or in other words to make it unnecessary that they should buy the *Gazette* and the *Chronicle*).

The *Mirror* marked the occasion with a supplement devoted entirely to Arctic discoveries. It provided an overview of developments since the sixteenth century, with detailed summaries of the expeditions of Phipps, Ross, Parry, and Franklin. Along with a wood engraving based on an illustration from Parry's first narrative and a reproduction of the diagram of an igloo in Franklin's book, the issue included a map engraved on steel, showing the discoveries made since 1818 (see figure 8). Although the supplement was 'got up at great expense,' the price was the same as for ordinary issues. Limbird and Byerley evidently hoped to make their profit from a very large volume of sales, and from advertisements on the wrapper in which the issue was enclosed.[11] The public response was presumably favourable, since in early January 1824 the *Mirror* inaugurated a new feature, 'Select Biographies,' with an account of Parry's life.

Because Parry's second expedition achieved far less than his first in terms of geographical discovery, the degree of interest and attention is somewhat surprising. Parry had attempted to follow the continental coastline westward from Hudson Bay, but the strait between the mainland and Baffin Island (named Fury and Hecla Strait after his ships) proved to be extremely narrow and choked with heavy ice. After two winters in the Arctic Parry was once again forced to return home unsuccessful. The *Mirror* assured its readers that this setback was of relatively little consequence, and that the quest for the Northwest Passage was 'one of the most important geographical problems that yet remains to be solved.' There was, in fact, 'none more deserving of the attention of the first maritime power in the world: the Doges of Venice were wedded to the humble Adriatic, but the King of Great Britain has the ocean for his bride: and we know of no better use that can be made of our naval supremacy and wealth, than in endeavouring to enlarge the boundaries of science, and thus to enable us to continue the first in arts, as we are in arms.' Some commentators 'slighted' northern discovery, 'on the ground of the very questionable advantages that would result from it'; the *Mirror's* writer, however, expressed his hope that the government would continue 'to send out one expedition after another.' He explained: 'To a nation like this, such expeditions are honourable, even in their failure; and ... the least successful contributes something towards a more correct knowledge of the Arctic Regions, and thus paves the way for future discoveries.'[12] The *British Critic's* reviewer agreed that

> the bare question as to the actual existence of any such passage or not, [is] one of very minor importance; and we have been ready to meet the *cui bono* interrogatories of self-complacent utility-mongers, as to the object of these expeditions, on much wider and more extensive grounds. Every step by which geographical knowledge is enlarged, redounds to the honour, not only of the immediate individual by whom it is gained, but of the country by which he is sent forth ... The greatest naval power which the world has ever beheld, is only fittingly and decorously employed in resolving intricate maritime problems[.][13]

The two journals agreed that the detractors of Arctic enterprise were correct in saying that little practical benefit could ensue even were the passage found; they also agreed that this was of no consequence. Such critics were dismissed as people of a limited, purely commercial cast of mind, incapable of understanding the moral foundations on which their nation's greatness had been built. Their carping was no longer attributed to radicalism, but rather to the more vulgar aspects of the commercial spirit: they were merely 'self-complacent utility-mongers.' Over the decades to come, the word *utilitarian* would replace *radical* in Arctic discourse as a term of abuse, while the romance of exploration was represented as a means of nourishing the nobler aspects of the British character, which were in danger of being lost in a mercenary age.

The idea of a long, yet exciting, story destined to unfold slowly over many years evidently had considerable appeal to journalists. The possible profits to be gained would, of course, have been a major factor from their point of view, and the level of public interest must indeed have been high for shrewd men of business such as Limbird and Byerley to believe that it would be sustained over a protracted time. There was good reason for their optimism: the *Mirror*'s success had demonstrated that 'amusing and instructive' non-political periodical literature had immense appeal among all classes (Byerley boasted in 1825 that the *Mirror* could be 'found in the cottage of the peasant, on the loom of the manufacturer, in the counting-house of the merchant, in the parlour windows of the affluent, and in the carriages of the nobility'),[14] and a serial epic of discovery was perfectly suited to this form of publication. Through Barrow's *Chronological History* and the periodical articles based on it, readers had been conditioned to see Arctic exploration as an ongoing story, which had begun with the Elizabethans, and in which apparent failure should not be taken at face value. '[I]t would be difficult to suppose,' the *British Critic* remarked, 'that any of our readers are unacquainted with the slow advances in discovery made from the attempt of Martin Frobisher in the time of Queen Elizabeth to the recent failure of Captain Ross.'[15] But where Frobisher, Baffin, and Ross had failed, Parry at last succeeded. The strenuous, repeated efforts required of those who engaged in the Arctic quest were not proof that their aim would never be fulfilled; instead, the long story demonstrated that perseverance was one of the most strongly developed traits in the British national character.

And, when striking geographical discoveries were lacking, periodical accounts could focus on the scenery and inhabitants of the Arctic world. In contrast to Parry's first voyage, throughout his second expedition the explorers were in frequent contact with the Inuit, and descriptions of this previously almost unknown people proved to be of great interest to the public. The extracts from Parry's narrative printed in the *Mirror* in April 1824 were concerned mainly with the 'Esquimaux' and their ways.[16] However, many readers evidently found all aspects of the new episode compelling: one wrote to Byerley enclosing more extracts, on a wider variety of topics, which the editor obligingly printed.[17]

Parry set out again in 1824, Franklin in 1825. In an attempt to circumvent the obstacle of Fury and Hecla Strait, Parry was instructed to sail north and west of Baffin Island, then turn south towards the mainland through the most promising channel he could find. Franklin's task was to travel overland to the Hudson's Bay Company territories once more, then descend the Mackenzie River to the coast. Next, he was to sail westward towards Bering Strait in boats, while a second party, under Richardson, explored the coastline between the Mackenzie and the Coppermine River. At the same time, a third expedition, commanded by Frederick Beechey, would enter Bering Strait from the Pacific Ocean and attempt to meet with Franklin's party.

Parry's expedition proved to be another frustrating failure. He attempted to make his way south through Prince Regent Inlet, but this route brought him into dangerous waters, where the *Fury* was wrecked. The expedition returned in the autumn of 1825. Despite the inevitable disappointment, tales of shipwreck and survival always had their own appeal. Parry brought all his men home safe and well from their perilous voyage, and this in itself could be seen as no small achievement. Once again, Arctic articles proliferated.[18] The *Mirror* dedicated most of its December 1825 supplement to Parry, and in September 1826 it printed extracts from his narrative.[19]

Franklin's departure attracted particular attention owing to the personal tragedy that accompanied it. Eleanor Franklin had been in poor health since her marriage. She gave birth to a daughter in June 1824 and thereafter her condition rapidly deteriorated. It soon became apparent that she was suffering from tuberculosis, and that there was little chance she would recover. Nevertheless, she insisted that plans for the new expedition should go forward. To one of his sisters Franklin explained that his wife was 'as warm in the cause of Arctic Discoveries as I can possibly be. Her mind indeed is so thoroughly English that she would cheerfully make any sacrifice to promote our national character and more particularly where my professional fame may be concerned.[20] Franklin left England in the middle of February 1825; Eleanor died a week later. The news reached him during the early stages of the expedition.

In June 1825, when the first reports from Franklin were received, the *Mirror* published an issue taken up mainly with an account of his life and achievements, along with a tribute to Eleanor Franklin, whose literary talents were described as 'of the highest order.'[21] Since 1824 each volume of the *Mirror* had included one portrait of a famous public figure, engraved on steel (unlike most of the illustrations, which were cheaper wood engravings). Each portrait first appeared in a supplement, then served as a frontispiece to the bound volume. Proof impressions of the portraits could also be purchased separately for framing.[22] The first such portrait was of Lord Byron and the second of George Canning.[23] Now Franklin was selected for the honour. Parry was chosen for the next volume, after his third expedition had returned (see figures 2 and 5).

An abundance of published letters and reports provides further testimony of the keen public interest felt in Franklin's new venture. They included 'Extract from a letter from Dr. Richardson on the progress of the Overland Arctic Expedition to Professor Jameson' in the July 1825 issue of the *Edinburgh Philosophical Journal*; dispatches from 'Captain Franklin's Arctic Land Expedition' in the *Gentleman's Magazine*, June 1826; letters from Franklin and Richardson in the *Literary Chronicle*, 17 June 1826; 'Intelligence from the Land Arctic Expedition under Captain Franklin and Dr. Richardson' in the *Edinburgh New Philosophical Journal*, April–July 1826; a letter from Richardson in the *Times*, 14 August 1826; dispatches in the *Times*, 30 June 1827; a 'letter from a gentleman connected with the expedition' in the *Gentleman's Magazine*, July 1827; reports on the 'North American Expedition' in the *Literary Gazette*, 14 July 1827, and the *Literary Chronicle*, 28 July 1827; and a letter from Beechey in the *Times*, 16 July 1827.[24] The explorers returned to England on 26 September 1827.

The expedition was a striking success. Through far more careful planning than had been bestowed on their first venture, Franklin and Richardson were able to avoid any extreme hardships, and an impressive amount of coastline was mapped (although the junction with Beechey's expedition failed by a very narrow margin). Franklin's second book was published in 1828. The *Edinburgh Review* had not published notices of any Arctic narratives since 1819; now, however, it printed an article in which Barrow's most enthusiastic claims were echoed. The reviewer (possibly geographer Hugh Murray)[25] began by declaring, 'Ever since the grand era of the discovery of America, and the rise of Britain into maritime greatness, her views have been steadily and zealously directed towards the discovery of a Northern passage to India. In this attempt, many of her most celebrated navigators acquired their glory, and have had their names almost canonized by a grateful people.' To the list that began with Frobisher and Baffin, other names, 'scarcely less distinguished,' had 'recently been enrolled.' Although the enterprise might be 'tinged with somewhat of a chimerical character,' its 'very hazards and improbability' had made it 'attractive in the eyes of a people to whom such enterprises are congenial.' The nation had been rewarded not by material gains but by far more valuable benefits: 'The naval energy – the spirit of enterprise – the love of knowledge and adventure, which Britain has displayed beyond any other people, have been greatly owing, we are persuaded, to the stern and severe struggles which she has so long maintained with the tempests and snows of the north.' Since 1818 the passage had been sought with a perseverance 'of which there is no former example,' and the expeditions 'made singular displays of the prowess and hardihood of British seamen.' Though it had not yet been found, Franklin had at least brought the continental coastline 'pretty completely within the domain of geographical science.'[26]

This article demonstrates the extent to which earlier political divisions and controversies had subsided into a broad general admiration for the explorers and their deeds. There was, however, one attempt to revive a more partisan approach to Arctic exploration. The Benthamite *Westminster Review* began publication in 1824 and soon rivalled the *Quarterly* and the *Edinburgh* in prestige. It was a highly political quarterly journal, devoted to spreading the ideas of philosophic radicalism. Romanticism in literature was severely frowned upon because of its Tory associations.[27] For the review's first few years Arctic narratives were ignored, but an unfavourable evaluation of Franklin's second book (along with Parry's narrative of his 1827 attempt to reach the North Pole) appeared in April 1829. It is of interest mainly as an anomaly: no other journals seconded the views expressed, nor did the *Westminster* publish any subsequent articles in the same vein.

The reviewer did not venture to criticize the explorers themselves, though he made unflattering references to Barrow. He did, however, condemn their writing. Though he described both Parry and Franklin as 'sensible and well-informed men,' in his opinion their books were

the most dreary set of quartos that ever issued from the press in any civilized country. In empty prolongation, vapidity, wearisomeness, there is scarcely a parallel ... Certainly, we have read them all, because it was our duty; but it has been the hardest and the driest task ever imposed upon us, and we know not, that we would not have rather performed Captain Parry's last journey with him, for nought but the voyages themselves can be the parallel to the books in which they have been for so many running years recorded … not one of these volumes, is either of a popular character or of an entertaining description … There is a pervading dullness in the very manner, as well as in the facts and the notation of facts that runs through the entire set.[28]

. The reviewer thus singled out for severe criticism those aspects of the books that others had praised. The plain, empirical style, with its slow accumulation of factual detail, was in most reviewers' eyes precisely what made the narratives so worthy of implicit belief. Any obvious attempt to entertain or to appeal to the popular taste would have deprived them of this status. That reading the books was the imaginative equivalent of living through the expeditions was for most reviewers no drawback at all. The *Westminster*'s writer also noted the ongoing nature of the story, continuing as it had 'for so many running years' through narratives that, despite their different authors, constituted a unified 'set' with readily identifiable common characteristics. Again, in the view of other commentators, and apparently to much of the reading public, this was a strength rather than a weakness.

The review returned again and again to the claim that the narratives were almost unendurably dull. This claim alternated with criticisms of the romantic metanarrative in which they were embedded. There was certainly no 'pervading dullness' or lack of popular appeal in this aspect of the Arctic story, but it too was condemned, on the grounds that the public was being enticed into absurdly romantic delusions. The controversies of 1818–19 were revived, and the reviewer criticized the whole enterprise of Arctic exploration from much the same point of view as had John Leslie. The North Pole was described as 'this long wished-for and mysterious Nothing, where there was to be found, who knows what – yet something assuredly never dreamt of, even by the romancers of the eastern tales. An actual pole made of diamond, or possibly … of an immense magnet … was perhaps the smallest conclusion that would have satisfied the people.' Once this was found, 'another pole, bearing the flag of George IV king of the seas and the faith, was to be stuck upon its summit.'[29]

As for the Northwest Passage, the name was merely 'an idle phrase which still misleads the people, and somewhat dazzles the brains of their betters': since it could not regularly be used for commercial purposes, even 'though it were passed, it can never be a passage, any more than the entrance made by a burglar can be termed the house door.' There was nothing to be gained by success, other than '[g]eographical reputation and national honour': both these goals were deemed 'laudable ... though we need not repeat the usual "heart of oak" canting about British seamen and British spirit.' But 'it is idle to speak of utility ... Nothing has been gained, and nothing will.'[30] In a Benthamite review, there could be no stronger reason for condemnation.

Despite the reviewer's irreverent and often very perceptive comments, he did not succeed in demolishing the Arctic explorers as national symbols. He apparently did not ask himself why, if the explorers' narratives were dull and Barrow's writings full of romantic exaggeration, the Arctic quest had been able to win public attention and hold it for so long. He identified some of the key elements of the metanarrative and criticized them in isolation from one another. However, it was the relationship between its different parts that made the Arctic story so appealing and effective. In Arctic literature, empiricism and romanticism intertwined and interacted with one another in a remarkable way. For all his intelligence, the *Westminster* reviewer could not fully enter into the state of mind in which so many of his compatriots read Arctic narratives. Yet at many points in the article it is evident that even for the most sceptical reader, the story had an appeal that was difficult to resist. The reviewer admitted that he had 'seldom been more interested' than he was by the early newspaper and periodical accounts of Franklin's first journey (though he hastened to add that the narrative had disappointed him). When he came to recount the details of the two narratives under review, he could not withhold his admiration of the explorers' 'patience and perseverance': indeed, he could only 'wonder at the courage which endured' so many hardships. And, though he began his article by stating his belief that there need be no more Arctic voyages, he ended by discussing the merits of various proposed routes. John Ross was about to depart on yet another expedition, and the reviewer concluded with the remark: 'we only speak the sentiments of the public at large, in wishing [him] success.'[31]

Since the *Westminster* reviewer's purpose was evidently to diminish the influence of Arctic literature on the public mind, it is surprising that he chose to focus on the supposed literary shortcomings of the narratives. Whether they were dull or not was to some extent irrelevant,[32] since throughout the 1820s Arctic literature in book form lagged well behind its wide dissemination in both older periodicals and newer, more innovative productions like the *Mirror*. Lower- and middle-class readers had ready access to extracts and secondary accounts, but not to the narratives themselves.

Publishers in the mid- and late 1820s were increasingly aware of the potential mass market for cheap books as well as cheap periodicals. Limbird was a pioneer in this area also,[33] and in 1825 Byerley boasted that in the 'new era' inaugurated by the *Mirror*, reprints of standard works could be purchased 'at less than one third of the usual price of the most ordinary editions; by this means ... the temple of knowledge is thrown open to all.'[34] However, Arctic narratives did not become widely available in an inexpensive form. That they should be brought within the reach of more readers had been suggested from the beginning; the *British Critic*, for example, remarked in its review of Parry's first narrative that 'the work will certainly allow of abridgement with advantage.'[35] The reviewer felt that while the many scientific and nautical details recorded by Parry were well worthy of publication, there should also be a shorter, less expensive version for general readers. An enterprising publisher, Samuel Loxton, wrote to Parry in 1824 requesting his permission to produce an abridged edition of the second narrative, 'conceiving, that were it brought into a smaller compass, it would prove highly serviceable & interesting to a very large portion of the community, whose pecuniary circumstances deprive them of the gratification of possessing it.'[36] Parry replied that the copyright had been sold to John Murray.

Murray attempted to respond to the new currents in the publishing world. He produced abridged editions of Parry (1827) and Franklin (1829). These illustrated sets in sextodecimo format were intended to present 'an uninterrupted narrative of each Voyage or Travels ... always in the Author's own words'; all details 'uninviting to the general reader' were omitted, leaving the 'interesting and amusing particulars' intact. Readers were assured that while they would find little on scientific matters or navigational techniques in the abridged volumes, all 'accessions to our general and geographical knowledge' had been retained.[37] The price was still fairly high at £1 per set,[38] but the books provided very good value for the money. As physical objects, these small volumes roused an enthusiasm almost equal to that felt for the original quartos: Parry wrote to Murray that his wife had 'laid her hands upon the little volumes of Voyages the instant she saw them.'[39] Isabella Parry added that, 'in common with every body who has seen this Edition,' she thought it 'a very beautiful and valuable little work.'[40] Barrow too expressed his approval of 'the beautiful little Edition of Cap: Parry's Voyages.'[41]

The Franklin set seems to have had only one printing. The Parry volumes were reprinted in 1828, and in 1831 there was a new edition incorporating the narrative of Parry's attempt to reach the North Pole. The second edition was reprinted in 1835. Perhaps this greater popularity was because Parry's exploits provided more suitable reading for children than did Franklin's tale of starvation and cannibalism. The young Princess Victoria read the Parry books soon after their publication in 1827. In 1839, schoolboy Clements Markham turned to them for amusement while in bed with the mumps. He later attributed his lifelong enthusiasm for polar exploration to this experience.[42]

Despite the enthusiastic reception accorded to these less expensive books, there were no more such ventures in Arctic publishing by Murray. Possibly the very quality of the books was, in commercial terms, their flaw. This was the case with Murray's Family Library series, published between 1829 and 1834. The fifty-three volumes in the series were mainly new non-fiction titles and were priced at 5 shillings each. Murray refused to compromise on the quality of the books, and despite initial success he lost money on the venture.[43] Thereafter, the firm showed little interest in producing cheap books. There was no other inexpensive edition of Franklin until 1910, when his first narrative was reprinted in the Everyman's Library.

However, another publisher was able to attain major success with a new kind of Arctic book, priced, like those in the Family Library, at 5 shillings. Arctic reading matter in book form was thus brought well within the reach of middle-class readers. In 1830 the Edinburgh firm of Oliver and Boyd inaugurated its Edinburgh Cabinet Library series with *A Narrative of Discovery and Adventure in the Polar Seas and Regions: with Illustrations of their Climate, Geology, and Natural History; and an Account of the Whale Fishery*, by John Leslie, Robert Jameson, and Hugh Murray. Either by conscious strategy, instinct, or luck, these three authors successfully combined the most appealing elements of previous Arctic literature in a single book. They offered impeccably researched, readable chapters on Arctic 'climate, geology and natural history' along with a romantic and colourful account of northern exploration. The volume was 'most respectfully dedicated' to Barrow, 'the chief promoter of discovery in the polar seas and regions.' In the historical section of the book, Barrow's metanarrative was concisely summarized and his own achievements were described in a most flattering light. The authors wrote that in the sixteenth century 'Britain had seen other nations carry off all the great prizes in naval discovery. She had scarcely a vessel on the ocean, when the nations of the Iberian peninsula laid open new worlds, and appropriated the golden treasures of the east and of the west.' But '[h]er energies being once roused, her efforts were from the beginning bold and adventurous.' The Northwest Passage was sought with ardent devotion, even though with inadequate means. Then the reigns of George III and George IV 'formed the era which decided both [Britain's] maritime supremacy and her special eminence in the department of discovery. She achieved almost entirely the exploration of the vast expanse of the South Sea ... leaving to the rival exertions of France only a scanty gleaning.' Northern voyages were undertaken by Cook and Phipps. After the Napoleonic wars, Britain 'looked again to this theatre of her former glory.' Because 'the northern seas, as a theatre of adventure, had been unoccupied for half a century,' there was 'a general impression, that so many expeditions undertaken in vain had set the great question at rest.' However, 'when Mr Barrow applied to it the powers of his vigorous and penetrating judgment, he became sensible that this conclusion was quite groundless,' and so the epic was resumed.[44] Jameson and Murray had already shown through their articles in the *Monthly* and the *Edinburgh* that they found the romantic vision of exploration compelling, but to read such a passage in a book co-authored by his former antagonist Leslie must have afforded Barrow considerable satisfaction.

The book was enthusiastically reviewed by geographer W.D. Cooley in a new periodical, the *Athenaeum*. He described it as 'an excellent addition to our pleasant literature'[45] and remarked that though 'admirably adapted to become popular,' it was 'by no means trivial.'[46] Cooley also noted that the book – in 'small octavo' format, nicely bound in cloth – was 'one of those volumes you cannot handle or open without satisfaction.'[47] *Discovery and Adventure in the Polar Seas and Regions* met with the success Cooley thought it deserved and was promptly followed by Patrick Fraser Tytler's *Historical View of the Progress of Discovery on the more northern Coasts of America, from the earliest Period to the present Time* (1832). In a preface to this volume, the publishers remarked that the first book's popularity had 'afforded a gratifying proof, both of the interest felt by the public in the subject, and of its having been treated in a satisfactory manner.' The new work, 'when studied in combination with the "Polar Seas and Regions," of which it may be regarded as the sequel, will be found to supply a complete account of the whole series of Northern Discoveries by land and water.' The publishers stated in an advertisement that they were at first unable to meet the 'rapid and increasing demand' for the series, but they assured readers that 'arrangements have now been made on a scale commensurate with the ample and flattering encouragement afforded by the Public.'[48]

Oliver and Boyd exploited their success shrewdly. *Discovery and Adventure in the Polar Seas and Regions* was not merely reprinted, but frequently revised and updated as news of the most recent expeditions was received. There were new editions in 1831, 1832, 1835, 1840, and 1846; then, during the period of the Franklin search, the book went on to even greater heights of publishing success, passing by 1860 through no fewer than twenty-one editions. In the twenty-first edition, the story was brought to its conclusion by novelist R.M. Ballantyne. Given this long publishing history, it seems likely that readers who already owned one edition were sometimes willing to buy yet another: at only 5 shillings each, such volumes were a very practical way for middle-class readers to obtain all the latest Arctic news in a well-organized, compact, and durable format. A new kind of Arctic 'serial' had been born, and whatever the difficulty of obtaining the original narratives cheaply, *Discovery and Adventure in the Polar Seas and Regions* (along with its imitators, which are discussed in chapters 7 and 8) ensured a steady supply of affordable Arctic books.

During the 1830s several newly founded periodicals were quick to demonstrate an interest in Arctic matters. The *United Service Journal* and the *Nautical Magazine and Naval Chronicle*, which began publication in 1829 and 1832, respectively, had obvious reasons for their interest in northern exploration. Arctic developments were regularly recorded by both, and naval officers frequently addressed letters to the *Nautical Magazine* when controversies arose on Arctic matters. The *Athenaeum*, a literary weekly, began publication in early 1828 and merged with the *Literary Chronicle* in the summer of that year. From the beginning, it opposed the utilitarianism of the *Westminster Review*. The contributors, many of whom were members of the Cambridge 'Apostles,' were strong champions of both romanticism and moral earnestness in literature. Despite the high quality of its contents, the new journal struggled financially until 1830, when John Wentworth Dilke took over as editor. Soon the *Athenaeum* was a serious rival to the *Literary Gazette*, and, as a result, both the profits and the influence of the *Gazette* began to decline.[49] It was the *Athenaeum*'s policy to review books on all subjects, but Arctic literature was accorded an especially high place. There were a number of reasons for this: the *Literary Chronicle* had already established a tradition of Arctic coverage, and the Arctic metanarrative conformed well to the *Athenaeum*'s literary ideals.

Finally, it is possible that a family connection with one of the Apostles played some role. Alfred Tennyson was a member of the group; his brother Charles married Franklin's niece Louisa Sellwood in 1836. At the wedding, Alfred fell in love with Louisa's sister Emily, and they soon became engaged (although, because her father disapproved of the poet's bohemian life, they were not married until 1850). By 1845, when Charles Richard Weld began his long career of writing on Arctic topics in the *Athenaeum*, it was well established as one of the most respected and influential sources of commentary on Arctic expeditions and narratives. Weld too had a family connection with Franklin: he married a third Sellwood sister, Anne, in 1842. A young barrister who decided that the law was not his true vocation, he became assistant secretary and librarian of the Royal Society in 1845 and published a history of the society in 1848.

Another authoritative source came into being when the Royal Geographical Society (RGS) was founded in 1830. The society's journal published information on Arctic expeditions from the planning stages onward. It quickly became an established practice for explorers to give lectures to the society both before they left England and after their return, and these were printed in the journal. After 1830 Arctic news was first presented to the public through the RGS rather than the *Quarterly Review*. (Barrow maintained his leading role, since he was one of the society's founders.) Though only fellows of the society received the journal, the lectures were widely reported and reprinted in newspapers and magazines. One such lecture appeared in an early number of Charles Knight's *Penny Magazine*,[50] which in March 1832 joined the *Mirror* as a cheap source of 'instruction and amusement.'

Knight, a member of the publications committee of the Society for the Diffusion of Useful Knowledge (SDUK), believed that a cheap magazine could do more than anything else to promote self-improvement, hard work, and good conduct among the labouring classes.[51] The *Penny Magazine* presented factual information on a wide variety of topics, along with woodcuts of far higher quality than those in the *Mirror*. Its Arctic articles were less frequent than the *Mirror*'s, and the tone was more sober and scientific. Arctic facts, not Arctic romance, were emphasized. The SDUK's founder, Henry Brougham, was a firm utilitarian;[52] he forbade Knight to print fiction in the *Penny Magazine*, and it is to this restriction that Richard Altick attributes its eventual demise (it ceased publication in 1845). Nevertheless, a substantial amount of information on northern discovery appeared in this periodical and, especially in its early days, it reached a very wide audience. The circulation in 1833 was 200,000 and even in later years it stood at 40,000.[53] Patricia Anderson's study of the correspondence columns of the *Penny Magazine* and similar journals shows that the majority of their readers were likely 'clerks, shopkeepers, and the more prosperous strata of the working class.'[54]

The story of Arctic exploration during the 1830s was on the whole less eventful and exciting than it had been in the 1810s and 1820s; nevertheless, the interest of both explorers and the public was maintained. This was the case even though after Franklin's return in 1827, official enthusiasm for the quest waned.[55] A great deal of public money had been spent, for what seemed to be little result. Much had indeed been learned, especially in the western Arctic, where the coastline had been mapped from Bering Strait to Point Turnagain, with the minor exception of the gap between Franklin's farthest west and Beechey's farthest east. Yet on the eastern side lay an area of great geographical complexity – the labyrinth of land, water, and ice that had baffled Parry on his second and third voyages. The problem of the Northwest Passage had been defined as that of finding a way through this maze to the relatively clear sailing along the coastline mapped by Franklin. Both the difficulty of the enterprise and its lack of practical utility inclined the Admiralty to turn to other projects.

Franklin's proposal for a third expedition was refused. He married Jane Griffin in November 1828 and spent a few years on half-pay, travelling with his new wife. Both Franklin and Parry were knighted in April 1829, and it seemed as if this honour was intended to mark the end of their Arctic careers. In 1830 Franklin returned to active service as captain of H.M.S. *Rainbow*. After two more years of half-pay in 1834–6, he accepted a civil appointment as governor of Van Diemen's Land (Tasmania).

It was left to John Ross, eager to redeem his mistake about Lancaster Sound, to undertake further exploration in the archipelago. With the help of a wealthy patron, distiller Felix Booth, Ross organized a private expedition that set out in 1829. After Parry's unsuccessful third voyage, geographical opinion was divided as to whether Prince Regent Inlet was the key to the Northwest Passage or a dead end. There was certainly land on its western side that lay very close to the mainland, but whether this was a peninsula or an island separated from the continent by a narrow strait remained unknown for many years. If it was a peninsula, efforts by this route would necessarily be blocked; if an island, a passage would likely be found, unless the strait dividing it from the mainland was, like Fury and Hecla Strait, filled with ice. (It is, in fact, a peninsula, now known as Boothia.) Ross hoped that Prince Regent Inlet would indeed prove to be the long-sought gateway.

According to W.D. Cooley, Ross's venture caught the public imagination precisely because of its unofficial nature. His initiative in taking up the abandoned quest and his courage in venturing forth unsupported by the government were widely admired. 'There was in Captain Ross's adventure something so personal in its origin ... that he was followed to the scene of peril by a national anxiety never before extended to any scientific expedition,' Cooley wrote.[56] Parry called it 'a bold, public-spirited undertaking';[57] both he and Franklin visited Ross's ship, the *Victory*, before the expedition sailed, though Barrow refused to accompany them.

Unfortunately, the *Victory* was frozen into a harbour on the east coast of Boothia for four years. Ross and his crew were eventually forced to take to the ship's boats, in which they reached Lancaster Sound and were rescued by a whaling ship. But despite their difficult situation, they did much more than stay alive: they explored much of Boothia and ventured still farther westward. Ross's nephew, James Clark Ross, located the north magnetic pole on the western coast of Boothia and, on the other side of the strait which now bears his name, he found new land, which he named King William Land after William IV. However, the Rosses did not make their way far enough south to determine whether Boothia was joined to the mainland.

Ross's long absence led to fears for his safety (according to Cooley, 'the thrill of fear which originated in the warm affections of relatives and friends, was soon propagated among all classes'),[58] and a relief expedition commanded by George Back set out in 1833. Given the difficulties of the eastern approach, Back chose to travel overland to the Hudson's Bay Company territory and down the Great Fish River to the coast. The exact location at which this river flowed into the sea had not previously been known, but from its general direction it seemed to be the best pathway towards Prince Regent Inlet. As it turned out, the mouth of the river was west of Boothia and not far from King William Land. Since the news of Ross's safe return had reached Back before he began the final stage of his journey, he did no more than travel to the coast and carry out a brief reconnaissance.

Back attempted to solve the problem of the eastern Arctic in 1836-7. He sailed into Foxe Channel, intending to winter at Repulse Bay or Wager Bay (small inlets on the west side of Hudson Bay), then carry boats overland to the western end of Fury and Hecla Strait. In other words, he was to reach the southern part of Prince Regent Inlet by another, and presumably less dangerous, route than that attempted by Parry and Ross. If Boothia proved to be an island, he was then to explore the coastline westward towards Franklin's Point Turnagain. However, his ship, H.M.S. *Terror,* was trapped in the ice before he could reach Repulse Bay. The ship was so badly damaged that Back barely managed to return home.

These three expeditions were more than sufficient to keep public interest in northern discovery alive. Ross and his men had been given up for dead, and their dramatic reappearance after four years made them the heroes of the hour. Even Barrow seemed inclined to give credit where credit was due: Ross's funds were not sufficient to pay his crew the full wages they were owed, and Barrow recommended that the Admiralty pay them. A grant of £4,580 was accordingly made, and Ross was also awarded £5,000 by Parliament. However, with a remarkable lack of judgment, he promptly revived old controversies and started new ones. In his narrative, he made vague and contradictory claims about his 1818 expedition, in an apparent effort to prove that he had not, in fact, made any mistakes at all. Barrow privately called the book 'trashy' and 'not worth a moment's notice';[59] publicly, in the *Quarterly,* he denounced Ross as vulgar, vain, mercenary, and a liar.[60] Another naval officer commented that Barrow had taken full advantage of the opportunity 'so amply afforded him by the vanity and inaccuracy of such a work as Captain Ross has given to the world.'[61]

Nor was Barrow's the only critical voice; the *Literary Gazette* described Ross's narrative as a 'huge quarto humbug' and remarked that whatever his failings as an explorer, when it came to using his exploits for monetary gain, 'the gallant captain has gone further ... than any body ever went before.'[62] Such remarks were provoked both by the contents of the narrative and by the circumstances of its publication. They demonstrate that when prevailing ideas about how an exploration narrative should be written were ignored or flouted, even by a man who had endured and achieved much, the level of critical censure could be devastating.

Ross failed utterly to achieve the expected modest and empirical narrative voice. Indeed, he seemed unaware that any such expectation existed. To the present-day reader, Ross's highly idiosyncratic and individual writing has its charm. At some points he appears absurdly pompous and self-satisfied, but at others shrewd and unfettered by conventional ideas. However, to most of his contemporaries, Ross was simply 'not a gentleman.' He unhesitatingly placed himself at the centre of the stage, extolling his own achievements and belittling those of other explorers.

Even before his narrative was published, Ross was lampooned by William Maginn in *Fraser's Magazine*, one of the liveliest new publications of the 1830s. Ross had evidently been enjoying his success as the lion of the season a little too blatantly. Maginn observed cruelly, 'In one respect it will be admitted that he is well qualified for shewing off; for both in movement and countenance he bears no small similitude to a walrus.' He made a sly reference to rumours that Ross's survival was due in part to the amount of brandy he had consumed: 'when we all thought him dead, he was not only alive, but in excellent spirits, and making gallant battle against the cold.' As for Ross's achievements as an explorer, 'He had failed once, and that should have been quite satisfactory. We take it for granted that he will never think of failing a third time. He should now be satisfied with the full glory that he has proved, if not exactly that there is no north-west passage at all, yet that he decidedly is not the man to find it.' Maginn noted that 'considerable doubt' existed as to whether Ross's narrative would be of any interest or value.[63]

The narrative proved to its readers that Maginn's remarks, though harsh, were not completely unwarranted. Parry had never published a word in denigration of Ross, but Ross wrote that if there were any blame in the matter of Lancaster Sound, it should fall on Parry rather than on himself. It was, he argued, a junior officer's duty to prevent his captain from making mistakes. Ross then went on to state that as the leader of the expedition he should be given the major part of the credit for his nephew's discovery of the north magnetic pole. His egotism appeared not only in these claims but in many minor passages of the narrative. When describing auroras and other atmospheric phenomena, most explorers spoke with reverence of the wonders of nature and the power of God; Ross, on the other hand, confided to his readers that a parhelion reminded him of the jewelled insignia worn by members of the Order of the Bath. He believed it was a divine message foretelling that he would be honoured with a CB, and he solemnly noted that the prophecy had been fulfilled (he was also knighted, to Barrow's great displeasure).[64]

No reviewer could refrain from comparing passages like these with the writings of Parry and Franklin. What Ross himself evidently regarded as a quite normal and acceptable degree of ambition for a naval officer appeared, in this context, as the crudest kind of vanity. Moreover, even though Arctic literature was expected to be free of overt political content, Ross made several highly topical references to the question of reform. His expedition spanned the period of intense agitation surrounding the passage of the First Reform Bill in 1832. On his return, Ross was appalled by what had happened. His narrative contained a steady stream of negative remarks about progress, natural rights, and the education of the lower classes.[65] With regard to his own crew, he wrote that, owing to 'the paltry, fantastical, and pretending, ultra philanthropy of these days of ruinous folly,' sailors 'think much more than they did in the days of my junior service, and, most assuredly and certainly, are "all the worse" for it.'[66] (Ross also attempted to carry the battle beyond the purely literary sphere and stood as a Tory in the 1835 general election. According to a contemporary newspaper account, 'All the cold he felt at the pole was nothing to the coldness of his reception by the electors.')[67] Even for those who wholeheartedly agreed with Ross's political opinions, their inclusion in his narrative seemed highly improper. From a more liberal point of view, David Brewster observed sternly in the *Edinburgh* that 'Captain Ross's name does not belong to faction, but to his country; and ... [he] should not have disseminated the elements of that political fanaticism which denounces the reformers of our institutions as the authors of anarchy.' Brewster commented, 'That Captain Ross should be the enemy of knowledge, or unfriendly to its diffusion, is indeed strange,' and he enquired pointedly whether Ross would be displeased 'if the instruction and amusement which his own costly narrative conveys, and the lessons of patience and pious resignation which it reads, should be communicated to the humble artisan and the lowly peasant' through publications like the *Penny Magazine.*[68]

Ross's attempt to secure the greatest possible financial return from his book became notorious. John Murray, who was known for generous treatment of his authors, had offered to publish it,[69] but Ross wanted to 'keep the property entirely in my own hands.'[70] He therefore published it himself and hired agents to solicit subscriptions. This frankly commercial approach dismayed Ross's friends and gave his enemies the perfect chance to attack him. Ross's subscription agents were so aggressive that Franklin, who was originally eager to purchase a copy, 'declined to have anything to do with it' after one called on him. Jane Franklin described the agent's behaviour as 'disgraceful.'[71] In the *Quarterly*, Barrow referred sarcastically to the 'brazen-faced bagmen' Ross had sent 'to knock at every gentleman's door in town and country, not humbly to solicit, but with pertinacious importunity almost to force, subscriptions.'[72] The *Literary Gazette* commented: 'the concoction of this work and all the circumstances attending it ... shew that had [Ross] not been bred to the navy, he would have been the most eminent travelling Number-man.'[73]

At the end of the *Gazette's* review, several of Ross's more boastful utterances were quoted. He wrote that the money, praise, and honours he and his men received were 'but a small reward, after all, for what every one endured; and sweet as it may be, it requires much forgetfulness of our past sufferings not to feel that it was dearly purchased, while it would be hard indeed were this tribute withheld from such enterprise, such patient endurance, such toils and sufferings so long continued, and such a spirit of hope and energy, amid circumstances capable of sinking almost any heart into the depths of despair.' Such comments had, of course, often been made about Arctic explorers, but not by the explorers themselves. The *Gazette's* writer commented: 'this is the tone which has disgusted us with Captain Ross's book ... It is offensive to see the interest taken in this expedition so ungratefully abused; and ... we emphatically denounce and reprobate it.'[74]

Reviewers turned with relief to Back's narratives, published by Murray in 1836 and 1838. As an author, Back followed in the footsteps of Parry and Franklin, but with greater liveliness and spirit. He was both modest and more entertaining than any other Arctic explorer. Barrow hailed the first of the two narratives as 'an honest book – the production of a plain, straightforward, veracious traveller ... depicting artlessly and unconsciously the noble mind and character of its author.' He added, 'As a literary composition, indeed, it may perhaps rank higher than any former volume of that valuable *library* which we owe to the Marine Worthies engaged in the Northern expeditions.'[75] The *Edinburgh* agreed: 'As a composition, it is superior to every similar work ... The style ... is simple and elegant, the observations and reasonings judicious and sound, and every page breathes a spirit of truth.'[76] The *Gazette* called it 'the simple narrative of as gallant and admirable an exploit as ever redounded to the honour of [the] English character.'[77] Like its author, the book was 'manly, straightforward, modest, and intelligent ... the only portions of it which are not full enough, are those which another pen would have told of the enduring courage and constancy, and the fine skill and judgment displayed throughout by the author himself.'[78] The *Penny Magazine* had ignored Ross altogether. Back's second narrative, however, was given a long and appreciative review. According to the reviewer, Back had demonstrated excellent qualities of character in the face of many perils,[79] and though his expedition in the *Terror* failed, he showed a 'manly and Christian spirit' throughout.

The book itself was described as 'amongst the most interesting of the interesting narratives of Polar expeditions.'[80]

Back's 1833–5 expedition introduced a new figure, Dr Richard King, to the reading public. King, who during the Franklin search would stir up many Arctic controversies, wrote his own narrative. Back published only praise of King, but King, following Ross's example, included criticisms of Back's leadership.[81] He also disagreed with Back's conclusions on Arctic geography, believing correctly that Boothia was a peninsula, while Back was more inclined to think it was an island.[82] King eagerly campaigned to be put in command of a new expedition. In this he was unsuccessful, and he developed a strong sense of grievance, feeling that he had been slighted by Back, the Admiralty, and the Royal Geographical Society.

During the late 1830s there were no further naval expeditions, but Peter Warren Dease and Thomas Simpson of the Hudson's Bay Company came very close to linking the coast mapped by Franklin with the discoveries of the Rosses. In three boat journeys during the summers of 1837, 1838, and 1839 Dease and Simpson explored the continental coastline. In 1839 they sailed eastward as far as Castor and Pollux Bay on the southwest coast of Boothia. The exact geography of Boothia and King William Land remained a mystery: it still was not definitely known whether Boothia was an island or a peninsula, or whether King William Land was connected to it. Like Back, Dease and Simpson themselves erroneously believed that Boothia was an island, and that the entrance to the Northwest Passage therefore lay at the southern end of Prince Regent Inlet.

It seemed that the problem of the passage had been solved. Following a meeting of the RGS at which Barrow echoed this belief, King stated his doubts in letters to the press, and it had to be conceded that the matter was not proven.[83] Still, Dease and Simpson had come so close to the area explored by the Rosses in 1829–33 that it appeared almost certain a ship from the east could, in fact, make its way through the 'labyrinth' to the western Arctic. Their exploits were therefore accorded high praise in the *Quarterly*, where a new Arctic reviewer, Francis Egerton, the first earl of Ellesmere, commended Simpson as an 'unpretending,' 'masculine and modest' author, whose name was the latest addition to 'the long list of British worthies which begins with Frobisher.'[84] The *Westminster* and the *Penny Magazine* also published very favourable accounts.[85] (The father of sixteen-year-old Robert Ballantyne looked up from a newspaper article about Dease and Simpson and asked his son, 'How would you like to go into the service of the Hudson's Bay Company and discover the North-west Passage?' 'All right, father,' Ballantyne replied; and so he became a clerk in Rupert's Land. Ballantyne's boyhood reading included the *Penny Magazine*.)[86]

During the early 1840s naval efforts turned to the south polar regions with James Clark Ross's extremely successful Antarctic voyage (1839–43). After Ross returned, Barrow proposed that his ships, *Erebus* and *Terror*, should be employed on another Arctic expedition.[87] Rumours about this proposal were evidently current. In a series of remarkably discourteous letters to Barrow, published in the *Athenaeum*, King claimed that Arctic expeditions by sea were of little use. Success could be hoped for only if a land expedition, led by himself, was sent out at the same time, to determine once and for all that Boothia was a peninsula. The editor of the *Athenaeum* commented that though he did not like the 'tone and temper' of King's writing, King deserved a public hearing for his views.[88]

King apparently believed that the new sea expedition would be ordered to try the Prince Regent Inlet route once again. Barrow's plans did not, in fact, involve Prince Regent Inlet. King was ignored and, whether coincidentally or not, the Hudson's Bay Company now decided to send one of its employees, John Rae, to complete the survey of Boothia. Despite this news, King sent yet another letter, this time to the secretary of state for the colonies, Lord Stanley,[89] which ended with a plea that he, as well as Rae, should be sent out.[90] Once again, he was refused.

Barrow's proposed expedition was approved, and the command was given to Franklin, now almost fifty-nine and recently returned from Tasmania. Since the expedition was to be a voyage rather than an overland trek, his age was not considered an insuperable obstacle. His second-in-command was Francis Crozier, who had been in the Arctic with Parry and in the Antarctic with Ross. The third officer, James Fitzjames, was a young man of exceptional abilities, and he had been encouraged to believe that he would be given the command. His friend Clements Markham admired the cheerfulness with which Fitzjames, in spite of his disappointment, accepted a subordinate position.[91] Fitzjames was a talented writer, whose letters and journal give a vivid account of the expedition's early days.

Joining together the known areas of the Arctic by ship involved traversing a relatively small blank space on the map. What Franklin had to do was to enter the archipelago by way of Lancaster Sound and then turn southward or southwestward towards the continent. Prince Regent Inlet was deemed likely to prove impassable, so Franklin was instructed to look for another channel farther to the west. If, however, he sailed as far to the west as Parry had done on his first voyage, he would be stopped by the heavy ice off Melville Island. West of Prince Regent Inlet and east of Melville Island, therefore, Franklin was to look for a way to the mainland. There was always the possibility that no such channel existed, or that it would be filled with ice. In that case, Franklin was given the option of going to the north, up Wellington Channel (which had been discovered, but not explored, by Parry on his first voyage), in the hope that a way around the Melville Island ice barrier might be found in that direction. These instructions were not published until 1848, and the public therefore had no information about the expedition's probable movements.

Franklin himself was guardedly optimistic, recognizing that the unknown area might contain formidable obstacles. The shortest possible course to take would be southwest from Cape Walker on the island of North Somerset directly towards Bering Strait. If this course led across open sea, perhaps containing small, scattered islands, success would be relatively easy. On the other hand, if the unknown area proved to be (as in fact it is) taken up mainly by large islands, the matter became much more problematic.[92] In letters to both Parry and Richardson, Franklin mentioned this possibility.[93] He asked Richardson to reassure his wife and daughter if the expedition was not heard of for a prolonged period. 'Your own experience will suggest to them many causes of detention quite consistent with our being in perfect safety and health,' he wrote.[94]

The Erebus and the Terror sailed in May 1845. Their departure was most memorably recorded in the Illustrated London News, which had begun publication three years earlier and was now inaugurating what would prove to be a long and profitable tradition of Arctic coverage. The ILN's article was accompanied by four drawings: one of Franklin, one of the two ships, one of Franklin's cabin, and one of Fitzjames's cabin (see figures 9 and 10).[95] 'I am writing at the little table you will see in the Illustrated News,' Fitzjames remarked in his first letter home. 'I commence to-night, because I am in a good humour. Every one is shaking hands with himself.'[96] Reports from Greenland duly made their appearance in the press that autumn. 'We hear that this is to be a remarkably clear season, but have had as yet no good authentic intelligence,' an unnamed officer wrote. 'However clear or not clear, we must go ahead, and if we don't get through, it won't be our fault.' There was slightly later news from the whaling ships: one captain

reported that on 19 July he 'saw two barques no doubt the Discovery
Ships ... and unquestionably in my opinion they would meet with no
interruption from ice to Lancaster Sound. They passed Pernawick
Island about 10 to 15 miles off, and not a bit of ice to be seen from the
highest part of the land.'[97]

Publishers clearly anticipated an increased demand for Arctic books.
In 1846 Barrow produced a new historical account, outlining developments since 1818, titled *Voyages of Discovery and Research within the Arctic
Regions, from the Year 1818 to the present Time: under the command of the several naval Officers employed by Sea and Land in search of a North-West Passage
from the Atlantic to the Pacific, with two Attempts to reach the North Pole,
abridged and arranged from the official Narratives, with occasional Remarks.*
His remarks on Franklin's first expedition took the form of quoting
from his *Quarterly* review of the narrative, thus making the passage on
the perseverance and faith of British sailors readily available to a new
generation of readers.[98] Oliver and Boyd brought out a sixth edition of
Discovery and Adventure in the Polar Seas and Regions. The Society for the
Promotion of Christian Knowledge contributed to the field of Arctic
literature with *Winter in the Arctic Regions.* 'While waiting the results of
[Franklin's] exertions, let us consider ... the dangers and difficulties ...
which ... British sailors are wont to overcome with bravery, or submit to
with patience,' the author of the latter book suggested.[99]

In the following spring, fears about the expedition's safety were
allayed by the statement that Franklin had asked his officers and men to
tell their families they would not likely be heard from before October
1847.[100] The expedition had carried provisions sufficient for three
years. In May the *Athenaeum* revealed that Richardson was superintending the shipment of stores to Rupert's Land, in case a relief expedition
proved necessary in 1848.[101] News was eagerly awaited in the summer
and fall of 1847. In his *Quarterly* review of James Clark Ross's Antarctic
narrative, Lord Ellesmere speculated that the *Erebus* and the *Terror* 'are,
perhaps, even now working their southward course through Behring's
Straits into the Pacific.'[102] King, on the other hand, published a letter to
the new colonial secretary, Earl Grey, in which he dramatically declared
that the explorers 'are at this moment in imminent danger of perishing
from famine.'[103] King alone had the knowledge to save them: though
ignorant of Franklin's orders, he concluded that the explorers were in
the vicinity of North Somerset, and that the best way to reach them
would be by an expedition down the Great Fish River. He himself was, of
course, the obvious leader for such a venture.

King's proposals for a relief expedition led by himself continued to appear in the *Athenaeum* until December 1848,[104] when a letter from Alexander Kennedy Isbister was published in the same journal. Isbister, who was born in Rupert's Land, pointed out that the logistics of overland northern travel, combined with the scarcity of food then prevailing in the northwest, made it impossible for King to carry enough supplies for his own and Franklin's men. If King found the explorers, and if they were indeed starving, the new arrivals would be no more than extra mouths to feed.[105] King seemed to have been refuted, but there was still no news. In 1848 three relief expeditions were sent out. A new era in both Arctic exploration and Arctic literature was about to begin. In the next decade the Arctic would occupy a larger place in the public mind than ever before. The terms *epic* and *romance* would take on new meaning and resonance. And, at a time of unprecedented expansion in the reading public, the Arctic story would increasingly be perceived as belonging not only to 'the nation' but to 'the people.'

7 The Knight-errantry of Our Day, 1848–1852

Hardship, and even repeated failure, do not damp the ardor of our officers in competing for the command of ships sent to the Arctic regions in search of Sir John Franklin's party ... It is a noble and wholesome desire; it helps to maintain the high character of our navy; it furnishes the occasion for indulging the spirit of adventure which animates all true chivalry. Arctic expeditions are the knighterrantry of our day.

'Arctic Enterprise,' *Spectator*, February 1850

It was in the 1850s, according to Richard Altick, 'that the reading public could first be called a mass public in anything like modern terms ... the familiar phrase of "literature for the millions" ceased to be mere hyperbole and came to have a basis in sober fact.'[1] The enormous circulations attained by many cheap weeklies were a constant reminder that the masses were very numerous indeed. Among these mass circulation journals only the *Illustrated London News* was not radical in its politics. The *ILN* sold 67,000 copies per issue in 1850 and 123,000 by 1854, just before the 'taxes on knowledge' were finally abolished. The *News of the World* sold 56,000 in 1850, rising to 110,000 in 1854; the figures for *Lloyd's Weekly Newspaper* in the same years were 49,000 and 96,000. In 1855 *Reynolds's Miscellany* was selling 200,000, the *Family Herald* 300,000, and the *London Journal* close to 450,000.[2]

Many of these papers followed the Franklin search closely. Editors and journalists were themselves likely to have read cheap Arctic literature in their youth, and they seemed confident that their readers in turn were familiar with and keenly interested in the story of northern exploration. In 1851, for example, the *News of the World* recommended that its readers visit the new Arctic panorama. '[A]s the interest attaching to all that relates to Sir John Franklin and the Arctic Regions is so great with all classes, a visit to this panorama will materially aid the spectator in gaining knowledge of the scenes and localities he is already familiar with from reading,' the writer commented.[3] (Like the material in the *Mirror of Literature, Amusement, and Instruction*, such remarks are, of course, at best indirect evidence: though the cheap weeklies were directed at a working-class audience, most of the writers were likely middle-class liberals and radicals.)

Criticism of the government's conduct of the search abounded both in the cheap weeklies and in the more expensive and prestigious journals of opinion. The latter included the long-established liberal *Spectator* and *Examiner* and, after 1855, the very successful *Saturday Review*, which quickly rivalled the *Athenaeum* as a maker of educated opinion. None of these journals achieved a high circulation, but the practice of reprinting made their views known to a very wide range of readers. For example, an article published in the *Examiner* (which had a circulation of only about 4,000) in January 1856 was quickly reprinted in the *News of the World* and so became available to a vast audience.[4] Charles Dickens's *Household Words*, which had a circulation of about 40,000,[5] followed the search from its early issues on, and published a number of vividly written and emotionally charged articles. The *Leader*, a new weekly dedicated to bringing middle- and working-class radicals together,[6] also demonstrated a keen interest in the story, and was always quick to condemn Admiralty decisions. Though its circulation was small (only about 1,500),[7] it scored a publishing coup in 1852 with James Fitzjames's journal of the first few months of the lost expedition.[8]

Fitzjames, an orphan, had been brought up in the family of William Coningham. Coningham was Fitzjames's junior by three years, so the two men were like brothers. Coningham left a career in the army for Radical politics (he was eventually elected to parliament as the member for Brighton in 1857). His political opinions can be deduced from the titles of the pamphlets he published, which included 'The Betrayal of England, Addressed to the Working Classes,' 'Palmerston: What Has He Done? By "One of the People"' and 'The Self-Organised Co-Operative Associations in Paris and the French Republic.' Fitzjames's journal had been sent to Coningham and his wife, Elizabeth. It was an exceptionally vivid piece of writing, with poetic yet refreshingly quirky descriptive passages such as: 'The sea is of the most perfect transparency – a beautiful, delicate, cold-looking green, or ultramarine. Long rollers, as if carved out of the essence of glass bottles, came rolling towards us; now and then topped with a beautiful pot-of-porter-looking head.'[9] The Coning-hams presumably decided to publish the journal in order to bolster support for the search, and they must have felt that their greatest chance of success lay in an appeal to the *Leader's* target audience.

It is very clear that populist writing was increasingly common in both middle- and working-class periodicals, and that the Franklin search provided a congenial theme for journalists extolling the virtues of the people. (That Franklin himself was a merchant's son rather than an aristocrat or even a member of the upper middle class made him especially well suited for a place in the popular culture of a new and more democratic era.) It was repeatedly claimed that the government was neglecting its duty towards the nation's Arctic heroes, and that only the voice of the people could compel reluctant bureaucrats to continue the search. Since the publication of Patrick Joyce's *Visions of the People* in 1991, mid-Victorian populism has received much scholarly attention. Unlike E.P. Thompson, who believed that workers had developed their own entirely distinctive class identity by the 1830s, Joyce argues that the political language of constitutionalism was shared by the middle and lower classes well into the second half of the nineteenth century. In shaping their sense of identity, workers continued to draw on the belief that the common people had rights guaranteed by the constitution; in Joyce's words, they 'inflect[ed] shared discourses with their own meaning.'[10] During the 1870s and 1880s these discourses formed a cultural bridge between Gladstone's Liberals and the working class. It seems that in the 1850s the Arctic story served a similar function.

In Joyce's view, 'populism cannot be viewed as static, conservative or traditional (as opposed to the "modernity" of class): on the contrary, it is the capacity of populism to mutate that is striking.'[11] Arctic newspaper and periodical coverage certainly demonstrates that disaffected writers in both middle- and working-class publications were eager to present the search for Franklin's lost expedition as a popular crusade.[12] The origins of this development lay in the early 1830s. In 1823 John Barrow had triumphantly described Franklin's first narrative as a refutation of all the 'Hunts and [the] Hones' of radical journalism. Twelve years later, David Brewster countered the embittered Toryism in Ross's book with the claim that explorer-authors, as representatives of their country, by definition were not entitled to publicly express the views of any political faction. Instead, Ross had a duty to his countrymen of every class and every party. 'It was for knowledge ... that he exposed himself to the horrors of four Arctic winters; it is to knowledge that he owes his professional and social rank,'[13] Brewster pointed out. This knowledge could not be kept as the special preserve of Ross's own class: it belonged to the nation, and the nation must be defined as the nation itself, not Ross alone, chose to understand the term.

According to the *Literary Gazette*, even though Ross's expedition was originally undertaken at private rather than public expense, the interest and sympathy shown by the public and the later grant of public money created an obligation which Ross had failed to honour. Any of his words that showed a self-serving, boastful spirit were thus subject to severe censure in the public sphere of periodical writing, and the *Gazette* felt that it was entitled to 'emphatically denounce and reprobate' his behaviour. Ross had accepted his honours and rewards as no more than his due: many journalists, on the other hand, were more concerned with the respect owed by Ross to the public. They believed that they spoke for the nation when they chastised him for his failure to make this respect the keynote of his literary endeavours. Barrow, who, like Ross, seemed in many ways still to live in 1819, harped on Ross's vulgarity and the unseemly behaviour of his subscription agents when dealing with their social superiors. For other periodical writers, however, the standards by which an explorer's literary work was to be judged were very different.

The apolitical nature of Parry's and Franklin's narratives had originally worked in favour of Tories like Barrow. However, the very success of this strategy meant that in the longer term the Arctic story could not be maintained as a Tory preserve. As a broad consensus of admiration for the explorers was established, the public came to believe that their deeds belonged equally to all Britons. Barrow was always credited as the official who had renewed the Arctic quest, but this did not entitle him to claim any monopoly of interpretation. In its broader outlines, the metanarrative of northern exploration he had created survived and even increased in strength during the Franklin search. However, new elements were added to it that might well have appalled him had he lived longer (he died in 1848).

These changes in the Arctic narrative suggest that, despite its many strengths, Linda Colley's treatment of the growth of the national identity may be somewhat misleading, ending as it does in 1837. Colley argues that the bitterness of the immediate post-war period evaporated as the nation's political life was transformed through the campaigns for Catholic emancipation, the abolition of slavery, and the First Reform Bill. By the time Queen Victoria succeeded to the throne, a new, more firmly based consensus had taken the place of the relatively fragile alliances formed between different groups under the pressing necessity of war.[14] Responses to Arctic literature in the 1820s and 1830s reflect this process of reconciliation, but beneath the surface, a largely unrecorded process was going forward. Middle- and working-class readers were quietly formulating a new, potentially subversive interpretation of the Arctic narrative, one that would find its way into print ever more forcefully as the Franklin search continued.

Both the search and its literature were extraordinarily complex. This was not a mere matter of geography: the convoluted windings of the labyrinth into which Franklin had vanished did indeed furnish matter for disputes that filled hundreds, even thousands, of printed pages. But to trace the connected narrative of the Arctic quest as a cultural phenomenon through these pages is at times extremely difficult, far more so than in the period from 1818 to 1848. This is because of the fluid and never fully resolved nature of the debates about the relationship between the explorers and the nation. The controversies surrounding Ross's second narrative brought to the surface assumptions about what the explorers owed their country; the Franklin search gave rise to disagreements about what the country owed the explorers. Precisely what obligations the nation had to Franklin and his men, and which of its representatives were responsible for fulfilling them, were questions not easily answered to the satisfaction of all.

The personnel, routes, and methods of the government search expeditions all were discussed at length in newspapers, magazines, and reviews. The question of whether the explorers could survive by living off the land was of especially great interest and was debated throughout the search period. These topics were linked by endless cross-references to other political and social issues of the day. The unifying theme of such discussions was the government's alleged dereliction of its duty, and the people's consequent obligation to intervene on behalf of the missing men, who were *their* heroes. Whatever the specific conclusions drawn by any author as to how long the lost explorers could survive without help, which part of the Arctic should be searched, or which men should be sent to carry out the task, there was a very broad underlying consensus that only the force of public opinion could ensure an adequate effort.

After several unsuccessful attempts, the government became increasingly reluctant to sponsor further expeditions, and after 1856 it adamantly refused to do so. Officials claimed that further risk to human life could not be justified; cynical journalists suggested that the cost of the search was the real deterrent. The quest was then carried on by Lady Franklin, who became a popular heroine. Her supporters were a rather strangely assorted group: they included, besides Parry, Richardson, and other well-known explorers, influential scientists like Roderick Murchison, conventional naval officers of established reputation like Francis Beaufort,[15] and ambitious junior officers such as Sherard Osborn and Leopold McClintock. Then there were the less easily categorized 'others': William Penny, a plain-spoken Scottish whaling captain with great practical ability but little knowledge of dealing with officialdom; William Kennedy, the son of a fur trader and a Cree woman; Joseph-René Bellot, a young French sailor of working-class origin; Henry Grinnell, a philanthropic American millionaire; another American, Dr Elisha Kent Kane; and John Arthur Roebuck, an MP whose 'radical and irreligious'[16] tendencies were deplored by Lady Franklin's shocked sister.[17]

Lady Franklin and her 'others,' especially Penny, Bellot, and Kane, became the objects of enthusiastic public acclaim. Both the new and the old elements of Arctic discourse worked in their favour. Penny, in particular, was constructed in the early years of the search as the people's hero, an ordinary but determined man who outshone the naval officers chosen by the government. At the same time, Barrow's romantic meta-narrative proved greatly to the searchers' advantage. Their quest was enveloped in an atmosphere of chivalrous adventure, with Jane Franklin perfectly filling her role as the lady who inspired her knights to set out on their journeys. As Clements Markham wrote, 'She gained her noble objects by arousing the chivalrous feeling of the devoted men who gathered round her. Only a woman could have achieved this. She introduced into the expeditions the element of chivalry, and it was this inspiration which gave to the searches the character of an epic.'[18] It is doubtful whether her energetic and well-organized public activities would have been so readily accepted if the narrative had not seemed to demand that a woman be involved (see chapter 8, below).

Jane Franklin was a lady in distress, her husband a hero imprisoned by the Arctic enchanter in a fortress of ice ('Fancy these men in their adamantine prison ... chained up by the Polar Spirit whom they had dared, – lingering through years of cold and darkness,' suggested a writer in the *Athenaeum*),[19] and the searchers her loyal knights. This interpretation placed the government in the role of a treacherous dragon. The decision not to carry the search through to the end, readily though it could be justified on economic and utilitarian grounds, was widely seen as a breach of a higher duty to both the explorers and the nation at large. According to this view, if even one of Franklin's men remained alive, he should not be abandoned by his country; if all the explorers were dead, it was due to them and to the nation that their story should be rescued from oblivion. Almost from the beginning of the search, there were complaints that the government was not adequately fulfilling either its obligation to seek the explorers at all costs or its duty to inform the public. Between 1856 and 1859 there was a strong feeling that in the absence of effective government action, the people were carrying forward the search of their own accord.

As early as 1850 William Scoresby claimed that 'not only is this a Government expedition, and therefore national, but by the general interest given to its objects, and the universal sympathy yielded to its perils, by the British public, *we*, as the people, *have recognised it as our own*.' It was therefore a public responsibility to ensure that 'the most *complete* measures of research' were taken.[20] In the later period, when the only expeditions in the field were privately funded, the contrast between public concern and official apathy became even more sharply drawn. The people, having assumed the responsibilities that more properly belonged to those in power, therefore represented the nation in a way that politicians could or would not.

Because criticism of government policy was an often explicit and always implicit part of the search for Franklin, many other forms of discontent almost inevitably became intertwined with advocacy of the search. However, it is hard to find any common political or philosophical assumptions linking Lady Franklin's supporters together. The MPs who spoke on her behalf in Parliament included old-fashioned Tories like Sir Robert Harry Inglis, one of the most diehard opponents of reform in any shape; more moderate conservatives like John Pakington, Thomas Acland, and Joseph Napier; Liberals, including Richard Monckton Milnes, William Mackinnon, and James Wyld; Irish nationalist Thomas Chisholm Anstey; and Radicals Richard Cobden, John Arthur Roebuck, and William Coningham.[21]

During the 1850s there was no lack of disaffection seeking a focal point. Political unrest was less marked than it had been in the 1830s and 1840s – the decades of the Reform Bill, the New Poor Law, the People's Charter, the Anti-Corn Law League, and the Irish potato famine. The economic downturn that began in 1836 ended in 1848, and the 'hungry forties' were followed by twenty years of unprecedented prosperity and growth. The Great Exhibition in 1851 seemed to mark the beginning of a more confident era. Yet discontent lay just under the surface among both the middle class and the workers. The nation's political life was in an awkward, transitional stage: Whigs and Tories were evolving into Liberals and Conservatives, but the change would not be fully achieved until the era of Gladstone and Disraeli. In the interval, confusion often reigned. Vernon Harcourt wrote in 1855, 'The struggle of Whiggism in these days to transmute itself into Liberalism is like the attempt of an old mail coachman to turn stoker. He fails because he was not born to the trade, and does not understand it – because it is alien to his nature, his habits, and his tastes.'[22] As for the Tories, they had been in disarray since the Corn Laws were repealed in 1846. Many Tories saw the repeal as a betrayal of their principles, and a faction led by Disraeli and Lord Derby immediately voted with the opposition, bringing down Sir Robert Peel's government. According to Harcourt, 'Since that fatal hour when, like an army falling upon itself in a midnight panic, the Tories committed suicide by overthrowing the Government of Sir Robert Peel, they have wandered like sheep without a shepherd, seeking for a leader, but finding none.'[23]

After 1832 legislation of a liberal, utilitarian nature had become more common. However, the first and perhaps the most notorious instance of this, the New Poor Law of 1834, convinced the workers that political power was being used against them by the newly enfranchised middle class. The result was the Chartist demand for universal male suffrage. Gareth Stedman Jones was the first to point out the Chartists' extensive use of constitutionalist language. They did not complain primarily of their economic exploitation as factory workers; instead, their central themes were corruption in government, the arbitrary use of power, and their own unjust exclusion from the political sphere.[24] Resentment of utilitarian reforms was expressed through a political rhetoric that was rooted in the eighteenth century. Though Chartist agitation ended in 1848, working-class grievances did not,[25] and the Chartists continued to express their outrage through constitutionalist rhetoric. Among middle-class reformers, resentment of aristocratic privilege remained strong, and the same language of corruption was extensively employed.

Through most of the 1850s the prime minister was Lord Palmerston, a Whig aristocrat born in 1784.[26] Despite his support of moderate reform, he retained many of the attitudes characteristic of his class in the eighteenth century, and he was notably lacking in the moral earnestness so greatly admired in the mid-Victorian years. There was a common perception that power was still largely monopolized by incompetent aristocratic placemen. In 1852 a leading article in the *Weekly Dispatch* complained that the 'splendid material force of the British Navy' was being undermined by 'class government.' The writer stated that reform of the naval administration and better treatment of sailors had been 'the themes of article upon article in our columns'; nevertheless, 'the dull obstinacy, the arrant idle stupidity of neglect' were 'shamefully and disastrously palpable.' Admiralty decisions were still characterized by 'the same deafness to reason, the same sluggish impediment to progress, the same reliance on the pitiful art of apology and excuse, the same trust in corrupt patronage and protection.' Such officials, the writer noted darkly, 'lead all who trust them to perish.'[27]

The blunders both military and administrative in the early phases of the Crimean War (1854–6) intensified the rhetoric.[28] Many advocates of the Franklin search were also critics of the management of the war – for example, Roebuck and Richard Cobden. Roebuck was first elected to parliament in 1832, and throughout his long career in politics he expressed unvarying contempt for the Whigs. He wrote in 1852 that they had 'ever been an exclusive and aristocratic faction, though at times employing democratic principles and phrases … When out of office they are demagogues; in power they become exclusive oligarchs.'[29] In January 1855 Roebuck introduced a motion for an inquiry into the management of the war. His action brought down Lord Aberdeen's coalition government and secured the resignation of the foreign secretary, Lord John Russell (a former Whig prime minister), who remained out of power and in disgrace for the next five years. Roebuck subsequently chaired the committee of inquiry.

Dickens responded to the Crimean revelations with a satire on entrenched bureaucratic incompetence in *Little Dorrit* (serialized in 1855–7). The novel's 'Circumlocution Office' is dominated by a single well-connected family, the Tite Barnacles. The follies committed in the Crimea and the nobility of the Franklin search were deliberately juxtaposed in Dickens's periodical *Household Words*. 'During the last year or two we have been accustomed to hear, without flinching, of as many men killed in a day by battle and by blunder as have perished in pursuit of knowledge or on missions of humanity at either pole … since the creation of the world,' Henry Morley pointed out in an 1857 article. Morley sarcastically contrasted the government's disregard for human life in the Crimea with its claim that another Arctic expedition would involve unjustifiable risk to the searchers. In Morley's view, it was essential 'to pay in full our debt of honour'; the government, on the other hand, apparently wished 'to leave it undischarged upon some plea of a statute of limitations.'[30] The implication was clear: just as it had done in the Crimea, the government was breaking faith with those who served it.

Middle-class reformers like Dickens were fierce in their denunciation of bureaucratic abuses. Yet it was not a simple matter of the rising middle class against the aristocracy. In many cases, it was one segment of the middle class against another, since utilitarianism in government could cause as much resentment as the remnants of aristocratic hegemony. Dickens's *Oliver Twist* (1837–9) exposed the inhumane practices instituted by the New Poor Law, and in *Hard Times* (1854) he portrayed the utilitarian philosophy of education as cold and soul-destroying. His Mr Gradgrind ('Now, what I want is, Facts. Teach these boys and girls nothing but Facts. Facts alone are wanted in life. Plant nothing else, and root out everything else') and Mr M'Chokumchild ('We hope to have, before long, a board of fact, composed of commissioners of fact, who will force the people to be a people of fact, and of nothing but fact. You must discard the word Fancy altogether')[31] are even more disquieting figures than the Tite Barnacles.

In Dickens's fictional world, the old bureaucracy is frivolously incompetent and the new bureaucracy heartless and soulless in its efficiency. His dislike of both seems to have been typical of many in his time. A fierce resentment of politicians and bureaucrats runs through the literature of Franklin search, but as in Dickens's novels, it cannot easily be reduced to issues of class, political philosophy, or party allegiance. Instead, there was a very broad division between 'us' and 'them,' 'the people' and 'the politicians.'[32] There was little consistency in the arguments employed: the government was sometimes denounced for inefficiency and sometimes for a heartless adherence to utilitarian principles. There was both a demand for and a distrust of action by the state. It is difficult, therefore, to make any broad generalization from this evidence; all that can be said with certainty is that during the 1850s the proper relationship between the individual citizen and the machinery of government was a fiercely contested issue.

It also seems clear that the appeal of romance was sustained and even heightened in the mid-Victorian years of great material prosperity. Dickens looked to the creative powers of imagination and emotion for the regeneration of society. In his mind, reform would be for the better only if it had as its aim a society where spiritual and moral elements would remain of paramount importance. Morley wrote in *Household Words* that such qualities were embodied most strikingly in the

heroes of Arctic knight-errantry. 'There are no tales of risk and enterprise in which we English, men, women, and children, old and young,
rich and poor, become interested so completely, as in the tales that
come from the North Pole,' Morley declared. This was because snow
and ice were 'emblems of the deeds done in their clime ... The history
of Arctic enterprise is stainless as the Arctic snows, clean to the core as
an ice mountain.'[33]

Somewhat paradoxically, the romance of the Arctic quest appealed
even to liberals who usually demonstrated a much more rationalist cast
of mind than Dickens. Harriet Martineau, for example, made her first
success with *Illustrations of Political Economy* (1832) and was subsequently
associated with Henry Brougham, Charles Knight, and the Society for
the Diffusion of Useful Knowledge. She strongly advocated the application of Benthamite principles to social problems and was a supporter of
the New Poor Law. During the 1850s she wrote leading articles in the
Daily News expressing admiration of Lady Franklin and recommending
that the search be continued.[34] The *Westminster Review* had taken a highly
sceptical line on Arctic romance in the 1820s, but in the 1850s it published favourable reviews of Arctic narratives by George Eliot and others.
Eliot wrote in 1857 that these books were 'of pre-eminent interest' not
merely because of the geographical discoveries they recorded, but for
their ability to rouse 'our intellectual and moral enthusiasm alike.'[35]

An even more unlikely example is provided by James Fitzjames
Stephen, the judge and legal scholar best known for his codification of
Indian law. Stephen was born into a family of evangelical reformers. His
father, Sir James Stephen, was a member of the Clapham sect and one of
the most powerful early Victorian civil servants: from 1836 to 1847 he
ruled the Colonial Office, where he was known as 'King Stephen' and
'Mr. Over Secretary Stephen.'[36] To all appearances, Fitzjames Stephen
was among the driest and most Gradgrind-like of utilitarians. He viewed
Dickens's sentimental social criticism with contempt, and wrote in the
Saturday Review, to which he was a frequent contributor, that Dickens
had gained a 'pernicious' influence on the 'intellectually weak' members of the public by preaching the 'flattering doctrine, that, by some
means or other, the world has been turned topsy-turvy, – so that all the
folly and stupidity are found in the highest places, and all the good
sense, moderation, and ability in the lowest.' 'Who is this man who is so
much wiser than the rest of the world that he can pour contempt on all
the institutions of his country?' Stephen demanded. Dickens had a vivid
imagination, but no practical experience of the realities of administration.

'Freedom, law, established rules, have their difficulties. They are possible only to men who will be patient, quiet, moderate, and tolerant of difference in opinion; and therefore their results are intolerable to a feminine, irritable, noisy mind,' he explained.[37]

Yet Stephen wrote of Arctic narratives and their appeal to the imagination with admiring enthusiasm. 'This is one of the books which form part of the nation's title-deeds to greatness,' he declared of Robert McClure's *The Discovery of the North-West Passage*. 'Captain M'Clure's narrative … may well take its place by the side of stories of the pious and gallant men who … navigated in the days of Elizabeth … The whole story is to the last degree grand and noble.' The Northwest Passage was of no practical value, but Arctic narratives were filled with unsurpassable 'moral grandeur,' expressed in a style of 'unaffected simplicity.'[38] A few weeks later, Stephen began his review of Kane's *Arctic Explorations* with the remark, 'Disastrous as Sir John Franklin's expedition may have been, it has at any rate occasioned the display of more heroism than any similar event of modern times.'[39] The combination of romanticism and stoicism in Arctic literature was likely the secret of its hold on Stephen's mind.

Only the *Times* was consistent and unyielding in its contention that Arctic expeditions were an unjustifiable expenditure of public money. 'Another expedition in search of Sir John Franklin is now meditated, and while it is yet time we would invoke the aid of public opinion to put a stop at once to so outrageous a proceeding,' a leader writer declared in the same month that Stephen's two reviews were published. 'We cannot, of course, prevent individuals from doing whatever they may please. If a party of gentlemen choose to sail a brig to the centre of the Atlantic, and there agree to scuttle her, and go down in a friendly manner together, who shall stop them? We do, however, most vehemently protest against the extension of any assistance from the public funds, or from the public establishments, to so preposterous a scheme.'[40] A young naval officer, Bedford Pim, replied in a letter to the editor that if the search was abandoned, future generations would 'read in the history of their country that two ships, with 138 public servants, were lost' and left to their fate by a heartless government.[41]

The advocates of the search had much on their side: as Cooley had noted of Ross's expedition, private ventures could catch the public imagination even more effectively than officially sponsored ones because there was 'something so personal' in them. However, as the reception of Ross's narrative demonstrated, there were dangers inherent in such enterprises as well. It was not merely that the search could be ridiculed as useless and quixotic: the charge that the searchers were ambitious and self-serving was potentially far more damaging. If they had placed themselves in the public eye with the ultimate aim of financial gain or professional advancement, then the matter took on a very different aspect. Like Ross, they would then be open to severe public criticism. The young naval officers who volunteered for Lady Franklin's private expeditions were in a particularly delicate position: success would undoubtedly forward their careers, but either failure or the appearance of self-interest might prove fatal.

Narratives and reviews of narratives became of greater importance than ever before, because the stakes were higher in so many ways. The words of explorers who appeared before the public as authors were very carefully scrutinized for evidence of their character and motives. Even those who chose not to publish narratives had to undergo this ordeal, since official reports and letters were now routinely printed for the information of the public. A modest, straightforward account would, as always, be received with enthusiasm, but any trace of egotism or boasting met with censure. From today's viewpoint, such criticism can appear excessive and almost irrational, couched as it often was in the politically charged rhetoric of corruption.

In most late twentieth-century accounts of the search, it is taken for granted that journalists and the public alike would accept only naval heroes, and that outsiders like John Rae were ridiculed or ignored for no better reason than that they were not navy men.[42] This is far from correct; the major factor determining public opinion was whether or not an explorer appeared egotistical and self-serving. A modest naval hero of British birth would inevitably win the greatest acclaim, but Penny, Kennedy, Bellot, and Kane all were accepted and admired, while some naval officers, particularly Horatio Austin and Edward Belcher, were the objects of scathing commentary in the press. Even James Clark Ross, usually a public favourite, received negative publicity after the failure of his 1848–9 search expedition.

Rae, as a member of one of the three expeditions sent out in 1848, was given very favourable press commentary in the early stages of the search. He returned from his survey of Boothia in October 1847, having ascertained that it was, in fact, a peninsula, and was quickly appointed to the overland search expedition. The nominal commander was John Richardson, but owing to his age, most of the work was carried out by Rae. In the summer of 1848 Richardson and Rae travelled down the Mackenzie River to the sea and searched the coast between the Mackenzie and the

Coppermine River. Richardson returned to England, while Rae continued the search in 1849 and 1850. Rae's account of his Boothia journey, *Narrative of an Expedition to the Shores of the Arctic Sea in 1846 and 1847*, was published in 1850 and received good reviews. The *Athenaeum*, for example, declared that to the 'gallant band' of 'explorers who have shed lustre on the country that sent them out ... is now to be added the name of John Rae; who with power of endurance combines excessive fortitude and coolness in the hour of danger. His high moral and physical qualities won the esteem and admiration of Sir John Richardson, – and the unpretending narrative now before us will tend to confirm the sentiment pre-existing in his favour.'[43] The *Spectator* spoke with admiration of both Rae's ability to endure 'hardships, toils, and short commons, that would have been death to less hardy and accustomed explorers' and his 'plain, brief style.'[44]

Private evaluations of Rae were also highly favourable at this time. Franklin's daughter, Eleanor, described him as an 'active, cheerful, young man, one who does not make difficulties & who is enured to fatigue & hardships.'[45] Richardson's wife, Mary, gratefully noted that Rae's ability and zeal had made it possible for her husband to return after only one year of exploration. 'I must always consider his selection of Mr Rae, as a peculiar providence to me and his family,'[46] she wrote. Richardson himself wrote two letters praising Rae in the most glowing terms to Roderick Murchison, the president of the Royal Geographical Society.[47] The Society awarded Rae its gold medal in 1852, just as he was preparing to set off on another surveying journey. His aim was to map northern Boothia, which was the last remaining uncharted portion of the North American coastline. He stated in a letter published in the *Times* that there was no possibility of finding Franklin survivors in the region to which he was bound.[48] Rae was therefore almost forgotten by the public until October 1854, when he made a dramatic return.

Unlike Rae, Richard King was viewed with distrust. The main reason for this was his exceptionally bombastic, egotistical language. In one of the letters printed in the *Athenaeum* (see chap. 6) King assured Earl Grey that he was the only person capable of the 'Herculean task' of rescuing the lost explorers: 'it is necessary the leader of such a journey should have an intimate knowledge of the country and the people through which he has to pass, – the health to stand the rigour of the climate, and the strength to undergo the fatigue of mind and body to which he will be subjected. It is because I have these requisites, which I conscientiously believe are not to be found in another, that I hope to effect my purpose.' King presented himself as an unsung hero, writing that he had 'been refused all character as a scientific traveller and all honourary acknowledgment of faithful service to my country ... I stand alone as a single individual, isolated from the heroes of the Pole in regard to reward for services.' He suggested that he was entitled to be given command of an expedition as 'a peace offering' from the government.[49]

King showed little or no appreciation of other explorers' work. While most commentators praised Rae's survey of Boothia, King cast doubts on its accuracy.[50] He also engaged in a controversy with John Ross in the pages of the *Athenaeum*.[51] King, who had never been in the archipelago, claimed to have discovered the only sure way of navigating through it. He insisted that the eastern coastlines of islands and peninsulas were invariably clogged with ice, while the western shores were free of it. Ross replied with a list of examples from his own and other navigators' experiences of ice-clogged western coasts and ice-free eastern ones. He contended, correctly, that the amount of ice depended 'materially, if not entirely, on the preceding winter – whether it has been mild or severe.'[52] King, however, stubbornly maintained that he knew far more about the matter than Ross. He professed to be utterly certain that the 'law' he had discovered would always hold true (with perhaps a few trivial exceptions), but Ross's theory was dismissed with the remark that observations carried out over many years would be necessary to substantiate it.[53] King's own convictions, on the other hand, apparently required no empirical testing at all. Even the editor of the *Athenaeum*, who was firm in his belief that King deserved a hearing, by November 1847 felt obliged to point out: 'Dr. King speaks his own language – and is responsible for his own statements and opinions.'[54]

In December the editor referred to reports of the distress King's letters had caused among the families of the lost explorers. '[W]e are in no way pledged to the statements or opinions of our correspondent,' he wrote. The letters had been published purely out of a concern that 'no measure of precaution should be neglected.' The editor agreed that it was still 'premature to talk of the Expedition as lost.'[55] The *Athenaeum* published nothing further by or about King in 1848. He too was all but forgotten until 1854, when his predictions about the locality where the explorers died were proved correct. His egotistical bombast would then be at least temporarily forgiven, while his adversarial stance towards the government was highlighted and held up for public admiration.

In practical terms, King's letters had already produced some effect. No one was convinced that he ought to lead an expedition, but Jane Franklin had considered his opinions. '[Y]ou will be thinking that

Dr. King has been exciting a most mischievous & unjustifiable influence on my mind. Of Dr. King himself I wish to say nothing. I do not desire that he should be the person employed,' she wrote to James Ross on 18 December, the day that the last in the series of King's letters, along with Alexander Kennedy Isbister's carefully reasoned critique of his plans, appeared in the *Athenaeum*. Despite King's unattractive personality, Lady Franklin realized that there was at least some plausibility in his theories, and she hoped the government would request the Hudson's Bay Company to send searchers to the mouth of the Great Fish River. This might be one of the more unlikely spots to find the missing explorers, but otherwise it would be left until 'other explorations have been made in vain. And then, does [King] *not* say truly, it will be *too late?*'[56] Throughout the search, Lady Franklin never neglected this possibility. The area was not visited until 1853; this, however, was because of a complex set of circumstances and not because those involved in the search refused to accept suggestions emanating from non-naval men.

After several fruitless letters to Earl Grey, King was advised to write to the Admiralty. He did so in February 1848.[57] His proposal was promptly sent to James Ross and Parry for their comments.[58] Preparations for searches in several directions were already well under way. Besides the expedition led by Richardson and Rae, other western Arctic searches would be carried out through Bering Strait by Henry Kellett in H.M.S. *Herald* (1848–50) and Thomas Moore in H.M.S. *Plover* (1848–51). James Ross was to take the eastern route through Lancaster Sound in the *Enterprise* and the *Investigator*. Both Parry and Ross agreed with King that the lost explorers might be in the vicinity of North Somerset. If forced to abandon their vessels anywhere in the eastern Arctic, they would likely make their way to this area, hoping to meet relief ships or whalers. However, there seemed to be no good reason for them to travel towards the mouth of the Great Fish River. Their only hope of succour in that direction would be at the Hudson's Bay Company posts. These were far distant, and the area to be traversed was one where it would be extremely difficult or impossible for such a large party to live off the land. Why would they turn their backs on the route most likely to lead to help? Ross intended to search the coasts of North Somerset by sledge and steam launch, and both he and Parry stated that this plan was far more likely to succeed than King's. Ross, like Isbister, pointed out that King 'would barely have sufficient provision for his own party, and would more probably be in a condition to require than afford relief.'[59] He also drew up a detailed list of queries on practical matters, showing that King's plan was vague in many important respects.

Unfortunately for Ross, his own expedition was perceived as a failure for which he personally was to blame. His return marked the true beginning of the search controversies, during which broad political and social resentments readily found expression through Arctic debates. Seemingly practical questions such as the choice of routes became fraught with intense meaning, and those who made unpopular decisions were frequently described as either self-seeking egotists or government placemen. Ross was the first explorer to undergo this ordeal.

During his expedition, he had many obstacles to contend with, including unusually bad ice conditions, poor quality provisions, and an outbreak of scurvy. Ross made his way to Lancaster Sound with some difficulty, wintered at Port Leopold on the island of North Somerset, and sent out several sledging parties. Among the sledgers was Leopold McClintock, then a twenty-nine-year-old lieutenant. He immediately began devising improvements to the equipment. In the summer of 1848 Ross and McClintock reached the hitherto unvisited western coast of North Somerset. A strait, which they named Peel Channel, led to the south, but it was so choked with heavy ice that, in McClintock's words, it seemed 'any attempt to force a ship down it would not only fail, but lead to almost inevitable risk of destruction.'[60] It was through this strait, however, that Franklin's ships had gone. In August 1849, Ross attempted to sail north to Wellington Channel, but the ships were almost immediately caught in heavy pack and drifted helplessly towards Baffin Bay. Once released, Ross returned to England, where he was met with disappointment and accusations.

Ross had been instructed to focus his efforts on the area west and south of North Somerset, but he was also to attempt a search of Wellington Channel if possible. While he was away, the public became aware that there was reason to believe Franklin might have preferred the northern route. Franklin's instructions had not previously been made public, but in 1848 they were printed,[61] along with a huge mass of other Arctic documents and correspondence. It now became known that Wellington Channel had been named as a possible route to Bering Strait. Barrow's oldest son, also named John and also an Admiralty official, brought forward a letter he had received from Fitzjames in 1845, in which Fitzjames expressed the opinion that Wellington Channel might be the most likely path to success.[62] This letter, too, was printed and seized on by eager journalists. As a result, the public expected to hear on Ross's return that the channel had been searched and the missing expedition, or some trace of it, found.

When it was learned that Ross had made only a brief effort to reach Wellington Channel, he became the target of extremely harsh criticism. Journalists suggested that he had gone to the Arctic with the intention of continuing his 1829–33 explorations in the Boothia-North Somerset area, using the search for Franklin merely as a pretext to advance his own reputation as an Arctic discoverer. Parry described one of the most extreme attacks, in the weekly *Nautical Standard and Steam Navigation Gazette*,[63] as 'atrocious, abusive, and ignorant.'[64] A more moderately phrased, but nevertheless highly critical, commentary appeared in the *Examiner.* The author noted that a whaling ship had been close to Wellington Channel during the period when Ross's men were sledging southwest from Port Leopold. He claimed that he pointed this out only

> with much pain, implying a reflection, as it seems to do, on a most deservedly distinguished officer. But the facts exact it from us. Sir James Ross might not have known the circumstances which strengthen our belief that Sir John Franklin had passed through Wellington Strait; but he could not have been ignorant of the grounds that exist for believing he intended to pass that way. Sir James was ordered by the Admiralty to examine it. Yet he confined his exertions to the southern side of Barrow's Straits. The accounts of his proceedings which have been allowed to appear, bear marks of his having been less anxious in the direction of the specific search, than to extend his land journeys in a S.W. and then in a S.E. direction, till he should reach, by another track, the extreme limit he had attained in a former expedition – his 'f[a]rthest.'[65]

The unfortunate result of these developments was what one periodical writer would later call the 'Wellington Channel mania,'[66] during which the main search efforts were directed north rather than southwest.[67] It certainly seems ironic that James Ross, the object of so much undeserved abuse, was the only one among the early searchers who came close to the right track. Bitterly hurt, Ross retired from active participation in the search. And, as attention turned to the north, King and his theories sank for the time being into oblivion.[68]

Many periodical writers expressed a strong belief that Franklin's men were still alive, having survived on the resources of the country after the supplies brought from England were exhausted, and they demanded that more expeditions be sent out, whatever the risk. The *Examiner* conceded that search expeditions entailed risk: 'the recovery of the missing ships and crews ought of necessity to lead to visits to the most dangerous places, as it is in them that the ships are likely to have been locked or cast away.' Nevertheless, 'while a rational chance of success remains ... the idea of leaving Franklin and his gallant companions to perish is not to be borne ... We have no right to count the cost.'[69]

Despite such comments in the press, the government was slow to announce its future plans. On New Year's Day 1850 Osborn made his first appearance in print with a letter to the *Times*, signed 'An Observer.' He attributed the failure of the searches to bureaucratic delay and mismanagement, and suggested that it was time to bring the matter out from behind the closed doors of the Admiralty and into the public sphere. 'The Admiralty,' he wrote, 'are, like other public offices, too much inclined to dose [*sic*] over their plans, for even purely professional points to be left entirely to their decision; and surely, after two years and a half spent in futile attempts, it is high time the public stepped in and called them to account for their stewardship upon the question of Sir John Franklin's relief.' Franklin and his men, '138 as noble fellows as ever trod a plank,' had gone out 'determined not to return but with honour and renown'; but in 1847, when questions about their safety were first raised, the government did not take prompt action. 'As is too often the case in England, every arrangement was left unquestioned to the judgment of the Admiralty and some Arctic oracles. The consequence was ... failure and disappointment, I might almost say disgrace,' Osborn wrote. He made a dramatic appeal for help, insisting that Franklin and his men were still alive, and that they would 'struggle manfully with their sufferings and hardships, for they will believe that their country and their profession will not let them sink into the sleep of death without having tried every means to save them.'[70]

A week later, when the government still had made no announcement, Osborn returned to the attack. In this second letter, he made more extensive use of the language of corruption, yet he also strongly denounced the concept of utility. He referred to 'cold-blooded remarks,' typical of 'these utilitarian days,' that he had heard in conversation. In Osborn's view it was 'so un-English to coldly reason upon the advisability of seeking Franklin, merely because other lives may be risked in doing so, that had I not heard it advanced, I could not have believed such indifference could exist.' The story of John Ross's 1829–33 expedition was irrefutable evidence that explorers could live off the resources of the country; if the public believed Franklin's men must be dead, then the government had failed in its duty. 'Shame be on those who, standing in high places, have thrown from the very first a blight upon the endeavours of the more hopeful and more earnest, by useless expressions of despair,' Osborn exclaimed. 'They damped the ardour, I fear, of those who went to save, and at any rate gave them some authority for being lax in their endeavours.' He hoped that 1850 would be 'the year to redeem our tottering honour.'[71]

Osborn's sentiments and his tone were echoed in an anonymous pamphlet titled *Observations on the missing Ships of the Arctic Expeditions, under Sir John Franklin, with some Propositions and Considerations for their Relief and Extrication from the Ice, by an old Officer of the Royal Navy*. According to its author, 'The nation is ... willing to a man; and it has deposited its will, and its power, and its means, in appointing hands to perform its behests. It looks to those hands for a prompt, a judicious, and a successful employment of these.' Yet all efforts had ended in failure. 'Where glory ends, shame begins,' the author warned. 'Let us look, then, well to our managers, and ask, What have they done – what are they doing – what will they yet do?' Like Osborn, he pointed to John Ross's survival as proof that there were no grounds for despair. The nation as a whole must act: 'It is not the affair of an office; it is not the affair of a profession; it is not the affair of *one* man; but it is the affair of the nation, and the affair of every individual in it. Let every Englishman, then, interest himself in it, and let one and all *see that it be done*.'[72]

Some periodical writers evidently shared the official sentiments deplored by Osborn. While admitting that the search could not yet be abandoned, they now described the entire enterprise of Arctic discovery in critical terms. One such article appeared in the January issue of the *New Monthly Magazine*. The author has been identified as geographer William Francis Ainsworth, a cousin of the magazine's editor, William Harrison Ainsworth. 'Without doubt,' Ainsworth proclaimed, 'the most wondrous of all voyages made for geographical purposes, since the discovery of the New World, have been the expeditions in search of a north-west passage. They are wondrous for the zeal, the endurance, and the perseverance with which they have been carried out. They are still more wondrous for the misplaced and perverted direction in which such qualities, and the material necessary to give them effect, have been brought to bear.' After the inevitable summary of expeditions from the sixteenth century to Franklin's departure, Ainsworth went on to the failure of the 1848–9 searches. He compared the ice that carried James Ross's ships away from Wellington Channel to 'the all-powerful arm of nature, which appeared in this case as if to forbid the accomplishment of a long-ambitioned project' and remarked that Ross's failure demonstrated 'the total inutility of exploratory voyages in those distant and desolate regions of eternal ice, from which man and his interests seem for ever banished.'[73]

Nevertheless, Ainsworth admitted that there must be more expeditions. His tone shifted abruptly as he turned to the question of survival. The likelihood that some of Franklin's men were still alive was in his opinion very high, since 'the stock of provisions might be greatly augmented' by hunting and fishing. He pointed to the success of 'that most intrepid and enduring traveller Mr. Rae' during his 1846–7 expedition as proof that living off the resources of the country was possible. This being the case, it was 'our bounden duty' to search further. Then, in another change of tone, Ainsworth ended his article by complaining that 'reasonable and feasible projects have been neglected' for the sake of useless Arctic ventures.[74] The particular project he had in mind was the building of a canal through the isthmus of Panama, which it seemed likely would soon be accomplished by the Americans.

A similar utilitarian comment was made in the February issue of the *British Quarterly Review* (an evangelical, Nonconformist journal that began publication in 1845). The anonymous author wrote indignantly of the proposed canal, 'The honour ... of achieving this grand undertaking, in which the commercial interests of mankind are essentially involved, is now ... wrested from our hands.' It would instead be built by the Americans: '*they*, and not *we*, will have the high credit of having opened a passage by sea from the western to the eastern world.' As for the Northwest Passage, 'It is time now to ask how many more ships' crews are to be immolated in the prosecution of this object? ... Our science may do much, but the laws of nature are not to be subdued by it. The icy latitude of the polar regions must remain for the most part her own solitary and impenetrable domain.'[75]

The *Spectator* replied to these articles with a vigorous defence of Arctic expeditions as one of the best schools for the national character. 'Those who demand tangible utility in all human enterprise would ... expunge the great van-leaders of civilization,' the writer argued. '[Arctic adventures] are amongst the few which remain to us, fitting with the peaceful character of the times, which test the hardihood of our seamen. These seamen *desire* to be tested ... It is a noble and wholesome desire; it helps to maintain the high character of our navy; it furnishes the occasion for indulging the spirit of adventure which animates all true chivalry. Arctic expeditions are the knighterrantry of our day.'[76] Here a romantic popu-list vision opposed the language of utility. The impetus for the search was said to have its origin not in the wisdom of the government, but in the innate urges of the sailors' hearts. That their instinct to seek adven-ture should be gratified was not only for their own good but for the good of the nation.

In late January Richard Collinson in the *Enterprise* and Robert McClure in the *Investigator* sailed for Bering Strait. On 31 January a lead-ing article in the *Times* suggested that this venture was 'a last effort,' since James Ross's failure had proved that further searches in the east-ern Arctic would be futile.[77] 'Surely never was argument more illogical than this,' C.R. Weld objected in a letter to the *Athenaeum*. Many explor-ers had passed through Lancaster Sound, and Ross's difficulties were the exception rather than the rule.[78] On 6 February Weld gave a lecture on the search at the Royal Institution, which was later published in Murray's Home and Colonial Library.[79] At the conclusion of the lecture, a 'messenger balloon,' designed to scatter printed notices of the loca-tion of the relief ships far and wide across the Arctic, was exhibited.[80]

The day before the lecture, Lady Franklin's main advocate in the House of Commons, Sir Robert Harry Inglis, had requested copies of all Admiralty papers relating to the search plans, clearly stating that his intention was to put pressure on the government to make further rescue attempts. Before long it was announced that there would be an eastern expedition in 1850. Weld (writing this time in *Fraser's Magazine* rather than in the *Athenaeum*) attributed the decision to renew the eastern search to the influence of public opinion.[81] The first lord of the Admi-ralty, Sir Francis Baring, was evidently annoyed by the public criticism to which he and his colleagues had been subjected. He commented testily that 'everyone had his own project: but it would be the endeavour of the Admiralty to adopt that which they really believed to be most efficient for the purpose.'[82]

The command of the expedition was subsequently given to Captain Horatio Austin. He was sent to Lancaster Sound, with much the same orders as those previously given to James Ross. This was the largest search expedition so far, consisting of four ships: *Resolute, Assistance, Intrepid,* and *Pioneer.* The *Intrepid* and the *Pioneer* were powerful steamers, intended to carry supplies and to tow the sailing ships through the ice if necessary. The *Athenaeum* reported that the number of volunteers for this expedition was greater than on any other occasion. Osborn, who had first volunteered for Arctic service in early 1849,[83] was appointed to command the *Pioneer*. McClintock was first lieutenant of the *Assistance* and Clements Markham served as a midshipman, also in the *Assistance*.

Lady Franklin's private expedition under Captain Penny was now placed under Admiralty orders: Penny was to act in cooperation with Austin, and he was 'particularly charged with' the examination of Wellington Channel.[84] (Two other private expeditions also set out for the eastern Arctic: a British venture commanded by John Ross and an American expedition sponsored by Henry Grinnell.) The decision to unite the Austin and Penny expeditions set the stage for a wider acceptance of the populist interpretation. Penny was a man of determined character with a great deal of self-confidence, and he was not prepared to accept Austin's authority to the extent that a naval subordinate would have done. That he was an enterprising man of the people seems to have been part of Penny's self-concept long before the expeditions set sail. (His father, the son of a tenant farmer, had risen from ship's carpenter to master of a whaling vessel; Penny himself made his first whaling voyage when he was twelve and was a master by the age of twenty-five.)[85] This conviction shaped Penny's behaviour both during and after his time in the Arctic.

Ainsworth hastened to comment on the latest developments and to clarify his own stance in a second *New Monthly* article, published in March. 'We have made our readers so perfectly acquainted with the progress of research in the Arctic Regions, that it may be very fairly expected, in a case where interest is so intense and so widely diffused, that we should persevere in our chronicle of enterprise and adventure,' he began. This opening suggests that since the publication of his first article, Ainsworth had been impressed by the intensity of popular support for the search. He had also evidently read Osborn's letters in the *Times*: in his first paragraph, he repeated the description of Franklin's crew as '138 as noble fellows as ever trod a plank.' He went on to assure his readers, 'We by no means wish to say that such an expedition as that sent out under Captain Collinson ought not to have been undertaken ... We only wish to point out ... the real difficulties of the case.' Whatever the obstacles, continued action was necessary to 'wipe away the stain to our national honour that would be sustained by leaving the devoted and gallant crews of two ships to an unknown fate in unknown regions.'[86]

At this point, Dickens's new periodical, *Household Words*, entered the Arctic debate. The fifth number (27 April) contained a poem, 'Arctic

Heroes,' by Richard Horne. Here the missing explorers were shown waiting and hoping for relief, while at the same time resolved that if none came,

> We, to the last
> With firmness, order, and considerate care,
> Will act as though our death-beds were at home ...
> So future times shall record bear that we,
> Imprisoned in these frozen horrors, held
> Our sense of duty, both to men and God.[87]

In May, Frederick Knight Hunt's description of 'A Visit to the Arctic Discovery Ships' appeared. Hunt conducted his readers on a tour of the *Pioneer* in dry dock at Woolwich. He offered vivid word pictures of an Arctic ship in the process of being filled with so many supplies that dangerous items like gunpowder had to be stored in Osborn's cabin. Hunt concluded by describing 'an inscription that glittered in the sunshine of that April afternoon, for the words were carved in letters of brass on the steersman's wheel ... ENGLAND EXPECTS EVERY MAN TO DO HIS DUTY.'[88]

Penny's ships sailed on 13 April and Austin's on 3 May. On 5 June they were followed by Lady Franklin's private expedition in the *Prince Albert*, commanded by a naval officer, Charles Forsyth. Lady Franklin was still haunted by the fear that King might be right, and Forsyth's orders were to make sledge journeys across North Somerset and Boothia, in order to meet the lost explorers should they be attempting to reach Lancaster Sound from the area of the Great Fish River. However, ice conditions made this impossible. Forsyth returned in October, bringing the news that Austin's squadron had discovered traces of Franklin's expedition on Beechey Island, in Lancaster Sound near the entrance to Wellington Channel. (The next year, Lady Franklin sent the *Prince Albert* out again on the same mission, this time under the command of William Kennedy.)

Forsyth's report was based on a note left at the scene by Captain Ommanney of the *Assistance*, who had continued to the west after making his discoveries. Forsyth also brought back a few items found by his own men, such as a piece of rope manufactured at the Chatham naval yard. The trail had been discovered at last, and in some quarters this was regarded as proof that had the government acted more promptly, the lost explorers would already have been restored to their homes. 'Certain it is that the official people have displayed a shameful backwardness in performing their duty – a backwardness wholly unworthy of the country that produces men like Franklin and his companions, or the gallant sailors now out on the search – eager to be sent. The object in Whitehall seemed to be to try how little trouble or cost "would do,"' the *Leader* commented shortly after Forsyth's return.[89]

Throughout 1851 interest in the search was high. Ainsworth published another Arctic article in the February issue of the *New Monthly*, titled 'The Track of Sir John Franklin.' The opinion had frequently been expressed that the discovery at Beechey Island meant the *Erebus* and *Terror* had indeed gone up Wellington Channel. Ainsworth was inclined to agree, but he wondered whether the discovery had come too late. 'Hope itself grows pale at the idea of our starving countrymen, if still alive, lingering in their icy prison for one more winter of cold, and darkness, and want!' he reflected.[90] An article published by Weld in *Fraser's Magazine* was slightly more optimistic. Although Weld conceded that 'great mortality must have taken place,' he considered it 'not only possible, but probable, that a few survive, and that we shall hear from living lips the strangest record of endurance and suffering that have yet befallen the mariners of any nation.'[91]

At about the same time, journalist Peter Lund Simmonds, the former editor of the *Colonial Magazine*,[92] published *Sir John Franklin and the Arctic Regions*, a book similar to *Discovery and Adventure in the Polar Seas and Regions*, but without the chapters on scientific subjects. Since 1849 *Discovery and Adventure* had been published by Thomas Nelson in London; in 1851 the sixteenth edition appeared. Evidently believing that there was a large market for inexpensive compilations of Arctic material, Simmonds produced a volume of his own. In the first half of the book, the narratives published from 1819 on were summarized. Here he drew heavily on Barrow, whose *Quarterly* articles and other writings were admiringly referred to.[93] The second half of the book outlined the progress of the search. It consisted mainly of reprinted reports and official correspondence from the Arctic blue books; as well, there were several poems about the missing expedition.[94] Simmonds's own commentary was kept to a minimum, for the most part serving merely to link these items into a coherent narrative of events. Forsyth's report made an effective conclusion, with its promise that more new developments were soon to follow. The book's 375 pages thus contained a great deal of important information arranged in a straightforward chronological fashion, and it was priced at only 2 shillings and sixpence (the price of later editions fell to 1 shilling and sixpence).[95] The *Weekly Dispatch* called it 'a most admirable volume.'[96] Like Leslie, Jameson, and Murray, Simmonds frequently revised his book as new information became available, and there were nine editions between 1851 and 1860.

In May 1851 the *Prince Albert* sailed from Aberdeen on yet another attempt to search the Boothia-North Somerset area. The commander, William Kennedy, wished to save Franklin because in his view Franklin had once 'saved' him. During Franklin's first winter in Rupert's Land, he taught young Kennedy to read. He also regularly conducted church services on Sundays; by Franklin's own account, these were the first Christian services ever held at the northern posts.[97] Kennedy confirmed, 'It was from that good man I received my first impression of what a Christian Sabbath and worship should be.'[98] Lady Franklin eagerly responded to the romance represented by this volunteer from a far-off land, and his mixed blood only enhanced his appeal in her eyes. 'He is a remarkable & most favorable specimen of the half European, half Indian race,' she told Murchison. 'The Indian character is strongly developed in Mr K's face & now & then in his character when the wrongs of his maternal race are brought to his memory – At these times, he needs only, as I tell him, the tomahawk in hand & the single lock on the scalp to be the [illegible] of an Indian warrior. At all others, he is the gentlest and most humble-minded of good Christians, but in every phase of character, faithful, generous, devoted & true.'[99] The press reacted just as favourably: 'This gentleman has crossed the broad Atlantic to undertake the duty, and has gone without fee or reward, animated by a pure devotion to the service,'[100] the *Leisure Hour* informed its readers.

Kennedy's second-in-command, Ensign Joseph-René Bellot of the French navy, was an equally unusual volunteer and met with equal, if not greater, public acclaim. The son of a blacksmith, Bellot had obtained his education through scholarships. After his untimely death, a writer in the *Dublin University Magazine* wondered how this 'stranger, of humble rank' had gained so great a place in the affection of the British public. It was, he concluded, because of Bellot's romantic enthusiasm, his 'geniality of heart, earnestness of purpose, and devoted loyalty'[101] to Lady Franklin and her cause. The public appeal of Kennedy's venture was completed by the presence of John Hepburn, who, like Richardson, was determined to go in search of his former commander despite his advancing years.

Interest in the search rose to greater heights than ever when Austin and Penny returned in September 1851. Class issues now came to a head, and Penny's energetic search efforts were contrasted (both by

Penny himself and by journalists) with Austin's greater concern for protocol and the safety of public property. Perhaps predictably, Austin and
Penny had clashed, and in Penny's perception Austin's naval rigidity
had prevented an effectual search from being carried out. Some of the
naval men themselves shared this view, with Osborn's support of Penny's
cause being especially strong. To Lady Franklin, Osborn reported that
Austin had 'treated with flippant indifference' or 'checked in the most
arbitrary manner'[102] all plans of search that differed from his own.

Penny, who reached England before Austin, brought the important
information that Beechey Island had been Franklin's winter quarters in
1845–6. No records indicating the expedition's planned course in the
summer of 1846 had been found. However, the proximity of Beechey
Island to Wellington Channel seemed in itself to indicate that the northern route was a definite possibility. This idea was strongly reinforced by
Penny's findings to the north. In the summer of 1851, while Austin's
men made westward sledging journeys, Penny had travelled up Wellington
Channel. At a spot he named Point Surprise, in latitude 76° north,
Penny was thrilled to discover that the ice-bound channel gave way to
open water. He saw a new channel, which he named Queen's Channel
after Queen Victoria, leading to the northwest. As further exploration
would have to be done by water, Penny at once returned to the ships
and dragged one of the boats north on a sledge.

In August, Penny returned to the ships once again, having found no
trace of Franklin. However, he firmly believed that conditions to the north
were such as to permit living off the land for a very long period. Franklin
might therefore have progressed far in that direction. Penny attempted to
convince Austin that the expedition should remain for another year, and
that one of the steamers should be used to pursue the northern search.
After a heated argument, Austin refused, and he asked Penny to state in
writing that no further search of Wellington Channel was required. (This
incident was omitted from the early reports.) Unwilling to take sole
responsibility for detaining the expedition in the Arctic, Penny did so, but
immediately after his return to England he urgently requested that the
Admiralty provide him with a steam vessel in which he might resume his
efforts. He hoped to return to the Arctic immediately, so that he could
begin operations as early as possible the following spring. The suggestion
was promptly rejected.[103] The Admiralty went on to solicit opinions about
the course it should now take from all the recognized Arctic experts and
from Austin, Penny, and Ommanney. An official report was submitted on
20 November, and released to the public on 5 December.[104]

Meanwhile, the news about Beechey Island and Queen's Channel created a press sensation, and the search gained even more attention as the conflicts between Austin and Penny became public knowledge. The earliest accounts appeared in the *Illustrated London News* and the *Athenaeum*,[105] based mainly on information provided by Penny. The *New Monthly* rushed into print with a commentary in its October issue. On the basis of the early reports, Ainsworth was somewhat sceptical of Penny's claim that Franklin had gone up Wellington Channel, but after reading more detailed material, he was convinced. In a note which he apparently added just as the magazine went to press, Ainsworth took a positive and enthusiastic view. 'With such favourable prospects before us, and considering how safely, and in what good health all the recent expeditions have carried on their explorations, it is surely worth while sending out at once an efficient steamer,' he thought.[106]

During October, the Admiralty released the letters exchanged between Austin and Penny in August (including Penny's statement that there was no need for further searches of Wellington Channel) in an apparent effort to influence public opinion against new expeditions. In November, Weld vehemently condemned both Austin and the Admiralty in *Fraser's*. He informed his readers of Austin's refusal to give Penny a steamer and the ensuing stormy scene, stating that he had heard this story from a 'high authority.' Weld also claimed that the Admiralty had suppressed a letter in which Penny forcefully expressed his view that Queen's Channel should be searched. He suggested that the Admiralty's effort to make the public believe Penny had willingly acquiesced in Austin's decision should be regarded as a deliberate attempt to mislead. Weld described Austin's behaviour as 'apathetic' and commented, 'It is, indeed, a fearful reflection, that the ships so liberally sent out to rescue our unfortunate countrymen, should have discovered their traces, and returned to us, leaving the dark mystery which clings to their fate still unsolved; and it is even more terrible to think, that the arm of help may have been almost within their grasp when it was recalled.'[107]

In early October, a letter from Rae to the New York *Albion*, written during Richardson's search expedition, was widely reprinted in the British press. Rae strongly opposed the belief 'that to continue the search for Sir John Franklin beyond the summer of 1850 would be a useless waste of time, labour and money.' He himself was firmly convinced that 'a part, or all, of Sir John's party may still exist,' and he cited his own experience in 1846–7 as proof that their survival was possible. Rae and his men, though only two were good shots, 'by our own exertions, in a country previously totally unknown to us, obtained the means of subsistence for twelve months. Why may not Sir John Franklin's party do the same?' If the expedition had 'providentially been thrown on or near a part of the coast where reindeer or fowl are at all numerous, surely out of so many officers and men sportsmen may be found,' who could provide for the party.[108]

Fraser's reprinted this letter, with the added comment that Penny had described Wellington Channel as an area teeming with bird and animal life. 'With such resources,' Weld believed, 'it would not be difficult to prolong life for many years; and until we have positive evidence of the death of the party, we are not warranted in arriving at this melancholy conclusion.'[109] The *Spectator* pointed out that in fifteen months, Rae's party had consumed only three months' worth of the small stock of supplies they carried with them. The lost expedition had three years' supplies, so 'at the same ratio, Franklin's provisions might serve for fifteen or twenty years.'[110] The *Leader* exclaimed, 'Brave John Rae! Heartily we wish that success may attend thy persevering and gallant efforts ... John Rae and the Hudson's Bay Company shame John Russell and the Lords of the Admiralty!'[111]

Weld concluded his November 1851 *Fraser's* article with the hope that Penny would be put in charge of the next expedition. It was implied, though not stated, that Austin had proved himself unworthy of command. The *Daily News* took an even stronger line. In a leading article on 9 December, Austin was described as a narrow-minded man more concerned with his own rank and power than with finding Franklin. The leader writer declared that Arctic naval officers 'ought to be given to understand that they are engaged on an exceptional service, in which all mere *martinet* must be left out of account.'[112]

The opinions presented by Scoresby and Richardson to the government's Arctic Committee were strongly in favour of another expedition. The possibility of survival, so important to the emotional impact of the searchers' cause, was emphasized by both. Scoresby firmly declared, 'That Sir John Franklin, or some portion of his associates, *may* still survive, is a position which cannot be controverted ... The Esquimaux ... live out, not six or seven winters merely, but a fair portion of the ordinary life of man. Why then may not hardy enterprizing [*sic*] Britons, sustained, over and above, by ... moral courage and Christan hope ... not be yet surviving?' Richardson stated that he thought it 'probable' some of Franklin's men were still alive, because the 'existence of Eskimos up to the 77th parallel' was 'in itself sufficient evidence of the means of subsistence being produced in these latitudes.' Richardson felt that the expedition's fate would depend mainly on the nature of the region in which its progress had been stopped. If it was a good hunting area, all was likely well, while if there was little game, then clearly most or all of the missing men must be dead. He mentioned the possibility that scurvy might have taken its toll, but ended by reiterating that life could 'be maintained in the most Arctic lands under circumstances, at first sight, seemingly the most hopeless.' In a final optimistic note, he added, 'I may also adduce the success of Mr. Rae ... as another proof of the possibility of sustaining a party on the products of an Arctic country.' Austin and Ommanney, on the other hand, spoke against such ideas. (Austin also flatly denied that Penny had asked for a steamer to explore Queen's Channel.)[113]

In late December, Penny provided further evidence supporting the theory that the explorers might still be alive. In a letter to the *Times*, he revealed that another whaler, Captain Robert Martin of Peterhead, was the last European to speak with the lost explorers. Franklin had informed Martin that he thought it was possible to make his provisions last as long as seven years, since he intended to use as much fresh game as possible. Martin (described by Penny as 'a man of the strictest integrity') had not wished to bring public attention to himself at the time, but he now realized his story might be of importance in influencing decisions about the search.[114] Penny's letter was widely reprinted,[115] and in early January Captain Martin provided a formal deposition attesting to the truth of the story.[116] Penny commented that Martin's evidence 'must give us the greatest hopes';[117] Simmonds, reprinting the deposition in a new edition of his book, wrote that it was 'not impossible, perhaps not improbable, that Sir John Franklin may yet make his appearance, coming down from those ice-bound regions bringing with him his noble ships and their daring crews, and giving joy to thousands upon thousands who are watching with intense interest the unraveling of the mystery of his absence.'[118]

This evidence of Franklin's determination to live off the land to the greatest extent possible, together with Penny's report of Queen's Channel and its abundant animal life, sparked a round of highly optimistic commentary. During 1852 articles about Franklin came thick and fast. The dominant theme was that of survival: as a writer in the *Dublin University Magazine* recorded, the searchers had been 'inspired with the growing hope, which we are glad to share,' that Franklin and his crews were watching for the relief ships.[119] The abundant journalistic commentary on this subject constantly reinforced the mental image of living explorers, hoping and waiting for proof that their countrymen had not forgotten them. One of the most interesting of these articles appeared in the 7 February number of *Chambers's Edinburgh Journal*. *Chambers's* had been published since 1832, but until this point it had shown little interest in the Arctic – far less than its two early rivals in the area of cheap weekly publication, the *Mirror* and the *Penny Magazine*. From 1852 on, however, *Chambers's* provided regular contributions to the connected narrative. The timing makes it seem likely that Penny, a forthright Scottish man of the people, appeared as the type of Arctic hero a journal aimed at the working classes could proudly celebrate.

The anonymous author of 'Food of the Arctic Regions – Franklin's Expedition,' who claimed to have personal experience of the Arctic, heaped scorn on those who argued that the lost expedition must have perished soon after the supplies brought from England were exhausted. He pointed out that 'all over these icy regions isolated tribes of natives are to be met with; and they do not exist in a starved and almost famished condition ... but in absolute abundance.' To the possible objection that Europeans could not live like natives, he replied, 'It is incredible how soon a man becomes reconciled to, and healthful under, a totally different diet from that to which he has been all his life accustomed, so long as that change is suitable to his new home. We ourselves ... were quite amazed at the rapid and easy way in which nature enabled us to enjoy and thrive on food at which our stomach would have revolted in England.' The author went on to confidently claim:

> In every country in the world ... the food eaten by the natives is that which is incomparably best suited to the climate ... In Britain, we read with disgust of the Greenlander eagerly swallowing whale-oil and blubber; but in his country, it is precisely what is best adapted to sustain vital energy. Europeans in the position of Franklin's crew would become acclimatised, and gradually accustomed to the food of the natives, even before their own provisions were exhausted; and after that, we may be very sure ... they would necessarily and easily conform to the usages, as regards food, of the natives around them.[120]

Not all commentaries were quite so optimistic as this one, but even the gloomier articles mixed considerable hope with the fear that seven years was too long an interval for even the most intrepid explorers to have endured.

The *Leisure Hour*, a new weekly published by the Religious Tract Society, first appeared in January 1852 and achieved wide circulation among middle- and lower-class readers, in part through its distribution in Sunday schools.[121] Its first issue contained an article on Franklin's 1819–22 expedition, emphasizing the religious faith of the explorers in terms very similar to those in Barrow's *Quarterly* review. The author assured his readers that he would 'take an early opportunity' of discussing the search expeditions,[122] and this promise was fulfilled in a two-part article published in February. Here Austin's 'unaccountable decision' not to search Queen's Channel was severely censured. It was implied that the last chance of saving Franklin might thus have been lost; however, the author held out some degree of hope. 'The probabilities of Sir John Franklin's preservation and ultimate rescue are not to be easily calculated,' he pointed out. He considered it 'satisfactory to know that those who have devoted most attention to the subject feel that the time for despair has not yet arrived.'[123]

A new strand was added to the optimists' argument by geographer Augustus Petermann's 'Notes on the Distribution of Animals Available as Food in the Arctic Regions.' Petermann pointed out that 'animal life is found as much in the Polar as in the tropical regions, and though the number of species is decidedly inferior to the number in the latter, yet, on the other hand, the immense multitudes of individuals compensate for the deficiency in the former respect.'[124] Petermann's observations, along with Richardson's and Scoresby's replies to the Arctic Committee and other key documents from the now voluminous Arctic blue books, were reprinted by Simmonds in a new edition of *Sir John Franklin and the Arctic Regions* and by James Mangles in another compilation, *Papers and Despatches Relating to the Arctic Searching Expeditions.*

The reading public was therefore well provided with very detailed information on Arctic plans and theories. In earlier decades, official documents like those in the blue books would have been available only to insiders; now, not only were they made public, but they could readily be obtained in convenient digests at a very low price. By all accounts, the resulting level of public knowledge and concern was very high. The *Leisure Hour*'s writer related, 'Sir John Franklin is ... the hero of the day. Is he alive, or has he perished? and if alive, where is he? are questions which pass from lip to lip, and are eagerly discussed ... around ... firesides.'[125] An Edinburgh landlady encountered by Lady Franklin and Sophia Cracroft in 1849 described how her daughter had brought home the latest newspaper report on the search, '& called her from the top of the house, to hear it.' The report suggested that Franklin would return alive, and the landlady 'could have cried for joy.'[126] According to *Chambers's Journal*, by 1852 such responses were extremely common: 'every rumour purporting to come from the fields of arctic enterprise is caught at with breathless eagerness … every record of arctic adventure is studied with deepest interest.'[127] The majority evidently supported continued searches. The *Dublin University Magazine* declared in the spring of 1852: 'We know … we speak the feeling of the public when we say, that an exhaustive search … should at once be attempted' by every possible route.[128]

The government now decided to send yet another expedition to Lancaster Sound, this time under Captain Sir Edward Belcher. He was given five ships: *Assistance*, *Resolute* (commanded by Henry Kellett), *Intrepid* (McClintock), *Pioneer* (Osborn), and the supply vessel *North Star*. His orders were to explore Wellington and Queen's channels and also to search westward for traces of either Franklin or Collinson and McClure, who had not been heard from since they passed through Bering Strait. This plan met with public approval, but controversy still surrounded Austin and Penny. Though Austin was not given command of the new venture, he had received an official commendation of his conduct, and the report of the Arctic Committee endorsed his version of the conflicts with Penny. Penny, on the other hand, received no commendation or thanks, and the Admiralty had not replied to his offer of further service. On 12 March questions were raised in Parliament.

The Tories under Lord Derby had recently assumed office, and Lady Franklin seems to have hoped that Penny would receive better treatment at their hands than he had from Russell and the Whigs. If so, her hopes were quickly dashed. In answer to a question from Chisholm Anstey, Augustus Stafford (the newly appointed secretary of the Admiralty) replied that Penny would receive no commendation or reward, and the government did not intend to employ him again. Robert Inglis, though himself a Tory, angrily remarked that officialdom seemed unwilling to acknowledge the services of those who came from humble backgrounds. He compared Penny to Cook, and reminded his colleagues that the latter had 'rendered the name of England dignified by the discoveries he had made.'[129] He also pointedly questioned the official refusal to refer to Penny as 'Captain' (in the opinion of the Admiralty, command of a mere whaling ship was insufficient to earn this title). Penny himself responded to the news with a letter to the *Times*, in which he publicly expressed his disappointment. Employing the trope of the plain-spoken man of action to its fullest advantage, he declared: 'I am willing to meet any jury of my countrymen ... but I am not willing ... to have my tongue tied by respect to etiquette, which those who most require it are the last to observe towards me.'[130]

In the April issue of the *New Monthly*, Ainsworth – now an ardent advocate of the romantic populist interpretation – commented that the opinions of Penny, Scoresby, Richardson, and Petermann were 'of the highest importance,' while Captains Austin and Ommanney demonstrated 'the bias of men who have failed ... and, therefore, despair of everything.' He went on to criticize the government for its refusal of Penny's services. 'There is no doubt,' Ainsworth reflected,

> that Captain Penny allowed his temper to get the better of his discretion, in his final intercourse with Captain Austin, after the discovery of Queen's Channel; but it is difficult to say how far he was driven to such extremes by the tone too often assumed by persons in office, or what latent jealousy may not have been manifested at his ... success. There are some points in Captain Penny's conduct decidedly open to censure; but they fade away into insignificance before the magnitude of his services. Sir Robert Inglis happily remarked, upon the paltry denial by official etiquette to the gallant mariner of his hard-earned title and reputation of captain, that gentlemen of the present day were apt to forget we had a Captain Cook.[131]

However, there was little to be done in practical terms, other than to await the outcome of Belcher's voyage. Throughout the rest of 1852 and most of 1853 commentary was confined mainly to reviews of search narratives. Two, Richardson's *Arctic Searching Expedition: A Journal of a boat Voyage through Rupert's Land and the Arctic Sea, in search of the discovery Ships under command of Sir John Franklin* and William Parker Snow's *Voyage of the Prince Albert in Search of Sir John Franklin: a Narrative of every-day Life in the Arctic Seas*, were published in late 1851; in 1852 they were followed by Osborn's *Stray Leaves from an Arctic Journal* and Peter Sutherland's *Journal of a Voyage in Baffin's Bay and Barrow Straits in the Years 1850–51 performed by H.M. Ships Lady Franklin and Sophia under the command of Mr. William Penny in Search of the missing Crews of H.M. Ships Erebus and Terror: with a Narrative of sledge Excursions on the Ice of Wellington Channel*. Sutherland's book, in particular, provided ample opportunity for critical remarks on government policy. Journals including the *Leisure Hour*, the *Examiner*, the *Spectator*, and the *New Monthly* strongly upheld Penny's cause, showing what wide appeal the populist vision of Arctic discovery now held.

The *Leisure Hour* repeated its earlier censure of Austin's decision not to remain in the Arctic another year and predicted that Belcher's expedition would vindicate Penny.[132] The *Examiner* stated that there was a strong belief among the public that Penny would have been successful 'if her majesty's government, or her majesty's orthodox officers, could have been content to let such an unorthodox fellow as a whaling master keep the lead that he had taken.'[133] The *Spectator* credited Penny with an intuitive understanding of the problem at hand, developed by his long experience in northern waters. His 'trusting faith' in his instincts formed 'a strong contrast to the more critical conclusion of Captain Austin.' Austin might technically have been right to return, but 'the critical or sceptical faculty is not the faculty for action.'[134] In the writer's opinion, better results would likely have been achieved by following Penny's lead.

The most glowing evaluation of Penny was published in the *New Monthly*. Ainsworth, who began in 1850 as a detached, sceptical critic of Arctic exploration, now portrayed Penny as a true hero of the people. Like Cook, Penny lacked 'the refinements of education and the nice conventionalisms of society,' but he possessed instead 'a rare experience, sound and extensive practical knowledge, an enlarged spirit of enterprise, [and] great perseverance.' Ainsworth predicted that Penny's name would 'be enrolled among those of the distinguished navigators of Great Britain,' and he thought that this honour was 'far more creditable than a disputed "captainship" or a barren knighthood.' The 'chivalry of modern times, which impelled the hardy Scot to buffet waves and storms, to force his way over icy wildernesses, and navigate an unknown Polar sea in the cause of suffering humanity' was true 'knight-errantry' of the highest order. Penny 'left all his rivals ... of the service and without the service, far in the rear in the amount of discovery effected, and in the important bearing of his researches.' Yet because he was '[w]ithout rhetoric, and unsophisticated,' his 'fearlessly expressed opinions' had 'terrified the officials.' It could only be hoped that Belcher would make his way north along the path Penny had blazed, though nothing but '"the relics" of our lòst countrymen' might remain to be found. Yet it was not impossible that, if that the naval commander followed the lead of the man of the people, all would still be well.[135]

As it turned out, however, the Belcher expedition only exacerbated the class-based conflicts of interpretation. The world of Admiralty officialdom was never in such low public repute as it was in the period from Belcher's return in 1854 to McClintock's departure in 1857.

8 The Duty of a People, 1852–1857

[I]f it be churlishly left to one woman to do the duty of a people, then will the one woman accept her fate. She will prepare as well as equip her own vessel. Volunteers will man it; and will bring home, we trust, such tidings as shall put our Admiralty Lords to eternal shame.

Henry Morley, 'Official Patriotism,' *Household Words*, April 1857

The period when Sir Edward Belcher's expedition remained in the field was an interval of relative calm before the storms of 1854. In the fall of 1854 issues of class and race sparked debates of a bitterness not previously known in Arctic literature. In 1852 and 1853, however, the yearly news from the north was of a generally positive nature.

William Kennedy returned in the fall of 1852. He could report only that extensive sledge journeys had been undertaken in Boothia and North Somerset, again without finding Franklin or any hint of his whereabouts. However, the length of Kennedy's journeys was cited in *Chambers's Repository* as proof of 'what it is in the power of a really intrepid traveller by skilful and judicious management to effect.'[1] The author of this article, published in early or mid-1853,[2] was convinced that even after eight years Franklin's men might still be alive. D.T. Coulton, reviewing several Arctic books in the March 1853 number of the *Quarterly Review*, agreed that though the searchers had as yet failed to find the lost explorers, their narratives proved 'that Franklin and his crews, if detained in some remote region of thick-ribbed ice, might not, even to this date, be reduced to utter extremity for want of food.'[3] Kennedy also brought back the encouraging report that Belcher had taken the *Assistance* and the *Pioneer* north through open water in

Wellington and Queen's channels. Captain Henry Kellett of the *Resolute*, meanwhile, was in command of the westward search.

In the autumn of 1853 Commander Edward Inglefield returned from a supply voyage in H.M.S. *Phoenix* with the sad news that Joseph-René Bellot, who had gone back to the Arctic as one of Inglefield's crew, was dead (he had drowned while travelling over the sea ice near Beechey Island). Bellot was mourned as one of the most chivalrous of all Arctic explorers, and a publicly funded monument was raised in his memory at Greenwich.[4]

Inglefield also brought the unexpected and sensational report that sledge parties sent to the west by Kellett had visited Parry's old winter quarters on Melville Island, where they found a message from Robert McClure. The *Investigator* was frozen in on the northern coast of Banks Island. A relief party was sent, and the *Investigator's* crew journeyed on foot to the *Resolute* and *Intrepid*, thus becoming the first men to cross from one ocean to another across the top of North America. The Northwest Passage had at last been traversed, though not in a ship. (Richard Collinson, meanwhile, had voyaged along the northern coast of the continent as far as Victoria Island, then returned to Bering Strait.) Though he and his men were still in the Arctic with Belcher and Kellett, McClure immediately became famous as the discoverer of the passage. A narrative based on his journal was written by Sherard Osborn, and published in 1856.

However, Belcher's own return in the autumn of 1854 was one of the deepest disappointments of the entire search. He had established a base far to the north, in latitude 77° 52', but had discovered no traces of Franklin. Four of his five ships were immobilized by ice during the summer of 1854. Rather than stay in the north for another season, Belcher decided to abandon the vessels and return on board the supply ships sent from England. The decision earned him much unfavourable press commentary. '[T]he motives given for the abandonment of the ships will appear to all who have carefully followed the proceedings in the Arctic regions to be perfectly inconclusive and unsatisfactory,'[5] was the judgment of an anonymous writer in *Bentley's Miscellany*. It was not merely that Belcher was unsuccessful in the search and had abandoned his ships – an act traditionally considered to disgrace any naval officer unless the extenuating circumstances were extremely strong. His conduct of the expedition seemed to confirm the worst that journalists had said about the arrogance of some naval captains.

Belcher was on very poor terms with his subordinates and demonstrated little concern for the welfare of his men. Osborn privately spoke of his 'want of judgment, consideration, or humanity.'[6] Belcher showed jealousy of those under his command who had more Arctic experience than he himself possessed, and was reluctant to consider their opinions. His conflicts with Osborn became so severe that Osborn was placed under arrest. In addition, Belcher did not adequately consult his officers before deciding to abandon the ships. The general suspicion of his motives was so high that Captain Kellett was careful to obtain explicit written orders before leaving the *Resolute*. Any commander who abandoned his vessel faced court martial, and Kellett was determined that it should be clear the full responsibility rested with Belcher.

The courts martial took place in October 1854, when the reading public was in a state of growing indignation over the bureaucratic and military incompetence detailed in *Times* correspondent William Howard Russell's despatches from the Crimea.[7] All the Arctic officers were acquitted; McClure and Kellett were commended by the court for their behaviour, but Belcher was not. A long and extremely indignant letter in the *Daily News* suggested that he should have been condemned, and that only the Admiralty's reluctance to admit its own mistakes had saved him. 'The Admiralty ... ought not to be allowed to stifle inquiry, to save themselves or their *protégés*,'[8] the writer fumed. Belcher was almost uniformly condemned by journalists as well. One 1855 article observed sardonically, 'Sir Edward ... holds an equal rank among Arctic navigators to that which Falstaff held among the captains on Shrewsbury field.'[9]

Harriet Martineau used the courts martial as the occasion for a summing-up of Arctic enterprise in a *Daily News* leading article. Of Franklin's men Martineau wrote: 'we must not now hope to see or hear of them again ... We cannot pay the usual honours to the dead bodies of our heroes; but we can pay very unusual honours to their immortal memories.'[10] Then on 23 October an entirely unexpected report from John Rae appeared in the *Times*.

While crossing Boothia in the spring of 1854, Rae had encountered a band of Inuit carrying articles that clearly had once belonged to Franklin's crew. On being questioned, they told him that they had obtained these items from other Inuit, who had taken them from the dead bodies of white men, near the mouth of the Great Fish River. There were about thirty-five bodies, and some were mutilated in such a way that the Inuit concluded the white men 'had been driven to the last resource – cannibalism – as a means of prolonging existence.'[11]

Rae's report was printed beside a letter responding to Russell's revelations about the appalling mortality among wounded soldiers in the inadequately equipped hospital at Scutari. 'To the roll-call of perished heroes, to the lists now daily swelling with noble names, of brave men battling against fearful odds, and dying in the performance of their duty, are to be added the names of the Arctic voyagers,' the *Examiner* lamented [12] The charge of the Light Brigade took place two days later and was quickly immortalized in verse by Tennyson. (His poem was printed in the *Examiner* on 9 December.) Journalists at once seized on Franklin's dreadful fate as evidence that here, too, 'someone had blundered.' In both cases, the heroism of soldiers and sailors was contrasted to the incompetence of the superiors who had so heedlessly sent them out to die. 'The most glaring apprehensions have been verified,' wrote the *Sun*, 'and what renders the fearful result even more deplorable is, that we now know that a large proportion of the party might have been rescued had the authorities at home displayed any degree of energy or activity.'[13] The *Atlas* charged that Franklin and his men had 'died of official pigheadedness and Admiralty neglect.'[14] The *Daily News* declared that the explorers 'might have been rescued had they been sought for in the right direction at the proper time'; but instead, 'unsuccoured ... they perished in the snow, after enduring the most horrible of all sufferings.' Their fate could only 'render more heavy than ever the moral responsibility' of the Admiralty.[15] The next day, the *News* repeated its condemnation. '[Franklin's] blood,' the article concluded dramatically, 'and the blood of his brave companions is on their heads!'[16]

October 1854 proved to be the hour of glory for which Richard King had waited so long: he was now hailed as a neglected prophet, whose warnings had gone unheeded by the arrogant, blinkered Admiralty. All these articles pointed to King, 'the Cassandra of this sad business,' as the one man who had realized the truth.[17] 'Dr. King has shewn that he knows more about Polar Discovery than any one else,'[18] wrote the *Observer*. The discomfort formerly caused by his vanity and self-promotion was forgotten, and the *Sun* went so far as to claim that '[e]very newspaper in England' had supported King's plans in 1847.[19] It was therefore with bureaucrats, and with bureaucrats alone, that responsibility for Franklin's death rested. The public was apparently willing to accept such claims. A letter to the editor of the *Sun* declared that the stain of the Admiralty's guilt could 'never, never' be washed off.[20] King himself referred to Franklin and his men as the 'Polar Victims,' and he drew up a list of the members of the Board of Admiralty between 1847 and 1854 in order to show, 'in a statistical form,' the 'exact amount of guilt which lies at each man's door.'[21]

The animosity demonstrated towards Rae at this time has often been pointed out in histories of Arctic exploration, but the vehement press criticism of the Admiralty is rarely even mentioned, and it is never examined in any detail. Nor is the sudden transformation of King's public image given much weight. For the time being, this former outsider was the people's hero, and if Rae was the object of public scorn, so too were the lords of the Admiralty. Once again, it is evident that the key distinction in the public mind was not between naval and non-naval explorers, but between those who represented the people and those who apparently thought only of their own ambition.

However, unlike King's rise from outcast to hero, Rae's fall from hero to outcast was not instantaneous. The process spanned the weeks from his return until the end of 1854. Initial press reactions centred on the accuracy of King's predictions and the guilt the Admiralty had incurred by ignoring him; the allegation that the lost explorers had committed cannibalism was not at first subjected to scrutiny. Instead, it was implied·that the desperate straits to which Franklin's men had been reduced proved the magnitude of the Admiralty's crime: had proper care been taken, such horrible events could never have taken place. 'We refrain from harrowing the feelings of our readers by repeating the condition in which their honoured remains were found; we would spare them and their friends such a recital. There is, however, a blood-stain somewhere,' declared the *Sun* on 25 October.[22] But it was not long until second thoughts and reservations came to the fore, and the manner in which the cannnibalism story was made public became a focus of attention.

It had not been Rae's intention to publicize the matter immediately on his return. He had already sent a report to Sir George Simpson of the Hudson's Bay Company in Montreal; on his arrival in England, Rae delivered another report to the Admiralty and wrote a letter to the *Times*. His two reports mentioned cannibalism, while the letter merely stated that 'a portion (if not all) of the then survivors of Sir John Franklin's long-lost, and ill-fated party perished of starvation in the spring of 1850 on the coast of America.'[23] Admiralty officials promptly gave Rae's report to the press. In it, Rae claimed his information proved 'beyond a doubt' that Franklin's men had met 'a fate as terrible as the imagination can conceive.'[24] Both the report and the letter were printed in the *Times* on 23 October. Further details about the condition of the bodies, presumbly elicited from Rae during an interview, followed the two documents.

Having declared on the 23rd that the report 'may be fairly considered decisive,'[25] the *Times* quickly voiced its full support of the government

point of view, stating in the next day's issue, 'The blame does not rest
upon the shoulders of any one at home.' The leader-writer preferred
not to 'dwell upon the horrors which obscured the dying hours of so
many noble-hearted men.' He regretted that it had not 'been in the
power of their countrymen to extricate them from their awful situation'
and insisted that he could 'in fairness say that we did all we could for
their relief.'[26] On the 26th, however, the *Times* expressed doubts about
Rae's claim. Whether these doubts stemmed only from a belated unwillingness to believe that Englishmen could be cannibals or from an
uncomfortable awareness of how effective a weapon the story was likely
to be for the Admiralty's critics must remain a matter for speculation. 'Is
the story told by the Esquimaux the true one?' a leader writer asked.
'Like all savages, they are liars.'[27]

Other journalists readily agreed that the second-hand information
conveyed by Rae was not sufficient to establish the fact of cannibalism.
(It should be remembered that Rae's informants had not themselves
seen the bodies.) The *Daily News* had remarked as early as 24 October
that reports from the Crimea 'show how easily even civilised and educated men can distort the truth, and work up incomplete oral com-
munications into adventurous romances.'[28] The *Examiner* noted on
28 October that the evidence was 'quite imperfect as to the manner of
the death, or as to the shocking incidents assumed to have preceded
it.'[29] On the same day the *Athenaeum* maintained, 'The suggestion about
the last despairing acts of the party seems to us absolutely unwarrant-
able on the evidence in court.' Like the *Times*, the *Athenaeum* implied
that Rae might have been duped by the Inuit, who, '[l]ike all savages ...
lie without scruple.'[30] Press criticism began to focus on Rae himself only
after a letter from the brother of an officer of the *Terror*, signed with the
initials E.J.H., appeared in the *Times* on 30 October. The writer, later
identified as the Reverend E.J. Hornby, stated: 'Dr. Rae has been deeply
reprehensible either in not verifying the report which he received from
the Esquimaux, or, if that was absolutely out of the question, in publishing the details of that report, resting, as they do, on grounds most weak
and unsatisfactory. He had far better have kept silence altogether than
have given us a story which ... pains the feelings of many.' Hornby also
asked, in phrases that echoed those used by Rae himself in 1850,
'Where the Esquimaux can live – where Dr. Rae's party could find abundant means – what should have prevented Sir John Franklin from
subsisting too?' And why, if the explorers were starving, should they
have troubled to carry with them the silver spoons and other articles

Rae had purchased from the Inuit? Hornby suggested that it was far more likely the Natives had plundered the abandoned ships, and that their story was a fabrication produced to account for their possession of the white men's belongings.[31]

Rae might have defended himself by pointing out that the Admiralty had released the news without consulting him. This would have been both a simple statement of fact and an effective way for Rae to deploy the now well-established trope of the Admiralty's callous arrogance. It would also certainly have been wise to show some compassion for the explorers' relatives, who had been given no forewarning whatever. Instead, Rae chose to attack the Reverend Hornby, employing a superior and sarcastic tone. Rae declared that he had been 'deeply pained and not a little surprised' by Hornby's letter. It would have been 'no difficult matter' for him to have verified the Inuit story, but doing so would have involved spending another winter in the Arctic, and he had considered it more important to stop further search expeditions. As for the question of why Franklin's men had been starving, 'No man but one perfectly unacquainted with the subject could ask such a question,' since '[t]hat portion of country near to, and on which a portion of Sir John Franklin's party was seen, is, in the spring, notoriously the most barren of animal life of any of the Arctic shores.' In his concluding sentences, Rae assumed the stance of the injured party. 'I trust,' he wrote, 'that any of the relatives of the lost navigators who may, in future, wish to make severe remarks on the mode in which I have acted ... will first do me the favour of communicating with me, and, if I cannot satisfy their doubts, it will then be quite time enough to make their opinions public. Such would be the more fair and satisfactory course.'[32]

The *Sun* had already noted, after the publication of Hornby's letter, that 'The more we reflect ... the less we are inclined to believe that this noble band of adventurers resorted to cannibalism.' Such an allegation required 'stronger proof, clearer evidence' than Rae could offer, and it was 'deeply to be regretted that Dr. Rae, upon such slender evidence, should have so summarily decided their fate, and turned ... when the distance between him and all that was mortal of our gallant immortal countrymen was *scarcely forty miles*.'[33] The *Sun* now reprinted Rae's response, adding the comment, 'We confess we do not like the tone of Dr. Rae's defence ... If Dr. Rae places so high a value upon his own judgement that he has a right to stand paramount, we do not.' Rae deserved 'all credit for boldness of character and unwearied industry,' but 'there is something about [his] language ... to which we strongly object':[34] Rae's sole aim seemed to be to enhance his own reputation, at no matter what cost in emotional terms to the dead explorers' families.

The *Times* tried to stem the movement towards condemnation of Rae, while pointing out that Hornby deserved more sympathy than Rae had shown him. 'It would be cruel to criticize harshly the opinions of a gentleman who writes under the influence of such deep and distressing feelings; but we cannot but hope that a little consideration will show him that he has been hasty in his strictures,' declared a leading article on 2 November. Turning to the question of cannibalism, the leader writer observed, 'We would fain touch as lightly as may be upon the most terrible portion of Dr. RAE's narrative. Of what avail, indeed, is any remark in such a case, beyond a brief and heartfelt expression of sympathy and sorrow?' He suggested that further discussion should be suspended until definite proof became available: 'The story may or may not be true, but it would be cruel indeed to harrow up the feelings of friends and relatives by premature speculation upon the truth or falsehood of so distressing a tale.'[35]

King (who had already demanded that he should be placed in command of an expedition to retrieve Franklin's records)[36] now joined the debate with a letter to the *Examiner*, in which he stated that Rae had 'formed an opinion solely upon his pantomimic conversation with the Esquimaux' and was 'still striving to maintain that opinion, solely, and irrespective of all others.' King himself was convinced that the explorers had been massacred by the Inuit.[37] He was not the only one to entertain such extreme suspicions: *Bentley's Miscellany* agreed that not only were the Inuit unreliable witnesses, but '[t]he horrible addition of mutilated bodies and cannibalism appears as if suggested by the fate experienced by the unfortunate travellers at the hands of the savage natives. It was the story which first suggested itself to shield the crimes they had committed.'[38]

Hornby, meanwhile, had written directly to Rae in polite and conciliatory terms. He apologized for any harsh words that might have caused Rae pain, but firmly reiterated that, as cannibalism had not been definitely proven, the allegation should not have been made public. Rae sent this letter to the *Times* for publication along with his reply, in which he asserted that Hornby's first letter had been 'both harsh and unjust.' He offered no sympathy for Hornby's distress at the publication of the report, but he did point out that it had been his duty to inform the Admiralty of the Inuit stories, 'leaving it for them to publish as much, or as little, of such report as they considered right and proper.'[39]

At the same time as Rae made these public statements, in private he aroused the dislike and opposition of Lady Franklin and the explorers associated with her. None had originally questioned his report of cannibalism. John Richardson, for example, wrote to Franklin's daughter Eleanor on 23 October, 'The only consolation I can offer to you, beside that devout resignation to God's will which I know has hitherto been your stay, is the reflection that your Father must have sunk either previous to the abandonment of the ships or under the fatigues of the early part of the spring journey,' and so he almost certainly had not been present at 'the last sad scene.'[40] Other friends and relatives also accepted the story. 'Painful tidings of the Arctic expedition,' was Emily Tennyson's short journal entry.[41]

Many of Lady Franklin's supporters met with Rae, expecting that he would help them to promote other searches. At the request of Sir Francis Beaufort, Rae drew up a plan for a new expedition, and a copy was sent to the *Times* for publication.[42] Lady Franklin, however, was far from satisfied with Rae's proposal. They seem to have met on several occasions, and he repeatedly told her that, although only thirty-five bodies had been seen by the Inuit, there could be no doubt that all the explorers had died at the mouth of the Great Fish River. He also said he was certain the ships had been crushed in the ice. Lady Franklin thought the explorers might well have broken up into small parties, travelling in different directions to increase their chances of survival, and she did not agree that the destruction of the ships had been proved.

Rae's plan was to send two canoes down the Great Fish River; nothing was said about making a search either for the ships or for men who might have attempted to escape by other routes. The Admiralty was not willing to send naval officers, but instead requested the Hudson's Bay Company to organize the search (which the government, however, would pay for). In a letter to Murchison written on 6 November, Jane Franklin declared that it was 'most unreasonable' to assume there had been no other detachments. 'And think what the finding of the ships, if they be still in existence, involves!' she exclaimed. 'I do not mean the rescue of any human being, but surely the ships could hardly fail to disclose some memorials of their history.'[43] Her niece Sophia Cracroft (Lady Franklin's closest confidante) also wrote to Murchison, at much greater length, on the same day. She assured him that her aunt's objections did 'not originate in any tendency to disparage Mr. Rae'; Lady Franklin was merely frustrated to find that 'he has formed certain very positive conclusions from the information he has obtained, and to these he clings with infinite tenacity.' Cracroft pointed out, 'With assumptions so positively maintained on the part of Mr Rae, it is hardly to be expected that [the searchers] … will either look for the ships or for any other of the unfortunate parties.' Neither of these letters contained any criticism of Rae for having made the allegation of cannibalism, or any statement to indicate that Jane Franklin had rejected the story out of hand. Indeed, Cracroft wrote that only two of Rae's conclusions were important: 'the one that the ships have been crushed; the other, that the party reported to him were the sole survivors of the expedition.'[44] The next day, Cracroft wrote again, stating that Lady Franklin was 'convinced strong pressure will be required' to organize 'an *effectual* search,' unless these two conclusions could 'be combated successfully.'[45]

Such private criticism of Rae paled before the remarks made publicly by King. Rae's report to the Hudson's Bay Company, sent to Sir George Simpson in Montreal, had been made public on 21 October, and was printed in the Montreal *Herald*. When copies reached London, it appeared in many British newspapers. King pounced on the new report, pointing to a passage in which Rae stated that he had heard the Inuit story while on his outward, rather than his return, journey. It therefore appeared that Rae might have abandoned the survey and devoted himself to investigating the Inuit report, without there being any need to pass another winter in the Arctic. According to King, Rae had wished to have the renown of making fresh geographical discoveries in Boothia. '[I]nstead of directing his steps to the tragedy before him … he turned his back upon these painfully interesting lands, and … proceeded upon his paltry discovery,' King accused. 'Although I had always my misgiving of Dr. Rae's ability as a traveller, I always gave him credit for enterprise and manly bearing; I am therefore astonished beyond measure that he could have written such language to "E.J.H." in the face of his statements to Sir George Simpson.'[46]

Rae now stood publicly accused of duplicitous, self-serving behaviour, to which was soon added the suspicion that he had returned mainly in order to claim the large reward the Admiralty had offered for news of Franklin's fate. Rae had been invited to lecture to the Royal Geographical Society on 13 November, and Murchison (who could not be present, owing to illness) wrote a frantic letter urging that 'poor Dr Rae' be treated courteously.[47] In the end, Rae did not appear. Instead, a second, longer report to the Hudson's Bay Company,[48] written mainly after Rae's return to England, which had been forwarded to the Society by the HBC, was read on his behalf. Rae now stated that though he had first encountered the Inuit on his outward journey, it was not until his return to his base that he had the opportunity to question them in detail. Only then did he realize that the location referred to was the mouth of the Great Fish River.[49] Many of Rae's critics professed to find this explanation unsatisfactory, asking why he had proceeded with his survey when he might have taken the time to elicit fuller information at once.

In December 1854 the main focus of public attention shifted. This was due to the intervention of Charles Dickens, whose article 'The Lost Arctic Voyagers' appeared in the 2 and 9 December issues of *Household Words*. Dickens staunchly defended Rae on all points but one. He began by clearly stating that he was 'fully convinced' of 'the propriety of [Rae's] immediate return to England with the intelligence he had got together.' As a man of 'sense and humanity,' Rae had 'perceived that the first and greatest account to which [the news] could be turned, was, the prevention of the useless hazard of valuable lives' in further searches up Wellington Channel. As for the release of the report, it was indeed Rae's simple duty to inform the Admiralty of the allegations; therefore, 'it is quite clear that if it were an ill-considered proceeding to disseminate this painful idea ... Dr. Rae is not responsible for it.'[50]

Now that the matter had been made public, if Rae believed the stories of cannibalism, he had 'all the rights to defend his opinion which his high reputation as a skilful and intrepid traveller of great experience in the Arctic Regions – combined with his manly, conscientious, and modest personal character – can possibly invest him with.' However, Dickens stated his own conviction that it was 'in the highest degree improbable that such men as the officers and crews of the two lost ships would, or could, in any extremity of hunger, alleviate the pains of starvation by this horrible means.' Dickens intended to make as strong a case against Rae's conclusions as he could, and he hoped his article would 'tend to the consolation of those who take the nearest and dearest interest in the fate of that unfortunate expedition.' He stated that the Inuit evidence was 'given, at the very best, at second-hand'; he then went on to claim that 'every savage [is] in his heart covetous, treacherous, and cruel.' It seemed to him highly likely that, as King had suggested, the Inuit had murdered the explorers. Dickens then turned to a discussion of Franklin's character, which in his opinion provided the strongest available proof that the Inuit stories could not be true. The remainder of the article was taken up mainly by a summary of and quotations from Franklin's first narrative. Dickens described the book as 'one of the most explicit and enthralling in the whole literature of Voyage and Travel. The facts are acted and suffered before the reader's eyes.'[51]

Dickens may have read the narrative in its entirety, but according to the editors of the 1853–5 volume of his letters, he did not own a copy. He did, however, have Barrow's *Voyages of Discovery and Research* in his library, and it was apparently from the copious extracts reprinted in this volume that he took the material for 'The Lost Arctic Voyagers.'[52] Here Dickens would also have read the passage from Barrow's *Quarterly* review. Barrow's interpretation of the narrative clearly influenced Dickens: the latter ended his series of quotations with Richardson's statement that Michel Teroahauté had killed his comrades because he lacked the religious faith which alone could have sustained him through his ordeal. As Barrow had done, Dickens explained that the Englishmen were able to behave more heroically than others because of their strong moral code.

In the second instalment of the article, Dickens detailed other cases in which Englishmen had been exposed to severe temptation, but preferred to suffer and even die rather than eat human flesh. Inevitably, he included the story of the *Méduse* (see chap. 4) in order to demonstrate once more that lesser men, of other nations, might find such temptation beyond their ability to resist. He pointed out that many of the French soldiers on the raft were ex-convicts, 'the scourged and branded sweepings of the galleys of France'; it was surely absurd to compare these men to 'the flower of the trained adventurous spirit of the English Navy.' Dickens also argued that because cannibalism was so horrible a crime, any accusation required 'the most direct and positive evidence ... even as occurring among savage people, against whom it was in earlier times too often a pretence for cruelty and plunder.' In conclusion, he reminded his readers of the fortitude shown by the members of Franklin's first expedition. According to Dickens, the 'foremost question' was 'not the nature of the extremity; but, the nature of the men.' He argued that the memory of the lost Arctic explorers was 'placed, by reason and experience, high above the taint of this so easily-allowed connection; and ... the noble conduct and example of such men, and of their own great leader himself, under similar endurances, belies it, and outweighs by ... the weight of the whole universe the chatter of a gross handful of uncivilised people, with a domesticity of blood and blubber.' Invoking the traditional metanarrative of Arctic exploration against the new elements introduced into the story by Rae, Dickens made a moving appeal to his countrymen: 'Because no Franklin can come back, to write the honest story of their woes and resignation, read it tenderly and truly in the book he has left us ... teach no one to shudder without reason, at the history of their end ... confide with their own firmness, in their fortitude, their lofty sense of duty, their courage, and their religion.'[53]

Dickens's racism, which has often been remarked on,[54] is evident, as is the great cultural power of the Arctic narrative. According to Dickens, Franklin's words 'outweighed by the weight of the whole universe' the Inuit stories, which were merely 'the chatter of a gross handful of uncivilised people.'[55] Yet this flagrantly racist article was not, as many twentieth-century writers have claimed, an inevitable development. In many ways, the Arctic narrative had been growing ever more flexible and inclusive over the decades. When Rae's news was first published, journalists and the reading public did not immediately assume that there could be no truth in what the Inuit said. While questions were raised about the second-hand nature of the account, initial responses, both public and private, did not deny the possibility that the story was true. Some journalists, indeed, were eager to accept it in order to blacken the Admiralty. Despite the pain the story caused them, Richardson, Lady Franklin, and other friends and relatives of the missing explorers also accepted (or at least did not deny) it at first. Racism and denial, in other words, were not central to Arctic discourse before 1854. In earlier years, Franklin and Richardson had represented Akaitcho and his hunters in a very favourable light, while refusing to entirely condemn the cannibal Teroahauté. Although Barrow's interpretation of the Arctic story was based on the contrasts he drew between Britons and 'others,' the most important 'others' were Franklin's voyageurs. Any criticism of the Natives encountered by Franklin and Parry was expressed in relatively restrained terms. But Dickens, with the imaginative power of a great writer, constructed a stark dichotomy between heroic explorers and treacherous, lying savages.

Dickens was evidently motivated by a profound and sincere admiration for Franklin's character. He also seems to have had an unusually strong abhorrence of cannibalism. Harry Stone has speculated that, for psychological reasons, Dickens's feelings about it were particularly intense.[56] The causes of his response, therefore, lay more in his individual psyche than in the wider culture of his time. However, his shaping of the Arctic narrative was to have far-reaching negative effects. It increasingly seemed essential that the Inuit story should be rejected in order to protect the explorers' reputations. On the subject of cannibalism, a rigid, hostile cast of mind became common. Rae's rebuttal of

Dickens, published in *Household Words* on 23 and 30 December, did little to remedy this and, in fact, only exacerbated the situation. His
response to Hornby had already shown that, like John Ross, Rae had
little awareness of the constraints imposed upon his public utterances
by the conventions of Arctic discourse.[57] As a result, he made several
serious blunders.

His article, like Dickens's piece, was published in two parts, and the
first makes a much better impression than the second. Rae began by
assuring readers that he had scrutinized the Inuit stories 'with the
utmost caution' and that 'not one material point ... was published to
the world without my having some good reason to support it.' As proof
of the reliability of Inuit information, he reported that his discoveries in
Boothia coincided almost perfectly with maps the Natives had drawn for
John and James Ross. Moreover, although over twenty years had passed
since the *Victory* expedition, Inuit who had never actually met the Rosses
were able to describe them in such accurate detail 'that any one
acquainted with these officers could have recognised them.' Their
knowledge of the events of the Ross expedition was equally comprehensive. Rae had mentioned in passing that all the white men had returned
safely to England; the Inuit 'immediately remarked, "that this was not
true, for some of the men had died at the place where the vessel was
left." I, of course, alluded only to that portion of the party who had got
away from Regent's Inlet in safety.' Rae pointedly observed that only
'those who know them not' could regard the Inuit as 'uneducated savages ... little better than brutes,' and he asked 'what possible motive'
they could have for inventing the cannibalism story.[58]

These were excellent points, not easily refuted, but the article also contained some less convincing arguments. Rae claimed that his interpreter,
William Ouligback, was entirely reliable and trustworthy. However,
because Rae himself had not the slightest knowledge of Inuktitut and
therefore no means of evaluating Ouligback's veracity, he made enquiries
about him before the beginning of the expedition. He was told that
Ouligback was an excellent interpreter and could be trusted without
reserve in most circumstances, but 'when he had any personal object to
gain, he would not scruple to tell a falsehood to attain it, but in such a
case the untruth was easily discovered by a little cross-questioning.' Rae
reported that this description had proved to be 'perfectly true.' He therefore implicitly admitted that Ouligback had been detected in a lie or lies,
and his own confidence that there had been no undetected deceptions
would not necessarily have been shared by his readers. Another of Rae's

claims seemed strange and unconvincing: he insisted that it was precisely because the information was not first-hand that it was so reliable. 'Had it been obtained from the natives who had seen the dead bodies of our countrymen, I should have doubted all they told me, however plausible their tale appeared,' Rae wrote. This was because 'had they, as they usually do, deposited any property under stones in the neighbourhood, they would have had a very excellent cause for attempting to mislead me.'[59]

These admissions that both Ouligback and the other Inuit were capable of deception did not help Rae's cause. The point was emphasized again in the second instalment of his article, which began with the statement: 'When the Esquimaux have an object to gain, they will not hesitate to tell a falsehood, but they cannot lie with a good grace; they cannot "lie like truth," as civilised men do. Their fabrications are so silly and ridiculous, and it is so easy to make them contradict themselves by a slight cross-questioning, that the falsehood is easily discovered.'[60] Rae, therefore, believed the Inuit not so much because he considered them honest as because he considered himself well able to see through them when they lied: surely an exaggerated claim from a man who, for all his long northern experience, had spent relatively little time with these people and did not understand their language.

Rae's other commendations of the Inuit were also somewhat unusual. He remarked that the Inuit of Labrador were considered good and reliable servants by the missionaries who lived among them, and that the men of his own expedition had found the Natives 'decorous, obliging, unobtrusive, orderly, and friendly.' Then, for no apparent reason, he defended his men against the possible charge that they had spoken so well of the Inuit only because they were sexually involved with the women. He declared that this was not the case, whatever might have occurred on other expeditions. 'I firmly believe, and can almost positively assert,' he exclaimed, 'that no case of improper intercourse took place between them and the natives of Repulse Bay ... which is more, I suspect, than most of the commanders of parties to the Arctic Sea can truthfully affirm.' This broad innuendo about other expeditions was followed by specific criticism of Franklin's crews. 'Much stress is laid on the moral character and the admirable discipline of the crews of Sir John Franklin's ships,' Rae remarked. 'What their state of discipline may have been I cannot say, but their conduct at the very last British port they entered was not such as to make those who knew it, consider them very deserving of the high eulogium passed upon them in Household Words.'[61] This referred to an incident at Stromness, where four sailors, after drinking whisky smuggled on board the *Erebus*, attempted to desert.[62] It was hardly enough to condemn two entire crews, but Rae declared he was far from certain 'that the men, in extreme cases of privation, would maintain that state of subordination so requisite in all cases, but more especially during danger and difficulty.' He referred to the dissensions on Belcher's expedition and demanded why it should be assumed that 'comparatively uneducated' seamen would conduct themselves heroically. If Franklin's officers, like Belcher's, had been unable to agree among themselves, would this not have contributed to a breakdown in discipline? And besides, 'seamen generally consider themselves, when they have lost their ship and set foot on shore, as being freed from that strict discipline to which they would readily submit themselves when on board.'[63]

Rae therefore appeared to be suggesting that Franklin's officers were incapable of maintaining order, and that his crews were a lustful rabble, likely to have rebelled almost as soon as the ships were abandoned. Presumably, the cannibals had been sailors and the officers their victims. In a time of heated class disputes, this implication would not have endeared Rae to the mass of his countrymen, and his gratuitous slurs against dead men did nothing to promote the idea that he would not make accusations without good reason. (Rae, of course, likely did not intend to insult the memory of the lost explorers, but his remarks were certainly interpreted in that way.)

Rae concluded his article by drawing a contrast between Dickens, 'a writer of very great ability and practice,' and himself, a plain-spoken man of action. 'To oppose [him], I have nothing but a small amount of practical knowledge of the question at issue, with a few facts to support my views and opinions; but, I can only throw them together in a very imperfect and unconnected form, as I have little experience in writing, and, like many men who have led a wandering and stirring life, have a great dislike to it,' Rae wrote.[64] This was a trope of exploration discourse that should have been greatly to his advantage. However, the speculations and unproven accusations contained in the later part of the second article had made the role of the plain, honest man unavailable to Rae. The author of an exploration account was expected to show generosity of spirit and to praise rather than speak ill of other explorers. A man of feeling, no matter what his rank or occupation, would instinctively respect the ties of family affection. Rae's defence of the Inuit might well have succeeded had it not been accompanied by unnecessary aspersions on Franklin's men. Dickens's logic and his facts were unquestionably inferior to Rae's; however, his fervent admiration of Franklin, his generous praise of Rae's accomplishments, and his warmhearted impulse to relieve the mental suffering of the explorers' relatives had greater public appeal than Rae's apparent lack of empathy.

Rae's public image would never recover from the damage inflicted on it by these articles. Other circumstances combined to make it difficult for him to rehabilitate himself. Some were not of his choosing; for example, the Hudson's Bay Company had put forward a claim to the Admiralty reward on Rae's behalf, and Rae was informed that, since he was clearly entitled to this large sum of money, it did not seem necessary for the company to reward his services. He was denied even his regular pay, since he had returned to England without completing the whole of his survey.[65] HBC officials apparently reasoned that, since Rae had left the Arctic to carry information to the Admiralty, he had become more the Admiralty's employee than the company's, and therefore the Admiralty should pay him.[66] The matter of the award was to cause Rae many problems, as it could so easily be used to make him appear self-serving. However, because of the HBC's parsimonious attitude, he had little alternative but to pursue the claim.

In addition, Rae offended Lady Franklin and her friends when he decided not to return her husband's belongings to her. Instead, he presented them to the Admiralty, and they were put on display in the Painted Hall of the naval hospital at Greenwich. Rae was later given some of the items to keep (he was frequently photographed with them),[67] but the original owners' families received nothing.[68] Through such actions, Rae become firmly associated with the Admiralty in the public mind, and among the adherents of the populist interpretation, explorers who were thought to court favour in the corrupt world of officialdom were always suspect.

Finally, Rae's credibility received a serious blow early in 1855, when an article first printed in the Toronto *Christian Guardian* on 3 January reached England. Missionary Thomas Hurlburt reported that one of Rae's men, a Cree named Thomas Mistegan, had told him it was possible that a few of the lost explorers were still living among the Inuit. According to Hurlburt, Mistegan also claimed that Rae's Inuit informants had possessed many articles made of oak wood, and obviously taken from the two ships. Rae had earlier denied that he saw wood or any other indication that the Inuit had visited the ships.[69] As a result, published references to Rae grew increasingly sceptical and sometimes even contemptuous. He was frequently criticized for his failure to investigate the scene of the alleged cannibalism.[70] Rae protested through letters to the press, but in vain.[71] Private references were also negative and sceptical: Osborn, for example, reported to Lady Franklin in June 1856 that at a meeting of the Royal Geographical Society, 'Rae pledged himself as to the gentle truth telling disposition of his amiable Esquimo's [sic] or if they ever told a lie the facility with which he could always unravel it.'[72] John Ross had earlier written that he was 'quite convinced of the truth of [Rae's] statements,' but neither he nor any other Arctic explorer came forward publicly in support of Rae.[73]

Negative evaluations of both Rae and the Inuit had become standard. But if the Arctic narrative was growing more rigid on issues of race in the mid-1850s, at the same time it broadened with regard to gender. After Belcher's return, government involvement in the search came to an end. This left the field open for individual initiative, and that the search continued was due mainly to Lady Franklin. King was far too eccentric and combative to keep the public's favour for long, and he soon faded from view. Jane Franklin, on the other hand, received ever more extensive publicity. She had been in the public eye since 1848, when she offered a reward of £1,000 to any whaling captain bringing news of the lost expedition,[74] and she had frequently been praised for her diligent devotion to her husband's cause. In April 1849 she wrote to the president of the United States, Zachary Taylor, appealing for American help in the search. The letter was described as beautiful and touching (speaking in the House of Commons, Robert Harry Inglis called it 'one of the most eloquent letters which has ever been written'),[75] and the chivalrous tone of the American reply was also widely remarked on.[76] In addition, she organized the two expeditions in the *Prince Albert* and Inglefield's voyage to Baffin Bay. These expeditions were paid for by a combination of public subscriptions and Lady Franklin's own money.

All this had gained her the reputation of being an 'estimable lady,'[77] so affectionate and devoted to her duty as a wife that she was willing to make 'unceasing sacrifices'[78] in order to bring her lost husband home. 'What energies she has put forth, what anxieties she has endured, and how noble has been her conduct throughout!' exclaimed the *News of the World* in 1851.[79] However, the most fervent applause had until now gone to the explorers themselves. It was only after 1854 that Jane Franklin took a truly central role and was constructed not only as the ideal of English womanhood, but as the embodiment of the spirit of the people. Her unwavering devotion was contrasted with the government's indifference. 'Lady Franklin, we understand, contemplates the renewal of a

task which it would be a disgrace to the country to leave to her. Already
… its official representatives have tarnished their honour by their treatment of this lady,' wrote the *Spectator* in November 1854. The author
noted that, while Jane Franklin fulfilled her obligations as a wife to the
utmost of her ability, the government's duty had been only reluctantly
and negligently carried out: 'Did Franklin go out in the service of his
wife, or of his country? Did he encounter death in any mission of hers,
or in adding to that knowledge which he had already procured for his
country? Domestic affection pointed out her duty; public virtue should
point out another kind of duty towards a public servant.'[80]

The perceived significance of Jane Franklin's actions was that her
duty as a wife, which under normal circumstances would have been carried out entirely in the private sphere, had through no choice of her
own forced her into the realm of public action. An individual woman,
seeking only to fulfil personal obligations, was able to perform far better
than the men who should have held themselves responsible for the lost
explorers' safety. 'Domestic affection' had lessons to teach in 'public virtue.' Lady Franklin was therefore the representative of all those ordinary men and women whose lives were lived in relative obscurity and
whose best qualities were exercised in the privacy of their homes. She
was a symbol of the people and their collective virtues. In 1856 she was
described as 'that sublime Lady Franklin, whose conduct … does honour to a whole epoch and a whole nation.'[81]

Ironically enough, Jane Franklin's unyielding determination caused
serious conflicts with her friends and family. Her private life was the
scene of a bitter feud with her stepdaughter, Eleanor. Nevertheless, to
the public she embodied all that was good in English domestic life, and
the readers of Arctic literature seem to have fervently supported the
idea that in order for the nation to prosper, the domestic virtues must
be brought into the public sphere.

The active role taken by Lady Franklin was not seen as a threat to conventional constructions of femininity because, like her husband and his
fellow explorers, she reiterated at every opportunity that she felt quite
unfit for, and indeed disliked, a public role. Only necessity and deep
emotion, she claimed, could have brought her to address the public.
She wrote to President Taylor that she felt 'misgivings' lest her 'intense
anxieties' might have 'led me to press too earnestly on your notice the
trial under which we are suffering.' Yet, she concluded, 'if you deem this
to be the case, you will still find, I am sure, even in that personal intensity of feeling, an excuse for the fearlessness with which I have thrown

myself on your generosity.'[82] Lady Franklin was therefore always credited with great modesty – an essential feminine characteristic – and she was accorded all the more respect because her efforts were made despite her 'natural' feminine timidity and reserve. It was assumed that only the most profound conjugal love could be the motive for her sacrifice of both money and natural feeling. The rare spectacle of such intimate private emotion finding expression in the public sphere had an appeal similar to that of fiction, and, like the exploration narratives written by men, it was all the more moving and powerful because the story was true.

Lady Franklin was both pitied for the public role that bureaucratic incompetence forced upon her and enthusiastically admired for the intelligence and ability with which she approached her uncongenial task. In 1859 a reader using the pen name 'Hampden' wrote to the *News of the World*, declaring that Lady Franklin, who fulfilled the highest ideal of womanhood, was a figure 'to contemplate, to admire, and to bow down to with all the homage and devotion that a human being may bestow.'[83] Her strength was accepted and even extolled because she was always careful to surround it with an aura of feminine softness. William Kennedy referred to her 'truly feminine yet heroic spirit.'[84] According to Clements Markham, the young men who rallied to Lady Franklin's cause were 'impressed by her remarkable intelligence and by her gentle and very prepossessing manner.'[85] Tennyson, her nephew by marriage, thought that 'Aunt Franklin' was 'charming, so clever yet so gentle & such a lady.'[86] She always deferred (or seemed to defer) to male opinion and turned to men to speak for her when her views were likely to arouse opposition. Her letters provide ample evidence of how carefully she had to manoeuvre and how essential it often was for her to employ the most indirect and subtle methods.[87]

Even so, at first she met with some disapproval. Soon after the announcement of the 1849 *Prince Albert* voyage, rumours spread that Lady Franklin and Miss Cracroft intended to go to the Arctic themselves. Parry was aghast. '*[T]his must not be*,'[88] he wrote to Eleanor Franklin. Jane herself carefully explained that she and Sophia had never so much as considered the possibility, since two women would 'cut a very poor figure' on an exploring expedition.[89] She protested that she had acted only after careful deliberation, and with the advice of experienced men.

Much of the initial support she received was, in fact, reluctantly given. Parry, for example, explained to Eleanor Franklin that her stepmother had *not* consulted him before announcing her plan, and that had she done so, he would have advised against it. However, as she was so determined, he thought it best to help her.[90] The enthusiastic public response soon secured Lady Franklin's position, and whatever the reservations felt by those whose Arctic reputations were already established, aspiring explorers eager to make their names gathered around her. In the early 1850s Penny, Kennedy, and Bellot were the best known of her protégés. Their popularity, great though it was, could not rival that later achieved by Elisha Kent Kane.

In the aftermath of Rae's allegations, Kane did much to reassure the public that the great tradition of Arctic heroism was not dead. He served on the first American search expedition in 1850–1, then led the second in 1853–5. Kane took his ship, the *Advance*, to Smith Sound at the northern end of Baffin Bay, seeking a way into Barrow's 'open polar sea.' The *Advance* was frozen into winter quarters on the coast of Greenland for two years; in the summer of 1855 Kane led his men on a 1,000-mile march south to the Danish settlements. (On his arrival there, he was greeted with the news that Sebastopol had not fallen. 'Where and what [is] Sebastopol?' was his response.)[91] A key feature of the expedition's survival during its second polar winter was the adoption of a diet similar to that of the Inuit. Kane's resourcefulness and his success in adapting to the northern environment were seen as proof that Mistegan's report of possible Franklin survivors might be true.

In 1856 and 1857 Jane Franklin's appeals and Kane's narrative together would keep interest in the Arctic search alive. However, there was a hiatus for most of 1855. Discussion was necessarily suspended until news came from James Anderson, the leader of the Hudson's Bay Company expedition down the Great Fish River, and Arctic publications were scantier in this year than in any other of the decade. Indeed, a reviewer in *Tait's Edinburgh Magazine* suggested that the Arctic story was now over.[92]

Despite the diminished level of Arctic activity and interest, with only two expeditions remaining in the field, the process of literary extraction and compilation still continued in a seemingly endless cycle, with the publication of such new books as Fanny Mayne's *Voyages and Discoveries in the Arctic Regions.* (It appeared in the Longman Travellers' Library series in 1855, with new editions in 1856 and 1862.) At the same time, a new element was added with the writing and publication of the first Arctic biographies. The subjects were Bellot, Franklin, and Parry. Bellot's journal of the second *Prince Albert* expedition, prefaced by a biographical memoir, appeared in 1855. The memoir, written by Julien Lemer, emphasized Bellot's humble origin, his loving devotion to his family, and his chivalrous support of Lady Franklin. A reviewer in the *Dublin University Magazine* commented, 'Being dead he yet speaketh, teaching, by his own story, the uses, personal and social, of legitimate and honourable ambition.'[93]

A short but extremely influential biography of Franklin was written by John Richardson in late 1855 or early 1856. It was published both in the eighth edition of the *Encyclopaedia Britannica* and in pamphlet form. In his account of the last expedition, Richardson ignored the question of cannibalism, emphasizing instead that the men who reached the Great Fish River had traversed the last unknown part of the Northwest Passage. In a phrase which was to be widely quoted, he wrote that the 'last link' of the passage 'was forged by Franklin's party with their lives.' In his concluding paragraph, Richardson explained to his readers that his account had been 'written by one who served long under [Franklin's] command, who during upwards of twenty-five years of close intimacy had his entire confidence, and in times of great difficulty and distress, when all conventional disguise was out of the question, beheld his calmness and unaffected piety. If it has in some passages assumed the appearance of eulogy, it has done so not for the purpose of unduly exalting its subject, but from a firm conviction of the truth of the statements.'[94] Lady Franklin sent a copy of the pamphlet to Dickens, who was deeply moved by this first-hand account of his hero's character. 'I think Richardson's manly friendship, and love of Franklin, one of the noblest things I ever knew in my life. It makes one's heart beat high, with a sort of sacred joy,' he wrote to his friend John Forster.[95]

Parry died in 1855 and a biography written by his son was published early in 1857.[96] It was extremely popular, going through nine editions between 1857 and 1868. For the first time, Parry's deep religious faith was made public. As one approving reviewer noted, 'it is not chiefly as a navigator, a discoverer, or a man of science and enterprise, that we are called to survey this simple but faithful portraiture of a true British sailor. His useful and eventful life is filled with incidents that must arrest attention; but combined with all these noble qualities which the world admires, his character rested on the solid basis of a pure and living Christianity.' Parry's faith was 'active and practical,' showing that religion was anything but 'inconsistent with the zealous and efficient discharge of every public and private duty.'[97]

As the lives and characters of dead Arctic heroes assumed a clearer shape in the public mind, living explorers continued to figure prominently in the news. In the autumn of 1855 Kane returned from

Greenland, and his exploits were widely publicized. In January 1856 the report of Anderson's expedition was published. The HBC party had searched the mouth of the Great Fish River without making any effort to venture farther afield. Only nine days were spent in the area. Anderson found clear indications that Franklin's men had been on Montreal Island, including tools, wood chips and shavings, a piece of wood with 'Terror' carved on it, and pieces of rope. However, he saw no bodies at all, on either the island or the mainland.[98] Osborn wrote to Lady Franklin that Anderson's report had 'awakened more hopes & fears than I like to give utterance to.'[99] Anderson himself, however, staunchly refused to admit that his findings gave any reason to question Rae's report. Instead, he argued that the explorers had likely died near the shore, and that their bodies had been either washed away by the tide or slowly covered over by wind-blown sand. Anderson stated that the chips and shavings had been produced when the Inuit, finding the possessions left by the dead explorers, cut up their boat in order to make the wood into sledges. The explanation was clearly a weak one, since it was difficult to image how bodies could disappear while wood chips and shavings remained in place. 'Anderson's sole object, as might be expected, was to confirm Rae's story of their having perished in a partr spot, tho' he brings no new proof of it but quite the reverse,' an exasperated Lady Franklin wrote to Murchison.[100] Osborn later criticized Anderson's version of events in a lengthy appendix to his narrative of McClure's voyage.[101]

Jane Franklin and her supporters were more exasperated still when an article from the Montreal *Herald* reached England in mid-January. It showed that the Hudson's Bay Company was determined to present Rae's story as conclusive and unquestionable. The HBC's spokesman had informed reporters that Rae's account 'was received by the public in England with great hesitation, arising, probably, from an unwillingness to believe the mournful facts.' Because Rae's 'proceedings and conclusions' had been 'frequently called into question,' it would be 'the more gratifying to him, now that they are fully corroborated,' even to minute details of locality &c. in which he might possibly have been mistaken.' Anderson's expedition was lavishly praised for its perfect organization and efficiency. In conclusion, the spokesman defiantly asserted that no more would ever be determined about the expedition's fate.[102]

The Admiralty had previously informed Rae that a decision on his claim to the reward must be deferred until Anderson was heard from. The company's motive for insisting that Anderson had 'fully corroborated' Rae, and that no further search was necessary to determine Franklin's fate, was clearly to ensure that Rae received the money. The Admiralty, not wishing to prolong the search, was ready enough to agree. On 22 January the *London Gazette* contained the announcement that Rae's claim would be adjudicated in three months, and that anyone wishing to enter a rival claim must do so within that time.

Dr King, irascible as ever, promptly wrote yet another in his seemingly endless series of letters to the Admiralty. 'Has everything, in the power of the English Government, been done to obtain evidence of the death of The Franklin Expedition? I unhesitatingly answer in the negative,' he declared.[103] He then published *The Franklin Expedition from First to Last*, a volume containing all his letters and many articles from the press. King concluded the book by denouncing the Admiralty for having delegated the search to 'a commercial company, notoriously ignorant of all things except rat skins and cat skins, utterly indifferent as to the mode in which they performed the task.'[104]

Lady Franklin's response was slower in coming, and far more dignified. She had already told Murchison privately that her main concern was 'that my last expedn receives no blow of discouragement from this contemplated act.'[105] In a long and carefully reasoned letter to the Admiralty, dated 12 April, she argued that Rae had not, in fact, determined the fate of the expedition, since so much remained a matter for conjecture, and she protested that to give him the award might deter further searches. She spoke of Rae with respect, praised his achievements, and suggested that he be rewarded, but not with the full £10,000. She stated that Anderson himself had visited her and had expressed 'his decided opinion that a vessel should be sent out to King William's Land to pursue the search.' She also made it clear that no matter what the government's decision might be, she would not abandon the cause. 'Here I feel compelled to state,' she wrote, 'that, though it is my humble hope and fervent prayer that the Government of my country will themselves complete the work they have begun, and not leave it to a weak and helpless woman to attempt the doing that imperfectly which they themselves can do so easily and well, yet, if need be, such is my painful resolve, God helping me.' It might seem like 'presumption' for her to address the Admiralty, but it was 'due to a set of men who have solved the problem of centuries by the sacrifice of their lives and in the very act of dying, that their remains should be sought for ... and that ... the records of their five long years of adventure and suffering ... should be the aim of persevering exertion and held out as a fitting object for reward.'[106]

The letter was printed in pamphlet form for private circulation, along with an extract from a letter by Kane,[107] in which he stated his opinion that though all the explorers were likely dead, it was not impossible that some had gone native and remained alive. 'It was my final intention, to have taken to Esquimaux life, had Providence not carried us through in our hazardous escape,' Kane wrote.[108] An anonymous pamphlet, *The Great Arctic Mystery*, echoed Lady Franklin's arguments about the reward and pointed to the 'late wonderful Expedition of Dr. Kane' as proof that 'private energy' remained a strong force, and that enterprising individuals would continue the search if the government failed in its duty.[109] Another pamphlet, *Arctic Rewards and Their Claimants*, insisted that Rae's claim involved far more than 'the paltry consideration of the reward of a sum of money'; it raised 'the far more important question, whether our account with Franklin and his gallant followers is now and for ever to be closed ... Dr. Rae is fully aware that, in advancing his ignoble claims, he is doing what in him lies to quench the search so long and so ardently followed, the object of which – stripped perhaps of some of its glory, but never to be stripped of its obligations – is now at last fairly within our grasp.'[110]

In June a memorial recommending another search, signed by eminent scientists, geographers, and Arctic officers, was presented to Lord Palmerston by Murchison. No answer was received by either Lady Franklin or the authors of the memorial. At the end of June it was announced that Rae would receive the reward. The Admiralty then made half-hearted enquiries about organizing an expedition, but concluded that nothing could be done that year. On 11 July Jane Franklin wrote again, pointing out that she had 'not been honoured with any reply' to her earlier appeal, and that the government's delay in coming to a decision meant that it was too late for her to organize her own expedition.[111] Questions were raised in the House of Lords, and vague assurances were given that the government would eventually act. On 2 December the *Times* reiterated, 'There must be an end to all things; we have paid our debt.'[112]

Lady Franklin wrote yet again to Lord Palmerston on the same day. 'I trust I may be pardoned for pressing ... for a decision, since by further delay even my own efforts may be paralyzed,' she argued. 'Surely ... I may plead ... that a careful search be made for any possible survivor, that the bones of the dead be sought for and gathered together ... and above all, that their last written words, so precious to their bereaved families and friends, be saved from destruction.' A last search was necessary

to 'satisfy the yearnings of surviving relatives and friends' and to safeguard what was 'justly of higher import to your Lordship, the credit and
the honor of the country.'[113] A pamphlet containing this letter went
through two editions,[114] but still Lady Franklin received no answer.

Throughout 1856 few periodical articles directly addressed the
search controversy. It might seem that the war of words was fought out
mainly in letters and pamphlets. But, as had always been the case,
reviews of Arctic narratives contained much lively and opinionated
commentary. Belcher's narrative was published in late 1855; McClure's
and Kane's books appeared in 1856. Reviews of Belcher's *The Last of the
Arctic Voyages* were an ideal forum in which to express disapproval of
the Admiralty. As the senior officer who, despite his lack of any Arctic
experience, had been chosen over such seasoned explorers as Penny,
Osborn, and McClintock, Belcher was clearly a placeman. The *Edinburgh
Review* called the title of the book 'pompous' and described Belcher's
style as 'at once vulgar, querulous, and incorrect … His language in
every page of this narrative is equally absurd and unintelligible.'
Belcher had 'add[ed] nothing to the annals of Arctic discovery' and
'established nothing beyond the utter unfitness of [the] author for the
task he undertook.'[115] The *British Quarterly Review* complained of 'the
pompous and petulant tone of the writer,' whose apparent motive was
constantly to remind the reader 'that he is dealing with no less a
personage than Sir Edward Belcher, Knight, C.B., Commander of the
Arctic Searching Expedition.' The article ended with a summary of
Rae's and Anderson's reports and an attempt to imagine the feelings of
the last forlorn survivors, hoping against hope for relief.[116] By implication, the shortcomings of Belcher's narrative showed where the blame
for their sad end should be placed.

Kane's *Arctic Explorations*, on the other hand, was described in *Chambers's Journal* as 'a tale of endurance and noble effort, which has had no
parallel, at least since the days when the lamented object of the search
made good his retreat from the outskirts of the remorseless frost-
land.'[117] In the *Saturday Review*, Fitzjames Stephen wrote that the book
'enlarges our notions of the powers of human endurance. We know of
no more terrible record of suffering, nor of any more glorious memorial of an indomitable tenacity of purpose and courage.' If it were not
for 'the grand lessons which it reads us,' the story would be 'almost too
horrible to read.' Because of the inspiring example of heroism it provided, Stephen could not 'but feel proud that the English language
should be the mother tongue of the hero of such a tale.'[118]

David Brewster's article in the *North British Review* was strongly focused on the need for another expedition. Kane had emphasized that Europeans could adapt to the Arctic climate, and the American explorer wrote in his narrative, 'My mind never realizes the complete catastrophe, the destruction of all Franklin's crews. I picture them to myself broken into detachments ... I think of them ever with hope.'[119] Brewster did not accept Rae's claim that all the explorers had died. Instead, he was 'disposed to adopt the more sanguine views of Dr. Kane.' Even if the hope of finding survivors was deemed 'extravagant,' it was still a national duty 'to ascertain the mysterious fate of men who have nobly perished in the service of their country.'[120]

The *British Quarterly Review* did not agree that survivors were possible, but it warmly commended Kane's book, which the reviewer considered far superior to Belcher's 'pompous [and] flatulent production.' 'A more interesting narrative of Arctic research than Dr. Kane's does not exist,' he declared. 'He must be fastidious indeed who does not yield to the fascinations of the book, or who permits his attention to grow cold before the last chapter is completed ... when a writer gives us such a delightful narrative, couched in so modest a strain, we can only thank him for his magnificent volumes.' In the last paragraph of the review, the author insisted that there should be another search for the lost expedition's records. '[T]hough Franklin and his comrades could no longer benefit by [the searchers'] generous exertions, yet, if they could return with his Journal, we have no doubt that its discovery would excite more interest than the announcement ... that the burning of the Alexandrian Library was a pure fiction, and that the whole of that splendid collection had been exhumed,' he wrote.[121]

This claim put a high value indeed on the possible results of a continued quest. The article was published in the spring of 1857, soon after the government definitely refused to sponsor another expedition. In February 1857 Arthur Roebuck and Joseph Napier had once again initiated discussion in Parliament. The first lord of the Admiralty, Sir Charles Wood, then stated that, in his opinion, no 'reasonable person entertained the expectation that any of the men of Sir John Franklin's expedition could be found alive.'[122] Wood also thought that the discovery of records was highly unlikely, as they would have been first carried away from the ships and then either left to the mercy of the elements as the explorers died one by one or hidden away in a cache that might never be located. With so little to be expected in the way of results, the risk could not be justified. The next day Lady Franklin, relieved that 'the cruel suspense in which I have been kept' had at least ended, began her preparations for a private expedition.[123]

Household Words published two articles strongly supporting the search in February and April 1857, both written by Henry Morley. The first, 'The Lost English Sailors,'[124] summarized the arguments put forward by naval officer Bedford Pim in his pamphlet *An Earnest Appeal to the British Public on behalf of the missing Arctic Expedition,* published by Hurst and Blackett in the previous month. The second, sarcastically titled 'Official Patriotism,' was written after Wood's announcement. In it, Morley indignantly rebuked the government. Lady Franklin's two letters to the Admiralty and her later appeal to Palmerston were quoted at length, and Morley remarked that her words 'should be read and felt by every household in the kingdom.' 'The matter cannot possibly rest where it now stands,' he declared. 'The Arctic story cannot close with the rejection of a plea like this from such a pleader. Certainly it cannot be closed with such an answer to the claims of humanity and justice in this case, as was given by the First Lord of the Admiralty.' Wood's argument that the records would be almost impossible to find was rejected. Morley was convinced that the ships remained intact, and that they 'would inevitably contain notes, explanations, letters to wives, children, and parents, copies of logs, even though for the original papers belonging to the expedition some safer place of deposit may have been found.' He ended with the prophecy that Lady Franklin's last devoted effort would bring 'such tidings as shall put our Admiralty Lords to eternal shame.'[125] The contrast between the noble behaviour of Franklin's wife and the corrupt indifference of the government had never been more sharply drawn.

9   A Sacred Sorrow, 1857–1860

McClintock came back, bringing with him a story ... the sorrow with which it fills you is not the vain and selfish sorrow that degrades, but the sacred sorrow that purifies, strengthens, and exalts. The end of the epic draws tears ... but these tears are such as a man is the better for shedding.

Joven, 'The End of an Epic,' *Sharpe's London Magazine*, November 1859

The quest on which Leopold McClintock set out in the summer of 1857 was to bring the story of Arctic exploration to a noble and fitting end. He might possibly rescue survivors, but it was far more likely that he would carry home only the last words left behind by dead men. To save these words from oblivion seemed to be an almost sacred mission because they were so fraught with personal and national significance. 'The deepest interest must attach to this undertaking,' declared the *New Monthly*. 'M'Clintock goes forth, single-handed, to complete the search.'[1] McClintock himself later wrote in his narrative, 'How could I do otherwise than devote myself to save at least the record of faithful service, even unto death, of my brother officers and seamen?'[2] By discovering the written record from Point Victory and the relics of the lost expedition, McClintock provided the final chapter in the Arctic story.

McClintock's success was seen as bringing two great quests to an end: the quest for news of Franklin's fate, and the far longer 300-year search for the Northwest Passage. Although his return precipitated a massive journalistic outcry in which the Admiralty's heartlessness was denounced more bitterly than ever before, by early 1860 (when most of the reviews of his narrative appeared), the tone of hostility was already fading, and in the end the more vehement rhetoric of the search period was forgotten.

It was replaced by a sense of pride in British achievements, resembling the consensus achieved after the publication of Parry's first narrative. That this could occur was, of course, due to many factors. The sheer cultural power exerted by literary paradigms should not be ignored: the widespread sense that the end of the story had at last been reached seemed in itself to mark the need for quieter, less partisan reflection. A great historical process had reached its consummation, and the nation should accordingly be united in its pride. McClintock's own intentions as an author also seem to have played a key role. Although specific evidence on this point is scanty, the overall impression produced by his actions and his writings alike is that he was determined to promote a sense of reconciliation.

Before 1857 McClintock had been one of the least publicized Arctic heroes. He served in three naval search expeditions, under James Ross, Horatio Austin, and Edward Belcher. Throughout the period from 1848 to 1854, he took a leading role in the improvement of sledging equipment and techniques, extending the length of sledge journeys from 500 to 1,400 miles. Although his achievements were well known to the public, he was far less of a popular hero than William Penny, Joseph-René Bellot, Robert McClure, or Sherard Osborn. To a large extent, this was due to McClintock's own cautious, reticent character. As one of the least financially secure of the naval officers involved in the search, he deeply feared arousing the anger or distrust of Admiralty officials. He therefore made few public statements and shunned journalists.

The review of *The Voyage of the 'Fox'* in the *Dublin University Magazine,* written by Samuel Haughton, may reflect McClintock's own opinions on the press. Haughton was professor of geology in the University of Dublin, a fellow of the Royal Society, and president of the Geological Society of Dublin. He and McClintock were close friends[3] and would likely have discussed the matter. In his summary of the search expeditions, Haughton described the response to James Ross's failure in 1849 as 'a most unfair clamour,' and he deplored the 'cruelty and baseness' of the insinuation that Ross had been motivated by self-interest. Of Austin's expedition Haughton wrote, 'All in the Expedition, both of the Royal Navy and the Merchant Marine, had done their duty, and done it well; but on their return home ... excused themselves to an exacting country by bandying charges of neglect and incompetence among themselves: the navy officers blaming the arrogance of the merchant sailors ... and the merchant officers returning the compliment, by enlisting the unreasoning aid of the public press against their naval comrades.' Following this characterization of journalistic comment on the Austin and Penny disputes as 'unreasoning' and unjust, Haughton went on to claim, 'The English care for nothing but success; and woe betide the public servant who fails to glut their ravenous maw with the requisite amount of this commodity ... The soldier and the sailor of England alike fight her battles, not merely in the cold shade of her aristocracy, but with the rope of an exacting and relentless taskmaster tied about their throats.'[4] If this last chilling remark did have its origin in conversations with McClintock, it casts an intriguing light on the difficulties he encountered in negotiating his public role. It would certainly appear that he did not believe either his status as a naval officer or his impressive record in the Arctic ensured lasting public approval.

McClintock's attitude to both the Admiralty and the public was strongly tinged with wariness, an attitude that likely stemmed from his insecure financial position. He was the oldest of twelve surviving children in a family of impoverished Anglo-Irish gentry. When at the age of eleven he was offered a place in the navy by a relative, the chance was too good to be refused, although McClintock was very small for his age (his biographer Clements Markham records that on the day of his entry, he was found to be 4 feet 6 inches tall and to weigh 68 pounds). As soon as McClintock reached the rank of lieutenant and had a salary that did more than meet his own immediate needs, he made an allowance to his mother, by then widowed with several unmarried daughters dependent on her. Doing so required that he himself live very frugally, and self-denial became second nature to him.[5]

As an adult, McClintock had 'a short, slender, but wiry and muscular frame.' His manner was 'controlled and cautious'; he was 'always calm to outward seeming, and inclined to be reticent' about his feelings,[6] unlike his friend Osborn, who had an exceptionally warm, enthusiastic, open manner. A fellow officer wrote of McClintock, 'I could not have conceived so much calmness to have been the property of any one man. In the greatest difficulties, and under the most aggravating circumstances, his face would not alter a muscle.'[7] McClintock was thus ill suited to court newspaper publicity, even had he wished to do so. While more colourful and outspoken heroes such as Penny and Osborn were available, he was far less popular than his very substantial achievements warranted. Nevertheless, he was the Franklin searcher who had most fully internalized the traditional values of Arctic heroism. When his time in the public eye finally came, his calm stoicism and tendency to quiet understatement served him well.

McClintock felt some reservations about accepting the command of Lady Franklin's expedition.[8] While his later claim that he joined 'cheerfully' because 'my whole heart was in the cause,'[9] need not be viewed with undue cynicism, it was not the full truth. In April 1857 McClintock wrote to James Ross, asking detailed questions about private expeditions and the Admiralty's attitude towards them. 'I do not wish to be so impolitic as to act contrary to their wishes!' he observed. He made it clear that he had a very pragmatic reason for wanting to return to the north, pointing out that unless the search was brought to a successful conclusion, the Arctic officers might never receive the credit they deserved.[10] He apparently hoped that a last, successful search led by a naval officer would heal the antagonisms created during the years of Arctic controversy. Though his participation in a private search was an implicit criticism of the Admiralty, McClintock's aim was to do so in a way that would ultimately restore the unity between explorers and officialdom. Unlike Osborn, McClintock was unwilling to incur the risks involved in an openly critical stance.

While he viewed the popular press with distrust, McClintock shrewdly realized that 'the countenance of scientific bodies'[11] would do much to lend credibility to a private venture. Though McClintock made little effort to cultivate the favour of journalists, he had quietly built up a solid base of support among scientific men, especially in his native Ireland. During the period of strident controversy after the return of Austin's expedition, McClintock carefully held himself aloof from the press. After volunteering for the next expedition, should there be one, he left London and returned to his mother's home in Dublin. There he experimented with different kinds of fuel for Arctic cooking equipment. It was at this time that he made Haughton's acquaintance. Through Haughton, McClintock soon came to know other scientific men, who were very favourably impressed by his practical, enquiring mind.[12]

As it became clear that the leadership of Lady Franklin's last expedition would likely fall to him, McClintock made a public statement among scientific men in Ireland, rather than to journalists in London. In late January 1857 he lectured to the Royal Dublin Society on the subject of Arctic sledge travel, ending his talk with a strong plea for a last search. The lost explorers 'were public servants, engaged in the faithful discharge of a public duty,' he pointed out. Because of the better techniques of Arctic travel developed during the search, 'It is in our power to rescue the survivors, or, at least, to ascertain their fate, *without periling a single life*, and at a comparatively trifling expense. That we refuse to do so is most assuredly a deep national disgrace.'[13] The lecture was printed in the February issue of the society's journal, along with an account of Arctic geology by Haughton. Haughton's article reinforced the idea that scientific curiosity as well as patriotic sentiment motivated McClintock. Although the *Fox* expedition was necessarily on a much smaller scale than the naval efforts of the past, McClintock nevertheless planned an extensive scientific program.[14] In particular, he approached the Royal Society with a request for the equipment needed to carry out magnetic observations.

While McClintock was away in the Arctic, very little about his expedition was published in newspapers or periodicals. This lack of coverage does not necessarily indicate that there was no public interest in his venture. Instead, it was likely the result of McClintock's own preference. Excessive publicity might in the end prove an embarrassment if he had to return empty-handed, as so many searchers had done before. Letters from McClintock to his family did, however, find their way into the *Natural History Review*, a new journal in which the proceedings of several Irish scientific societies were published.[15] The *Review* had not previously given notices to Arctic narratives, but during 1858 three articles surveyed all the northern literature published in the last few years.[16] Every opportunity to mention McClintock was taken by the reviewer. From McClintock's cautious point of view, this was surely a more desirable form of publicity than the highly polemical popular journalism of earlier years.

The most striking Arctic article published between McClintock's departure and his return was 'The Last Leaves of a Sorrowful Book' in Dickens's new periodical *All the Year Round*. (*Household Words* had ceased publication after Dickens quarrelled with the publishers, Bradbury and Evans.) William Coningham had printed James Fitzjames's journal-letter in a small pamphlet for private circulation among family and friends. At the same time, Coningham ensured a wide public circulation when he sent a copy to Dickens, along with 'permission to make what literary use [he thought] fit' of it (far wider than the journal had achieved through publication in the *Leader*: the circulation of *All the Year Round* was 120,000).[17] Dickens printed extracts in the 30 July 1859 number, along with a running commentary. (The article is not signed,[18] but given Dickens's deep interest in Arctic matters, it seems very possible he wrote it himself.)

In the commentary, earlier controversies were referred to only very briefly and indirectly. The article focused instead on the diary itself. The commentator noted the vivid quality of Fitzjames's writing and the powerful illusion of immediacy it created: reading it 'place[s] us on board ship by the writer's side.' The eager young explorer had possessed the 'happy facility' of conveying his thoughts and observations 'plainly, unaffectedly, and graphically to others.' His words re-created the day-to-day life of the expedition 'in its most familiar and most domestic aspect.' The author observed: 'How delightfully the little strokes of character in the journal open the view to us of the cheerful, simple-hearted social intercourse of the sailor-brotherhood!' It would be impossible, the commentator thought, for anyone to read the journal without 'a heightened admiration and a closer sympathy for Sir John Franklin, for Captain Fitzjames, and for their brave companions.' This officer's letter allowed readers a privileged glimpse not only of their countrymen in the far-off Arctic, but of men, now dead, as they had been in the vanished past. The cheerful tone of the journal was all the more poignant when it was remembered that Fitzjames's 'simple, warm-hearted words are the last that reach us, before the endless and the awful silence that follows.'[19]

Here, as in the response to Lady Franklin, the interaction of private and public exerted a strong fascination. Fitzjames's journal was a private document, privately published, recounting the everyday, domestic side of expedition life; the commentator repeatedly reminded his readers of this, but at the same time he suggested that the journal was 'a relic of public interest, associated with a public bereavement.' In his private life, Fitzjames was 'loved, honoured, and trusted by all who knew him.'[20] The same qualities that had earned him such personal esteem were now revealed to the public, as the best possible refutation of Rae's aspersions.

Rae himself was not mentioned by name, nor were there any criticisms of the Admiralty, either explicit or implicit. The simple contrast between Fitzjames's lively, optimistic account and the 'awful silence' that followed was evidently deemed a more effective device than any other. Again, this was the sort of publicity McClintock favoured. It is possible that McClintock and Dickens had discussed such matters, since Dickens attended the farewell dinner given to McClintock by the Royal Geographical Society in May 1857. He made a speech on behalf of 'Our Periodical Literature and the Press,' but there is no record of what he said.[21] McClintock would presumably have taken the opportunity to express his own views to one of the most influential journalists of his time.

However, when McClintock returned, the handling of his news by the Admiralty and the *Times* ensured that controversy would break out

afresh in its most strident form. The *Weekly Dispatch* observed sarcastically, 'The gentlemen who administered our naval affairs between the
year[s] 1845 and 1854 have now the pleasure of knowing, that the reasons why the companions of Sir John Franklin were starved and frozen
to death were, next to cold and hunger, the official insolence and corruption of the Lords of the Admiralty.'[22] Not all press responses were so
harshly phrased, but the *Times*'s dismissive response was widely interpreted as a callous insult to the nation's Arctic heroes.

The journalists who rushed to McClintock's defence were quick to
describe him, like Penny, as a man of the people, allied with Lady Franklin and his fellow searchers against the cold-blooded, cold-hearted
bureaucrats. 'Logically, Lady Franklin and Capt. McClintock should
never have acted as they did,' wrote Joven in 'The End of an Epic.' They
were 'warned against their folly; but Lady Franklin was not convinced,
and Capt. McClintock was not daunted. And this hardy gentleman has
succeeded! The wilderness has given up its secrets, the graves of the dead
have spoken, and mystery that seemed buried beneath a winding-sheet
of snow is a mystery no longer.'[23]

Joven defiantly suggested it was all for the best that the government
had refused to be involved. McClintock's venture in the *Fox*, one of the
smallest ships employed in the search, had 'a chivalry, a romance about
[it], which we would not readily lose.' Joven was pleased that 'the task
which had baffled larger ships was achieved by this little yacht.' The
story of McClintock's adventure carried readers back to the days of the
Elizabethan worthies, who 'sailed across the ocean in their cock-boats.'
Like Sir Humphrey Gilbert, 'McClintock, too, could say, "In this behalf,
mutare vel timere sperno": and so he went forth, like a knight of old, at a
lady's call. Style the enterprise Quixotic, if that is any consolation to you,
O sublime officials of the Admiralty ... There were many men, despite
sublime officiality, who *felt* he that would succeed; and ... [w]e now
know on whose side lay the truth.'[24] McClintock's resolve and the faith
of his supporters were thus contrasted with the cynical, superior pose of
'sublime officiality': McClintock represented the devotion of the people, who were collectively determined to see the quest through to the
end. In his little ship, he was like a throwback to the era in which the
roots of Britain's greatness lay.

McClintock's positive relationship with his subordinates was emphasized in his report to the Admiralty, and it was given even greater prominence by Joven. Joven quoted McClintock's statement that without the
'enthusiastic spirit and cheerful obedience' of his crew, 'our small

number – twenty-three in all – would not have sufficed for the successful performance of so great a work.' In Joven's opinion, 'McClintock and his crew were worthy of the men they sought.' However, he also pointed out that they were in many ways merely ordinary citizens. Their exploits were romantic and daring, but McClintock was 'not a big man, they tell me – not a hero of romance, to look at, by any means; and I dare say that his crew are but fair samples of the better class of English sailors. At which I hugely rejoice. If all that such men have endured and achieved can be borne and done by ordinary Englishmen ... why the more reason we have to be proud of our race.'[25] Arctic heroes were not aloof demi-gods to be admired from a distance; rather, they showed what potential for heroism lay within all their countrymen. The *Illustrated London News* agreed, observing: 'The heart of the people has beat more proudly on reflection that these men were their countrymen and their fellow-citizens ... There is but one speck on the brightness of the picture – the cold, stolid, selfish apathy of the Government.'[26] Osborn sounded the same notes in his *Blackwood's* review. 'It is truly wonderful to read how so small a party in a little yacht, only 170 tons burden, could do so much in seas where huge expeditions have often failed ... To such men, under the energetic and persevering M'Clintock, all things were possible,' he wrote. The 'gallant captain and crew' had done their work 'without any flourish of trumpets, but calmly, as if no other measures were possible.'[27] They had demonstrated the quiet heroism of the people as they persevered and succeeded where Belcher had hesitated and turned back.

Privately, however, Osborn was not well pleased with McClintock. The details remain vague, but his discontent apparently centred on McClintock's determination to conciliate the Admiralty. Lady Franklin, Osborn, and others believed that McClintock should receive full naval pay for his time in the *Fox* and were apparently ready to commence a campaign to get it. Early in January McClintock wrote to Sophia Cracroft, warning her that he would be 'exceedingly annoyed' if the matter was raised in Parliament.[28] 'I don't feel at all in love with his policy and must let him work it out himself,' Osborn declared a few weeks later. 'I believe he thinks himself conscientious, but there is too much calculation and too little generousness to touch me – I know he has thirteen in his family and that he has behaved very nobly to them in more ways than one – but I cannot understand his want of independence of a parcel of besotted old gentlemen in the Admiralty – and it simply riles me to hear him talk of trusting to them.'[29] McClintock's trust did, however, prove to be a successful tactic from his point of view. In March

1860, Lord Palmerston spoke in Parliament, extolling McClintock's achievements and Lady Franklin's devotion. McClintock and his crew were later granted a reward of £5,000, of which McClintock himself received £1,500.[30] A further £7,000 was allocated for a monument to Franklin.[31] With his share of the reward and the money he had earned by his narrative,[32] McClintock was financially secure for the first time in his life. He then went on to a distinguished naval career: he served as commander-in-chief of the North American and West Indian station in the early 1880s and achieved the rank of full admiral before he retired.

It is very clear that McClintock would do nothing to promote any interpretation of his work which posited an opposition between himself and the Admiralty. The role of the people's hero held no such appeal for him as it undoubtedly would have possessed for Osborn or Penny, had either of them been in McClintock's place. And, after the initial hostility aroused by the *Times* in September 1859 had subsided, many journalists were willing to take a more moderate stance. 'All question of the wisdom of the Government in ceasing when it did to pursue the search [for] Sir John Franklin is laid aside in presence of the fact, that there could be no nobler end to the best chapter in the history of England than that furnished by the events that are narrated in this volume,' asserted the *Examiner*'s review of *The Voyage of the 'Fox'*. Not all commentators agreed: from Ireland, the *Natural History Review* fumed indignantly, 'A most dishonest attempt has been made ... to appropriate the credit, which belongs only to Lady Franklin and the volunteers who manned her yacht, to the glorification of the Admiralty and the great Anglo-Saxon race!'[33] In general, however, it seemed reasonable that now the 'end of the great, romantic, melancholy, story of Arctic Discovery has at last arrived,'[34] the controversies of the past decade should come to an end as well. It was difficult to construct a noble picture of the Franklin expedition's last days while at the same time perpetuating the squabbles and recriminations that had characterized Arctic journalism for so long.

McClintock's narrative made three central points: the lost explorers had discovered the Northwest Passage; there was no evidence that they had committed cannibalism; and the record found on King William Island, though brief, indicated they had met their fate with courage and resignation. Other evidence, particularly the religious books taken on the last march, also promoted the belief that the explorers had died in a spirit of noble endurance. The end of the epic thus presented a highly edifying spectacle, rather than a picture of misery and horror. As a result, it no longer seemed necessary to emphasize the Admiralty's guilt.

The discovery of the passage was indisputably proved by a skeleton seen by McClintock a few miles beyond the cairn raised by Peter Dease and Thomas Simpson at Cape Herschel on the southern coast of King William Island. Though McClintock, like James Anderson, searched Montreal Island and the nearby mainland, he saw no bodies there. The Cape Herschel skeleton and two others, found in a boat on the western side of King William Island, provided no evidence of cannibalism. Nor did the Inuit accounts carefully collected by McClintock mention it.[35] Several books were found in the boat that contained the two skeletons; all but one (*The Vicar of Wakefield*) were religious. In particular, there was a small Bible with many marginal notes and underlined passages. These provided important if indirect proof that in 1848, as in 1821, Britain's Arctic heroes had been sustained by faith.

There was no reason to think the explorers had been murdered by the Inuit. That they should have died of starvation was inevitable, since McClintock's journey proved to him that the western side of King William Island was an exceptionally barren and desolate region, almost totally devoid of animal life. They must have been suffering from scurvy as well as hunger, and their attempted retreat to the Great Fish River had quickly turned into a death march. In the words of one of McClintock's Inuit informants, 'they fell down and died as they walked along.'[36]

The major focus of public attention was the record from Point Victory, written immediately after the abandonment of the ships. A facsimile of the document appeared in the *Illustrated London News*, and it was also included in McClintock's narrative. It was a standard printed form, containing three messages in total. The first, written by Graham Gore and Charles Des Voeux on 28 May 1847, revealed that the expedition 'wintered in 1846–7 [evidently a careless mistake for 1845–6] at Beechey Island ... after having ascended Wellington Channel to lat. 77°, and returned by the west side of Cornwallis Island.' In 1846–7, the ships 'wintered in the ice' near King William Island. At the time the message was written, the explorers were 'All well.' Those who believed Franklin had gone up Wellington Channel were therefore correct. It was only in the expedition's second year that he took his ships to the southwest.

The second message was written by Fitzjames, and dated 25 April 1848: 'H.M. ships Terror and Erebus were deserted on the 22nd April, 5 leagues NNW of this [place] having been beset since 12th Septr. 1846. The officers & crews consisting of 105 souls under the command of Captain F[.] R[.] M. Crozier landed here ... Sir John Franklin died on the 11th June 1847 and the total loss by deaths in the expedition has been to this date 9 officers & 15 men.' A short note added by Crozier stated that they would 'start on tomorrow 26th for Backs Fish River.' 'In the short space of twelve months how mournful had become the history of Franklin's expedition; how changed from the cheerful "All well" of Graham Gore!' McClintock wrote. 'A sad tale was never told in fewer words. There is something deeply touching in their extreme simplicity, and they show in the strongest manner that both the leaders of this retreating party were actuated by the loftiest sense of duty, and met with calmness and decision the fearful alternative of a last bold struggle for life, rather than perish without effort on board their ships.'[37]

Journalists uniformly agreed that the laconic record formed part of the great tradition of Arctic literature. That it was written by Fitzjames added to its interest. '[I]n a few words the firm hand of the gallant Captain Fitzjames reveals to us a thrilling tale of sorrow and suffering, heroically, calmly met,'[38] wrote Osborn in *Blackwood's*. In the *Dublin University Review*, Haughton told his readers that McClintock had 'scattered all ... crude conjectures' and 'placed the facts of the voyage before us in their simple grandeur.' He urged his readers to 'listen to the record of Fitzjames, the once lighthearted and still brave Fitzjames.' Haughton noted with reverent admiration that Crozier and Fitzjames had written and acted calmly, even though they must have known they were going to 'certain death.'[39]

The record also provided indirect evidence that Franklin had known before he died how close the expedition was to success. It was possible that Gore and Des Voeux had left the ships to lead a sledge party to Cape Herschel. If this had been the case, they might well have returned just before Franklin's death, in time to assure their dying commander that the fulfilment of the quest was within reach.[40] In his narrative, McClintock emphasized that this version of events was based on speculation; in his *Once a Week* article, however, Osborn transformed the suggestion of a triumphant death for Franklin into a dramatic scene. He pictured Gore and Des Voeux 'casting one glance upon the long-sought shores of America' before hastening back to the ships. Then the 'shout of victory, which cheered the last hour of Nelson and of Wolfe, rang not the less heartily round the bed of the gallant Franklin, and lit up that kind eye with its last gleam of triumph. Like them, his last thought must have been of his country's glory.' Osborn also provided an account of Franklin's funeral, with 'Fitzjames, who had sworn only to part from him in death,' reading the burial service.[41]

The fate of those who had left the ships in 1848 was the subject of still more speculation. The *Leisure Hour* made particular mention of the religious books found in the boat. 'We dwell with mournful pleasure upon the possession of articles of this kind, as showing that, unutterably sorrowful as was the earthly fate of the owners, they had a sure guide with them to "a better country, that is, a heavenly,"'[42] the writer noted. The books and other relics were placed on display at the United Service Institute. The Bible was open 'at that most beautiful 15th chapter of St. Paul's Corinthians, in which doubtless these brave men read that their failing, perishing bodies together with their immortal souls, should survive that terrible ordeal, and rise again in glorious incorruption.'[43] Joshua Fitch recorded that it was 'an affecting thing to see the underscoring and the marginal lines which abound in these books, and to recognise in them tokens of the source from which proceeded the last rays of hope which shone on the hearts of these unhappy men.' He thought there could be no doubt 'that, in the icy solitude in which they dropped down to die, many a spirit was cheered by a sense of the Divine presence and tenderness, and was enabled to rejoice in the thought of an eternal resting-place.'[44]

A writer in the new religious periodical *Good Words* reflected that 'to the believer in the faith which upheld them in their severest trials,' Franklin and his men had 'bequeathed associations not soon forgotten; as with full heart he turns over the record of their wanderings: musing it may be, on the "Scripture Help" of Hood, preserved through all his weary journey to drop from his hand in death ... [or on] the Bible, marked and underlined in almost every page, in that lonely boat.'[45] Charles Weld was also convinced that, though they were 'reduced to a state of infantine weakness' and finally 'dropp[ed] as they struggled to escape from the barren shores of King William Land,' there could be no doubt 'that the religious influence present during Franklin's memorable journey across the North American shores, comforted the crews of the *Erebus* and *Terror*.' Moreover, it was likely that 'their last hours were cheered by the consciousness that they had done their duty ... and that they would always be remembered as having triumphed over difficulties which baffled ardent spirits during three centuries.'[46]

Joven recorded that though he was 'not addicted to tears,' his 'eyes were full of them' as he read the news. Though there was 'immense pathos in the story ... the sorrow with which it fills you is not the vain and selfish sorrow that degrades, but the sacred sorrow that purifies, strengthens, and exalts. The end of the epic draws tears, as I say; but these tears are such as a man is the better for shedding.'[47] Fiercely though Joven had railed against the Admiralty, in the end the emotional catharsis he described placed the matter on a level where such polemics seemed irrelevant. The end of a 300-year national epic was increasingly seen as a matter for quiet pride rather than carping.

The *Gentleman's Magazine* began its review of McClintock's narrative with the statement that, though 'we did once, in common with the public at large, feel humiliated at seeing the Government of the day, in deference to we know not what sinister influence, refuse to fulfil [its] plain duty,' such feelings had now dissipated. Only the thought of the mental suffering inflicted on Lady Franklin and the other relatives by the government's refusal prevented the reviewer from 'rejoic[ing] at the decision that was then come to,'[48] for the result was a magnificent story of British courage and initiative. In the February 1860 issue of *Macmillan's Magazine*, Franklin Lushington (a friend of the Tennysons), surveyed 'Arctic Enterprise and its Results since 1815.' 'Whoever wishes to see a great result summed up as shortly and simply as possible, need only glance at an Arctic chart of the date of the Peace of 1815, and then look at one drawn in the last half-year,' he proudly began. With the notable exceptions of Bellot and Kane, 'the whole cycle of the Arctic discoveries of this century is the work of our own countrymen. British names mark every channel, cape and inlet: and a history is to be read in almost every name.' It was 'impossible to overrate in imagination the toil, the danger, the hardships and privations, the noble daring, and the unflinching endurance, the unselfish devotion and the high sentiment of professional duty, which have been necessarily involved in the accomplishment of such a task.' No reader could 'follow the narrative of any single Arctic voyage or journey, and not feel throughout an admiring wonder.' 'As long as our naval officers are trained in the school which has ripened such men as ... McClintock, whose character is written on every page of their journals, we need never fear for the behaviour of the British navy,'[49] Lushington affirmed triumphantly.

The *Leisure Hour* wrote in its review of McClintock that 'to poets it may now be left to celebrate the wild romance of the modern Odyssey, and to sing the praises of the Penelope of England,'[50] and it was not long before the poets took up the challenge. Their elegiac words evoked a sense of sorrow mixed with contentment and pride that the great story had now reached its end. 'History shrines them with her mighty dead, / The hero-seamen of this isle of Britain,'[51] declared Thomas Hood in 'The Lost Expedition.' 'Sleep! Martyrs of discovery, sleep!' wrote Nicholas Michell in the *New Monthly*.

> Your winding-sheets the Polar snows;
> What though the cold winds o'er ye sweep,
> And on your graves no flowret blows,
> Your memories long shall flourish fair,
> Your story to the world proclaim
> What dauntless British hearts can dare;
> Sleep! lost ones, sleep! embalmed in fame.[52]

A schoolboy, Spencer Smith, wrote,

> To thee, brave Franklin, and thy gallant crew,
> Are England's praise and England's sorrow due;
> Who braved at Duty's call the Arctic wave,
> And led by Science, found the untimely grave.

Then he asked,

> Dread spirits of the misty Northern sky,
> Lights of these darksome realms, say did they die
> Racked in convulsive pangs, or fall asleep,
> Lulled by the music of the pitying deep?

The answer was provided by McClintock's narrative:

> Immortal Faith! when human aids were far,
> In the last conflict of the life-long war,
> 'Twas thine upon the sacred page to show
> The bright reflection of the heavenly glow;
> To fix their love upon the world on high,
> Shew them its joys, and teach them how to die.[53]

'Thus fell a hundred heroes, but their name shall never die,' explained Owen Vidal, a student at Trinity College, Oxford.[54] He was the winner of a £50 prize for the best student poem on the set topic of that year: 'The Life, Character and the Death of the heroic seaman, Sir John

Franklin, with special reference to the time, place, and discovery of his death.' The second place in the competition went to young Algernon Charles Swinburne,[55] who wrote,

> This is the end. There is no nobler word
> In the large writing and scored marge of time
> Than such endurance is …
> These chose the best; therefore their name shall be
> Part of all noble things that shall be done,
> Part of the royal record of the sea.[56]

Whatever his feelings about Swinburne's later works might have been, of this early effort Barrow undoubtedly would have approved. The connected narrative he inadvertently began in 1818 reached a remarkable conclusion when 'McClintock came back, bringing with him a story' that could unite so many disparate elements of Victorian society.

Notes

Introduction

1 Stephen Leacock, introduction to Stefansson, *Unsolved Mysteries of the Arctic*, vi.
2 Raffan, *Summer North of Sixty*, 144–54.
3 Academic work since the 1970s that takes a critical view of Franklin includes MacLeod and Glover, 'Franklin's First Expedition'; MacLaren, 'Retaining Captaincy of the Soul,' 'Aesthetic Mapping of Nature,' 'Discovery as Misperception,' 'Aesthetic Map of the North,' 'From Exploration to Publication'; Davis, 'Vision and Revision,' 'Thrice-Told Tales,' 'History or His/Story?' Introductions to *Franklin, The First Arctic Land Expedition* and *Franklin, The Second Arctic Land Expedition*, 'Once Bitten, Twice Shy'; Collis, 'Voyage of the Episteme'; Warkentin, introduction to *Canadian Exploration Literature*.
4 Davis, introduction to *Franklin, The First Arctic Land Expedition*, lxxxi; review of Wiebe, 97–8.
5 Mowat, *Ordeal by Ice*; Newman, *Company of Adventurers*; Berton, *Arctic Grail*; Richler, *Solomon Gursky Was Here*; Wiebe, *Playing Dead*; Struzik, *Northwest Passage*; Wiebe, *Discovery of Strangers*; Atwood, 'Concerning Franklin'; McGoogan, *Fatal Passage*.
6 Monchuk, 'Franklin "Insensitive" Choice.'
7 Davis, review of Wiebe, 98.
8 See Cavell, 'Second Frontier.'
9 Grant, 'Myths of the North,' 15, and *Sovereignty or Security?* 3; Grace, *Canada and the Idea of North*. For an opposing view, see Cavell, 'Second Frontier,' and Hulan, *Northern Experience*.
10 Davis, review of David, 180–1.

11 The introduction to Franklin, *The First Arctic Land Expedition*, provides the most extensive statement of Davis's theoretical assumptions.

12 Grace, *Canada and the Idea of North*, 24.

13 Foucault, 'Nietzsche, Genealogy, History,' in *Language, Counter-Memory, Practice*, 162, 142. See also Weeks, 'Foucault for Historians'; Taylor, 'Foucault on Freedom and Truth.'

14 Scott, 'Evidence of Experience.'

15 See the appendices in Cavell, 'Tracing the Connected Narrative.' Appendix 2 has been published as 'The Hidden Crime of Dr Richardson' and appendix 3 as 'Representing Akaitcho.' The appendices examine three issues that have been accorded prominence in recent Canadian Arctic literature. In all three cases, inadequately substantiated claims about the British explorers have been used to promote the idea that Arctic narratives were constructed with the intention of distorting events and deceiving the public. The hidden truth, it is alleged, is that Franklin and his followers suffered only because of their own mistaken perceptions of the northern environment; that Franklin's closest friend and associate John Richardson was guilty of a secret crime; and that when writing his narratives, Franklin constructed northern Aboriginal people as childlike savages. The appendices and articles cited above include historical data that are seriously at odds with these claims. Again, my intention is not to suggest that British narratives should be regarded as purely factual and entirely reliable sources of historical truth, but rather to emphasize the element of construction in twentieth-century Canadian representations of Arctic history.

16 I have sometimes employed the term *fact*. By 'fact' I mean a discrete piece of information about a historical event, without any implication that there is an essential, timeless meaning or significance attached to such information. Facts take on their perceived significance only as they are integrated into narratives of historical meaning. Historical data that cannot be reconciled with a certain narrative, and so are ignored by its author, are important clues in the analysis of cultural construction, because they point to the possible alternative meanings the author wished to exclude. Some facts that appear in the British discourse are absent from Canadian representations. See Cavell, 'Hidden Crime'; 'Representing Akaitcho'; and 'Tracing the Connected Narrative,' appendices. However, this does not mean that one is real and the other 'merely constructed.'

17 Butler, 'Culture's Medium.'

18 Pocock, 'European Perceptions,' 28. See also Majeed, *Ungoverned Imaginings*, which places James Mill's representation of India in the context of the European intellectual and political debates of his time.

19 Iser, *Act of Reading*.

20 Chartier, 'Popular Appropriations: The Readers and Their Books,' in Chartier, *Forms and Meanings*, 92–3, 89.

21 Rose, 'Rereading the English Common Reader,' 49, 51, and 'How Historians Study Reader Response: or, What Did Jo Think of *Bleak House*?' in Jordan and Patten, *Literature in the Marketplace*, 195. See also Hume, 'Texts within Contexts.'

22 The classic statement is Tanselle, 'Editorial Problem.' Such theories were disputed by McGann in *Critique of Modern Textual Criticism*, *Textual Criticism*, and *Textual Condition*. On the initial response by the authorial intention school to work by McGann, Robert Darnton, and D. F. McKenzie, see Sutherland, 'Publishing History.' For Tanselle's later evaluation of McGann and others, see 'Textual Criticism and Literary Sociology' and 'Textual Criticism and Deconstruction.'

23 Barker, 'Intentionality and Reception Theory,' in Barker, *Potencie of Life*, 200. See also Thomas R. Adams and Nicolas Barker, 'A New Model for the Study of the Book,' in the same volume.

24 Chartier, 'Figures of the Author,' in Chartier, *The Order of Books*, 28–9.

25 Thompson, 'Reception Theory,' 257.

26 Magnuson, *Reading Public Romanticism*, 37–8, 3.

27 Ginzburg, *Cheese and the Worms*, xxi.

28 John Richardson, in Franklin, *Second Expedition, 1825–26–27*, 237.

29 John Franklin to John Richardson, 11 August [1823], Richardson-Voss Papers, SPRI 1503/5/1–13.

30 Individual narratives and collections of Portuguese, Spanish, and French voyages were available in translation before the first English narratives were published from the 1550s on. See George B. Parks, 'Tudor Travel Literature: A Brief History,' in Quinn, *Hakluyt Handbook*, 98–9.

31 See Helgerson, *Forms of Nationhood*, chap. 4; Payne, '"Strange, remote, and farre distant countreys": The Travel Books of Richard Hakluyt,' in Myers and Harris, *Journeys through the Market*.

32 See Edwards, *Story of the Voyage*, chap. 2.

33 G.R. Crone and R.A. Skelton, 'English Collections of Voyages and Travels, 1625–1846,' in Lynam, *Richard Hakluyt*.

34 Whether Walter was, in fact, the main author of the book or whether the majority of the work was done by Benjamin Robins (a mathematician and political pamphleteer) is a matter of dispute. See Williams, *Prize of All the Oceans*, appendix I.

35 Williams, '"To Make Discoveries,"' 22–3.

36 See Pearson, 'Hawkesworth's Alterations,' on changes to the content; Percy, 'In the Margins,' on changes in style.

37 Cook, *Journals: Voyage of the Endeavour,* ccxlvi; Beaglehole, *Cook the Writer,* 11–12.

38 'Hawkesworth's Account of the Voyages for making Discoveries in the Southern Hemisphere, &c.,' *Monthly Review* 49, pt 1 (August 1773): 138. Emphasis in original.

39 'Account of Books,' *Annual Register* (1773): 267–8.

40 Beaglehole, *Life of Captain James Cook,* 459.

41 'Navalis,' letter to the editor, *Baldwin's London Weekly Journal,* 22 May 1773, reprinted in *Carteret's Voyage Round the World,* Vol. 2, 497–8. On the public response to Hawkesworth, see also Smith, *European Vision,* 28–35.

42 Cook, preface to *Voyage towards the South Pole.* However, the narrative was not purely and entirely Cook's work. He acknowledged in his preface that others had helped him to prepare it for press. The alterations made by Dr John Douglas were in fact more extensive than Cook's statement implied. Douglas edited the manuscript for punctuation, paragraphing, spelling, and grammar. He also revised many passages to improve the style. Cook's version of the preface read: 'It is a work for information and not for amusement, written by a man, who has not the advantage of Education, acquired, nor Natural abilities for writing; but by one who has been constantly at sea from his youth, and who, with the Assistance of a few good friends [has] gone through all the Stations belonging to a Seaman, from a prentice boy in the Coal Trade to a Commander in the Navy. After such a Candid confession he hopes the Public will not consider him as an author, but a man Zealously employed in the Service of his Country and obliged to give the best account he is able of his proceedings.' *Journals: Voyage of the Resolution and Adventure,* 2. Douglas later wrote that 'the Journal if printed as the Captain put it into my Hands, would have been thought too incorrect, & have disgusted the Reader.' Quoted in ibid., cxliv.

43 'Cook's Voyage round the World,' *Monthly Review* 57 (July 1777): 18, 20, 21. Emphasis in original.

44 'Advertisement from the Editor,' in Vancouver, *Voyage of Discovery,* Vol. 1.

1: The End of an Epic, 1859–1860

1 Second leader, *Illustrated London News* 35 (1 October 1859): 316.

2 Franklin Lushington, 'Arctic Enterprise and its Results since 1815,' *Macmillan's Magazine* 1 (February 1860): 277.

3 [Joshua Fitch], 'Arctic Explorations,' *London Quarterly Review* 14 (April 1860): 226, 261. Unless otherwise indicated, attributions of authorship are from Houghton, *Wellesley Index.*

4 'Fate of Sir John Franklin's Expedition. Return of Captain McClintock, R.N.,' *Times*, 23 September 1859, 7.

5 McClintock to Lady Franklin, 21 September [1859], in Jane Franklin, *Life, Diaries and Correspondence*, 144–6. The original is in SPRI MS 248/439/22-36.

6 'Fate of Sir John Franklin's Expedition.'

7 Fourth leader, *Times*, 23 September 1859, 6–7.

8 On the relationship between the government and the *Times*, see Cook, *Delane of 'The Times'*, 269–76. On mid-Victorian ideas about newspapers and public opinion, see Jones, *Powers of the Press*, 87–92.

9 Col. John Barrow to Sir Roderick Murchison, 27 November 1856, BL Add. MS 46125 f.111–15.

10 Leopold McClintock to Sophia Cracroft, 9 March 1857, SPRI MS 248/439/9-22.

11 'An Arctic Navigator,' 'The Search for Sir John Franklin' (letter to the editor), *Times*, 26 September 1859, 10.

12 Joven, 'The End of an Epic,' *Sharpe's London Magazine*, n.s. 15 (November 1859): 242–6.

13 'The Arctic Regions of North America,' *Weekly Dispatch*, 13 November 1859, 2.

14 C.R. Weld, 'Franklin's Fate, and the Voyage of the "Fox,"' *Fraser's Magazine* 61 (February 1860): 227.

15 'The Fate of Sir John Franklin,' *United Service Magazine* 375 (February 1860), 218.

16 Advertisement in the *Saturday Review* 8 (31 December 1860). Darwin's *The Origin of Species* and Samuel Smiles's *Self Help*, both published by Murray a month earlier, at the end of November, had by the same time sold 5,000 and 6,000 copies, respectively. Work on a second, revised edition of *The Voyage of the 'Fox'* began in January 1860, and it was published in March.

17 John Brown, quoted in Owen, *Fate of Franklin*, 400.

18 Second leader, 1 October 1859, 316.

19 Altick, *English Common Reader*, 163.

20 Graham, *English Literary Periodicals*, 301.

21 'Death in the Inkpot,' *Chambers's Journal*, 3rd ser. 12 (29 October 1859): 275.

22 *London Journal* No. 769, quoted in Browne, *North-West Passage*, 75.

23 Tennyson, *Lady Tennyson's Journal*, 141. On this issue, see also Maunder, '"Discourses of Distinction"'; Altick, *English Common Reader*, 359.

24 Early hopes that the passage might be used for commercial purposes were based on the inaccurate assumption that the coastline of North America took a fairly direct line westward from Hudson Bay to Bering Strait. The only area of scientific research that seemed likely to have truly practical results was terrestrial magnetism.

25 Hughes and Lund, *Victorian Serial*, 1–2. Serialized fiction was not popular throughout the entire period of this study. Publication in parts was a format of long standing, but it was Dickens's *Pickwick Papers* (1836–7) that first demonstrated its immense potential to nineteenth-century publishers. However, to judge from the responses to Arctic literature in the 1820s (see chap. 6, below), the reading public had long been ready to welcome stories whose 'instalments' extended over many years.

26 Hayward, *Consuming Pleasures*, 35–6; Vincent, *Literacy and Popular Culture*, 208–9. On Mayhew, see Hayward, 36.

27 [Elizabeth Rigby], '*Vanity Fair* – and *Jane Eyre*,' *Quarterly Review* 84 (December 1848): 153. *Vanity Fair* was first published as a serial, but *Jane Eyre* was not. *Jane Eyre* created an unusual public stir because of its unknown author ('Currer Bell') and its 'scandalous' themes, described by Rigby with considerable disapproval.

28 'Sir J. Franklin – the North-West Passage,' *British Quarterly Review* 11 (February 1850): 111.

29 Scoresby, *Franklin Expedition*, 7. This pamphlet was based on a series of articles published in the *Morning Herald* on 1, 14, and 26 December 1849. Emphasis in original.

30 Joven, 'End of an Epic,' 243.

31 Osborn, *Career, Last Voyage*, 26.

32 'Fate of the Franklin Expedition,' *Leisure Hour* 417 (22 December 1859): 812, 816.

33 'The Last of the Arctic Voyages,' *New Monthly Magazine* 106 (January 1856): 51.

34 For example, see 'The Arctic Expeditions,' *Saturday Review* 8 (1 October 1859): 387–8.

35 'The Fate of Sir John Franklin,' *Illustrated London News* 25 (28 October 1854): 421; 'Fate of the Franklin Expedition,' 812n.

36 Altick, *English Common Reader*, 263, 312–14.

37 In the currency of the time, 12 pence made 1 shilling and 20 shillings made a pound. A guinea was 21 shillings. Four guineas was therefore £4 4s. This was a very substantial amount: £500 a year was a comfortable income, and a family with £1,000 a year or more was considered wealthy.

38 'Parry's Voyage of Discovery,' *Gentleman's Magazine*, 91, n.s. 14, pt 1 (June 1821): 538.

39 John Wilson Croker to John Murray, quoted in Altick, *English Common Reader,* 298.
40 Leopold McClintock to Robert Cooke, 1 November 1874, John Murray Archive.
41 Richard D. Altick, 'English Publishing and the Mass Audience in 1852,' in Altick, *Writers, Readers and Occasions,* 148. Altick estimates that out of an adult population of 11.5 million, 'the market for ordinary trade books ... was limited to the 27,000 or so families with an annual income of more than £400, and that for the one- or two-shilling reprints, the cheapest books published, to the 110,000 families with more than £150 a year.'
42 Altick, *English Common Reader,* 393; Ellegård, *Readership of the Periodical Press,* 35.
43 Jerdan, *Autobiography,* 2: 187.
44 'Captain Parry's Voyage,' *Blackwood's* 9 (June 1821): 290.
45 On the law of copyright at the time, see Feather, *Publishing, Piracy and Politics,* 5.
46 'Account of the Expedition to the North Pole,' *Blackwood's* 4 (October 1818): 95–8.
47 'Letter from an Officer Concerning the Polar Expedition,' *Blackwood's* 4 (November 1818): 193–8.
48 'North-West Passage: Expedition under Captain Ross and Lieutenant Parry, in the Isabella and Alexander,' *Blackwood's* 4 (December 1818): 338–44.
49 'J.R.,' 'Letter from the Arctic Land Expedition,' *Blackwood's* 6 (December 1819): 305–7.
50 'J.R.,' 'Letter from the Arctic Land Expedition,' *Gentleman's Magazine* 90, n.s. 13, pt 1 (February 1820): 132–24.
51 'Overland Northern Expedition,' *Gentleman's Magazine* 91, n.s. 14, pt 1 (January 1821): 3–5.
52 'Northern Expedition,' *Literary Chronicle* 96 (17 March 1821): 171.
53 'Arctic Land Expedition,' *Literary Gazette* 253 (24 November 1821): 748.
54 'Notice of the Progress of the Arctic Land Expedition under the Command of Lieutenant Franklin. In a Letter to Professor Jameson,' *Edinburgh Philosophical Journal* 4 (January 1821): 141–4.
55 'The Arctic Expedition,' *New Monthly Magazine* 10 (October 1818): 240–3.
56 'Arctic Expedition,' *New Monthly Magazine* 10 (November 1818): 333–6.
57 'The Arctic Expedition,' *New Monthly Magazine* 10 (December 1818): 430–3.
58 'Northern Expedition,' *New Monthly Magazine* 3 (September 1821): 448–9.
59 McClintock to Col. John Barrow, *Times,* 4 November 1857, 9.
60 McClintock to Richard Collinson, *Times,* 24 August 1858, 7; McClintock to Col. John Barrow, *Times,* 28 August 1858, 10; two letters from McClintock

to his brother Dr Alfred McClintock, *Natural History Review* 5 (1858): 165–7, 168. Selections from the journal of the expedition's surgeon, David Walker, appeared in the *Belfast News-Letter*, 8 September 1858, and were reprinted in the *Natural History Review* 5 (1858): 171–82.

61 McClintock to Col. John Barrow, *Times*, 4 October 1858, 4; McClintock to Alfred McClintock, *Natural History Review* 5 (1858): 182–3.

62 For example, see Sherard Osborn, 'The Voyage of the "Fox" in the Arctic Seas,' *Blackwood's* 87 (January 1860): 119–20, and Samuel Haughton, 'The Voyage of the "Fox" in the Arctic Seas,' *Dublin University Magazine* 55 (February 1860): 214–15.

63 Gerin, *Branwell Brontë*, 28–9.

64 Roper, *Reviewing*, 41–3.

65 Fish, *Is There a Text in This Class?* Roger Chartier has developed this concept; see 'Communities of Readers,' in Chartier, *Order of Books*, 1–23.

66 Scoresby, *Franklin Expedition*, 7.

67 'The Open Polar Sea,' *Chambers's Journal*, 4th ser. 178 (25 May 1867): 324.

68 Hughes and Lund, *Victorian Serial*, 12.

69 Joven, 'End of an Epic,' 242. Emphasis in original.

70 The issue (vol. 28, no. 56) is dated January 1823, but it was not published until July. Cutmore, Early Quarterly Review Page (accessed 5 January 2002).

71 Parry to Franklin, 23 October 1823 (copy), SPRI MS 248/453/10.

72 Second leader, *Illustrated London News*, 1 October 1859, 316.

73 Ibid.

74 An older study dealing with the Franklin search is Marlow, 'Fate of Sir John Franklin.'

75 David, *Arctic in the British Imagination*, chap. 4.

76 David strongly criticizes Francis Spufford, an earlier writer on the subject, for considering only literary works produced by the educated elite. While it is undoubtedly true that visual images, especially those published in the illustrated press, are of at least equal if not greater significance because of their place in popular culture, David leaves a vast area of print culture almost completely unexamined. The quarterly reviews, the monthly magazines, and the more literary weekly journals receive only a few scattered references in his book. David's study therefore falls short of what could have been achieved by an examination of the full range of nineteenth-century publications.

77 David, *Arctic in the British Imagination*, 85–6.

78 See Cook, *Delane of 'The Times*,' 289, on the 'high authority' and 'almost pontifical influence' of the *Times* leaders.

79 Riffenburgh, *Myth of the Explorer*, 27, 26.

80 Smith, *Imagining the Pacific*, chaps 7 and 10.

81 David, *Arctic in the British Imagination*, 10–11, 19–20, 82.

82 Said, *Orientalism*, 43, 204; see also Pratt, *Imperial Eyes*, introduction and chap. 3.

83 See Stephen and Lee, *Dictionary of National Biography*; Clive Holland, 'Sherard Osborn,' in Brown, *Dictionary of Canadian Biography*, vol. 10; obituaries in the *Times*, 10 May 1875; *Geographical Magazine* 2 (June 1875), 161–70; *Athenaeum* 2481 (15 May 1875): 657.

84 Markham, *Life of McClintock*, 280. Markham (1830–1915), like McClintock and Osborn, served in Austin's search expedition. He then left the navy, becoming a civil servant and geographer. He was a lifelong advocate of polar exploration. See Markham, *Life of Sir Clements R. Markham*.

85 'Sherard Osborn,' *Blackwood's Magazine* 117 (June 1875): 790.

86 W.A.B. Hamilton to Osborn, 6 May 1854, in Sherard Osborn scrapbook, NMM BGR/ 5.

87 Markham, *Life of McClintock*, 279.

88 Sherard Osborn to Sophia Cracroft, 26 January 1860, SPRI MS 248/488/1-5.

89 McClintock, *Voyage of the 'Fox'*, v.

90 Sherard Osborn to John Murray, 9 October 1859, Murray Archive.

91 Leopold McClintock, 'Journal of the Fox, sent to Lady Franklin and containing her amendments,' NMM MCL/ 17. In fact, relatively few of the corrections are in Lady Franklin's handwriting. 'Capt McClintock / With S. Osborn's compliments' is written on the back of the first page. Overall, Osborn's contribution seems to have lain primarily in a heightening of the style in descriptive and reflective passages, making them more forceful and vivid, and in the clarification of geographical references for easier understanding by readers.

92 Sherard Osborn to John Murray, 24 November 1859, Murray Archive.

93 Cracroft to Richardson, 14 October 1859, Richardson-Voss Papers, SPRI 1503/59 (1).

94 The *Blackwood's* review is attributed to Osborn in Houghton, *Wellesley Index*, and this is confirmed by an undated letter from Osborn to John Murray. The same letter proves his authorship of the *Times* review. 'I ... will if you like arrange my review in the Times so as to make it appear the day the book is supplied to the trade – rather than give the other reviewers cause to complain,' he wrote. Murray Archive.

95 Jane Franklin to Roderick Murchison, 9 March 1857, BL Add. MS 46126, f. 257–58.

96 [Osborn], 'The Voyage of the Fox,' *Times*, 30 December 1859, 8.

97 Osborn, 'Voyage of the "Fox" in the Arctic Seas,' 118, 119.

98 Sherard Osborn, 'The Last Voyage of Sir John Franklin,' *Once a Week* 1 (22 October 1859): 338.

99 Sherard Osborn, 'The Last Voyage of Sir John Franklin,' *Once a Week* 1 (29 October 1859): 367.

100 Sherard Osborn, 'The Search for Sir John Franklin,' *Once a Week* 1 (5 November 1859): 387.

101 Osborn to Murray, undated, Murray Archive.

102 [C.R. Weld], review of *The Career, Last Voyage, and Fate of Captain Sir John Franklin, Athenaeum* 1683 (28 January 1860): 131. Attributions of authorship in the *Athenaeum* are from 'The Athenaeum Index of Reviews and Reviewers: 1830–1870,' www. athenaeum.soi.city.ac.uk (accessed 2 March 2002 and 11 May 2003).

103 'Arctic Exploration,' *New Monthly Magazine* 118 (1860): 231–2.

104 [Fitch], 'Arctic Explorations,' 238–42.

105 [Osborn], 'Voyage of the "Fox" in the Arctic Seas,' 117.

106 [Osborn], 'Voyage of the Fox,' 8.

107 McClintock was, in truth, a man of exceptionally upright character; the issue is not whether he was shown in an undeservedly favourable light, but the literary strategies Osborn employed in presenting him to the public.

108 McClintock to Murchison, 20 October 1859, BL Add. MS 46127, f. 138–9.

109 McClintock, *Voyage of the 'Fox'*, xxvii.

110 McClintock to Murray, 29 November 1859, Murray Archive.

111 Markham, *Life of McClintock*, 240.

112 Decades later, after the turn of the century, Markham still described polar exploration as a 'tale of derring-doe.' Clements Markham, 'Address to the Royal Geographical Society, 1903,' *Geographical Journal* 22 (July 1903): 13.

113 'Last of the Arctic Voyages,' *British Quarterly Review* 23 (April 1856): 363. For other reviews of Belcher, see chap. 8, below.

114 'Dr. Kane's Arctic Explorations,' *Chambers's Edinburgh Journal*, 3rd ser. 6 (20 December 1856): 390.

115 For some exceptions, see Nigel Leask, *British Romantic Writers and the East* (Cambridge: Cambridge University Press, 1992); Richardson and Hofkosh, *Romanticism, Race*; and Fulford and Kitson, *Romanticism and Colonialism*.

116 Said, *Orientalism*, 3, 176–7, 204.

117 See Berlin, 'The Counter-Enlightenment,' in *Against the Current*. See also Brown, 'Romanticism and Enlightenment.'

118 See Cobban, *Edmund Burke*; Mulhauser, 'Tradition of Burke'; Pocock, 'The Varieties of Whiggism from Exclusion to Reform,' in *Virtue, Commerce and History*, especially 280–3.

119 Burke, *Reflections*, 281, 128, 147, 144.

120 Markham, *Life of McClintock*, 35.
121 [David Brewster], 'Arctic Searching Expeditions,' *North British Review* 16
     (February 1852): 260. Brewster (1781–1868) invented the kaleidoscope
     and did his most important work on the polarization of light. He wrote
     many articles for the *Edinburgh Review* and the *North British Review*. See
     Stephen and Lee, *Dictionary of National Biography*.
122 McClintock, *Voyage of the 'Fox'*, 95.
123 [Fitch], 'Arctic Explorations,' 261, 259.
124 Review of *The Voyage of the 'Fox' in the Arctic Seas, Examiner*, 31 December
     1859, 836.
125 'An Observer' [Sherard Osborn], letter to the editor, *Times*, 9 January 1850,
     5. The letter is attributed to Osborn in Day, *Search for the Northwest Passage*.
126 Second leader, *Illustrated London News*, 1 October 1859, 316.

2: The Dreams of Romance, 1818–1820

  1 The issue (vol. 21, no. 41) was dated January 1819, but it was not published
     until 4 June. Cutmore, Early Quarterly Review Page. The *Quarterly* usually
     appeared well behind schedule.
  2 Other journalists referred to Barrow's authorship of the *Quarterly* articles as
     if to a widely known fact; for example, see the review of his *Chronological
     History of Voyages into the Arctic Regions* in the November 1818 issue of
     Blackwood's Magazine.
  3 [John Barrow], 'Ross's *Voyage of Discovery*,' *Quarterly Review* 21 (January
     1819): 213–14.
  4 Ibid., 214.
  5 Graham, *English Literary Periodicals*, 238–9.
  6 Roper, *Reviewing*, 32.
  7 See Habermas, *Structural Transformation*; 'Further Reflections on the Public
     Sphere,' in Calhoun, *Habermas*, 421–57. For a discussion of Habermas's
     ideas in relation to British periodical writing in the Romantic era, see
     Magnuson, *Reading Public Romanticism*, chap. 1.
  8 Quoted in Ross, *Polar Pioneers*, 69.
  9 This was Markham's description of Parry, in *Lands of Silence*, 205.
 10 Lloyd, *Mr. Barrow*, 11.
 11 [John Barrow], 'Burney – Behring's Strait and the Polar Basin,' *Quarterly
     Review* 18 (January 1818): 457–8, 456.
 12 [Barrow], 'On the Polar Ice and Northern Passage into the Pacific,' *Quar-
     terly Review* 18 (October 1817): 213, 212–13.
 13 See chap. 1, n. 72.

14 'State of Public Affairs,' *Quarterly Review* 22 (January 1820): 493, 495.

15 For example, see [Barrow], 'On the Polar Ice,' 204, 215; 'Burney – Behring's Strait,' 449.

16 [Barrow], 'Burney – Behring's Strait,' 431.

17 Clive, 'The *Edinburgh Review*,' 120.

18 Roper, *Reviewing before the* Edinburgh, 24.

19 Clive, 'The *Edinburgh Review*,' 119. This circulation was exceeded only by the *Methodist Magazine* and the *Evangelical Magazine*, both of which stood at 18,000–20,000. Altick, *English Common Reader*, 392.

20 Murray to Canning, 25 September 1807, in Smiles, *A Publisher and His Friends*, 36.

21 Lloyd, *Mr. Barrow*, 168.

22 Colley, *Britons*, especially chap. 4; Thompson, *Making of the Working Class*, 178–9, 197–9, 683, 807–8.

23 See Gilmartin, *Print Politics*.

24 Altick, *English Common Reader*, 392, 381–2.

25 Klancher, *Making of English Reading Audiences*, Introduction, chap. 2; Hayden, *Romantic Reviewers*, chap. 2.

26 Klancher, *Making of English Reading Audiences*, 48.

27 'State of Public Affairs,' 554, 556–7.

28 Lloyd, *Mr. Barrow*, 167.

29 Barrow to Murray, 9 June, no year, annotated '? 1836,' Murray Archive. Greek letters in original.

30 Scott to George Ellis, 2 November 1808; Scott to Murray, 2 November 1808; Murray to Scott, 15 November 1808; quoted in Smiles, *A Publisher and His Friends*, 41, 42, 47.

31 [Barrow], 'Lord Selkirk, and the North-West Company,' *Quarterly Review* 16 (October 1816): 144, 141, 159, 160–1, 163.

32 Ibid., 153, 166–8, 169.

33 Ibid., 170n.

34 'Extract of a Letter from Mr Scoresby, Jun. M.W.S. &c. to Professor Jameson,' *Blackwood's* 2 (October 1817): 20–1. Dated 27 August 1817.

35 [Barrow], 'O'Reilly's Voyage to Davis's Strait,' *Quarterly Review* 19 (April 1818): 209–10.

36 The letter is printed in Weld, *History of the Royal Society*, 2: 274–77.

37 Lloyd, *Mr. Barrow*, 124; Bravo, 'Science and Discovery,' 7–8, 11–17, 43–4, 58, 60–3, 85–6.

38 Printed in Weld, *History of the Royal Society*, 2: 279.

39 See Wright, 'Open Polar Sea.'

40 [Barrow], 'On the Polar Ice,' 219.

41 Cutmore, Early Quarterly Review Page.

42 [Barrow], 'On the Polar Ice,' 220.

43 Smiles, *A Publisher and His Friends*, 48, 44.

44 'Expeditions to the North Pole,' *Literary Gazette* 58 (28 February 1818): 130.

45 'Some Account of Captain Ross's Voyage of Discovery, for the Purpose of Exploring Baffin's Bay, and Inquiring into the Probability of a North-West Passage,' *Edinburgh Magazine* 4 (April 1819): 329.

46 'Accounts of Greenland, and of Arctic Voyages,' *Monthly Review* 88 (January 1819): 62.

47 Porden, *Arctic Expeditions*, 6, 7–8.

48 John Franklin to Hannah Booth, 18 April 1818, Derbyshire Record Office D3311/ Unlisted box 1, family letters.

49 John Franklin to Isabella Cracroft, 6 April 1818, SPRI MS 248/298/1-20.

50 Quoted in Woodward, *Portrait of Jane*, 156.

51 'Barrow's Voyages into the Arctic Regions,' *Blackwood's Edinburgh Magazine* 4 (November 1818): 188.

52 [Leslie], 'Polar Ice, and a North-West Passage,' *Edinburgh Review* 30 (June 1818): 5. The article is attributed to John Leslie in the *Dictionary of National Biography*. It was well known at the time that he was the author: see a letter to the editor in *Blackwood's* 6 (May 1819): 152. Leslie (1766–1832), a professor of mathematics at the University of Edinburgh, wrote for both the *Edinburgh* and the *Monthly Review*. On the scientific dimension of the controversy, see Bravo, 'Science and Discovery,' 92–107.

53 Duff, *Romance and Revolution*, 10.

54 Ibid., 27, 31–33, 12.

55 [Leslie], 'Polar Ice,' 2.

56 Jameson (1774–1854), was Regius Professor of natural history at the University of Edinburgh. He took a keen interest in Arctic geology. In 1819 he and David Brewster founded the *Edinburgh Philosophical Journal*. See Stephen and Lee, *Dictionary of National Biography* and Sweet, 'Jameson and the Explorers.'

57 [Robert Jameson], 'Account of the Expedition to Baffin's Bay, under Captain Ross and Lieutenant Parry. Drawn up from Captain Ross's Account of the Voyage, and other Sources of Information,' *Edinburgh Philosophical Journal* 1 (June 1819): 151. The article is attributed to Jameson in Day, *Search for the Northwest Passage*.

58 'The Arctic Expedition,' *New Monthly Magazine* 10 (October 1818): 241.

59 'Barrow's Voyages,' *Blackwood's*, 188.

60 'Arctic Expedition,' 241.

61 'Intelligence from the Discovery Ships,' *British Review* 12 (November 1818), 530. Emphasis in original.

62 Dodge, *Polar Rosses*, 73–5; Ross, *Polar Pioneers*, 52–3, 68–9.

63 Barrow was attacked on this score in an anonymous pamphlet; see 'A Friend to the Navy,' *A Letter to John Barrow, Esq., on the Subject of the Polar Expedition.*

64 'North-West Passage. Expedition under Captain Ross and Lieutenant Parry, in the Isabella and Alexander,' *Blackwood's* 4 (December 1818): 342–3.

65 Peter Heywood to John Ross, 25 January 1819; quoted in Ross, *Polar Pioneers*, 57.

66 'Baffin's Bay. North-West Passage,' *Literary Gazette* 103 (9 January 1819): 23.

67 [Alexander Fisher], 'Journal of a Voyage of Discovery to the Arctic Regions, performed between the 4th of April and the 18th of November, 1818, in His Majesty's Ship Alexander, Wm. Edw. Parry, Esq. Lieut. and Commander, by an Officer of the Alexander,' *New Voyages and Travels* 1 (1819), 73. Nine · volumes of this series were published in monthly parts between 1819 and 1823.

68 'Barrow's Voyages,' *New Monthly Magazine* 11 (February 1819): 63.

69 For example, those in the *Monthly Review* and the *New Monthly Magazine*.

70 'Barrow's Voyages,' 63.

71 For example, [Hugh Murray?], 'North-West Passage. Expeditions to the Polar Sea,' *Edinburgh Review* 48 (December 1828): 423–50; [W. Francis Ainsworth], 'The Arctic Voyages,' *New Monthly Magazine* 88 (January 1850): 83–99; 'The Recent Arctic Expeditions,' *United Service Magazine*, repr. *Littell's Living Age* 24 (2 February 1850): 193–202; [Joshua Fitch], 'Arctic Explorations,' *London Quarterly Review* 14 (April 1860): 226–61.

72 Barrow had arranged for the publication immediately after Ross's return and before relations between them deteriorated. Ross later complained that Barrow had tried to write the narrative for him. He described a dramatic moment when, after a disagreement, Barrow stalked out of Murray's office, saying to Ross, 'I'll have nothing more to do with you.' (Ross, *Polar Pioneers*, 52–3). The second edition was published by Longmans.

73 Sabine, 'Account of the Esquimaux,' 93–4.

74 'Ross's Voyage of Discovery, &c.,' *Monthly Review* 89 (August 1819): 337–56.

75 'On the Practicability of Effecting a North North East, or North West Passage into the Pacific Ocean, with Observations on the Voyage of Captain Ross and Lieutenant Parry,' *New Monthly Magazine* 11 (May 1819): 312–20.

76 'Captain Ross, and Sir James Lancaster's Sound,' *Blackwood's* 5 (May 1819): 150.

77 [Jameson], 'Account of the Expedition to Baffin's Bay,' 150–9.

78 'Captain Ross's Voyage of Discovery,' *British Review* 13 (May 1819): 418, 414, 419.

79 'Captain Ross's Voyage to Baffin's Bay,' *Edinburgh Review* 31 (March 1819): 336–7.
80 The *Wellesley Index* (Houghton) suggests that either Hugh Murray or Sydney Smith may have written the article.
81 'Captain Ross's Voyage to Baffin's Bay,' 337, 360, 363, 353.

3: The Threshold of a World Unknown, 1820–1821

1 'The Arctic Expedition,' *Literary Gazette* 161 (19 February 1820): 126.
2 'Discovery Ships,' *Literary Gazette* 198 (4 November 1820): 714.
3 'Northern Expedition,' *Literary Gazette* 199 (11 November 1820): 729.
4 'Captain Parry and Mr Fisher's *Journals of a Voyage of Discovery to the Arctic Regions,*' *Edinburgh Philosophical Journal* 5 (July 1821): 178.
5 Barrow to Murray, 5 November 1820, Murray Archive.
6 Parry to Murray, 7 November 1820, Murray Archive.
7 The chart was printed in a number of periodicals, including the *Literary Gazette* 201 (25 November 1820), *Blackwood's* 8 (November 1820), the *Gentleman's Magazine*, n.s. 13, pt 2 (December 1820), and the *Edinburgh Philosophical Journal* 4 (January 1821).
8 For example, see 'Arctic Voyages,' *Eclectic Review* 16 (July 1821): 56.
9 Parry to Murray, 7 November 1820, Murray Archive. Emphasis in original.
10 'Letters written during the late Voyage of Discovery in the Western Arctic Sea. By an Officer of the Expedition,' *New Voyages and Travels* 5 (July 1821).
11 'Literary and Philosophical Intelligence,' *Monthly Magazine* 51 (June 1821): 450.
12 'Critical Notices of Books of the Month,' *Monthly Magazine* 51 (June 1821): 457.
13 Jerdan, *Autobiography,* 2: 187; 3: 110.
14 *Literary Gazette* 202 (2 December 1820): 779. Jerdan states in his autobiography that he was the author of earlier Arctic articles, so it seems highly likely he also wrote the reviews.
15 *Literary Gazette* 226 (19 May 1821): 314; 227 (26 May 1821): 325–6.
16 '*North Georgia Gazette, and Winter Chronicle,*' *Literary Gazette* 227 (26 May 1821): 325.
17 Jerdan, *Autobiography,* 3: 110–11; *Literary Gazette* 225 (12 May 1821): 293–5.
18 'North Polar Passage,' *Literary Chronicle* 80 (25 November 1820): 753–5; 81 (2 December 1820): 778–9; 83 (16 December 1820): 807–10; 84 (23 December 1820): 824–6.
19 *Literary Gazette* 226 (19 May 1821): 314.
20 'Captain Parry's Journal,' *Literary Gazette* 227 (26 May 1821): 323.

21 Jerdan, *Men I Have Known*, 132.

22 *Literary Chronicle* 105 (19 May 1821): 305.

23 'Captain Parry's Voyage,' *Blackwood's* 9 (June 1821): 290.

24 'Captain Parry's Journal,' *London Magazine* 3 (June 1821): 642, 647.

25 'Arctic Voyages,' 65.

26 'Queen Mab. By Percy Bysshe Shelley,' *Literary Chronicle* 107 (2 June 1821): 344–5.

27 *Literary Gazette* 227 (26 May 1821): 323.

28 'Captain Parry and Mr Fisher's *Journals*,' 196.

29 'Captain Parry's Voyage,' *Blackwood's*, 294.

30 'Captain Parry's Voyage,' *British Critic*, n.s. 15 (June 1821): 619.

31 'Q,' review of Parry, *Examiner* 699 (27 May 1821): 333.

32 Parry, *Journal of a Voyage for the Discovery of a North-West Passage*, xv.

33 Although Parry has been subject to much less debunking than Franklin, the views expressed by A.G.E. Jones in 'Parry: A Different View' have had some influence.

34 See Croker, *Croker Papers*, 1: 25.

35 [J.W. Croker], 'Frankenstein, or the Modern Prometheus,' *Quarterly Review* 18 (January 1818): 382, 385, 381. Attribution by Cutmore, Early Quarterly Review Page.

36 'Parry's Voyage of Discovery,' *Monthly Review* 96 (October 1821): 148.

37 'Q,' Review of Parry, 332.

38 'Captain Parry's Voyage,' *British Review* 18 (September 1821): 78.

39 'Arctic Voyages,' 51.

40 'Captain Parry's Voyage,' *British Review*, 65–6.

41 'Parry's Voyage of Discovery,' *Gentleman's Magazine*, n.s. 14, pt 1 (June 1821): 539, and supplement, 616.

42 See Lukács, *Historical Novel*, 29–69. For more recent assessments of Scott, see Trumpener, *Bardic Nationalism*, chap. 3; Chandler, *England in 1819*, 11–13, 131–51, 211–36. Trumpener argues that Scott did not, as Lukács claims, invent the historical novel; rather, he drew on the work of several less famous contemporaries. However, his great popularity must nevertheless earn him a unique place in the cultural history of the era.

43 Scott himself had an interest in the supernatural and occasionally made it an element in his plots; reviewers, however, usually disapproved of this practice. The supernatural aspect of Scott's second novel, *Guy Mannering*, was severely rebuked: in the *Quarterly*, Croker called it a 'monstrous absurdity.' 'Guy Mannering, or the Astrologer,' *Quarterly Review* 12 (January 1815): 507. Attribution by Cutmore, Early Quarterly Review Page.

44 'Waverley; or, 'tis Sixty Years Since,' *Quarterly Review* 11 (July 1814): 377. Emphasis in original. Cutmore suggests Croker or Gifford as the author of this review.

45 Ruskin, *Praeterita*, 5, 30.

46 [Nassau William Senior], 'Novels, by the Author of Waverley,' *Quarterly Review* 26 (October 1821): 127. Attribution by Cutmore, Early Quarterly Review Page.

47 See Girouard, *Return to Camelot.*

48 'Remarks on Captain Parry's Expedition,' *Blackwood's* 8 (November 1820): 221.

49 See the extracts from Fisher's narrative in 'Fisher's Voyage to the Arctic Regions,' *Literary Gazette* 226 (19 May 1821): 314–15.

50 'Parry's Expedition,' *New Monthly Magazine*, 1821 pt 1: 719.

51 Quoted in 'The Arctic Regions,' *New Monthly Magazine* 13 (May 1820): 539.

52 For example, see Franklin to Sarah Sellwood, 12 April 1823, in Davis, '"… which an affectionate heart would say,"' 205; Franklin to Richardson, 20 November [1823], DRO 3311/ unlisted box 1, letter 94.

53 'Arctic Voyages,' 63.

54 [Barrow], 'Parry's Voyage of Discovery,' *Quarterly Review* 25 (April 1821): 175, 177. This issue of the *Quarterly* did not appear until 28 June (Cutmore, Early Quarterly Review Page).

55 Ibid., 180.

56 [Barrow], 'Flinders' *Voyage to Terra Australis,*' *Quarterly Review* 12 (October 1814): 13.

57 [Barrow], 'Parry's Voyage of Discovery,' 215–16, 214–15, 177, 214.

58 Ibid., 214.

59 Osborn, *The Career, Last Voyage*, 1–2; Traill, *Life of Sir John Franklin*, 6–7.

60 Owen, *Fate of Franklin*, 27.

61 Mack, *Matthew Flinders*, 73–9.

62 John Franklin to Ann Flinders, 18 October 1810, NMM FLI/ 27.

63 John Franklin to Matthew Flinders, 1 November 1810, NMM FLI/ 1.

64 Mack, *Matthew Flinders*, 216–17, 220–1, 228.

65 In 1841, while governor of Van Diemen's Land, Franklin recounted a story about the Flinders expedition that showed just how ambitious and self-centred he was as a youth. One of the *Investigator's* boats had capsized with eight men on board. Franklin and several others were landed to search for bodies that might have washed up on shore. They were provided with flags to signal the ship if any were found. Franklin, in this situation, was less concerned with his mission than with the fact that he was on an unexplored shore with a British flag. He waved it simply for the sake of being able in

future to say that he had been the first to do so, and he made up a glib story of having thought he saw a body. His second wife, to whom the story was told, wrote disapprovingly that the action was 'not of the first order of merit.' Traill, *Life of Franklin*, 280–1.

66 Ibid., 2–3, 32–3; Owen, *Fate of Franklin*, 22–4. The wording of the account of Thomas Franklin's death quoted by Owen suggests that he committed suicide.

67 In the introduction to his Champlain Society edition of Franklin's journal, Richard Davis claims that, when writing his narrative, Franklin revised his original account so as to highlight what he perceived as the failings of the Native leader Akaitcho. In fact, a close analysis of the two texts shows that Franklin removed his original negative comments in order to give the British reading public a more favourable and just impression of Akaitcho's character and actions. In all other respects, the narrative follows the journal very closely; for periods when Franklin had made few entries, he drew on Richardson's journal, at some points reproducing it almost word for word. See Cavell, 'Representing Akaitcho.'

68 Franklin, *Narrative of a Journey*, xx (1969 repr.).

4: A Romance in Real Life, 1821–1824

1 For example, in a letter written in 1826, when Franklin was on his second overland expedition, Ann Flinders referred pointedly to 'those who plan such schemes & in a manner force others to execute them.' She added, 'Those now in power seem happily to grow weary of the cause, happily I say, because it may be the means of preserving some valuable lives.' Ann Flinders to Franklin, 22 April 1826, SPRI MS 248/382/1-2.

2 Ann Flinders to John Barrow, 11 November 1815, copy in Flinders private letter books, S1/57, Nov. 1810–May 1814 (Vol. 3), 311. Matthew Flinders Electronic Archive, State Library of New South Wales, www.slnsw.gov.au/flinders/archive.html (accessed 16 March 2003). She ended by asking Barrow 'to pardon this intrusion, a liberty I certainly shod. not have taken but from being informed that Mr. Franklin is not in possession of any written document from Capt. Flinders expressive of the high esteem in which he held him.'

3 John Franklin to Ann Flinders, 5 December 1815, NMM FLI/27.

4 'MS Memorandum from Sir John Franklin,' in Jerdan, *Men I Have Known*, 223. Franklin wrote this autobiographical sketch for Jerdan after his second expedition.

5 John Franklin to Ann Flinders, 18 February 1818, NMM FLI/27.

6 Traill, *Life of Franklin*, 64.

7 Weld, *History of the Royal Society*, 2: 283n. Weld does not name his source, refer-
ring to it simply as 'MS. Document,' nor does he provide any details of the
plan. The biographies of Franklin shed no further light on the matter.

8 In exploration narratives of the time, this band (a subgroup of the Dene
nation) is referred to as the Copper Indians or the Red Knives; they are
now usually called the Yellowknife or Yellowknives. See Helm, *Handbook of
North American Indians*, Vol. 6, *The Subarctic*.

9 Both William Law, *A Serious Call to a Devout and Holy Life, Adapted to the State
and Condition of All Orders of Christians* (1729) and Philip Doddridge, *The
Rise and Progress of Religion in the Soul* (1745) were very popular works, frequently reprinted throughout the eighteenth and nineteenth centuries.

10 Franklin to Henrietta Wright, date not given, in Traill, *Life of Sir John Franklin*,
77–9. See also Franklin's letter to J.B. Wright from Fort Enterprise, 18 October 1820, DRO D3311/115 (copy by Philip Lyttelton Gell, 1897).

11 Historian Richard Glover charged that Richardson was too quick to conclude that Teroahauté had killed Hood, and that the shooting of Teroahauté was motivated by the desire for revenge. Later writers have suggested that
perhaps Richardson himself had knowingly committed cannibalism. Such
claims are based on no evidence other than a vague statement by Wentzel
about unspecified wrongdoing on the part of one of the officers, written
before he had read Richardson's own account of events. See Cavell, 'Hidden
Crime of Dr Richardson.'

12 Franklin, *Narrative of a Journey*, 440 (1969 repr.).

13 John Franklin to Willingham Franklin, 8 April 1822, in Davis, '"… which an
affectionate heart would say,"' 202.

14 Hood and three others in the weakest group (Ignace Perrault, Jean-Baptiste
Belanger, and Vincenza Fontano) were almost certainly murdered by
Teroahauté, and Teroahauté was shot by Richardson. The Inuk interpreter
Junius and two voyageurs, Matthew Pellonquin (or Crédit) and Registe
Vaillant, had already died of starvation on the march. Two voyageurs,
Joseph Peltier and François Semandré, died of starvation at Fort En-
terprise. Another voyageur, Gabriel Beauparlant, died of starvation with
Back's advance party. Franklin, Richardson, Back, Hepburn, the Inuk inter-
preter Augustus, the Canadian interpreters Pierre St Germain and Jean-
Baptiste Adam, and the voyageurs Joseph Benoit and Solomon Belanger
survived.

15 John Franklin to Elizabeth (Betsey) Franklin, 10 October 1822, DRO 3311/
unlisted box 1, family letters. Davis prints this letter in '"… which an affectionate heart would say,"' 202–4, and claims that it is to Sarah Sellwood. It

begins simply 'My dear Sister,' but the outside direction is to 'Miss Franklin, Horncastle, Lincolnshire.' As Elizabeth was Franklin's only surviving unmarried sister, the letter must be to her. See Gell, *John Franklin's Bride*, xx. Franklin's report is in the files of the Colonial Office, with the date of receipt noted. Colonial Office 6/15 f.72, microfilm copy in Library and Archives Canada, MG 11, reel B-3004.

16 John Franklin to Isabella Cracroft, 10 October 1822, in Davis, "'… which an affectionate heart would say,'" 204.

17 Hearne placed the mouth of the river in latitude 71° 55' north, longitude 120° 30' west. Franklin's observations gave a latitude of 67° 48' north, longitude 115° 37' west. John Richardson, 'Digression concerning Hearne's Route,' in Back, *Arctic Land Expedition*, 148.

18 'North-Western Land Expedition,' *Times*, 4 October 1822, 2. Reprinted from the Montreal *Herald*, 17 August 1822. The report was received through 'a gentleman who has just arrived in this city, from a distant post in the north-west territory.'

19 'North-West Land Expedition,' *Times*, 18 October 1822, 2. Reprinted from 'the *Montreal Herald* of Sept. 11.' The article was, in fact, taken from the Montreal *Gazette*. The report apparently came from York Factory. The article recounted that the explorers 'were driven to the necessity of … feeding upon the tattered remnants of their shoes, and, we fear, upon a more forbidding and unpalatable fare.'

20 Ibid., 19 October 1822, 2. Reprinted from 'an Evening Paper.' It is likely that the article is by Barrow, as the phrasing resembles that used in his *Quarterly* review of Franklin's narrative.

21 Eleanor Porden to John Franklin, 19 October 1822, in Gell, *John Franklin's Bride*, 71–2.

22 'Arctic Land Expedition,' *Blackwood's* 12 (October 1822): 500; 'North-West Expedition by Land,' *Gentleman's Magazine* n.s. 15, pt 2 (October 1822): 364.

23 John Franklin to John Richardson, 24 October 1824, in *Franklin's Journals and Correspondence, 1819–1822*, 428.

24 'The American Overland Expedition,' *Literary Gazette* 303 (9 November 1822): 711–12. Jerdan accurately reported that Richardson, Hepburn, and Hood had been given human flesh to eat by Teroahauté, who claimed it was wolf meat. However, he also wrote that after Teroahauté had killed Hood, the voyageur 'was proceeding to devour his corpse, had not Dr. R. (coming back) rid the world of the insane and dangerous wretch, by shooting him dead on the spot.'

25 John Franklin to Willingham Franklin, 8 April 1822, in Davis, "'… which an affectionate heart would say,'" 202.

26 Willingham Franklin to John Franklin, 10 July 1822, SPRI MS 248/394 (copy).

27 Ibid. Emphasis in original.

28 John Franklin to Isabella Cracroft, 10 October 1822, in Davis, '"… which an affectionate heart would say,"' 204.

29 John Franklin to John Richardson, 24 October 1822, *Franklin's Journals and Correspondence, 1819–1822*, 428.

30 John Franklin to Isabella Cracroft, 10 October 1822, in Davis, '"… which an affectionate heart would say,"' 204.

31 John Franklin to Elizabeth Franklin, 10 October 1822, ibid., 203. Emphasis in original.

32 See John Franklin to Henry Sellwood, 21 November 1822, DRO 3311/ 115 (copy).

33 John Franklin to John Richardson, 23 October 1822, *Franklin's Journals and Correspondence, 1819–1822*, 428, 430.

34 See Eleanor Porden to John Franklin, 18 December 1822, in Gell, *John Franklin's Bride*, 83; John Franklin to Eleanor Porden, 16 June 1823, ibid., 182–3.

35 Eleanor Porden to John Franklin, 29 March 1823, ibid., 103–13, and 9 July 1823, ibid., 205.

36 John Franklin to Ann Flinders, 19 June 1824, SPRI MS 248/ 300.

37 Eleanor Porden to John Franklin, 29 March 1823, in Gell, *John Franklin's Bride*, 108.

38 John Franklin to Eleanor Porden, 16 December 1822, ibid., 81–2.

39 John Franklin to Eleanor Porden, 11 July 1823, ibid., 219.

40 Richardson, in Franklin, *Second Expedition*, 236–7.

41 Henry Elliott, 'Sir John Franklin,' *Nineteenth Century* 32, 185 (July 1892): 129.

42 John Franklin to Eleanor Porden, 19 June 1823, in Gell, *John Franklin's Bride*, 194.

43 Eleanor Porden to John Franklin, 9 July 1823, ibid., 207. Emphasis in original.

44 John Franklin to Eleanor Porden, 11 July 1823, ibid., 221.

45 Eleanor Franklin to John Franklin, 13 September 1824, ibid., 279.

46 'Review of Captain Franklin's Narrative,' *Christian Observer* 24 (March 1824): 172.

47 Franklin, *Narrative of a Journey*, 413 (1969 repr.).

48 In his 1839 biography of Anson, Barrow noted with disapproval the lack of religious sentiment in the narrative of Anson's voyage. He remarked that not a single expression in the book showed the author to be a Christian, or that he wrote with a Christian audience in mind. Barrow, *The Life of George*

Lord Anson, cited in Hamilton, 'Naval Hagiography and the Victorian Hero,' 387n15.

49 *Christian Observer* 2 (February 1824): 107–8; 2 (March 1824): 168.

50 'Franklin's Journey to the Polar Sea,' *British Review* 22 (May 1824): 24.

51 Richardson, in Franklin, *Narrative of a Journey*, 449.The book referred to is Edward Bickersteth, *A Scripture Help, Designed to Assist in Reading the Bible Profitably* (1816).

52 Richardson, in Franklin, *Narrative of a Journey*, 459.

53 Franklin, *Narrative of a Journey*, 417, 427.

54 John Franklin to Eleanor Porden, 11 July 1823, in Gell, *John Franklin's Bride*, 217.

55 Richardson, in Franklin, *Narrative of a Journey*, 458, 460.

56 [Barrow], 'Franklin's Journey to the Polar Sea,' *Quarterly Review* 28 (January 1823): 399. The issue was published on 8 July (Cutmore, Early Quarterly Review Page).

57 [Hugh James Rose], '*Apocryphal New Testament*,' *Quarterly Review* 25 (July 1821): 348. Attribution by Cutmore, Early Quarterly Review Page.

58 'Mr. Hone and the Quarterly,' *Examiner* 722 (4 November 1821): 697–8.

59 [John Matthews], 'Hazlitt's Table Talk,' *Quarterly Review* 26 (October 1821): 103–4. Attribution by Cutmore, Early Quarterly Review Page.

60 [George Taylor], 'Godwin and Malthus on Population,' ibid., 149. Attribution by Cutmore, Early Quarterly Review Page.

61 [William Sidney Walker], 'Shelley – *Prometheus Unbound*, &c.,' ibid., 189. Attribution by Cutmore, Early Quarterly Review Page.

62 'The Quarterly Review,' *Examiner* 733 (20 January 1822): 33. See also 'The Three Asses. – Wm. Gifford,' *Examiner* 731 (6 January 1822): 4; 'The Black Dwarf Against the Quarterly Review,' *Black Dwarf* 10 (18 March 1823): 413–18.

63 *Monthly Magazine* 55 (April 1823): 257. Richard Davis erroneously gives the date as June 1823 in 'History or His/Story?' 100.

64 Eleanor Porden to John Franklin, 1 May 1823, in Gell, *John Franklin's Bride*, 113–14.

65 *Literary Gazette* 326 (12 April 1823): 225–6.

66 Barrow to Murray, 14 December 1822, Murray Archive. Barrow persuaded Finden to lower his price, and Finden stated that he 'wd. rather do them at a loss than not do them at all, wishing to have his name to so respectable a work ... If you should still think the work will not afford it, Franklin must consent to strike out 8 or 10 – which I [illegible] would be a pity.' Selling the narrative at a higher price was evidently considered the better alternative. There were twenty-four illustrations, some aquatinted by hand.

67 Barrow to Murray, 25 December 1822, Murray Archive.

68 *Literary Gazette* 327 (19 April 1822): 247.

69 Franklin to Richardson, 24 July 1823, in *Franklin's Journals and Correspondence, 1825–1827*, 270.

70 Richardson to Franklin, 10 March 1824, DRO 3311/ unlisted box 1, letter #7.

71 Woodward, *Portrait of Jane*, 156.

72 *Literary Gazette* 327 (19 April 1822): 247.

73 *Literary Chronicle* 205 (19 April 1822): 241.

74 *Literary Chronicle* 208 (10 May 1823): 296.

75 'Capt. Franklin's Narrative,' *Gentleman's Magazine* n.s. 16, pt 1 (May 1823): 428, 432.

76 'Narrative of a Journey to the Shores of the Polar Sea,' *London Magazine* 7 (May 1823): 573.

77 'Franklin's Expedition,' *New Monthly Magazine* 7 (May 1823): 400.

78 'Franklin's Journey to the Polar Sea,' *Eclectic Review*, n.s. 19 (June 1823): 531, 521.

79 'Account of Franklin's Expedition to the Shores of the Polar Sea,' *Edinburgh Magazine* n.s. 12 (June 1823): 665.

80 John Franklin to John Richardson, 20 November [1823], DRO 3311/ unlisted box 1, letter #94.

81 [Barrow], 'Franklin's Journey to the Polar Sea,' 372, 373, 395, 397, 398, 399. Emphasis in original.

82 Ibid., 402.

83 Cutmore suggests that the review was written either by Barrow or by Robert William Hay. See Early Quarterly Review Page.

84 Barrow's emphasis on the 'otherness' of the French-Canadian voyageurs demonstrates the accuracy of Colley's argument that the British national character was defined primarily through confrontations with the French. Colley, *Britons*, 1–2. Contrasts between Britons and Natives, on the other hand, were of comparatively little interest to Barrow.

85 'Franklin's Journey to the Polar Sea,' *Monthly Review* 102 (September 1823): 1.

86 Ibid. (October 1823): 167–8, 176.

87 'Review of Captain Franklin's Narrative,' *Christian Observer* 24 (February 1824): 107–8.

88 Ibid. (March 1824): 166, 167, 167–8, 171–2.

89 Ibid., 172–3. Emphasis in original.

90 'Franklin's Journey to the Shores of the Polar Sea,' *British Review and London Critical Journal* 22 (May 1824): 1, 2, 4.

91 Ibid., 21, 16, 24.

92 Bellot, *Memoirs of Lieutenant Joseph-René Bellot*, 2: 238–9.

5: The Nelsons of Discovery

1 Besides his Arctic articles and books, Barrow's writings on naval topics included several articles in the sixth (1820–3) edition of the *Encyclopaedia Britannica*; *The Eventful History of the Mutiny and Piratical Seizure of H.M.S. Bounty* (1831); *The Life of Richard, Earl Howe* (1838); *The Life of George, Lord Anson* (1839).

2 See Helgerson, *Forms of Nationhood*, chap. 4.

3 See Glass, 'Image of the Sea Officer.'

4 Hamilton, 'Naval Hagiography.'

5 The only general study is Behrman, *Victorian Myths of the Sea*. Behrman takes a thematic rather than a chronological approach, and her book therefore does little to elucidate the historical development of the metanarrative, especially in the earlier half of the century. Most of her examples are drawn from the 1880s and 1890s. The naval narrative is briefly but deftly summarized and its reflection in novels analysed by John Peck in *Maritime Fiction*. Standard works on the navy in the Victorian era include Kennedy, *British Naval Mastery*; Bartlett, *Great Britain and Sea Power*; and Semmel, *Liberalism and Naval Strategy*.

6 Newman, *English Nationalism*, 127, 123, 124, 139–42. For a detailed catalogue of the traits considered to define the national character, see Langford, *Englishness Identified*.

7 Newman, *English Nationalism*, 125, 149–51.

8 Collini, 'Idea of "Character,"' 45.

9 'On the Genius and Character of Rousseau,' *Blackwood's Magazine* 11 (February 1822): 135, 138.

10 On Victorian hero-worship, see also Houghton, *Victorian Frame of Mind*, chap. 12; Cubitt and Warren, *Heroic Reputations*, especially the introduction and John MacKenzie, 'The Iconography of the Exemplary Life: The Case of David Livingstone,' 84–104.

11 Carlyle, *Sartor Resartus*, 239, 358.

12 Froude, 'Representative Men,' in *Short Studies on Great Subjects*, 1: 582. This essay, a review of Emerson's *Representative Men*, was first published in 1850.

13 Smiles, *Self Help*, 35, 360, 350–51. The book was the outgrowth of lectures Smiles had been giving since 1845. His ideas thus developed and found expression in the precise period covered by the Franklin search.

14 [Bulwer-Lytton], 'On Self-Control,' *Blackwood's Magazine* 93 (April 1863): 475, 472, 476.

15 'The Fate of Franklin,' *Good Words* 1, 8 (1860): 113.

16 On the 'unresolved tension between voluntarism and determinism,' see
   Collini, 'Idea of "Character,"' 34–7.
17 See Pocock, 'Burke and the Ancient Constitution.'
18 Thompson, *English Working Class*, 671–2.
19 Ibid., 457–9, 625, 756. See also Gilmartin, *Print Politics*, chap. 4; Vernon,
   Politics and the People, chap. 8.
20 Jordan and Rogers, 'Admirals as Heroes,' 211, 214.
21 Quoted in ibid., 224.
22 [Southey], 'Lives of Nelson,' *Quarterly Review* 3 (February 1810): 262.
23 Southey, *Life of Nelson*, lxxiv.
24 Southey, 'Lives of Nelson,' 248.
25 Barrow, *Chronological History*, 57–8.
26 Froude, *English Seamen*, 2, 3.
27 Glass, 'Image of the Sea Officer,' 584. As Glass points out, the contrast
   between Cromwell's officers and those given commissions by Charles II was
   a central focus of political debate at the time, and these seventeenth-
   century representations were given wide currency in the nineteenth century by Macaulay. Recent scholarship demonstrates that there was a gap
   between rhetoric and reality, but the depiction of aristocratic officers as
   foppish and incompetent was widely accepted both at the time and afterwards. In the nineteenth century, this representation served to heighten
   readers' awareness of the far higher professional standards attained by well-
   born officers in their own time.
28 Ibid., 597, 585.
29 Quoted in ibid., 595.
30 Edward Thompson, *A Sailor's Letters* (1767), quoted in Marcus, *Heart of Oak*, 75.
31 William Locker, *Memoirs of Celebrated Commanders* (1830), quoted in ibid., 77.
32 Ibid., 73.
33 Dening, *Mr. Bligh's Bad Language*, 61. See also 83–4, 123, 138–45.
34 Ibid., 138, 133, 145.
35 Barrow, *Voyages of Discovery*, viii, vii. Emphasis in original.
36 Ibid., 271.
37 Leslie, Jameson, and Murray, *Polar Seas and Regions*, 8.
38 Behrman, *Victorian Myths*, 116, 121.
39 First leader, *Illustrated London News* 35 (5 November 1859): 436.
40 For example, see Anderson, 'Growth of Christian Militarism'; Dawson,
   Soldier Heroes, especially chaps 4 and 5; Watson, 'Soldiers and Saints: the
   Fighting Man and the Christian Life,' in Bradstock et al., *Masculinity and
   Spirituality*, 10–26.

41 Behrman, *Victorian Myths*, 43, 111, 116, 121, 123.

42 'Captain Parry and Mr Fisher's *Journals of a Voyage of Discovery to the Arctic Regions*,' *Edinburgh Philosophical Journal* 5 (July 1821): 187–8. This review is likely by either Robert Jameson or David Brewster.

43 [Francis Egerton, earl of Ellesmere], 'Sir James Ross's *Voyage to the Antarctic Regions*,' *Quarterly Review* 81 (June 1847): 167.

44 Stevenson, 'English Admirals,' 75–6.

45 Admiral Thomas Pye to Lord Sandwich, quoted in Marcus, *Heart of Oak*, 277n4.

46 See Fulford, *Romanticism and Masculinity*, 1–9.

47 Southey, *Life of Nelson*, 4, 11–12, 122.

48 'Captain Parry's Voyage,' *Blackwood's* 9 (June 1821): 291. See also 'Captain Parry's Voyage,' *British Critic*, n.s. 15 (June 1821): 609.

49 'Arctic Voyages,' *Eclectic Review* 16 (July 1821): 62.

50 'Parry's *Voyage of Discovery*,' *Monthly Review* 96 (October 1821): 147.

51 This point has been made by Francis Spufford in the excellent chapter on women and exploration in *I May Be Some Time*, 103–4. Spufford's analysis, however, draws more on his own and other twentieth-century readings than on nineteenth-century historical sources. His main evidence comes from the essays written by two twentieth-century women, Ursula Le Guin and Doris Lessing, on their positive response to Antarctic narratives.

52 'Expeditions to the North Pole,' *Westminster Review* 10 (April 1829): 498.

53 Parry, *Memoirs*.

54 Dickens, *Speeches*, 290.

55 Smiles, *Self Help*, 376.

56 Back, *Arctic Land Expedition*, 180.

57 Franklin, *Narrative of a Journey*, 445, 465, 461, 468, 470–1 (1969 repr.).

58 'Narrative of a Journey to the Shores of the Polar Sea,' *London Magazine* 7 (May 1823): 578.

59 [Barrow] 'Franklin's Journey to the Polar Sea,' *Quarterly Review* 28 (January 1823): 402.

60 'Franklin's Journey to the Polar Sea,' *Monthly Review* 102 (October 1823): 166.

61 'Review of Captain Franklin's Narrative,' *Christian Observer* 24 (February 1824): 116–17, 170–1.

62 Franklin, *Narrative of a Journey*, 471.

63 Vance, *Sinews of the Spirit*, 7, 24.

64 Johnson, *Sir John Richardson*, 44.

65 'The Lost Mariners in the Polar Seas,' *Leisure Hour* 106 (5 January 1854): 9–10.

66 'Sir J. Franklin – The North-West Passage,' *British Quarterly Review* 11
(February 1850): 107.

67 'What is Heroism?' *Chambers's Edinburgh Journal* 3rd ser. 7 (9 May 1857): 298.

68 'Dr Kane's Arctic Explorations,' *Chambers's Edinburgh Journal,* 3rd ser. 6
(20 December 1856): 390.

69 'Captain Back's Expedition to the Polar Seas,' *Penny Magazine* 7 (11 August
1838): 311.

70 'Arctic Contributions to Science,' *Chambers's Edinburgh Journal* n.s. 18,
(11 December 1852): 374.

71 Southey, *Life of Nelson,* 2.

72 Quoted in Kennedy, *Nelson and His Captains,* 290.

73 Quoted in Guillemard, 'Franklin and the Arctic,' 240.

74 Austen, *Persuasion,* 19.

75 Marcus, *Heart of Oak,* 204.

76 Ibid., 79. Several examples are given on 79–81.

77 Southey, *Life of Nelson,* 99.

78 'Franklin's Journey to the Shores of the Polar Sea,' *British Review and
London Critical Journal* 22 (May 1824): 13.

79 Barrow, *Voyages of Discovery,* 105.

80 See Markham, *Life of Sir Clements Markham,* 127–8. Clements Markham, as a
midshipman in H.M.S. *Assistance* during the Franklin search, found this
aspect of Arctic discovery especially congenial. During his earlier naval service, he found it almost unbearable to witness floggings, and he later gave
distaste for such punishments as one of his reasons for leaving the service;
41–2, 49–51.

81 Davidoff and Hall, *Family Fortunes,* 30. See also Dror Wahrman, *Imagining
the Middle Class* (Cambridge: Cambridge University Press, 1995).

82 Joven, 'The End of an Epic,' 245.

83 William Thom, *Rhymes and Recollections of a Hand-Loom Weaver,* 3rd ed.
(1847), quoted in Rose, *Intellectual Life,* 17.

84 Ruskin, *Praeterita,* 5.

85 Rose, *Intellectual Life,* 42. A French volunteer on one of the Franklin search
expeditions was 'astonished to hear all the sailors talk to me of Shakespeare; one prefers Macbeth, another Hamlet.' Bellot, *Memoirs,* 1: 138–9.

86 Similar conclusions about readers in other periods have been reached by
Carlo Ginzburg and Janice Radway. See Ginzburg, *The Cheese and the Worms;*
Radway, *Reading the Romance.*

87 Dennett, *Voyages and Travels,* 1–2.

88 An 1845 article in *Chambers's Journal* provided a list of works that the editors
thought best suited for popular libraries, and that were available in cheap

editions. No Arctic narratives were included, but both Anson and Cook were listed, in editions costing 2 shillings and sixpence. 'Popular Libraries,' *Chambers's Edinburgh Journal* n.s. 3, 73 (24 May 1845): 333–5. Murray's abridged editions were priced at £1 for a multi-volume set (four volumes for Franklin, five for Parry).

89 Rose, *Intellectual Life*, 349.

90 Ibid., 372.

91 Altick, *English Common Reader*, 220. On the popularity of Anson and Cook, see also 218, 250, and 258, and Vincent, *Literacy and Popular Culture*, 59.

92 Dennett, *Voyages and Travels*, advertisement following title page.

93 Scoresby, *Franklin Expedition*, 15. Emphasis in original.

6: Their Tribute from the General Voice, 1823–1848

1 Topham, 'Thomas Byerley, John Limbird,' 82–3.

2 Ibid., 85.

3 Ibid., 76.

4 Ibid., 86.

5 *Mirror of Literature, Amusement and Instruction* 2 (17 November 1823): 418n.

6 'Memoir of Capt. Franklin,' *Mirror of Literature, Amusement and Instruction* 1 (26 April 1823): 405–6.

7 'The White Wolf and Dog-Rib Rock,' *Mirror of Literature, Amusement and Instruction* 1 (3 May 1823): 412.

8 'The Esquimaux Indians,' ibid., 426.

9 'The Falls of Wilberforce, in the Arctic Regions,' *Mirror of Literature, Amusement and Instruction* 2 (24 May 1823): 2.

10 'The Northern Expedition,' *Wesleyan Methodist Magazine*, 3rd ser. 2 (November 1823): 756.

11 'Captain Parry's Voyage,' *Mirror of Literature, Amusement and Instruction* 2 (8 November 1823): 400.

12 'History of North Polar Expeditions,' *Mirror of Literature, Amusement and Instruction* 2 (17 November 1823): 417.

13 'North-West Passage,' *British Critic* n.s. 21 (May 1824): 463–4.

14 Preface, *Mirror of Literature, Amusement and Instruction* 5 (January-June 1825): iii–iv.

15 'North-West Passage,' *British Critic*, 465.

16 'Captain Parry's Journal,' *Mirror of Literature, Amusement and Instruction* 3 (3 April 1824): 217–20.

17 'Captain Parry's Last Voyage,' *Mirror of Literature, Amusement and Instruction* 3 (1 May 1824): 279–82.

18 See the listing in Day, *Search for the Northwest Passage*, 366–8.

19 'Captain Parry, and his Last Voyage,' supplementary issue, *Mirror of Litera-ture, Amusement and Instruction* 6 (December 1825): 449–52; 'Captain Parry's Third Voyage,' *Mirror of Literature, Amusement and Instruction* 8 (2 September 1826): 140–2.

20 John Franklin to Sarah Sellwood, 2 December 1823, SPRI MS 248/318/ 1-2 (copy). The identification of Sellwood as the recipient must be an error, since she died soon after Franklin's return from his first expedition.

21 'A Biographical Memoir of Captain John Franklin, R.N., F.R.S.,' *Mirror of Literature, Amusement and Instruction* 5 (25 June 1825): 421.

22 'To Correspondents,' *Mirror of Literature, Amusement and Instruction* 7 (4 Feb-ruary 1826): 80.

23 Both were popular heroes of the day. Byron died in 1824 while fighting for the cause of Greek independence. Canning, one of the most liberal mem-bers of the administration, won acclaim when as foreign secretary he refused to involve Britain in the reactionary policies of the Holy Alliance.

24 For full references to these and other articles on the 1825–7 expedition, see Day, *Search for the Northwest Passage*, 373–5.

25 Houghton, *Wellesley Index.*

26 'North-West Passage,' *Edinburgh Review* 48 (December 1828): 423, 424, 429, 430, 433.

27 For a discussion of the standards by which the *Westminster* judged the books it reviewed, see Nesbitt, *Benthamite Reviewing.*

28 'Expeditions to the North Pole,' *Westminster Review* 10 (April 1829): 484.

29 Ibid., 485, 486–7, 488, 496, 499, 500, 496, 490.

30 Ibid., 487–8.

31 Ibid., 485, 497, 506.

32 Even Barrow privately thought that Franklin's second narrative was 'a very dull book.' Barrow to Murray, undated, Murray Archive.

33 Altick, *English Common Reader,* 266–7. A footnote to one of the *Mirror's* Arctic articles urged readers to purchase Limbird's edition of Cook, published in 1824. 'Biographical Memoir of Captain John Franklin,' 417.

34 Preface, 5: iii.

35 'Captain Parry's Voyage,' *British Critic,* 619.

36 Samuel Loxton to W.E. Parry, 25 March 1824, Murray Archive. Parry's reply is copied on the other side of the sheet.

37 Parry, *Journals,* advertisement, 1: i–ii, iii.

38 Prices from 'New Publications,' *Quarterly Review* 33 (March 1826): 582 (Parry), and 39 (January 1829): 254 (Franklin). The latter was advertised with the title *The interesting Narrative of Captain Franklin's Privations and Suf-ferings during his Voyages to the Polar Sea.* This was later changed to the less

sensational *Journey to the Shores of the Polar Sea in 1819–20–21–22, with a brief Account of the second Journey in 1825–26–27.*

39 Parry to Murray, 29 March 1827, Murray Archive.

40 Isabella Parry to Murray, on verso of Parry to Murray, 27 October 1827, Murray Archive.

41 Barrow to Murray, undated, Murray Archive.

42 List of books read by Princess Victoria, 1826–9, in Gail Turley Houston, 'Reading and Writing Victoria: The Conduct Book and the Legal Constitution of Female Sovereignty,' in Homans and Munich, *Remaking Queen Victoria,* 178–9; Markham, *Life of Sir Clements Markham,* 7.

43 Bennett, 'John Murray's Family Library,' 159–62. On the increasing popularity of books in series, see Howsam, 'Sustained Literary Ventures.'

44 Leslie, Jameson, and Murray, *Discovery and Adventure in the Polar Seas and Regions,* 223–4.

45 [Cooley], review of *Narrative of Discovery and Adventure in the Polar Seas and Regions,* pt 2, *Athenaeum* 153 (2 October 1830): 615. Cooley was the author of the three-volume *History of Maritime and Inland Discovery* (London: Longman, Rees, Orme, Brown, Green and Taylor, 1831), which contains a section on Arctic exploration.

46 [Cooley], review of *Discovery and Adventure,* pt 1, *Athenaeum* 152 (25 September 1830): 593.

47 Ibid., pt 2, 615.

48 Tytler, *Historical View,* 8.

49 Marchand, *The Athenaeum,* 11–12, 34–6.

50 'Arctic Land Expedition,' supplement, *Penny Magazine* 1 (December 1832): 386–9.

51 Altick, *English Common Reader,* 333; 'Reading for All,' *Penny Magazine* 1 (31 March 1832): 1. See also Anderson, *Printed Image,* chap. 5.

52 See Altick, *English Common Reader,* chap. 6. He suggests that 'Broughamism' would be a better term than 'Benthamism' for the utilitarian spirit as it was understood by many purveyors of cheap literature.

53 Ibid., 333–5.

54 Anderson, *Printed Image,* 140.

55 According to Richardson, the decision to end Arctic exploration was made by the duke of Clarence (later King William IV), for whom the office of lord high admiral was briefly revived in 1827–8. Richardson to Henrietta Kay, 22 June 1828, DRO 3311/ 101.

56 [Cooley], 'Captain Back's Expedition to the Arctic Regions,' *Edinburgh Review* 63 (April 1836): 287.

57 Quoted in Dodge, *Polar Rosses,* 119.

58 [Cooley], 'Back's Expedition,' 288.

59 Barrow to Murray, 3 December 1835, Murray Archive.

60 [Barrow], 'Captain Ross's *Second Voyage in Search of a North-West Passage*,' *Quarterly Review* 54 (July 1835): 3, 16, 25, 26, 30, 32, 37, 38.

61 Admiral Sir Robert Stopford to Admiral Sir Byam Martin, quoted in Ross, *Polar Pioneers*, 187.

62 Review of John Ross, *Narrative of a Second Voyage in search of a North-West Passage, and of a Residence in the Arctic Regions, during the Years 1829, 1830, 1831, 1832, 1833, Literary Gazette* 955 (9 May 1835): 289.

63 [Maginn], 'Gallery of Literary Characters. No. XLIV. Captain Ross,' *Fraser's Magazine* 9 (January 1834): 64.

64 Ross, *Narrative of a Second Voyage*, 51, 344, 128.

65 For example, ibid., xiv, 149–50, 158, 167, 277, 349.

66 Ibid., 435.

67 Quoted in Ross, *Polar Pioneers*, 181.

68 [Brewster], 'Ross's *Voyage to the Arctic Regions*,' *Edinburgh Review* 61 (July 1835): 444.

69 Ross, *Polar Pioneers*, 181–2.

70 John Ross to William Scoresby, 28 April 1835, quoted in ibid., 182.

71 Jane Franklin, journal, quoted in ibid., 182–3.

72 [Barrow], 'Captain Ross's *Second Voyage*,' 3, 38.

73 Review of Ross, *Literary Gazette*, 289.

74 Ibid., 292.

75 [Barrow], 'Back's *Journey to the Arctic Sea*,' *Quarterly Review* 56 (April 1836): 278, 296. Emphasis in original.

76 [Cooley], 'Back's Expedition,' 311.

77 Review of George Back, *Journal of the Arctic Land Expedition to the Mouth of the Great Fish River, and along the Shores of the Arctic Ocean, in the Years 1833, 1834, and 1835, Literary Gazette* 1007 (7 May 1836): 289.

78 'Captain Back's Journal, &c.,' *Literary Gazette* 1008 (14 May 1836): 309.

79 'Captain Back's Expedition to the Polar Seas,' *Penny Magazine* 408 (11 August 1838): 311.

80 'Captain Back's Expedition to the Polar Seas,' *Penny Magazine* 409 (18 August 1838): 319.

81 King, *Journey to the Shores of the Arctic Ocean*, 1: 12; 2: 204–5, 321.

82 Ibid., 2: 26–9.

83 For King's own account of this episode, see 'The Arctic Sea and North-West Passage,' *Athenaeum* 915 (10 May 1845): 462.

84 [Lord Ellesmere], 'Simpson's *Narrative of Discoveries by Officers of the Hudson's Bay Company*,' *Quarterly Review* 73 (December 1843): 113, 129, 113–14. Elles-

mere (1800–57), a politician, philanthropist, and man of letters, was president of the Royal Geographical Society in 1853–5. See *Dictionary of National Biography.*

85 [John Robertson], 'The Arctic Discoveries. Dease and Simpson's Narrative,' *London and Westminster Review* 29 (August 1838): 373–92; 'Discovery of the North-West Passage,' *Penny Magazine* 7 (28 April 1838): 154–6; 'Discovery of the North-West Passage,' *Penny Magazine* 9 (2 May 1840): 181–4.

86 Ballantyne, *Personal Reminiscences,* 3, 5.

87 His proposal, dated December 1844, is reprinted in Cyriax, *Franklin's Last Expedition,* 18–20.

88 'Polar Sea Expeditions and Polar Land Journeys,' *Athenaeum* 898 (11 January 1845): 40. This article reproduced two letters from King to Barrow (40–1); a third appeared in issue 901 (1 February 1845): 120.

89 All the overland expeditions were officially the responsibility of the Colonial Office rather than the Admiralty.

90 Richard King, 'Polar Sea Expeditions and Polar Land Journeys' (letter to Lord Stanley, dated 20 February 1845), *Athenaeum* 907 (15 March 1845): 269.

91 Markham, *Life of McClintock,* 36–8.

92 Franklin's first attempt to make his way southwest or south was apparently thwarted, since in the summer of 1845 the *Erebus* and the *Terror* sailed up Wellington Channel. After circumnavigating Cornwallis Island, the explorers returned to Lancaster Sound and spent the winter of 1845–6 at Beechey Island. In the summer of 1846 they at last made their way to the south, most likely via Peel Sound. Off the northwest coast of King William Island, they encountered the extremely heavy pack ice that drifts from the Beaufort Sea down McClintock Channel and into the heart of the archipelago. The ships were beset in the ice on 12 September 1846. They were only about 100 miles from the continental coastline, but movement was now impossible. Franklin died in June 1847, and in April 1848 the ships were abandoned. The surviving men (105 of an original 129), led by Crozier and Fitzjames, set out on foot for the Great Fish River; why they chose this direction – in which the only hope of relief lay at the far distant Hudson's Bay Company posts – rather than northeast to Lancaster Sound, is a matter of debate. It is possible that the lead poisoning discovered by Canadian anthropologist Owen Beattie had affected their judgment. See Beattie and Geiger, *Frozen in Time.*

93 Quoted in Cyriax and Wordie, 'Centenary of the Sailing of Franklin,' 175.

94 'Unpublished Letter of Franklin.'

95 'Departure of the "Erebus" and "Terror" on the Arctic Expedition,' *Illustrated London News* 6 (24 May 1845): 328.

96 Fitzjames, *Last Journals*, 1–2.
97 'Latest Intelligence from the Polar Ships,' *Nautical Magazine and Naval Chronicle* (October 1845): 541.
98 Barrow, *Voyages of Discovery*, 331–2.
99 *Winter in the Arctic Regions*, 12.
100 Our Weekly Gossip, *Athenaeum* 1016 (17 April 1847): 414.
101 Our Weekly Gossip, *Athenaeum* 1018 (1 May 1847): 466.
102 [Lord Ellesmere], 'Sir James Ross's *Voyage to the Antarctic Regions*,' *Quarterly Review* 81 (June 1847): 167.
103 King, 'Sir John Franklin's Expedition,' *Athenaeum* 1024 (12 June 1847): 621.
104 King, 'Sir John Franklin's Expedition,' dated 21 June, *Athenaeum* 1026 (26 June 1847): 671–72; 'Sir John Franklin's Expedition,' dated 5 July, 1028 (10 July 1847): 734; 'The Arctic Expeditions,' dated 25 November, 1048 (27 November 1847): 1220–1; 'The Arctic Expeditions,' dated 8 December, 1050 (11 December 1847): 1273–4; 'The Arctic Expeditions,' dated 16 December, 1051 (18 December 1847): 1302.
105 'The Arctic Expeditions,' dated 14 December, *Athenaeum* 1051 (18 December 1847): 1302–3. To be fair to King, he believed that a ship laden with supplies should be sent to Lancaster Sound, and he saw his own role as that of reaching Franklin in order to inform him where the relief ship could be found. However, he did not explain why he believed that he could find the lost explorers more readily than overland or boat parties sent out from the ship. He merely stated that such parties were bound to fail. 'The Arctic Expeditions,' *Athenaeum* 1048 (27 November 1847): 1221.

7: The Knight-errantry of Our Day, 1848–1852

1 Altick, 'English Publishing,' 142–3.
2 Altick, *English Common Reader*, 349, 394; 'English Publishing,'146.
3 'Exhibitions,' *News of the World*, 15 June 1851, 5. See also 'Panorama of the Arctic Regions,' *Weekly Dispatch*, 22 June 1851, 10.
4 'Last Tidings of Franklin,' *Examiner*, 12 January 1856, 17; *News of the World*, 20 January 1856, 6.
5 Altick, *English Common Reader*, 394.
6 See Brick, 'The *Leader*.'
7 Ellegård, *Readership of the Periodical Press*, 22.
8 'The Arctic Expedition. Extracts from a private Journal kept by an Officer on board the Erebus,' *Leader* 3 (10 January 1852): 32–3; continued in 3 (17 January 1852): 52–3; 3 (24 January 1852): 76–7; 3 (7 February 1852): 127; 3 (28 February 1852): 199. Reprinted in the *Nautical Magazine and Naval*

Chronicle 21 (March 1852): 158–65, and 21 (April 1852): 195–201, under the title 'Arctic Matters.'

9 'Arctic Matters,' 162.

10 Joyce, *Visions of the People*, 333. See also Joyce, *Democratic Subjects*; Epstein, 'The Populist Turn.'

11 Joyce, *Visions of the People*, 218.

12 On middle- and lower-class radicalism in the 1850s, see Finn, *After Chartism*, chap. 4. Finn emphasizes the divergences between the two. The middle-class radical interpretation of the Franklin search may have been intended to create a much needed sense of common cause.

13 [Brewster], 'Ross's *Voyage to the Arctic Regions*,' *Edinburgh Review* 61 (July 1835): 444.

14 Colley, *Britons*, chap. 8.

15 On Murchison's standing in the world of Victorian science, see Stafford, *Scientist of Empire*. Beaufort was the Hydrographer to the Navy and originator of the Beaufort wind force scale. See Friendly, *Beaufort of the Admiralty*.

16 Woodward, *Portrait of Jane*, 294.

17 An acquaintance wrote that Lady Franklin's parties were 'the most curiously interesting of the times; and from Earl Russell, then Lord John, to the roughest whaler – to anyone, indeed, who could "say his say" about the North – there was no telling who you would not meet round the chair of Lady Franklin.' Unidentified obituary, quoted in Owen, *Fate of Franklin*, 429.

18 Markham, *Life of McClintock*, 239.

19 'The Arctic Expeditions,' *Athenaeum* 1198 (12 October 1850): 1070.

20 Scoresby, *Franklin Expedition*, 15. Emphasis in original.

21 There are entries for all these men, except Coningham, in Stephen and Lee, *Dictionary of National Biography*. On Coningham, see Boase, *Modern English Biography*.

22 [Harcourt], 'The Last Doge of Whiggism,' *Saturday Review* 1 (1855), quoted in Bevington, *The Saturday Review*, 55.

23 [Harcourt], 'The Tories and Their Chiefs,' quoted in ibid., 56.

24 Jones, 'Rethinking Chartism,' 90–178.

25 For this period, see Finn, *After Chartism*, chap. 3.

26 The Tories under Sir Robert Peel governed from 1841 to 1846, Lord John Russell and the Whigs from 1846 to 1852. In 1852, after a brief period when Lord Derby led a minority Tory government, a coalition of Tories and Whigs was formed, with Lord Aberdeen as prime minister. Aberdeen's government fell in 1855, and Palmerston was prime minister from 1855 to 1858. There was another short-lived Tory government under Derby in

1858–9. Palmerston regained the prime ministership in June 1859 and held it until his death in 1865.

27 Third leader, *Weekly Dispatch*, 25 January 1852, 57.

28 On criticism of the conduct of the war, see Anderson, *Liberal State at War*, 97–162.

29 Quoted in 'John Arthur Roebuck,' in Stephen and Lee, *Dictionary of National Biography*.

30 [Morley], 'The Lost English Sailors,' *Household Words* 15 (14 February 1857): 145.

31 Dickens, *Hard Times*, 1, 5.

32 A rare instance of aristocratic protest is contained in an 1857 *Blackwood's* article. The author, G.C. Swayne, suggested that 'while Manchester made such a noise in the world with the racket of her spinning-jennies,' the military virtues belonging to those with Norman blood and the lust for adventure that characterized the descendants of the Danes were almost forgotten. The life of the nation was dominated by plodding Saxons bent only on making money. Then the Crimean War and the Franklin search provided welcome opportunities for gentlemen: '[p]olitically stifled, they were only too glad to assert their claims to vitality' in the Crimea and the Arctic. 'Arctic Adventure,' *Blackwood's* 81 (March 1857): 366.

33 [Morley], 'Unspotted Snow,' *Household Words* 8 (12 November 1853): 239.

34 For example, see the third leader, *Daily News*, 17 February 1857. The article is attributed to Martineau in Arbuckle, *Harriet Martineau*.

35 [Eliot], 'Contemporary Literature: History, Biography, Voyages, and Travels,' *Westminster Review* 67 (January 1857): 303, 305.

36 'Sir James Stephen,' and 'Sir James Fitzjames Stephen,' in Stephen and Lee, *Dictionary of National Biography*.

37 [Stephen], 'Mr. Dickens as a Politician,' *Saturday Review* 3 (3 January 1857), quoted in Bevington, *Saturday Review*, 156, 157.

38 [Stephen], 'The North-West Passage,' *Saturday Review*, 2 (8 November 1856): 617, 619. Attribution in Bevington, *Saturday Review*, 377.

39 [Stephen], 'Kane's Arctic Explorations,' *Saturday Review* 2 (22 November 1856): 660. Attribution in Bevington, *Saturday Review*, 377.

40 Fourth leader, *Times*, 27 November 1856, 6.

41 Pim, 'Another Arctic Voyage,' *Times*, 29 November 1856, 12. Throughout this period 138 was usually given as the number of Franklin's crew. In fact, several men were left in England for various reasons, and there were only 129 men on the two ships. This was ascertained by McClintock in 1859. McClintock to Eleanor Gell, 21 November 1859, pasted into scrapbook of press clippings, DRO 3311/ 95.

42 This widespread belief originated with Vilhjalmur Stefansson, who claimed that throughout the period of the search, Rae 'was ... in rather bad standing, for having behaved on his expeditions like a menial ... and for having lived like a savage ... This behaviour did not seem cricket to the British public.' The public preferred naval officers because they had heroism rather than mere survival as their goal. It mattered not at all to the public that these explorers' minds were 'inhibited by the outlook of their time and service.' *Unsolved Mysteries*, 126, 115. Popular historians in both Britain and Canada have repeated this view. Roland Huntford, for example, writes that Rae's 'success with small means was a standing reproach to the elaborate, costly and disastrous naval expeditions ... Because his methods differed from "official" ones he was derided and neglected at home.' Huntford, *Scott and Amundsen*, 77. According to Pierre Berton, 'To the gold-braided bluecoats of Arctic exploration, John Rae was an outsider ... he didn't consider it a stigma to go native.' Berton, *Arctic Grail*, 158. The belief that non-naval explorers had great difficulty in winning public approval also runs through academic works such as Wallace, *The Navy, the Company, and Richard King*.

43 Review of Rae, *Narrative of an Expedition to the Shores of the Arctic Sea in 1846 and 1847*, *Athenaeum* 1187 (27 July 1850): 784.

44 'Rae's Expedition to the Shores of the Arctic Sea,' *Spectator*, repr. *Littel's Living Age* 26 (21 September 1850): 572.

45 Eleanor Franklin to John Franklin, 29 April 1848, DRO 3311/ unlisted box 1, folder of family letters.

46 Mary Richardson to Eleanor Gell, 26 November 1849 (?), DRO 3311/106.

47 Richardson to Murchison, BL Add. MSS 46127, 4 March 1852, f. 438–41, 25 March 1852, f. 442–43.

48 Rae, 'Another Arctic Expedition,' *Times*, 27 November 1852, 6.

49 King to Earl Grey, 25 November 1847, 'The Arctic Expeditions,' *Athenaeum* 1048 (27 November 1847): 1220–1.

50 Ibid.

51 'Sir John Franklin's Expedition' (letter from Ross), *Athenaeum* 1025 (19 June 1847): 644–5; 'Sir John Franklin's Expedition' (letter from King dated 21 June 1847), 1026 (26 June 1847): 671–2; 'Sir John Franklin's Expedition' (letter from Ross dated 29 June), 1027 (3 July 1847): 702; 'Sir John Franklin's Expedition' (letter from King dated 5 July 1847), 1028 (10 July 1847): 734.

52 *Athenaeum* 1025 (19 June 1847): 624.

53 *Athenaeum* 1028 (10 July 1847): 734.

54 *Athenaeum* 1048 (27 November 1847): 1221.

55 *Athenaeum* 1051 (18 December 1847): 1302.

56 Quoted in Ross, *Polar Pioneers*, 302. Emphasis in original.

57 The letter is printed in *Arctic Expedition*, 41–3.

58 Ibid., 43–7.

59 Ibid., 45.

60 McClintock, 'Reminiscences of Arctic Ice-Travel in Search of Sir John Franklin and his Companions,' *Journal of the Royal Dublin Society* 1 (February 1857): 195.

61 *Arctic Expedition*, 1–7. The title page records that the papers were 'ordered to be printed' in April, but it seems that they were not actually available to the public until later in the year. An article in the December 1848 issue of *Fraser's Magazine* mentions that they had appeared 'recently.'

62 *Arctic Expedition*, 71. See also 'The Arctic Expeditions' (letter from John Barrow Jr), *Nautical Magazine and Naval Chronicle* 25 (April 1856): 106–7.

63 'The Expedition in Search of Sir John Franklin Critically Examined,' *Nautical Standard and Steam Navigation Gazette* 4 (17 November 1849): 721–5; 'The Expedition in Search of Sir John Franklin Further Examined,' 4 (24 November 1849): 737–40.

64 Quoted in Ross, *Polar Pioneers*, 315.

65 'The Search for Sir John Franklin,' *Examiner*, repr. *Littel's Living Age* 24 (9 February 1850): 280.

66 A.B.B., 'Reflections on Sir John Franklin's Expedition, and where his Ships were most probably beset in the Ice,' *Nautical Magazine and Naval Chronicle* 25 (March 1856): 129.

67 Though the idea that Franklin could find a Northwest Passage by sailing north now seems absurd, many scientists at the time believed in an 'open polar sea.' This notion, originally put forward by Barrow, gained new credibility after the publication of Humboldt's work on isothermal lines. Humboldt's treatise, published in German in 1817, was translated into English by David Brewster in 1819. Brewster hypothesized that there were two poles of maximum cold in each hemisphere, and that they bore some relation to the position of the magnetic poles. Brewster thought that the North American pole of maximum cold was in latitude 80° north, longitude 100° west, and that the isothermal lines formed concentric circles around this point. If his theory was correct, then the regions north of the 80th parallel would have a climate similar to that prevailing well to the south. Further support seemed to be given to Brewster's theory by the fact that Russian explorers had found large expanses of open water, which they called *polynyas*, off the coast of Siberia. Periodical writers often expressed the opinion that Franklin had found a *polynya* up Wellington Channel, where animal life abounded. However, it was thought that a ring of excep-

tionally heavy ice must surround the open sea, and those who found a way in would not necessarily be able to find a way out. See Edward Sabine, preface to Wrangell, *Expedition to the Polar Sea*; 'Baron Humboldt's *Kosmos, a General Survey of the Physical Phenomena of the Universe*,' *North British Review* 4 (November 1845): 235–6, 250; [Brewster], 'Arctic Searching Expeditions,' *North British Review* (February 1852): 258–9; Wright, 'Open Polar Sea.'

68 King later took his revenge on Ross by claiming, 'If ever one man sacrificed another, Sir James Ross sacrificed Sir John Franklin, and not only Sir John Franklin, but one hundred and thirty-seven noble hearts with him.' King then repeated the claim that Ross had acted out of self-interested ambition. According to King, Ross had prevented the Admiralty from accepting King's plans only so that he might glorify himself through new geographical discoveries. King, *The Franklin Expedition*, 72–4.

69 'Search for Sir John Franklin,' 279, 281.

70 'An Observer' [Sherard Osborn], 'Sir J. Franklin' (letter to the editor), *Times*, 1 January 1850, 3.

71 'An Observer' [Sherard Osborn], letter to the editor, ibid., 9 January 1850, 5.

72 *Observations on the missing Ships*, 453, 456. Emphasis in original.

73 [Ainsworth], 'The Arctic Voyages,' *New Monthly Magazine* 88 (January 1850): 83–4, 96, 99.

74 Ibid., 97–8, 99.

75 'Sir J. Franklin – The North-West Passage,' *British Quarterly Review* 9 (February 1850): 109, 102, 104. Emphasis in original.

76 'Arctic Enterprise,' *Spectator* (23 February 1850), repr. *Littel's Living Age* 25 (23 April 1850): 191. Emphasis in original.

77 Quoted in 'The Arctic Expeditions,' letter from C.R. Weld dated 31 January, *Athenaeum* 1162 (2 February 1850): 131.

78 Ibid.

79 Weld, *Arctic Expeditions*.

80 'Our Weekly Gossip,' *Athenaeum* 1163 (9 February 1850): 160.

81 [Weld], 'The Search for Sir John Franklin,' *Fraser's Magazine* 43 (February 1851): 198. Beaufort's efforts at the Admiralty seem to have also been a key factor, but this was not publicized at the time. See Ross, 'Admiralty and the Franklin Search,' 295.

82 Quoted in Stone, 'Franklin Search in Parliament,' 210.

83 Charles Eden to Osborn, 10 February 1849, in Sherard Osborn's scrapbook, NMM BGR/ 5.

84 Our Weekly Gossip, *Athenaeum* 1164 (16 February 1850): 182.

85 W. Gillies Ross, Introduction to Penny, *Distant and Unsurveyed Country*, xxvii–xxxiv. See also Holland, 'William Penny,' 25–43.

86 [Ainsworth], 'Arctic Expeditions,' *New Monthly Magazine* 88 (March 1850): 350, 353, 358.

87 [Horne], 'Arctic Heroes: A Fragment of Naval History,' *Household Words* 1 (27 April 1850): 109. All attributions of authorship for *Household Words* are taken from Lohrli, *Household Words*.

88 [Frederick Knight Hunt], 'A Visit to the Arctic Discovery Ships,' *Household Words* 8 (18 May 1850): 182.

89 'Sir John Franklin,' *Leader* 1 (12 October 1850): 684.

90 [Ainsworth], 'The Track of Sir John Franklin,' *New Monthly Magazine* 90 (November 1850): 375.

91 [Weld], 'The Search for Sir John Franklin,' 202.

92 See Griffiths, *Encyclopedia.*

93 Simmonds, *Sir John Franklin and the Arctic Regions* (1851), 6–7.

94 One, called 'A Ballad of Sir John Franklin,' contained these lines:

> Oh! think you, good Sir John Franklin,
> We'll ever see the land?
> 'Twas cruel to send us here to starve,
> Without a helping hand.
> 'Twas cruel, Sir John, to send us here,
> So far from help or home;
> To starve and freeze on this lonely sea
> I ween, the Lords of the Admiralty
> Had rather send than come.   Ibid., 279

95 Advertisements, *Weekly Dispatch,* 23 March 1851, 13, and *Daily News,* 6 February 1856, 8.

96 'Sir John Franklin and the Arctic Regions,' *Weekly Dispatch,* 4 May 1851, 6.

97 John Franklin to J.B. Wright, 18 October 1820, DRO 3311/ 115.

98 Quoted in Clark, 'Captain William Kennedy,' 449.

99 Jane Franklin to Roderick Murchison, undated, BL Add. MS 46126 f. 209–10.

100 'Sir John Franklin and the Arctic Expeditions,' *Leisure Hour* 1 (26 February 1852): 138.

101 'Lieutenant Bellot,' *Dublin University Magazine* 46 (December 1855): 712.

102 Sherard Osborn to Jane Franklin, 19 December [1851], SPRI MS 248/448/ 6–8.

103 W.A.B. Hamilton to Penny, 18 September 1851, printed in *Additional Papers,* 300.

104 *Report of the Committee.* Reprinted in the *Times,* 14 February 1852, 8–9, and Mangles, *Papers and Despatches.*

105 'Arctic Searching Expedition,' *Illustrated London News* 19 (13 September 1851): 330; 'The Arctic Expeditions,' *Illustrated London News* 19 (20 September 1851): 337–8; 'The Arctic Searching Expeditions,' *Athenaeum* 1247 (20 September 1851): 998–9.

106 [Ainsworth], 'Arctic Expeditions of Succour,' *New Monthly Magazine* 93 (October 1851): 201n.

107 [Weld], 'The Search for Sir John Franklin,' *Fraser's Magazine* 44 (November 1851): 505, 506, 508.

108 Repr. ibid., 509.

109 Ibid.

110 'Hope On,' *Spectator,* 4 October 1851, repr. *Littel's Living Age* 31 (29 November 1851): 404.

111 'Is Not Sir John Franklin Alive?' *Leader* 2 (4 October 1851): 939.

112 Leading article, *Daily News,* 9 December [1851], in a scrapbook of press cuttings belonging to Eleanor Gell, DRO 3311/ 134. Emphasis in original. For other commentaries critical of Austin, see 'The Recent Arctic Expedition, and Its Results,' *Nautical Standard and Steam Navigation Gazette* 6 (27 September 1851), and the *Morning Chronicle's* leading article, 26 September 1851.

113 *Report of the Committee,* 154–5, 174, 176, 164–7, 170–4. Emphasis in original. For an excellent analysis of the committee's bias in favour of Austin's evidence, see Holland, 'Arctic Committee of 1851.'

114 Penny, 'Sir J. Franklin' (letter to the editor), *Times,* 23 December 1851, 5.

115 For example, in the *Illustrated London News* 19 (28 December 1851) and the *News of the World,* 28 December 1851, 6.

116 'Sir John Franklin' (letter from C.R. Weld, enclosing a copy of the deposition), *Times,* 3 January 1852, 5. Repr. *Illustrated London News* 20 (10 January 1852): 35 and *Weekly Dispatch,* 11 January 1852, 28. See also 'The Arctic Expeditions,' *Athenaeum* 1264 (17 January 1852): 82–3.

117 Penny, 'Sir J. Franklin.'

118 Simmonds, *Sir John Franklin,* 396.

119 [James McGlashan], 'Sir John Richardson's Arctic Expedition,' *Dublin University Magazine* 39 (April 1852): 476.

120 'Food of the Arctic Regions – Franklin's Expedition,' *Chambers's Edinburgh Journal* n.s. 17 (7 February 1852): 91, 92.

121 Ellegård, *Readership,* 37. The circulation was estimated at 100,000.

122 J.K., 'Sir John Franklin's First Journey in the Polar Regions,' *Leisure Hour* 1 (1 January 1852): 10.

123 'Sir John Franklin and the Arctic Expeditions,' 137, 139.

124 'Scientific. Societies. Geographical,' *Athenaeum* 1271 (6 March 1852): 281. The article reports Petermann's lecture, given at the Royal Institution on 9 February. See also Petermann, 'Note on the Distribution of Animals

available as Food in the Arctic Regions,' *Journal of the Royal Geographical Society* 22 (1852): 118–27.

125 'Sir John Franklin's First Journey,' 10.

126 Quoted in Spufford, *I May Be Some Time*, 121.

127 'Arctic Contributions to Science,' *Chambers's Edinburgh Journal* (11 December 1852): 374.

128 [McGlashan], 'Sir John Richardson's Arctic Expedition,' 476.

129 Quoted in Stone, 'The Franklin Search,' 211.

130 Penny, 'Captain Penny and the Arctic Expeditions' (letter to the editor), *Times*, 29 March 1852, 5.

131 [Ainsworth], 'Curiosities of Arctic Travel,' *New Monthly Magazine* 94 (April 1852): 450, 451.

132 'The Probable Route of Sir John Franklin,' *Leisure Hour* 50 (9 December 1852): 793.

133 'Penny's Voyage in Search of Franklin,' *Examiner*, repr. *Littel's Living Age* 35 (2 October 1852): 30.

134 'Sutherland's Journal of Penny's Voyage in Search of Franklin,' *Spectator*, repr. *Littel's Living Age* 35 (2 October 1852): 32, 33.

135 [Ainsworth], 'Queen Victoria's Channel,' *New Monthly Magazine* 96 (September 1852): 10, 103, 111.

8: The Duty of a People, 1852–1857

1 'The Search for Sir John Franklin,' *Chambers's Repository*, No. 45, repr. (Toronto: Canadiana House, n.d.), 17.

2 The reprint gives the date as 1854, but as the news brought by Inglefield in October 1853 is not referred to, it must be from the earlier part of 1853. See 20–1.

3 [Coulton], 'Search for Sir John Franklin,' *Quarterly Review* 92 (March 1853): 393.

4 See 'Lieutenant Bellot,' *Leisure Hour* 114 (2 March 1854): 135–8.

5 'The Fate of Sir John Franklin,' *Bentley's Miscellany* 36 (1854): 581.

6 Sherard Osborn to Jane Franklin, 25 December 1854, SPRI MS 248/448/6-8.

7 Reprinted in Bentley, *Russell's Despatches from the Crimea*. On the *Times*'s role in forming public opinion about the war, see Anderson, *A Liberal State at War*, 70–93.

8 'Argus,' 'Courts-Martial at Sheerness' (letter to the editor), *Daily News*, 27 October 1854, 3.

9 [Horatio Mansfield], 'Arctic Enterprise,' *Tait's Edinburgh Magazine*, n.s. 22 (March 1855): 137.

10 [Harriet Martineau], second leader, *Daily News*, 17 October 1854, 4. Attributed to Martineau in Arbuckle, *Harriet Martineau*.

11 John Rae, letter to the editor, printed in 'The Arctic Expedition,' *Times*, 23 October 1854, 7.

12 Leading article, *Examiner*, 28 October 1854, repr. in King, *Franklin Expedition*, 136.

13 Leading article, *Sun*, 23 October 1854, repr. ibid., 150.

14 Leading article, *Atlas*, 28 October 1854, repr. ibid., 147.

15 'The Fate of Sir John Franklin,' *Daily News*, 23 October 1854, 4.

16 'The Fate of Franklin,' *Daily News*, 24 October 1854, 4.

17 *Examiner*, repr. in King, *Franklin Expedition*, 139. See also 'The Fate of Franklin,' *Cassell's Illustrated Family Paper* 1 (25 November 1854): 396–8, and 1 (2 December 1854): 404–6, 411.

18 Leading article, *Observer*, 29 October 1854, repr. in King, *Franklin Expedition*, 149.

19 Leading article, *Sun*, 25 October 1854, repr. ibid., 153.

20 Letter to the editor, *Sun*, 28 October 1854, repr. ibid., 163–4.

21 King, *Franklin Expedition*, 135, 133.

22 Repr. ibid., 152.

23 Rae, letter to the editor, in 'The Arctic Expedition,' *Times*, 23 October 1854, 7.

24 Rae, report dated Repulse Bay, 20 July 1854, in ibid.

25 'Arctic Expedition,' 7.

26 Second leader, *Times*, 24 October 1854, 6.

27 Third leader, *Times*, 26 October 1854, 6.

28 'Fate of Franklin,' *Daily News*, 4.

29 Quoted in King, *Franklin Expedition*, 137.

30 'The Fate of Franklin,' *Athenaeum* 1409 (28 October 1854): 1305.

31 E.J.H., 'Dr. Rae's Reports on the Arctic Expedition' (letter to the editor), *Times*, 30 October 1854, 10.

32 Rae, letter to the editor, *Times*, 31 October 1854, 8.

33 Repr. in King, *Franklin Expedition*, 156, 157. Emphasis in original.

34 Repr. ibid., 119–20, 120–1.

35 Fourth leader, *Times*, 2 November 1854, 6.

36 King to the secretary of the Admiralty, letter dated 26 October 1854, repr. in King, *Franklin Expedition*, 169.

37 Letter dated 8 November, repr. ibid., 114, 188–9.

38 'Fate of Sir John Franklin,' *Bentley's*, 583. See also the letters from 'Nauticus' and 'C.' in the *Daily News*, 24 October 1854, 2 and 28 October 1854, 2.

39 'Dr. Rae and the Arctic Expedition' (letters), *Times*, 8 November 1854, 7.

40 John Richardson to Eleanor Gell, 23 October 1854, DRO 3311/80.

41 Tennyson, *Lady Tennyson's Journal*, 39.

42 'Arctic Expedition,' *Times*, 27 October 1854, 8.

43 Jane Franklin to Roderick Murchison, 6 November 1854, BL Add. MS 46126, f. 220–22.

44 Sophia Cracroft to Roderick Murchison, 6 November 1854, BL Add. MS 46125, f. 428–32.

45 Sophia Cracroft to Roderick Murchison, 7 November 1854, BL Add. MS 46125, f. 433–36. Emphasis in original.

46 King, *Franklin Expedition*, 131, 129.

47 Quoted in Wallace, *The Navy, the Company*, 145.

48 The report is dated York Factory, 1 September 1854, but Rae's biographer Robert Richard states that it was completed in London. *Dr. John Rae*, 107.

49 'Rae's Arctic Exploration, with Information respecting Sir John Franklin's missing Party,' *Journal of the Royal Geographical Society* 25 (1855): 250–1, 255.

50 [Dickens], 'The Lost Arctic Voyagers,' *Household Words* 10 (2 December 1854): 361.

51 Ibid., 362, 363.

52 Dickens, *Letters of Charles Dickens*, Vol. 7, 470n5.

53 [Dickens], 'The Lost Arctic Voyagers,' *Household Words* 10 (9 December 1854): 388, 392.

54 For example, see Roberts, 'Dickens and the Arctic,' and Stone, '"The contents of the kettles,"' 7–16.

55 [Dickens], 'Lost Arctic Voyagers,' 392.

56 Stone, *Night Side of Dickens*.

57 Rae's narrative had been very well received by reviewers, but he himself complained that his friend Archibald Barclay, the HBC's secretary, to whom he had entrusted the manuscript, had made extensive changes in the published version. Barclay may have been primarily responsible for the tone of the published book, which coincided well with reviewers' expectations. Rae was duly praised for the narrative's modest, manly tone (see chap. 7, above). His letters to the press in 1854 may have been all the more of a shock to readers familiar with Arctic literature because they were written in a style so different from the narrative. Cooke, 'Autobiography of Dr John Rae,' 174.

58 Rae, 'The Lost Arctic Voyagers,' *Household Words* 10 (23 December 1854): 433, 435, 434.

59 Ibid., 433.

60 Rae, 'Dr. Rae's Report,' *Household Words* 10 (30 December 1854): 457.

61 Ibid., 458.

62 See Fitzjames, *Last Journals*, 14.

63 Rae, 'Dr. Rae's Report,' 458.

64 Ibid., 459.

65 He did not reach Bellot Strait, the goal of his journey, owing to adverse weather conditions.

66 See Rae, *John Rae's Correspondence*, lxxxviii–xcii (introduction by J.M. Wordie and R.J. Cyriax), 289–97, 345–7.

67 See Kerr, 'Rae's Franklin Relics,' 25.

68 As late as 1865 this caused sharp words between Rae and Sophia Cracroft. In answer to her reproaches, he wrote that he had paid the Inuit for the items and considered them his. Rae to Cracroft, 17 August 1865, SPRI MS 248/459/2.

69 See Our Weekly Gossip, *Athenaeum* 1424 (10 February 1855): 175; letter from Rae, *Athenaeum* 1425 (17 February 1855): 202.

70 For example, see King, *Franklin Expedition*, 131; *Great Arctic Mystery*, 8–9, 12; Pim, *An earnest Appeal*, 14.

71 Rae, 'Dr. Rae and the Arctic Expeditions' (letter), *Times*, 23 July 1856, 8; Veritas, 'Dr. Rae and the Arctic Expeditions' (letter), *Times*, 24 July 1856, 8; Rae, letter to the editor, *Times*, 25 July 1856, 5.

72 Sherard Osborn to Jane Franklin, 15 June 1856, SPRI MS 248/448/6–8.

73 Richard, *Dr John Rae*, 110.

74 See *Athenaeum* 1066 (1 April 1848): 341.

75 Quoted in Stone, 'Franklin Search,' 210.

76 For example, see 'The Arctic Expeditions,' *Nautical Magazine and Naval Chronicle* 18 (July 1849): 367–71; 'Search for Sir John Franklin,' *Chambers's Repository*, 13–16; [Brewster], 'Arctic Searching Expeditions,' *North British Review* 16 (February 1852): 255.

77 [Ainsworth], 'Progress of Arctic Exploration,' *New Monthly Magazine* 91 (February 1851): 236.

78 'The Franklin Search,' *Leader* 2 (12 April 1851): 345.

79 'The Arctic Expedition,' *News of the World*, 15 June 1851, 6.

80 'Lady Franklin,' *Spectator* 1378 (25 November 1854): 1232.

81 Bellot, *Memoirs*, 1: 44.

82 'Arctic Expeditions,' *Nautical Magazine*, 370. This article reprints both Lady Franklin's letter and the American reply.

83 Quoted in Woodward, *Portrait of Jane*, 302.

84 Kennedy, *Voyage of the Prince Albert*, 39.

85 Markham, *Life of McClintock*, 73.

86 Tennyson, *Lady Tennyson's Journal*, 214.

87 For example, see Lady Franklin's letters to Murchison, 20 and 22 June 1856, and undated, BL Add MS 46126 f. 239–40, 241–2, 249–50. In the last of these letters, she made a suggestion and then added, 'I know you were

thinking of some thing of the kind which encourages me to mention it.'
Another example is provided in a letter from Sophia Cracroft to Murchison.
Cracroft wrote: 'Mr. Cobden has urged [Lady Franklin] so strongly to write to
W. Mackinnon, that she feels almost obliged to follow his advice, the more
so as from what he said, we think Mr. Mackinnon may be led to expect a let-
ter from her.' 6 July 1855, BL Add MS 46125 f. 444–45.

88 Parry to Eleanor Franklin, 11 May 1849, DRO 3311/ 77. Double emphasis
in original.

89 Jane Franklin to Henrietta Kay, undated, DRO 3311/ 101. Kay was Eleanor
Porden's sister.

90 Franklin's friends were aware that his wife's plans might decrease his
daughter's financial well-being. Jane had her husband's power of attorney
and so could legally spend the income from Eleanor Porden's property (in
which he had a life interest) on her expeditions – provided that Franklin
was still alive. However, if he was in fact dead, the money belonged to
Eleanor Franklin. As Parry noted, Eleanor was placed in a very painful
position. In early 1854 Franklin's name was taken off the Admiralty books,
indicating that officially he was considered dead. Eleanor and her husband,
Philip Gell, then threatened to initiate legal action. A settlement was finally
arrived at in late 1855. Owen, *Fate of Franklin*, 362–3.

91 Kane, *Arctic Explorations*, 2: 292.

92 [Mansfield], 'Arctic Enterprise,' 119.

93 'Lieutenant Bellot,' *Dublin University Magazine* 46 (December 1855): 718.

94 Richardson, *Life of Sir John Franklin*, 15, 16.

95 Dickens to John Forster, 2 March 1856, in *Letters of Charles Dickens*, 8: 66. In
late 1856 and early 1857 Dickens threw much of his energy into the
production of Wilkie Collins's play *The Frozen Deep*, a tale of Arctic heroism
and survival. For a discussion of the place of the Arctic story in Dickens's
emotional life at this time, see Brannan, *Under the Management of Mr. Charles
Dickens*, 6–25.

96 Parry, *Memoirs*.

97 *A Brief Memoir*, 1, 2.

98 See Anderson and Stewart, *Searching for Franklin*.

99 Sherard Osborn to Jane Franklin, 15 June 1856, SPRI MS 248/448/6–8.

100 Jane Franklin to Roderick Murchison, 8 December [1855], BL Add MS
46126 f. 247–8.

101 Osborn, *Discovery of the North-West Passage*, 318–28. Frederick Schwatka's
1879–81 American expedition later found many skeletons on the mainland, at a spot he named Starvation Cove. This was likely the place the Inuit
had described to Rae. The men who reached Montreal Island may well, as

Osborn believed, have travelled some distance up the Great Fish River before they died. See also Pim, *An earnest Appeal*, 17.

102 The original article was published in the *Herald* on 24 December 1855 and reprinted in British daily newspapers on 9 January 1856. For example, see *Times*, 10, and *Manchester Guardian*, 4. The weeklies printed it on 13 January. See *Weekly Dispatch*, 5.

103 King to the Admiralty, 23 January 1856, repr. in King, *Franklin Expedition*, 219. The date on the title page of the book is 1855, but the inclusion of this letter shows that it cannot have been published until early 1856.

104 King, *Franklin Expedition*, 209–10.

105 Jane Franklin to Roderick Murchison, 26 January 1856, BL Add MS 46126 f. 234–37.

106 Franklin, *Letter to the Lords Commissioners*, 3, 4, 5.

107 Sophia Cracroft's account of how Kane's letter was included in the pamphlet reveals much about Lady Franklin's methods, and her reluctance to attribute anything she did solely to her own decision or initiative. 'You will find a very powerful letter from Dr. Kane to Mr. Grinnell accompanying my Aunts [*sic*] letter,' Cracroft told Murchison. 'It arrived a week after hers went in to the Admiralty, but we have had it also printed ... on account of its importance; and it would appear from the manner in which it was sent to us, that Dr. Kane wished it to be placed at my Aunts [*sic*] disposal, for the purpose of being usefully made known.' Sophia Cracroft to Roderick Murchison, 5 May 1856, BL Add MS 46125, f. 453–54.

108 Franklin, *Letter to the Lords Commissioners*, 6.

109 *Great Arctic Mystery*, 16.

110 *Arctic Rewards*, 24, 27.

111 There is a printed copy of this letter on a single sheet in the Gell collection, DRO 3311/ unlisted box 2, likely intended only for private circulation.

112 Fourth leader, *Times*, 2 December 1856, 6.

113 Repr. in McClintock, *Voyage of the 'Fox'*, 322, 326, 328.

114 Franklin, *Letter to Viscount Palmerston*. Lady Franklin's 12 April letter to the Admiralty was printed as a pamphlet, but apparently was intended only for private circulation. The printed version of her 11 July letter was also intended only for private circulation (see above); the letter to Palmerston was offered for sale. All the letters were also printed in the Arctic blue books, several months after they were written.

115 'Sir Robert McClure's Discovery of the North West Passage,' *Edinburgh Review* 103 (January 1856): 202. The *Wellesley Index* (Houghton) states that the review may have been written by Samuel Gurney Cresswell.

116 'Last of the Arctic Voyages,' *British Quarterly Review* 23 (April 1856): 363, 382–6.
117 'Dr Kane's Arctic Explorations,' *Chambers's Edinburgh Journal*, 3rd ser. 7 (9 May 1857): 387.
118 [Stephen], 'Kane's Arctic Explorations,' *Saturday Review* 2 (22 November 1856), 661.
119 Kane, *Arctic Explorations*, 1: 245–6.
120 [David Brewster], 'Dr. Kane's Arctic Explorations,' *North British Review* 26 (February 1857): 236–37.
121 'Arctic Adventures – Dr. Kane,' *British Quarterly Review* 25 (April 1857): 348, 353.
122 Quoted in Stone, 'Franklin Search,' 214.
123 Jane Franklin to Richard Monckton Milnes, 25 February 1857, printed in Lentz, 'The *Fox* Expedition,' 177.
124 [Morley], 'The Lost English Sailors,' *Household Words* 15 (14 February 1857): 145–7.
125 [Morley], 'Official Patriotism,' *Household Words* 15 (25 April 1857): 389, 385, 390.

9: A Sacred Sorrow, 1857–1860

1 'The Final Arctic Search,' *New Monthly Magazine* 112 (March 1858): 289.
2 McClintock, *Voyage of the 'Fox'*, 4. McClintock originally wrote, 'I wished to save at least the record'; this was altered by Osborn to 'How could I do otherwise than devote myself to save at least the record ...' MS 'Journal of the Fox,' NMM MCL/17, 3.
3 Markham, *Life of McClintock*, 137.
4 Haughton, 'The Voyage of the "Fox" in the Arctic Seas,' *Dublin University Magazine* 55 (February 1860): 209–10.
5 Markham, *Life of McClintock*, 8, 301.
6 Ibid., 77, 298, 49.
7 Charles Parry, quoted in ibid., 261.
8 On the factors that influenced Lady Franklin's choice of commander, see her notes, quoted in Owen, *Fate of Franklin*, 377. The other possible candidates, Osborn, Penny, and Kane, all had experienced poor health as a result of their Arctic service, and early in 1857 Kane died.
9 McClintock, *The Voyage of the 'Fox'*, 4.
10 McClintock to James Clark Ross, 4 April 1857, quoted in Ross, *Polar Pioneers*, 374–5.
11 Ibid.
12 Markham, *Life of McClintock*, 136–7.

13 McClintock, 'Reminiscences of Arctic Ice-Travel in Search of Sir John Franklin and his Companions,' *Journal of the Royal Dublin Society* 1 (February 1857): 238. Emphasis in original.

14 See Levere, *Science and the Canadian Arctic*, 228–34.

15 The Geological Society of Dublin, Dublin Natural History Society, Dublin University Zoological and Botanical Association, Royal Irish Academy, and Royal Dublin Society.

16 'Arctic Voyages,' *Natural History Review* 5 (1858): 34–49, 65–83, 119–26.

17 Altick, *English Common Reader*, 395.

18 Nor is the author identified in Oppenlander, *Dickens' All the Year Round*.

19 'The Last Leaves of a Sorrowful Book,' *All the Year Round* 1 (30 July 1859): 319, 321, 323.

20 Ibid., 319.

21 Dickens, *Speeches of Charles Dickens*, 236–7.

22 'Red Tape and Sir John Franklin,' *Weekly Dispatch*, 9 October 1859, 6.

23 Joven, 'The End of an Epic,' *Sharpe's London Magazine* n.s. 15 (November 1859): 244.

24 Ibid., 245.

25 Ibid., 242, 245.

26 Second leader, *Illustrated London News* 35 (1 October 1859): 316.

27 Osborn, 'The Voyage of the "Fox" in the Arctic Seas,' *Blackwood's* 87 (January 1860): 119, 120.

28 Leopold McClintock to Sophia Cracroft, 10 January 1860, SPRI MS 248/439/9–12.

29 Sherard Osborn to Sophia Cracroft, 26 January 1860, SPRI MS 248/448/1–5.

30 Markham, *Life of McClintock*, 236–7.

31 Stone, 'Franklin Search,' 215. It had been suggested that the money spent by Lady Franklin be reimbursed, but she let it be known that she would prefer the funds to be used for a public monument. The total cost of the *Fox* expedition was £10,000; £3,000 had been raised by public subscription and Lady Franklin paid the rest.

32 He was paid 1,000 guineas before the book was published. Receipt dated 23 November 1859, Murray Archive. Further royalty cheques were received through the years. See McClintock to Murray, 4 January 1861, 11 February [1862], 8 December 1863, 13 December 1864, 17 September [1868], 18 October 1889, Murray Archive.

33 'Captain M'Clintock – Arctic Voyages,' *Natural History Review* 6, pt 1 (1859): 60.

34 Leading article (unidentified source), quoted in Simmonds, *Arctic Regions*, 274.

35 Although further oral Inuit accounts of cannibalism were reported by Charles Hall in the 1860s and Frederick Schwatka in the 1880s, none of the bodies found by these explorers bore any trace of such acts. There was no physical proof until the 1990s, when amateur historian Barry Ranford discovered bones cut by a saw. See Keenleyside, Bertulli, and Fricke, 'Final Days.'

36 McClintock, *Voyage of the 'Fox'*, 249.

37 Ibid., 259, 260. These two passages are not in McClintock's manuscript, and therefore must have been added at a later stage, either by McClintock or by Osborn. McClintock's only comment in the manuscript is: 'Brief as these records are we must needs be contented with them; they are perfect models of official brevity, no logbook could be more provokingly laconic' (187).

38 Osborn, 'Voyage of the "Fox,"' 124.

39 Haughton, 'Voyage of the "Fox,"' 217, 218.

40 McClintock, *Voyage of the 'Fox'*, 258.

41 Osborn, 'The Last Voyage of Sir John Franklin,' *Once a Week* (20 October 1859): 366.

42 'Fate of the Franklin Expedition,' *Leisure Hour* 417 (22 December 1859): 815.

43 Browne, *The North-West Passage*, 78. The Biblical passage referred to is: 'So when this corruptible shall have put on incorruption, and this mortal shall have put on immortality, then shall be brought to pass the saying that is written, Death is swallowed up in victory. O death, where is thy sting? O grave, where is thy victory?'

44 [Fitch], 'Arctic Explorations,' *London Quarterly Review* 14 (April 1860): 259.

45 'The Fate of Franklin,' *Good Words* 1, 8 (1860): 113.

46 C.R. Weld, 'Franklin's Fate, and the Voyage of the "Fox,"' *Fraser's Magazine* 61 (February 1860): 227.

47 Joven, 'The End of an Epic,' 248.

48 'The Fate of the Franklin Expedition,' *Gentleman's Magazine* 208 (February 1860): 91.

49 Franklin Lushington, 'Arctic Enterprise and its Results since 1815,' *Macmillan's* 1 (February 1860): 268, 269, 278.

50 'Fate of the Franklin Expedition,' *Leisure Hour*, 816.

51 Thomas Hood, 'The Lost Expedition,' *Macmillan's Magazine* 3 (December 1860): 113.

52 Nicholas Michell, 'The Franklin Monument,' *New Monthly Magazine* 177 (November 1859): 317.

53 Spencer Smith, 'The Deserted Boat,' in *Repton School Prize Poems* (Derby: W. Bemrose, 1860), 11–12.

54 Vidal, *Life and Character of Sir John Franklin*, 27.
55 Swinburne, *The Swinburne Letters*, Vol. 1, *1854–1869*, edited by Cecil Y. Lang (New Haven: Yale University Press, 1959), 31n3.
56 Swinburne, 'Death of Sir John Franklin,' 1, 8.

Bibliography

Unpublished Manuscript Sources

British Library, London (BL)

Letters to Sir Roderick I. Murchison. Includes correspondence from John Barrow Jr, Francis Beaufort, Richard Collinson, Sophia Cracroft, Jane Franklin, Leopold McClintock, Sherard Osborn, John Rae, John Richardson, and C.R. Weld.

Derbyshire Record Office, Matlock (DRO)

Franklin Papers, Gell Collection. Includes family letters, correspondence between Franklin and Richardson, and a collection of Arctic books, pamphlets, periodical articles, and newspaper clippings.

John Murray Archive, 50 Albemarle Street, London (now in the National Library of Scotland)

Correspondence files for John Barrow, Jane Franklin, John Franklin, Leopold McClintock, Sherard Osborn, and William Edward Parry.

Library and Archives Canada, Ottawa

MG 11, microfilm copies of Colonial Office files, reels B-3004 and B-3005 (CO 6/15)

National Maritime Museum, Greenwich (NMM)

Matthew Flinders Papers, Leopold McClintock Papers, Sherard Osborn scrapbook.

Scott Polar Research Institute, Cambridge (SPRI)

Correspondence of Sophia Cracroft, Jane Franklin, John Franklin, Leopold
McClintock, Sherard Osborn, and John Richardson.

Published Primary Sources

*Additional Papers relative to the Arctic Expedition under the Orders of Captain Austin
and Mr. William Penny.* London: Eyre and Spottiswoode for HMSO, 1852.
Anderson, James, and James Stewart. *Searching for Franklin: The Land Arctic Search-
ing Expedition, 1855: James Anderson's and James Stewart's Expedition via the Back
River.* Edited by William Barr. London: Hakluyt Society, 1999.
Anson, George. *A Voyage round the World in the Years MDCCXL, I, II, III, IV by
George Anson; compiled from papers and other materials of the Right Honourable
George Lord Anson and published under his direction by Richard Walter.* London:
John and Paul Knapton, 1748.
*Arctic Expedition. Return to an Address of the Honourable the House of Commons dated
21 March.* Sessional Papers, Accounts and Papers, 1847–8, 41.
Arctic Rewards and Their Claimants. London: T. Hatchard, 1856.
Back, George. *Arctic Artist: The Journal and Paintings of George Back, Midshipman
with Franklin, 1819–1822.* Edited by C.S. Houston and I.S. MacLaren. Mon-
treal and Kingston: McGill-Queen's University Press, 1994.
– *Narrative of the Arctic Land Expedition to the Mouth of the Great Fish River and
Along the Shores of the Arctic Ocean, in the Years 1833, 1834, and 1835.* Repr.
Edmonton: Hurtig, 1970 [1836].
Ballantyne, R.M. *Personal Reminiscences and Incidents in Book-Making.* London:
Nisbet, 1893.
Barrow, John. *A Chronological History of Voyages in the Arctic Regions; undertaken
chiefly for the purposes of discovering a North-East, North-West, or Polar Passage
between the Atlantic and the Pacific: from the earliest periods of Scandinavian Naviga-
tion, to the departure of the recent Expeditions, under the Orders of Captains Ross and
Buchan.* Repr. Newton Abbott, U.K.: David and Charles, 1971 [1818].
– *Voyages of Discovery and Research within the Arctic Regions, from the Year 1818 to the
present Time: under the command of the several naval Officers employed by Sea and
Land in search of a North-West Passage from the Atlantic to the Pacific, with two*

Attempts to reach the North Pole, abridged and arranged from the official Narratives, with occasional Remarks. London: John Murray, 1846.

Bellot, Joseph-René. *Memoirs of Lieutenant Joseph-René Bellot ... with his Journal of a Voyage in the Polar Seas, in Search of Sir John Franklin.* 2 vols. London: Hurst and Blackett, 1855.

A Brief Memoir of Rear-Admiral Sir W. Edward Parry, Kt., &c., Lieutenant Governor of Greenwich Hospital. Reprinted from the "Record" of March 25th, 1857. King's Lynn, U.K.: Thew and Son, 1857.

Browne, James A. *The North-West Passage and the Fate of Sir John Franklin.* Woolwich, U.K.: W.P. Jackson, 1860.

Burke, Edmund. *Reflections on the Revolution in France.* Edited by Conor Cruise O'Brien. Repr. Harmondsworth: Penguin Books, 1986 [1790].

Carlyle, Thomas. *Sartor Resartus and On Heroes and Hero-Worship.* Repr. London: Dent, 1964 [1836, 1841].

Carteret, Philip. *Carteret's Voyage Round the World.* Edited by Helen Wallis. Cambridge: Hakluyt Society, 1965.

Cook, James. *The Journals of Captain James Cook on his Voyages of Discovery: The Voyage of the Endeavour 1768–1771.* Edited by J.C. Beaglehole. Cambridge: Cambridge University Press / Hakluyt Society, 1968.

– *The Journals of Captain James Cook on his Voyages of Discovery: II. The Voyage of the Resolution and Adventure 1772–1775.* Edited by. J.C. Beaglehole. Cambridge: Cambridge University Press / Hakluyt Society, 1968.

– *A Voyage towards the South Pole, and round the World.* London: Cadell, 1777.

Croker, J.W. *The Croker Papers: The Correspondence and Diaries of the Late Right Honourable John Wilson Croker, LL.D., F.R.S., Secretary to the Admiralty from 1809 to 1830.* 2nd ed. 3 vols. Edited by Louis J. Jennings. London: John Murray, 1885.

Davis, Richard. "'... which an affectionate heart would say": John Franklin's personal correspondence, 1819–1824.' *Polar Record* 33 (1997): 189–212.

Dease, Peter Warren. *From Barrow to Boothia: The Arctic Journal of Chief Factor Peter Warren Dease, 1836–1839.* Edited by William Barr. Montreal and Kingston: McGill-Queen's University Press, 2002.

Dennett, Frederick. *The Voyages and Travels of Captains Parry, Franklin, Ross, and Mr. Belzoni; forming an interesting History of the Manners, Customs, and Characters of various Nations, visited by enterprising Travellers.* London: J. Jaques and W. Wright, 1826.

Dickens, Charles. *The Letters of Charles Dickens.* Vol. 7, *1853–1855.* Edited by Graham Storey, Kathleen Tillotson, and Angus Easson. Oxford: Clarendon Press, 1993.

– *The Letters of Charles Dickens.* Vol. 8. *1856–1858.* Edited by Graham Storey and Kathleen Tillotson. Oxford: Clarendon Press, 1995.

– *The Speeches of Charles Dickens.* Edited by K.J. Fielding. Oxford: Clarendon, 1960.

Elliott, Henry. 'Sir John Franklin.' *Nineteenth Century* 32 (July 1892): 118–29.

Fitzjames, James. *The Last Journals of Captain Fitzjames, R.N., of the Lost Polar Expedition.* Edited by William Coningham. Brighton, U.K.: W. Pearce [1859].

Franklin, Jane. *Letter to the Lords Commissioners of the Admiralty.* Privately printed, 1856.

– *A Letter to Viscount Palmerston from Lady Franklin, with an Appendix.* London: Ridgeway, 1857.

– *The Life, Diaries and Correspondence of Jane Lady Franklin, 1792–1875.* Edited by Willingham Franklin Rawnsley. London: Erskine Macdonald [1923].

Franklin, John. *Journey to the Shores of the Polar Sea, in 1819–20–21–22, with a brief Account of the second Journey in 1825–26–27.* 4 vols. London: John Murray, 1829.

– *Narrative of a Journey to the Shores of the Polar Sea in the Years 1819, 20, 21 and 22.* Repr. Edmonton: Hurtig, 1969 [1823]. *Note*: All text and note page references are to this reprint edition.

– *Narrative of a Journey to the Shores of the Polar Sea in the Years 1819, 20, 21 and 22.* 3rd ed. 2 vols. London: John Murray, 1824.

– *Narrative of a Second Expedition to the Shores of the Polar Sea in the Years 1825–26–27.* Repr. Edmonton: Hurtig, 1971 [1828].

– *Sir John Franklin's Journals and Correspondence: The First Arctic Land Expedition, 1819–1822.* Edited by Richard C. Davis. Toronto: Champlain Society, 1995.

– *Sir John Franklin's Journals and Correspondence: The Second Arctic Land Expedition, 1825–27.* Edited by Richard C. Davis. Toronto: Champlain Society, 1998.

– 'An Unpublished Letter of Sir John Franklin.' *Polar Record* 5 (1947–50): 350.

'A Friend to the Navy.' *A Letter to John Barrow, Esq., on the Subject of the Polar Expedition, or, The Reviewer Reviewed.* London: James Ridgeway, 1819.

Froude, J.A. *English Seamen in the Sixteenth Century.* London: Longmans, 1895.

– *Short Studies on Great Subjects.* 4 vols. Repr. London: Longmans, Green, 1891 [1867].

The Great Arctic Mystery. London: Chapman and Hall, 1856.

Hargrave, Letitia. *The Letters of Letitia Hargrave.* Edited by Margaret Arnett MacLeod. Toronto: Champlain Society, 1947.

Hearne, Samuel. *A Journey from Prince of Wales's Fort in Hudson's Bay to the Northern Ocean in 1769, 1770, 1771, 1772.* Edited by Richard Glover. Toronto: Macmillan, 1958.

Hood, Robert. *To the Arctic by Canoe, 1819–1821: The Journal and Paintings of Robert Hood, Midshipman with Franklin.* Edited by C. Stuart Houston. Montreal and Kingston: McGill-Queen's University Press, 1974.

Jerdan, William. *The Autobiography of William Jerdan.* 4 vols. Repr. New York: AMS Press, 1977 [1852–3].

– *Men I Have Known.* London: George Routledge, 1866.

Kane, Elisha Kent. *Arctic Explorations: the Second Grinnell Expedition in Search of Sir John Franklin, 1853, '54, '55.* 2 vols. Philadelphia: Childs and Peterson, 1856.

Kennedy, William. *A short Narrative of the second Voyage of the Prince Albert in search of Sir John Franklin.* London: W.H. Dalton, 1853.

King, Richard. *The Franklin Expedition from First to Last.* London: John Churchill, 1855.

– *Narrative of a Journey to the Shores of the Arctic Ocean in 1833, 1834, and 1835; under the Command of Capt. Back, R.N.* 2 vols. London: Richard Bentley, 1836.

Lentz, John W. 'The *Fox* Expedition in Search of Franklin: A Documentary Trail.' *Arctic* 56 (2003): 175–84.

Leslie, John, Robert Jameson, and Hugh Murray. *A Narrative of Discovery and Adventure in the Polar Seas and Regions: with Illustrations of their Climate, Geology, and Natural History; and an Account of the Whale Fishery.* Edinburgh: Oliver and Boyd, 1830.

– *The Polar Seas and Regions, with a Narrative of the Present Expeditions in Search of Sir John Franklin.* 20th ed. London: Nelson, 1855.

Leslie, John, Hugh Murray, and R.M. Ballantyne. *Discovery and Adventure in the Polar Seas and Regions … with a Narrative of the recent Expeditions in Search of Sir John Franklin, including the Voyage of the 'Fox,' and the Discovery of the Fate of the Franklin Expedition.* 21st ed. London: Nelson, 1860.

Mangles, James. *Papers and Despatches relating to the Arctic Searching Expeditions of 1850–51–52.* 2nd ed. London: Francis and John Rivington, 1852.

Masson, L.F.R., ed. *Les Bourgeois de la Compagnie du Nord-Ouest.* 2 vols. Repr. New York: Antiquarian Press, 1960 [1889].

Mayne, Fanny. *Voyages and Discoveries in the Arctic Regions.* London: Longman, 1855.

McClintock, Francis Leopold. *The Voyage of the "Fox" in the Arctic Seas: A Narrative of the Discovery of the Fate of Sir John Franklin and his Companions.* Repr. Edmonton: Hurtig, 1972 [1859].

Observations on the missing Ships of the Arctic Expeditions, under Sir John Franklin, with some Propositions and Considerations for their Relief and Extrication from the Ice, by an old Officer of the Royal Navy. Repr. *Littel's Living Age* 24 (9 March 1850): 453–6.

Osborn, Sherard. *The Career, Last Voyage and Fate of Captain Sir John Franklin.* London: Bradbury and Evans, 1860.

– *The Discovery of the North-West Passage: from the Logs and Journals of Capt. Robert le M. McClure.* Repr. Edmonton: Hurtig, 1969.

– *Stray Leaves from an Arctic Journal; or, eighteen Months in the polar Regions, in search of Sir John Franklin's Expedition, in the Years 1850–51.* London: Longman, Brown, Green and Longmans, 1852.

Parry, William Edward. *Journal of a Voyage for the Discovery of a North-West Passage from the Atlantic to the Pacific: performed in the Years 1819–20, in His Majesty's Ships Hecla and Griper.* London: John Murray, 1821.

– *Journals of the first, second and third voyages for the discovery of a north-west passage from the Atlantic to the Pacific: in 1819–20–21–22–23–24–25 in His Majesty's ships Hecla, Griper and Fury, under the orders of Captain W. E. Parry.* 5 vols. London: John Murray, 1828.

– *Three Voyages for the Discovery of a North-West Passage from the Atlantic to the Pacific, and Narrative of an Attempt to Reach the North Pole.* 5 vols. London: John Murray, 1835.

Parsons, James. *Reflections on the Mysterious Fate of Sir John Franklin.* London: J.F. Hope, 1857.

Penny, Margaret. *This Distant and Unsurveyed Country: A Woman's Winter at Baffin Island.* Edited by W. Gillies Ross. Montreal and Kingston: McGill-Queen's University Press, 1997.

Pim, Bedford. *An earnest Appeal to the British Public on behalf of the missing Arctic Expedition.* London: Hurst and Blackett, 1857.

Rae, John. *John Rae's Correspondence with the Hudson's Bay Company on Arctic Exploration 1844–1855.* Edited by E.E. Rich and A.M. Johnson. London: Hudson's Bay Record Society, 1953.

– Letter to John Ballenden, 4 September 1854. In 'Two Franklin Documents,' *Beaver* 27 (September 1947): 47.

Report of the Committee appointed by the Lords Commissioners of the Admiralty to inquire into and report on the recent Arctic Expeditions in search of Sir John Franklin, together with the Minutes of Evidence taken before the Committee, and Papers connected with the Subject. London: Eyre and Spottiswoode, for HMSO, 1851.

Richardson, John. *Arctic Ordeal: The Journal of John Richardson, Surgeon-Naturalist with Franklin, 1820–1822.* Edited by C. Stuart Houston. Montreal and Kingston: McGill-Queen's University Press, 1984.

– *Life of Sir John Franklin.* Edinburgh: Adam and Charles Black [1856].

Ross, John. *Narrative of a Second Voyage in search of a North-West Passage, and of a Residence in the Arctic Regions, during the Years 1829, 1830, 1831, 1832, 1833.* Philadelphia: E.L. Carey and A. Hart, 1835.

Ruskin, John. *Praeterita.* Repr. Oxford: Oxford University Press, 1978 [1885–9].

Russell, William Howard. *Russell's Despatches from the Crimea 1854–1856.* Edited by Nicolas Bentley. London: André Deutsch, 1966.

Scoresby, William. *The Franklin Expedition: or Considerations on Measures for the Discovery and Relief of our absent Adventurers in the Arctic Regions.* London: Longman, Brown, Green, and Longmans, 1850.

'The Search for Sir John Franklin.' *Chambers's Repository* No. 45. Repr. Toronto: Canadiana House, n.d.

Simmonds, Peter Lund. *The Arctic Regions, and Polar Discoveries during the Nineteenth Century*. 10th ed. London: George Routledge and Sons, 1875.

– *Sir John Franklin and the Arctic Regions: showing the Progress of British Enterprise for the Discovery of the North-West Passage during the Nineteenth Century: with more detailed Notices of the recent Expeditions in Search of the missing Vessels under Captain Sir John Franklin*. London: George Routledge, 1851.

– *Sir John Franklin and the Arctic Regions*. Buffalo: George H. Derby, 1852.

Simpson, George. *Journal of Occurrences in the Athabasca Department*. Edited by E.E. Rich. London: Hudson's Bay Record Society, 1938.

Smiles, Samuel. *Self Help: with Illustrations of Conduct and Perseverance*. Repr. London: John Murray, 1958 [1859].

Southey, Robert. *The Life of Nelson*. Edited by E.R.H. Harvey. Repr. London: Macdonald, 1953 [1813].

Stevenson, Robert Louis. 'The English Admirals.' In *Virginibus Puerisque and Familiar Studies in Men and Books*. Repr. London: Dent, 1963 [1881–2].

Swinburne, Algernon Charles. *The Swinburne Letters*. Vol. 1, *1854–1869*. Edited by Cecil Y. Lang. New Haven: Yale University Press, 1959.

Tennyson, Emily Sellwood. *Lady Tennyson's Journal*. Edited by James O. Hoge. Charlottesville: University Press of Virginia, 1981.

Tytler, Patrick Fraser. *An Historical View of the Progress of Discovery on the more northern Coasts of America, from the earliest Period to the present Time*. Edinburgh: Oliver and Boyd, 1832.

Vancouver, George. *A Voyage of Discovery to the North Pacific Ocean and Round the World*. London: G.G. and J. Robinson and J. Edwards, 1798.

Weld, C.R. *Arctic Expeditions: A Lecture*. London: John Murray, 1850.

Winter in the Arctic Regions. London: Society for Promoting Christian Knowledge, 1846.

Wrangell, Ferdinand von. *Narrative of an Expedition to the Polar Sea, in the Years 1820, 1821, 1822 & 1823*. 2nd ed. London: James Madden, 1844.

Fiction, Poetry, and Drama

Austen, Jane. *Persuasion*. In *The Novels of Jane Austen*. Vol. 5. Edited by R.W. Chapman. 3rd ed. Oxford: Oxford University Press, 1933 [1818].

Brannan, R.L. *Under the Management of Mr. Charles Dickens: His Production of 'The Frozen Deep.'* Ithaca, N.Y.: Cornell University Press, 1966.

Dickens, Charles. *Hard Times*. Edited by George Ford and Sylvère Monod. New York: Norton, 1966 [1854].

Porden, Eleanor. *The Arctic Expeditions. A Poem.* London: John Murray, 1818.

Richler, Mordecai. *Solomon Gursky Was Here.* Markham, Ont.: Viking, 1989.

Smith, Spencer. 'The Deserted Boat.' In *Repton School Prize Poems.* Derby, U.K.: W. Bemrose, 1860.

Swinburne, Algernon Charles. 'The Death of Sir John Franklin.' In *The Complete Works of Algernon Charles Swinburne: Poetical Works.* Vol. 1. Edited by Edmund Gosse and Thomas James Wise. Repr. New York: Russell, 1968 [1925].

Wiebe, Rudy. *A Discovery of Strangers.* Toronto: Knopf, 1994.

Vidal, Owen A. *A Poem on the Life and Character of Sir John Franklin, with special Reference to [the] Time, Place, and Discovery of his Death: Recited in the Sheldonian Theatre Monday, July 2, at the Meeting of the British Association for the Advancement of Science.* Oxford: T. and G. Shrimpton, 1860.

Newspapers and Periodicals

All the Year Round

Annual Register

Athenaeum

Bentley's Miscellany

Black Dwarf

Blackwood's Magazine

British Critic

British Quarterly Review

British Review

Cassell's Illustrated Family Paper

Chambers's Edinburgh Journal

Christian Observer

Daily News

Dublin University Magazine

Eclectic Review

Edinburgh Magazine

Edinburgh Philosophical Journal

Edinburgh Review

Everybody's Journal

Examiner

Fraser's Magazine

Gentleman's Magazine

Geographical Journal

Geographical Magazine

Good Words

Household Words

Journal of the Royal Dublin Society

Journal of the Royal Geographical Society

Illustrated London News

Leader

Leisure Hour

Literary Chronicle

Literary Gazette

Littel's Living Age

London Magazine

London Quarterly Review

Macmillan's Magazine

Mirror of Literature, Amusement and Instruction

Monthly Magazine

Monthly Review

Montreal *Gazette*

Morning Chronicle

Natural History Review

Nautical Magazine and Naval Chronicle

Nautical Standard and Steam Navigation Gazette

New Monthly Magazine

New Voyages and Travels
News of the World
North British Review
Once a Week
Penny Magazine
Quarterly Review
Saturday Review

Sharpe's London Magazine
Spectator
Tait's Edinburgh Magazine
Times (London)
United Service Magazine
Weekly Dispatch
Westminster Review

Secondary Sources

Altick, Richard D. *The English Common Reader: A Social History of the Mass Reading Public, 1800–1900.* 2nd ed. Columbus: Ohio State University Press, 1998.

– *Writers, Readers and Occasions: Selected Essays in Victorian Literature and Life.* Columbus: Ohio State University Press, 1989.

Anderson, Olive. 'The Growth of Christian Militarism in Mid-Victorian Britain.' *English Historical Review* 86 (1971): 46–72.

– *A Liberal State at War: English Politics and Economics During the Crimean War.* London: Macmillan, 1967.

Anderson, Patricia. *The Printed Image and the Transformation of Popular Culture, 1790–1860.* Oxford: Clarendon, 1991.

Arbuckle, Elisabeth Sanders, ed. *Harriet Martineau in the London Daily News.* New York and London: Garland, 1994.

Atwood, Margaret. 'Concerning Franklin and His Gallant Crew.' In Atwood, *Strange Things: The Malevolent North in Canadian Literature.* Oxford: Clarendon, 1995.

Barker, Nicolas, ed. *A Potencie of Life: Books in Society; The Clark Lectures, 1986–87.* London: British Library, 1993.

Bartlett, C.J. *Great Britain and Sea Power, 1815–1853.* Oxford: Clarendon Press, 1963.

Beaglehole, J.C. *Cook the Writer.* Sydney: Sydney University Press, 1970.

– *The Life of Captain James Cook.* London: Hakluyt Society, 1974.

Beattie, Owen, and John Geiger. *Frozen in Time.* Saskatoon: Western Producer Prairie Books, 1987.

Beesley, A.H. *Sir John Franklin.* New York: H.M. Caldwell, 1881.

Behrman, Cynthia Fansler. *Victorian Myths of the Sea.* Athens: Ohio State University Press, 1977.

Belyea, Barbara. 'Captain Franklin in Search of the Picturesque.' *Essays on Canadian Writing* 40 (1990): 1–24.

Bennett, Scott. 'John Murray's Family Library and the Cheapening of Books in Early Nineteenth Century Britain.' *Studies in Bibliography* 29 (1976): 140–67.

Berlin, Isaiah. *Against the Current: Essays in the History of Ideas.* New York: Viking, 1980.

Berton, Pierre. *The Arctic Grail.* Toronto: McClelland and Stewart, 1988.

Bevington, Merle Mowbray. *The Saturday Review, 1855–1868: Representative Educated Opinion in Victorian England.* Repr. New York: AMS Press, 1996 [1941].

Boase, Frederic, ed. *Modern English Biography.* Repr. London: Cass, 1965 [1892–1921].

Bradstock, Andrew, Sean Gill, Anne Hogan, and Sue Morgan, eds. *Masculinity and Spirituality in Victorian Culture.* Basingstoke, U.K.: Macmillan, 2000.

Brake, Laurel. 'Star Turn? Magazine, Part-issue, and Book Serialisation.' *Victorian Periodicals Review* 34 (Fall 2001): 208–27.

Brake, Laurel, Aled Jones, and Lionel Madden, eds. *Investigating Victorian Journalism.* London: Macmillan, 1990.

Bravo, Michael. 'Science and Discovery in the Admiralty Voyages to the Arctic Regions in Search of a North-West Passage (1815–25).' Unpublished PhD dissertation, Cambridge University, 1992.

Brick, Allan R. 'The *Leader*: Organ of Radicalism.' Unpublished PhD dissertation, Yale University, 1957.

Brown, George W., ed. *Dictionary of Canadian Biography.* Toronto: University of Toronto Press, 1966–.

Brown, Lucy. *Victorian News and Newspapers.* Oxford: Clarendon Press, 1985.

Brown, Marshall. 'Romanticism and Enlightenment.' In Stuart Curran, ed., *The Cambridge Companion to British Romanticism.* Cambridge: Cambridge University Press, 1993.

Bullen, J.B., ed. *Writing and Victorianism.* London and New York: Longman, 1997.

Butler, Marilyn. 'Culture's Medium: The Role of the Review.' In Stuart Curran, ed., *The Cambridge Companion to British Romanticism.* Cambridge: Cambridge University Press, 1993.

Calhoun, Craig, ed. *Habermas and the Public Sphere.* Cambridge, Mass.: MIT Press, 1992.

Cavell, Janice. 'Comparing Mythologies: Twentieth-Century Canadian Constructions of Sir John Franklin.' In Norman Hillmer and Adam Chapnick, eds, *Canadas of the Mind: The Making and Unmaking of Twentieth-Century Canadian Nationalism.* Montreal and Kingston: McGill-Queen's University Press, 2007.

– 'The Hidden Crime of Dr Richardson.' *Polar Record* 43 (2007): 155–64.

– 'Representing Akaitcho: European Vision and Re-Vision in the Writing of John Franklin's *Narrative of a Journey to the Shores of the Polar Sea.*' *Polar Record* 44 (2008): 25–34.

– 'The Second Frontier: The North in English-Canadian Historical Writing.' *Canadian Historical Review* 83 (2002): 364–89.

– 'Tracing the Connected Narrative: The Literature of British Arctic Exploration, 1818–1860.' PhD dissertation, Carleton University, 2003.

Chandler, James. *England in 1819: The Politics of Literary Culture and the Case of Romantic Historicism.* Chicago: University of Chicago Press, 1998.

Chartier, Roger. *Forms and Meanings: Texts, Performances, and Audiences from Codex to Computer.* Philadelphia: University of Pennsylvania Press, 1995.

– *The Order of Books: Readers, Authors and Libraries in Europe between the Fourteenth and Eighteenth Centuries.* Translated by Lydia G. Cochrane. Stanford: Stanford University Press, 1994.

Clark, A.J. 'Captain William Kennedy.' *Canadian Magazine* 39 (1912): 446–53.

Clive, John. 'The *Edinburgh Review*: The Life and Death of a Periodical.' In Asa Briggs, ed., *Essays in the History of Publishing in Celebration of the 250th Anniversary of the House of Longman, 1724–1974.* London: Longman, 1974.

Cobban, Alfred. *Edmund Burke and the Revolt Against the Eighteenth Century.* London: Allen, 1960.

Colley, Linda. *Britons: Forging the Nation, 1707–1837.* New Haven: Yale University Press, 1992.

Collini, Stefan. 'The Idea of "Character" in Victorian Political Thought.' *Transactions of the Royal Historical Society* 5th ser., 35 (1985): 29–50.

Collis, Christy. 'The Voyage of the Episteme: Narrating the North.' *Essays on Canadian Writing* 59 (Fall 1996): 26–45.

Cook, Edward. *Delane of 'The Times'.* London: Constable, 1915.

Cooke, Alan. 'The Autobiography of Dr John Rae (1813–1893): A Preliminary Note.' *Polar Record* 14 (1968): 173–7.

Cooke, Alan, and Clive Holland. *The Exploration of Northern Canada: 500 to 1920, A Chronology.* Toronto: Arctic History Press, 1978.

Cubitt, Geoffrey, and Allen Warren, eds. *Heroic Reputations and Exemplary Lives.* Manchester: Manchester University Press, 2000.

Cunningham, Hugh. 'The Language of Patriotism, 1750–1914.' *History Workshop Journal* 12 (1981): 8–33.

Cyriax, Richard J. *Sir John Franklin's Last Expedition: A Chapter in the History of the Royal Navy.* Repr. Plaistow and Sutton Coldfield, U.K.: Arctic Press, 1997 [1939].

Cyriax, R.J., and J.M. Wordie. 'Centenary of the Sailing of Sir John Franklin in the *Erebus* and *Terror*.' *Geographical Journal* 76 (1945): 169–97.

David, Robert G. *The Arctic in the British Imagination, 1818–1914.* Manchester: Manchester University Press, 2000.

Davidoff, Leonore, and Catherine Hall. *Family Fortunes: Men and Women of the English Middle Class, 1780–1850.* London: Hutchinson, 1988.

Davis, Richard C. 'Exploration Literature in English.' *Canadian Encyclopedia,* 1985.

– 'History or His/Story? The Explorer Cum Author.' *Studies in Canadian Literature* 16, 2 (1991): 93–111.

– 'Once Bitten, Twice Shy: Cultural Arrogance and the Final Franklin Expedition.' *Polar Geography* 26, 1 (2002): 21–38.
– Review of Robert David, *The Arctic in the British Imagination 1818–1914*. *Polar Record* 38 (2002): 180–1.
– Review of Rudy Wiebe, *A Discovery of Strangers*. *Arctic* 49 (1996): 97–8.
– 'Thrice-Told Tales: The Exploration Writing of John Franklin.' In Jørn Carlsen and Bengt Streijffert, eds, *The Canadian North: Essays on Culture and Literature*. Lund: Nordic Association for Canadian Studies, 1989.
– 'Vision and Revision: John Franklin's Arctic Landscapes.' *Australian-Canadian Studies* 6, 2 (1989): 23–33.
Dawson, Graham. *Soldier Heroes: British Adventure, Empire and the Imagining of Masculinities*. London: Routledge, 1994.
Day, Alan E. *Search for the Northwest Passage: An Annotated Bibliography*. New York and London: Garland, 1986.
Dening, Greg. *Mr. Bligh's Bad Language: Passion, Power and Theatre on the Bounty*. Cambridge: Cambridge University Press, 1992.
Dodge, Ernest S. *The Polar Rosses*. London: Faber and Faber, 1973.
Duff, David. *Romance and Revolution: Shelley and the Politics of a Genre*. Cambridge: Cambridge University Press, 1994.
Eastwood, David. 'Robert Southey and the Intellectual Origins of Romantic Conservatism.' *English Historical Review* 104 (1989): 308–31.
Edwards, Philip. *The Story of the Voyage: Sea-Narratives in Eighteenth-Century England*. Cambridge: Cambridge University Press, 1994.
Ellegård, Alvar. *The Readership of the Periodical Press in Mid-Victorian Britain*. Göteborg: Göteborgs Universitets Årsskrift, 1957.
Epstein, James. 'The Populist Turn.' *Journal of British Studies* 32 (April 1993): 177–89.
Feather, John. *Publishing, Piracy and Politics: An Historical Study of Copyright in Britain*. New York: Mansell, 1994.
Finn, Margot C. *After Chartism: Class and Nation in English Radical Politics, 1848–1874*. Cambridge: Cambridge University Press, 1993.
Fish, Stanley. *Is There a Text in This Class? The Authority of Interpretive Communities*. Cambridge, Mass.: Harvard University Press, 1980.
Foucault, Michel. *The Archaeology of Knowledge*. New York: Pantheon, 1972.
– *The History of Sexuality*. Vol. 2, *The Use of Pleasure*. New York: Vintage, 1990.
– *Language, Counter-Memory, Practice*. Ithaca: Cornell University Press, 1977.
– *Power/Knowledge: Selected Interviews and Other Writings, 1972–1977*. Edited by Colin Gordon. New York: Pantheon, 1980.
Friendly, Alfred. *Beaufort of the Admiralty: The Life of Sir Francis Beaufort, 1774–1857*. London: Hutchinson, 1977.

Frye, Northrop. *Anatomy of Criticism*. Princeton: Princeton University Press, 1971.
– *The Secular Scripture*. Cambridge, Mass.: Harvard University Press, 1976.
Fulford, Tim. *Romanticism and Masculinity: Gender, Politics and Poetics in the Writings of Burke, Coleridge, Cobbett, Wordsworth, De Quincey and Hazlitt*. Basingstoke: Macmillan, 1999.
Fulford, Tim, and Peter J. Kitson, eds. *Romanticism and Colonialism: Writing and Empire, 1780–1830*. Cambridge: Cambridge University Press, 1998.
Galinsky, Hans. 'Exploring the "Exploration Report" and its Image of the Overseas World: Spanish, French, and English Variants of a Common Form Type in Early American Literature.' *Early American Literature* 12 (1977): 5–24.
Gell, Edith Mary. *John Franklin's Bride*. London: John Murray, 1930.
Gerin, Winifred. *Branwell Brontë*. London: Nelson, 1961.
Gibson, William. 'Sir John Franklin's Last Voyage.' *The Beaver* 17 (June 1937): 44–75.
Gilmartin, Kevin. *Print Politics: The Press and Radical Opposition in Early Nineteenth-Century England*. Cambridge: Cambridge University Press, 1996.
Ginzburg, Carlo. *The Cheese and the Worms: The Cosmos of a Sixteenth-Century Miller*. Baltimore: Johns Hopkins University Press, 1980.
Girouard, Mark. *The Return to Camelot: Chivalry and the English Gentleman*. New Haven: Yale University Press, 1981.
Glass, Robert E. 'The Image of the Sea Officer in English Literature, 1660–1710.' *Albion* 26 (Winter 1994): 583–99.
Glover, Richard. 'The Witness of David Thompson.' *Canadian Historical Review* 31 (1950): 25–38.
– 'A Note on John Richardson's "Digression Concerning Hearne's Route."' *Canadian Historical Review* 32 (1951): 252–63.
Grace, Sherrill. *Canada and the Idea of North*. Montreal and Kingston; McGill-Queen's University Press, 2002.
– 'Re-Inventing Franklin.' *Canadian Review of Comparative Literature* (Sept.-Dec. 1995): 707–23.
Graham, Walter. *English Literary Periodicals*. New York: Octagon Books, 1966.
Grant, Shelagh. 'Myths of the North in the Canadian Ethos.' *Northern Review* 3, 4 (1989): 15–41.
– *Sovereignty or Security? Government Policy in the Canadian North, 1936–1950*. Vancouver: University of British Columbia Press, 1988.
Griffiths, Dennis, ed. *Encyclopedia of the British Press*. New York: St Martin's Press, 1992.
Guillemard, F.H.H. 'Franklin and the Arctic.' *Blackwood's Magazine* 161 (February 1897): 238–56.

Habermas, Jürgen. *The Structural Transformation of the Public Sphere.* Cambridge, Mass.: MIT Press, 1991.

Hamilton, C.I. 'Naval Hagiography and the Victorian Hero.' *Historical Journal* 23 (1980): 381–98.

Hayden, John O. *The Romantic Reviewers, 1802–1824.* London: Routledge and Kegan Paul, 1969.

Hayward, Jennifer. *Consuming Pleasures: Active Audiences and Serial Fictions from Dickens to Soap Opera.* Lexington: University Press of Kentucky, 1997.

Helgerson, Richard. *Forms of Nationhood: The Elizabethan Writing of England.* Chicago: University of Chicago Press, 1992.

Helm, June, ed. *Handbook of North American Indians.* Vol. 6, *The Subarctic.* Washington, D.C.: Smithsonian Institution, 1981.

Holland, Clive .'The Arctic Committee of 1851: A Background Study.' *Polar Record,* 20 (1980): 3–17, 105–18.

– 'John Franklin and the Fur Trade, 1819–22,' in Richard Davis, ed., *Rupert's Land: A Cultural Tapestry.* Waterloo: Wilfrid Laurier University Press, 1988.

– 'William Penny, 1809–92: Arctic Whaling Master.' *Polar Record* 15 (1970): 25–43.

Homans, Margaret, and Adrienne Munich, eds. *Remaking Queen Victoria.* Cambridge: Cambridge University Press, 1997.

Houghton, Walter E. *The Victorian Frame of Mind, 1830–1870.* New Haven: Yale University Press, 1957.

– ed. *The Wellesley Index to Victorian Periodicals, 1824–1900.* 5 vols. Toronto: University of Toronto Press, 1966–89.

Howsam, Leslie. 'Sustained Literary Ventures: The Series in Victorian Book Publishing.' *Publishing History* 31 (1991): 5–26.

Hughes, Linda K., and Michael Lund. *The Victorian Serial.* Charlottesville and London: University Press of Virginia, 1991.

Hulan, Renée. *Northern Experience and the Myths of Canadian Culture.* Montreal and Kingston: McGill-Queen's University Press, 2003.

Hume, Robert D. 'Texts Within Contexts: Notes toward a Historical Method.' *Philological Quarterly* 71 (Spring 1992): 69–100.

Huntford, Roland. *Scott and Amundsen.* London: Hodder and Stoughton, 1979.

Iser, Wolfgang. *The Act of Reading.* Baltimore: Johns Hopkins University Press, 1978.

Johnson, Robert E. *Sir John Richardson.* London: Taylor and Francis, 1976.

Jones, A.G.E. 'Rear Admiral Sir William Edward Parry: A Different View.' *Musk-Ox* 21 (1978): 3–10.

Jones, Aled. *Powers of the Press: Newspapers, Power and the Public in Nineteenth-Century England.* Aldershot, U.K.: Scolar Press, 1996.

Jones, Gareth Stedman. 'Rethinking Chartism.' In Jones, *Languages of Class: Studies in English Working Class History, 1832–1982*. Cambridge: Cambridge University Press, 1983.

Jordan, Gerald, and Nicholas Rogers. 'Admirals as Heroes: Patriotism and Liberty in Hanoverian England.' *Journal of British Studies* 28 (1989): 201–24.

Jordan, John O., and Robert L. Patten, eds. *Literature in the Marketplace*. Cambridge: Cambridge University Press, 1995.

Joyce, Patrick. *Democratic Subjects: The Self and the Social in Nineteenth-Century England*. Cambridge: Cambridge University Press, 1994.

– *Visions of the People: Industrial England and the Question of Class, 1848–1914*. Cambridge: Cambridge University Press, 1991.

Karamanski, Theodore J. *Fur Trade and Exploration: Opening the Far Northwest, 1821–1852*. Norman: University of Oklahoma Press, 1983.

Keenleyside, Anne, Margaret Bertulli, and Henry C. Fricke. 'The Final Days of the Franklin Expedition: New Skeletal Evidence.' *Arctic* 50 (March 1997): 36–46.

Kennedy, Ludovic. *Nelson and His Captains*. London: Collins, 1975.

Kennedy, Paul. *The Rise and Fall of British Naval Mastery*. London: A. Lane, 1976.

Kent, Christopher. 'Victorian Social History: Post-Thompson, Post-Foucault, Postmodern.' *Victorian Studies* 40 (1996–7): 97–133.

Kerr, Robert. 'Rae's Franklin Relics.' *Beaver* 33 (March 1954): 25–7.

Klancher, Jon. *The Making of English Reading Audiences, 1790–1832*. Madison: University of Wisconsin Press, 1987.

Langford, Paul. *Englishness Identified: Manners and Character, 1650–1850*. Oxford: Oxford University Press, 2000.

Leacock, Stephen. Introduction to Vilhjalmur Stefansson, *Unsolved Mysteries of the Arctic*. New York: Macmillan, 1938.

Levere, Trevor. *Science and the Canadian Arctic*. Cambridge: Cambridge University Press, 1993.

Lloyd, Christopher. *Mr. Barrow of the Admiralty*. London: Collins, 1970.

Lohrli, Anne. *Household Words: A Weekly Journal, 1850–1859, Conducted by Charles Dickens. Table of Contents, List of Contributors and Their Contributions*. Toronto: University of Toronto Press, 1973.

Lukács, Georg. *The Historical Novel*. Repr. Harmondsworth, U.K.: Peregrine Books, 1969 [1962].

Lynam, Edward, ed. *Richard Hakluyt and His Successors*. London: Hakluyt Society, 1946.

Mack, James D. *Matthew Flinders, 1774–1814*. Melbourne: Nelson, 1966.

MacLaren, Ian S. 'The Aesthetic Map of the North, 1845–1859.' In Kenneth Coates and W.R. Morrison, eds, *Interpreting Canada's North*. Toronto: Copp Clark, 1989.

- 'The Aesthetic Mapping of Nature in the Second Franklin Expedition.' *Journal of Canadian Studies* 20 (1985): 39–57.
- 'Discovery as Misperception: The Case of Nineteenth-Century Arctic Exploration.' In Diana Macintyre Deluca, ed., *Essays on Perceiving Nature*. Honolulu: Perceiving Nature Conference Committee, 1988.
- 'From Exploration to Publication: The Evolution of a Nineteenth-Century Arctic Narrative.' *Arctic* 47 (1994): 43–53.
- 'Exploration/ Travel Literature and the Evolution of the Author,' *International Journal of Canadian Studies* 5 (Spring 1992): 39–68.
- 'John Franklin.' *Profiles in Canadian Literature* 5 (1986): 25–32.
- 'John Franklin.' In *Dictionary of Literary Biography*. Vol. 99, *Canadian Writers before 1890*, edited by W.H. New. Detroit: Gale Research, 1990.
- 'Retaining Captaincy of the Soul: Response to Nature in the First Franklin Expedition.' *Essays on Canadian Writing* 28 (Spring 1984): 57–92.
MacLeod, Margaret Arnett, and Richard Glover. 'Franklin's First Expedition as Seen by the Fur Traders.' *Polar Record* 15 (1971): 669–82.
Magnuson, Paul. *Reading Public Romanticism*. Princeton: Princeton University Press, 1998.
Majeed, Javed. *Ungoverned Imaginings: James Mill's The History of British India and Orientalism*. Oxford: Clarendon Press, 1992.
Makdis, Saree. *Romantic Imperialism: Universal Empire and the Culture of Modernity*. Cambridge: Cambridge University Press, 1998.
Marchand, Leslie A. *The Athenaeum: A Mirror of Victorian Culture*. Chapel Hill: University of North Carolina Press, 1941.
Marcus, G.J. *Heart of Oak: A Survey of British Sea Power in the Georgian Era*. London: Oxford University Press, 1975.
Markham, Albert. *The Life of Sir Clements R. Markham*. London: John Murray, 1917.
 –*The Life of Sir John Franklin*. London: G. Philip, 1891.
Markham, Clements. *The Life of Admiral Sir Leopold McClintock*. London: John Murray, 1909.
- *The Lands of Silence*. Cambridge: Cambridge University Press, 1921.
Marlow, James E. 'The Fate of Sir John Franklin: Three Phases of Response in Victorian Periodicals.' *Victorian Periodicals Review* 15 (Spring 1982): 3–11.
Maunder, Andrew. '"Discourses of Distinction": The Reception of the *Cornhill Magazine*, 1859–60.' *Victorian Periodicals Review* 32 (Fall 1999): 239–58.
McGann, Jerome. *A Critique of Modern Textual Criticism*. Chicago: University of Chicago Press, 1983).
- *The Textual Condition*. Princeton: Princeton University Press, 1991.
- *Textual Criticism and Literary Interpretation*. Chicago: University of Chicago Press, 1985.

McGhee, Robert. *The Last Imaginary Place: A Human History of the Arctic World.*
New York: Oxford University Press, 2005.

McGoogan, Ken. *Fatal Passage: The Untold Story of John Rae, the Arctic Adventurer
Who Discovered the Fate of Franklin.* Toronto: HarperCanada, 2001.

Monchuk, Judy. 'Franklin "Insensitive" Choice for Ship's Name.' *Ottawa Citizen*
20 May 2003, A3.

Moss, John. *Enduring Dreams: An Exploration of Arctic Landscape.* Toronto: Anansi,
1994.

– ed. *Echoing Silence: Essays on Arctic Narrative.* Ottawa: University of Ottawa
Press, 1995.

Mowat, Farley. *Ordeal by Ice.* Toronto: McClelland and Stewart, 1960.

Mulhauser, Frederick L. 'The Tradition of Burke.' In Joseph Baker, ed., *The
Reinterpretation of Victorian Literature.* New York: Russell and Russell, 1962.

Myers, Robin, and Michael Harris, eds. *Journeys through the Market: Travel,
Travellers and the Book Trade.* New Castle, Del.: Oak Knoll Press / Folkestone,
U.K.: St Paul's Bibliographies, 1999.

– *Serials and Their Readers, 1620–1914.* Winchester: St Paul's Bibliographies /
New Castle, Del.: Oak Knoll Press, 1993.

Nesbitt, George L. *Benthamite Reviewing: The First Twelve Years of the Westminster
Review, 1824–1836.* Repr. New York: AMS Press, 1966 [1934].

Newman, Gerald. *The Rise of English Nationalism: A Cultural History, 1740–1830.*
New York: St Martin's Press, 1987.

Newman, Peter C. *Company of Adventurers.* Markham: Viking Penguin, 1985.

Oppenlander, Ella Ann. *Dickens' All the Year Round: Descriptive Index and Contributor List.* Troy, N.Y.: Whitson, 1984.

Owen, Roderic. *The Fate of Franklin.* London: Hutchinson, 1978.

Parry, Edward. *Memoirs of Rear-Admiral Sir W. Edward Parry, Kt., F.R.S. etc., late
Lieutenant-Governor of Greenwich Hospital.* London: Longman, Brown, Green,
Longmans, and Roberts, 1857.

Philp, Mark, ed. *The French Revolution and British Popular Politics.* Cambridge:
Cambridge University Press, 1991.

Pearson, W.H. 'Hawkesworth's Alterations.' *Journal of Pacific History* 7 (1972):
45–72.

Peck, John. *Maritime Fiction: Sailors and the Sea in British and American Novels,
1719–1917.* Basingstoke and New York: Palgrave, 2001.

Percy, Carol E. 'In the Margins: Dr Hawkesworth's Editorial Emendations
to the Language of Captain Cook's *Voyages.' English Studies* 77 (1996):
549–78.

Pocock, J.G.A. 'Burke and the Ancient Constitution – A Problem in the History
of Ideas.' *Historical Journal* 3 (1960): 125–43.

– 'European Perceptions of World History in the Age of Encounter.' In Alex Calder, Jonathan Lamb, and Bridget Orr, eds, *Voyages and Beaches: Pacific Encounters, 1769–1840.* Honolulu: University of Hawaii Press, 1999.

– *Virtue, Commerce and History.* Cambridge: Cambridge University Press, 1985.

Pratt, Mary Louise. *Imperial Eyes: Travel Writing and Transculturation.* London and New York: Routledge, 1992.

Quinn, D.B., ed. *The Hakluyt Handbook.* Vol. 1. London: Hakluyt Society, 1974.

Radway, Janice. *Reading the Romance: Women, Patriarchy, and Popular Literature.* Chapel Hill and London: University of North Carolina Press, 1984.

Raffan, James. *Summer North of Sixty: By Paddle and Portage across the Barren Lands.* Toronto: Key Porter, 1990.

Richard, Robert. *Dr. John Rae.* Whitby, U.K.: Caedmon, 1985.

Richardson, Alan, and Sonia Hofkosh. *Romanticism, Race, and Imperial Culture, 1780–1834.* Bloomington and Indianapolis: University of Indiana Press, 1996.

Riffenburgh, Beau. *The Myth of the Explorer: The Press, Sensationalism, and Geographical Discovery.* London and New York: Belhaven Press, 1993.

Roberts, David. 'Dickens and the Arctic.' *Horizon* (January 1980): 64–71.

Roper, Derek. *Reviewing before the Edinburgh, 1788–1802.* Newark: University of Delaware Press, 1978.

Rose, Jonathan. *The Intellectual Life of the British Working Classes.* New Haven: Yale University Press, 2001.

– 'Rereading the English Common Reader: A Preface to a History of Audiences.' *Journal of the History of Ideas* 53 (1992): 47–70.

Ross, M.J. *Polar Pioneers.* Montreal and Kingston: McGill-Queen's University Press, 1994.

Ross, W. Gillies. 'The Admiralty and the Franklin Search.' *Polar Record* 40 (2004): 289–301.

– 'Nineteenth-Century Exploration of the Arctic.' In John Logan Allen, ed., *North American Exploration.* Vol. 3. Lincoln and London: University of Nebraska Press, 1997.

Sabine, Edward. 'An Account of the Esquimaux, who Inhabit the West coast of Greenland, above the Latitude 76°.' *Quarterly Journal of Science, Literature and Art* 7 (1819): 72–94.

– *Remarks on the Account of the Late Voyage of Discovery to Baffin's Bay. Published by Captain J. Ross, R.N.* London: Richard and Arthur Taylor, for John Booth, 1819.

Said, Edward. *Orientalism.* New York: Vintage, 1979.

Savours, Ann. *The Search for the Northwest Passage.* New York: St Martin's Press, 1999.

St Clair, William. *The Reading Nation in the Romantic Period.* Cambridge: Cambridge University Press, 2004.

Schofield, Thomas Philip. 'Conservative Political Thought in Britain in
    Response to the French Revolution.' *Historical Journal* 29 (1986): 601–22.
Scott, Joan. 'The Evidence of Experience.' *Critical Inquiry* 17 (1991): 773–97.
Semmel, Bernard. *Liberalism and Naval Strategy: Ideology, Interest and Sea Power dur-
    ing the Pax Britannica.* Boston: Allen & Unwin, 1986.
Shattock, Joanne, and Michael Wolff, eds. *The Victorian Periodical Press: Samplings
    and Soundings.* Leicester and Toronto: Leicester University Press / University
    of Toronto Press, 1982.
Smiles, Samuel. *A Publisher and His Friends: Memoir and Correspondence of John
    Murray, with an Account of the Origin and Progress of the House, 1768–1843.* Con-
    densed and edited by Thomas Mackay. London: John Murray, 1911 [1891].
Smith, Bernard. *European Vision and the South Pacific, 1768–1850: A Study in the
    History of Art and Ideas.* Oxford: Oxford University Press, 1960.
– *Imagining the Pacific in the Wake of Cook's Voyages.* New Haven: Yale University
    Press, 1992.
Spufford, Francis. *I May Be Some Time: Ice and the English Imagination.* New York:
    St Martin's Press, 1997.
Stafford, Robert A. *Scientist of Empire: Sir Roderick Murchison, Scientific Exploration
    and Victorian Imperialism.* Cambridge: Cambridge University Press, 1989.
Steele, Peter. *The Man Who Mapped the Arctic.* Vancouver: Raincoast Books, 2003.
Stefansson, Vilhjalmur. *Unsolved Mysteries of the Arctic.* New York: Macmillan,
    1938.
Stephen, Leslie, and Sidney Lee, eds. *Dictionary of National Biography.* London:
    Oxford University Press, 1921–22.
Stone, Harry. *The Night Side of Dickens: Cannibalism, Passion, Necessity.* Columbus:
    Ohio State University Press, 1994.
Stone, Ian R. '"The contents of the kettles": Charles Dickens, John Rae and Can-
    nibalism on the 1845 Franklin Expedition.' *Dickensian* 83 (1987): 7–16.
– 'The Franklin Search in Parliament.' *Polar Record* 32 (1996): 209–17.
Struzik, Edward. *Northwest Passage.* Toronto: Key Porter, 1991.
Suleiman, Susan, and Inge Crossman, eds. *The Reader in the Text: Essays on Audi-
    ence and Interpretation.* Princeton: Princeton University Press, 1980.
Sullivan, Alvin, ed. *British Literary Magazines: The Victorian and Edwardian Age,
    1837–1913.* Westport, Conn.: Greenwood Press, 1984.
Sutherland, John. 'Publishing History: A Hole at the Centre of Literary Sociol-
    ogy.' *Critical Inquiry* 14 (Spring 1988): 574–89.
– *Victorian Fiction: Writers, Publishers, Readers.* New York: St Martin's Press, 1995.
– *Victorian Novelists and Publishers.* London: Athlone Press, 1976.
Sutherland, Patricia, ed. *The Franklin Era in Canadian Arctic History, 1845–1859.*
    Ottawa: National Museums of Canada, 1985.

Sweet, Jessie M. 'Robert Jameson and the Explorers: The Search for the North-West Passage.' *Annals of Science* 31 (1974): 21–47.

Tanselle, G. Thomas. 'The Editorial Problem of Final Authorial Intention.' In *Selected Studies in Bibliography*. Charlottesville: University of Virginia Press, 1979.

– 'Textual Criticism and Deconstruction.' In *Literature and Artifacts*. Charlottesville: Bibliographical Society of the University of Virginia, 1998.

– 'Textual Criticism and Literary Sociology.' *Studies in Bibliography* 44 (1991): 83–143.

Taylor, Andrew. *Arctic Blue Books: British Parliamentary Papers on Exploration in the Canadian North*. Washington, D.C.: U.S. Government Printing Office, 1959.

Taylor, Charles. 'Foucault on Freedom and Truth.' *Political Theory* 12 (1984): 152–83.

Thompson, E.P. *The Making of the English Working Class*. London: Victor Gollancz, 1963.

Thompson, James. 'After the Fall: Class and Political Language in Britain, 1780–1900.' *Historical Journal* 39 (1996): 785–806.

Thompson, Martyn P. 'Reception Theory and the Interpretation of Historical Meaning.' *History and Theory* 32 (1993): 248–72.

Topham, Jonathan. 'Thomas Byerley, John Limbird, and the Production of Cheap Periodicals in Regency Britain.' *Book History* 8 (2005): 75–106.

Traill, H.D. *The Life of Sir John Franklin R.N.* London: John Murray, 1896.

Trumpener, Katie. *Bardic Nationalism: The Romantic Novel and the British Empire*. Princeton: Princeton University Press, 1997.

Vance, Norman. *The Sinews of the Spirit: The Ideal of Christian Manliness in Victorian Literature and Religious Thought*. Cambridge: Cambridge University Press, 1985.

Vann, J. Don, and Rosemary T. VanArsdel, eds. *Victorian Periodicals and Victorian Society*. Toronto: University of Toronto Press, 1994.

Vernon, James. *Politics and the People: A Study in English Political Culture, c. 1815–1867*. Cambridge: Cambridge University Press, 1993.

– ed. *Re-Reading the Constitution: New Narratives in the Political History of England's Long Nineteenth Century*. Cambridge: Cambridge University Press, 1996.

Vincent, David. *Literacy and Popular Culture: England, 1750–1914*. Cambridge: Cambridge University Press, 1989.

Wallace, Hugh N. *The Navy, the Company, and Richard King*. Montreal and Kingston: McGill-Queen's University Press, 1980.

Warkentin, Germaine. Introduction to *Canadian Exploration Literature*. Toronto: Oxford University Press, 1990.

Weeks, Jeffrey. 'Foucault for Historians.' *History Workshop Journal* 14 (Autumn 1982): 107–19.

Weld, Charles Richard. *A History of the Royal Society.* 2 vols. London: John W. Parker, 1848.

Wiebe, Rudy. *Playing Dead: A Contemplation Concerning the Arctic.* Edmonton: NeWest, 1989.

Williams, Glyndwr. ' "To Make Discoveries of Countries Hitherto Unknown": The Admiralty and Pacific Exploration in the Eighteenth Century.' In Alan Frost and Jane Samson, eds, *Pacific Empires: Essays in Honour of Glyndwr Williams.* Vancouver: UBC Press, 1999.

Williams, Glyndwr. *The Prize of All the Oceans: Commodore Anson's Daring Voyage and Triumphant Capture of the Spanish Treasure Galleon.* Harmondsworth, U.K.: Penguin, 2001.

Woodman, David. *Unravelling the Franklin Mystery: Inuit Testimony.* Montreal and Kingston: McGill-Queen's University Press, 1991.

Woodward, Frances. *Portrait of Jane: A Life of Lady Franklin.* London: Hodder and Stoughton, 1951.

Wright, John Kirtland. 'The Open Polar Sea.' In Wright, *Human Nature in Geography.* Cambridge, Mass.: Harvard University Press, 1966.

Web Sites

The Athenaeum Index of Reviews and Reviewers: 1830–1870. www.athenaeum .soi.city.ac.uk.

Cutmore, Jonathan. The Early Quarterly Review Page 1809–1824: Notes, Contexts, and Identification of Contributors. Originally accessed at www. dreamwater.com/edu/earlyqr. Now available at www.rc.umd.edu/ reference/qr.

Matthew Flinders Electronic Archive. www. slnsw.gov.au/flinders/archive.html.

Index

Bulwer-Lytton, Edward, 121
Bunyan, John, 138; *Pilgrim's Progress*, 139
Burke, Edmund, 50, 65, 81–2, 123
Burns, Robert, 138
Butler, Marilyn, 8
Byerley, Thomas, 141, 142, 143, 145, 146, 151
Byron, John, 16–17
Byron, Lord, 65, 147, 273n23

cannibalism, 15, 95–6, 111, 204, 206, 207–9, 210, 211, 212, 213–14, 217, 238, 239, 263n11, 264n19, 293n35
Canning, George, 58, 147, 273n23
Carlile, Richard, 59
Carlyle, Thomas, 120, 138
Carteret, Philip, 16–17
Cassell's Illustrated Family Paper, 38
Chambers's Edinburgh Journal, 25, 29–30, 34, 48, 134–5, 197, 199, 227, 271–2n88
Chambers's Repository, 202, 285n2
Chappell, Ann, 88. *See also* Flinders, Ann
Chappell, Edward, 62
charge of the Light Brigade, 205
Charles I, 123
Chartier, Roger, 9, 10, 252n65
Chartism, 174
chivalry, 28, 65, 82–4, 137–8, 172, 176–7, 187–8, 201, 236. *See also* romance
Christian Guardian (Toronto), 218
Christian Observer, 60, 103, 104, 112–13, 133
Clarence, duke of (William IV), 274n55
class, 125, 130, 134–40, 167–76, 192–3, 217, 269n27, 278n12, 279n32

Cobbett, William, 59, 123, 141
Cobden, Richard, 173, 175, 288–9n87
Colley, Linda, 8, 14, 58, 59, 77, 170–1, 267n84
Collini, Stefan, 119
Collinson, Richard, 188, 189, 199, 203
compilers, 16
compilations, 16, 139, 152–4, 191–2, 198
Coningham, Elizabeth, 168
Coningham, William, 168–9, 173, 234
constitutionalism, 122–3, 169, 174
Cook, James, 86–7, 93–4, 126, 130, 136, 153, 199, 200, 201, 273n33; as author, 15–16, 17, 248n42; as hero, 40; as model for other authors of exploration narratives, 19, 78, 79; popularity of narratives, 139, 271–2n88, 272n91
Cooley, W.D., 153, 157, 178, 274n45
Coppermine River, 73, 93–4, 95, 96–7, 146, 179–80, 264n17
Cornhill Magazine, 26
Corréard, Alexandre, 111
Coulton, D.T., 202
Cracroft, Isabella, 99
Cracroft, Sophia, 23, 42–3, 44, 198, 210–11, 221, 237, 288n68, 288–9n87, 290n107
Crimean War, 175–6, 204–5, 207, 222, 279n32, 285n7
Critical Review, 58
Croker, John Wilson, 58, 73, 79, 98, 100, 104, 260n43, 261n44
Cromwell, Oliver, 123, 269n27
Crozier, Francis, 21, 163, 239–40, 276n92

Daily News, 38, 177, 195, 204, 205, 207
Dampier, William, 16

STUDIES IN BOOK AND PRINT CULTURE

General Editor: Leslie Howsam